The National Institute of Economic and Social Research is an independent, non-profit-making body, founded in 1938. It has as its aim the promotion of realistic research, particularly in the field of economics. It conducts research by its own research staff and in co-operation with the universities and other academic bodies. The results of the work done under the Institute's auspices are published in several series, and a list of its publications up to the present time will be found at the end of this volume.

THE NATIONAL INSTITUTE OF
ECONOMIC AND SOCIAL RESEARCH

Economic and Social Studies
XV

THE STRUCTURE OF
BRITISH INDUSTRY

A SYMPOSIUM
VOLUME I

THE STRUCTURE OF BRITISH INDUSTRY

A SYMPOSIUM

EDITED BY
DUNCAN BURN

VOLUME I

CAMBRIDGE
AT THE UNIVERSITY PRESS
1958

PUBLISHED BY
THE SYNDICS OF THE CAMBRIDGE UNIVERSITY PRESS
Bentley House, 200 Euston Road, London, N.W. 1
American Branch: 32 East 57th Street, New York 22, N.Y.

©

CAMBRIDGE UNIVERSITY PRESS
1958

Printed in Great Britain at the University Press, Cambridge
(Brooke Crutchley, University Printer)

CONTENTS

CHAPTER III

INLAND CARRIAGE BY ROAD AND RAIL

By GILBERT WALKER

Professor of Commerce, University of Birmingham

and C. I. SAVAGE

Lecturer in Political Economy, University of St Andrews

TABLES

CHAPTER IV

THE COAL INDUSTRY

By A. BEACHAM

*Professor of Economics and Political Science,
University College of Wales, Aberystwyth*

CHAPTER V

THE OIL INDUSTRY

BY DUNCAN BURN

Formerly Lecturer in Economic History, University of Cambridge

CHAPTER VI

THE CHEMICAL INDUSTRY

By W. B. Reddaway

Director, Department of Applied Economics, University of Cambridge

TABLES

CHAPTER VII

STEEL

By Duncan Burn

TABLES

CHAPTER VIII

THE BUILDING MATERIALS INDUSTRY

By B. R. WILLIAMS

Professor of Economics, University College of North Staffordshire

TABLES

CHAPTER IX

THE MACHINE TOOL INDUSTRY

By M. E. Beesley

Lecturer in Commerce, University of Birmingham

and G. W. Troup

Formerly Research Officer, Board of Trade

TABLES

INTRODUCTION

This book is the outcome of a suggestion that with the assistance of Conditional Aid a survey of British industry should be made on the lines of the symposium of case studies on American industry edited by Professor Walter Adams.[1] The proposal met with favour: the support of Conditional Aid was obtained, and the National Institute undertook the responsibility of looking after the venture.

The book has been written, like Professor Adams' symposium, not merely for the professional economist but also for the 'intelligent layman'. Initially it was the intention that all the chapters should be contributed by economists already authorities on particular industries, who would write about their special industries and present in short compass the results of their past work. This would have made it possible to produce a book quickly, but the number of economists who had an industry, as it were, at their finger tips was limited, not all of these were free to co-operate, and the scope of the book would have been too narrow. The plan was therefore widened: economists having some familiarity with the problems involved, and in many cases having had also some war-time administrative experience, were asked to write on industries which they had hitherto not examined in detail. The book therefore has involved some fresh investigation—at points a great deal: it is not, as was first proposed, merely an assembly or distillation of work done hitherto. This has delayed its appearance: but it has greatly widened its scope and, it may be hoped, increased its usefulness.

The object of the book is to give an up-to-date picture of the structure of a group of British industries—the number, size, scope, and inter-relations of the firms or units within each industry, for instance, and their relation with industries overseas, and with the government—and to examine the effect of the structure of each industry on its economic performance, its adaptability to markets and to technical change, and its contribution to such change, and so on. Degree of monopoly has naturally been regarded as a matter of primary importance: but the intention has been not to isolate this or give it prominence disproportionate to its importance by the side of other factors. While every effort has been taken to keep a sense of scale the authors are not setting out to provide a statistical digest: this kind of thing is available elsewhere. The chapters have not been written to a pattern. What is of interest in different industries, and what is known about them, varies: the object has been to emphasize what is most significant in what is known. The

[1] W. Adams (ed.), *The Structure of American Industry*, rev. ed. (New York, Macmillan, 1954).

responsibility in this selection and emphasis has remained naturally with the authors individually.

The book remains far short of a complete picture of the structure of all British industry. The chapters cover manufacturing industries responsible in 1955 for nearly 40 % of the net income of all manufactures, though for only approximately one-third of employment in them. In addition it covers agriculture, building, rail and road transport and coal mining—and the total employment covered is well over 40 % of total industrial employment (including in this total the distributive trades which are hardly touched on in the book).

Incompleteness is implicit in the method of the book. Unless the scale of treatment is to be insubstantial only a limited number of case studies can be brought within the confines of a book—even in two volumes. The intention in planning was to make the sample fairly representative. Industries which differed widely in character and age and expansiveness were brought together. There was a slight bias in favour of the newer and rapidly expanding industries whose structures remain rather unfamiliar, such as the electronic, chemical and aircraft industries.

There is a brief concluding chapter: but this is not intended either to fill gaps arising out of the general construction of the book, or to provide a comprehensive summary of the other chapters. It draws together and discusses what is said in the book on some problems of common interest: criteria of efficiency, for example; the forms and effectiveness of competition, the functioning of very large and of rather small firms, the impact of cartel-like activities, the differential effects of the structure of the market for new capital and of some forms of taxation; and finally the impact of the State as owner, supervisor, subsidizer and buyer, with special reference to administrative problems and to the evolution of price and investment policies.

The ordering of the chapters is necessarily arbitrary but the broad principle has been to include those which provide basic raw materials or services in vol. I, those producing more highly finished products largely for consumption in vol. II. A short selective bibliography is included for each chapter. It should perhaps be mentioned that the chapters, which were drafted at different times from 1954 to 1956, were all revised late in 1956 or early in 1957. Also that the authors are individually responsible for their chapters: neither they nor the editor (still less the National Institute) have any collective responsibility.

The authors are greatly in debt to many people for help, advice and criticism; to innumerable firms in the industries covered, and to the officials of their trade associations, to members of several government departments, and to economic colleagues. To mention all individually is impracticable. It is hoped that those who have been so generous of their time will feel that the book bears some imprint of their labours on our behalf. Where other unpublished work has been made available this naturally is specifically acknowledged. The book has benefited greatly at all stages from the advice of Mr Bryan Hopkin, who was largely instrumental in starting it, and whose helpful interest has been invaluable throughout. He has at many points greatly lightened my task as editor and given me sound advice which I have been glad to take as contributor. Finally I am grateful for the help of several members of the staff of the National Institute, above all to the Librarian, Miss Clarke, who has been largely responsible for preparing the work for the printer and handling the proofs.

D. L. B.

LONDON
September 1957

NOTE ON ABBREVIATIONS AND BIBLIOGRAPHICAL CONVENTIONS

(A) ABBREVIATIONS

The following abbreviations for the names of organizations or publications most frequently referred to have been used in both volumes:

C.S.O.   Central Statistical Office.
D.S.I.R.   Department of Scientific and Industrial Research.
E.C.E.   Economic Commission for Europe, Geneva.
H.M.S.O. Her Majesty's Stationery Office.
O.E.E.C.   Organization for European Economic Co-operation, Paris.
S.I.C.   Standard Industrial Classification.

(B) BIBLIOGRAPHICAL REFERENCES

(i) A selective bibliography has been provided at the end of each chapter. These do not necessarily include all the references in the footnotes to the chapters concerned as they are not intended to be exhaustive but to be a fairly brief list of the more important literature on the industry concerned.

(ii) Where no publisher is given for a book, the publisher may be assumed to be the same as the author (as in the case of several organizations and firms).

(iii) The *Reports on the Censuses of Production* (published by H.M.S.O. for the Board of Trade) are often mentioned in the text; to avoid where possible the distraction of further footnotes, these have been referred to simply as the Census of Production, or the Census of Production Reports. The dates of the Censuses and the industry or product concerned are indicated in the context of each chapter.

CHAPTER I

AGRICULTURAL PRODUCTION AND MARKETING[1]

By John R. Raeburn

The structure of the industries engaged in agricultural production has remained one of numerous small firms. Interest in these firms stems partly from their persistence, partly from the wide differences amongst them, which are as significant as their smallness, partly from the fact that they are subjected to overseas competition in the home market, and partly from the extent to which the State has been drawn to intervene in their product and factor markets and even in their internal management.

There thus arise several questions of general importance in relation to the structure of industry. In attempting to answer them this chapter proceeds by considering, first, the sizes of the producing firms and the methods by which they are financed, then the conditions in their factor markets, paying particular attention to those for land and labour and to the effect of State intervention.

The second part of the chapter considers the structure of the industry in marketing, and the development of forward pricing arrangements with State guarantees and of Marketing Boards with State supervised monopoly powers.

Finally, in the third part an attempt is made to judge, by a set of general criteria, the economic efficiency of the industry in production and marketing, and to assess the effects of structure and changes in structure.

I. STRUCTURE OF PRODUCTION

(a) The sizes of the firms

The small size of the great majority of the firms in agricultural production is obvious. For the whole industry the gross revenue was about £1400 million in 1955–6, and the 'net farm income'[2] was about

---

[1] The author is indebted to his assistant, Mr W. Morgan, of the Economics Research Division of the London School of Economics and Political Science, for help in assembling material for this chapter.

[2] Returns for management and labour of farmers and their wives and for use of short- and medium-term capital ('tenant's' capital). Farm produce and stores used in the farm-house are included, usually at country wholesale prices, also rental values of the farm-house, use of the car, etc. Returns on 'landlord's' capital are charged as 'rent'.

£300 million. But the number of firms was well over 350 thousand. Net farm incomes exceeded £1800 on only 19 % of the farms within the Farm Management Survey of England and Wales in 1952–3 although this survey tends to include relatively more 'large' than 'small' farms. On 41 % of the farms included net farm incomes were less than £600.

Table 1. *Gross income and net income*
(Analysis by area of holding,*† England and Wales, 1952–3)

Area of holding (acres)		Percentage of total			
Range	Average	Number of holdings	Land acreage†	Gross income‡	Net income§
5–24	12	35	5	10	11
25–99	55	39	25	32	34
100–299	165	21	45	39	38
300–699	412	5	19	16	14
700 and over	1,035	‖	6	3	3
Total	—	100	100	100	100

* Holdings 'under the same occupancy and day-to-day management' and with 'a common source of labour, machinery and other permanent equipment' are here regarded as single units. Holdings of less than 5 acres of crops and grass are excluded.

† Excluding rough grazings.

‡ Including value of produce and stores consumed on the farm, rental value of farm houses and cottages, and government grants and subsidies.

§ Return for use of medium- and short-term capital, and for labour and management by farmers and their wives.

‖ Less than 0·5.

Sources: Based on Ministry of Agriculture and Fisheries, *National Farm Survey of England and Wales* (H.M.S.O. 1946), Tables 2, 27 and H, and *Farm Incomes in England and Wales 1952–53,* Farm Incomes Series, no. 6 (H.M.S.O. 1955), Tables 2, 3, 12 and 23.

The distribution of gross and net incomes over the basic units of official statistical enumeration—agricultural holdings—can be estimated for England and Wales (Table 1). The size classification of these holdings is by land area (excluding rough grazings). Of the holdings of 5 acres or over, those with only 5 to 25 acres numbered 35 % of the total number, used 5 % of the land, and were responsible for 10 % of the gross income and 11 % of the net farm income. Those with 700 acres or over numbered less than 0·5 % of the total number, used 6 % of the land and were responsible for only 3 % of the gross and net incomes. Wales and Northern Ireland have an even smaller proportion of large holdings (Table 2).

The range of sizes as measured by land area is not very different from that prevailing in France, Denmark or the United States and the distribution of holdings within this range is similarly skewed, the holdings with areas less than 50 acres being much more numerous than those with 50 to 99 acres or 100 to 149 acres (Table 3). But in France and Denmark so much as 38 and 40 %, respectively, of the land is in holdings of less than 50 acres (Table 3). In England and Wales together, the roughly comparable proportion is only 14 %; but 70 % of the agricultural area is in holdings of less than 250 acres. And for at least sixty years these percentages have changed very little.

Table 2. *Numbers and acreages of holdings*
(Analysis by area of holding, 1951)

Area of holding* (acres)	Percentage of total holdings					Percentage of total acreage (England and Wales)
	England	Wales	Scotland	Northern Ireland	United Kingdom	
1–4	23	13	23	15	21	1
5–14	19	23	25	23	21	3
15–49	21	31	19	41	25	10
50–99	15	20	13	15	15	17
100–149	8	8	8	3	7	16
150–299	10	5	9	2	8	28
300–499	3	†	3	1	3	14
500–699	1	†	—	—	—	5
700 and over	†	†	—	—	—	6
Total	100	100	100	100	100	100
Total holdings (thousands)	322	55	75	84	536	‡
Total acres (millions)	21·9	2·6	4·4	3·0	31·9	24·5

* Excluding acreage of rough grazings, except in Northern Ireland.
† Less than 0·5 %.
‡ Not applicable.
Sources: Based on Ministry of Agriculture, *Agricultural Statistics, 1950–1, England and Wales,* part 1 (H.M.S.O. 1954), Tables 61 and 63, and *Agricultural Statistics, 1950–1, United Kingdom,* part 1 (H.M.S.O. 1953), Table 25.

This persistent structure naturally limits the scope for specialization by individual manual workers or for concentration on managerial work by farmers themselves. During 1941–3, when a special survey was made, 44 % of the holdings of over five acres in England and Wales had, apart from the occupiers and their wives, no regular workers. One or two such workers were on 36 % of the holdings, and ten or more on only 3 %. Of the total area, excluding rough grazings, so much as 53 % was within holdings with less than three regular workers apart from the occupiers and their wives, and only 13 % was within holdings with ten or more.

Some allowance must be made for the fact that many agricultural holdings are not farms providing the main employment and chief source of livelihood of their occupiers. The special survey in 1941–3 showed that 15 % of the holdings over five acres in extent had 'spare-

Table 3. *Numbers and acreages of agricultural holdings*
(Analysis by area of holding)

Area of holdings (acres)	England and Wales*	France	Denmark	Netherlands	United States
	Percentage of total holdings				
Less than 15	41	37	22	66	12
15–49	23	43	50	31	24
50–99	15	} 16	20	1	20
100–149	8		5	2	14
150–249	9	3	3	†	15
250 and over	4	1	†	†	15
Total	100	100	100	100	100
	Percentage of total acreage				
Less than 15	4	5	6	17	†
15–49	10	33	34	45	3
50–99	17	} 40	34	26	7
100–149	16		13	8	7
150–249	23	7	10	1	14
250 and over	30	15	3	3	69
Total	100	100	100	100	100

* In England and Wales rough grazings are not included in the area of holdings, and holdings which are not farmed separately may be enumerated separately more often than in other countries.

† Less than 0·5 %.

Sources: Partly estimated, from Food and Agriculture Organization, *1950 World Census of Agriculture*, vol. 1 (Rome, 1955); K. H. Parsons and others (eds.), *Land Tenure*, Proceedings of the International Conference on Land Tenure and Related Problems in World Agriculture, Madison, Wisconsin, 1951 (University of Wisconsin Press, 1956).

time', 'hobby', or 'other' occupiers, and another 11 % had 'part-time' occupiers. Together these types of occupier farmed 12 % of the land area. The 'spare-time' and 'hobby' occupiers numbered 36,000: the 'part-time' farmers, 32,000. No strictly comparable figures are available for Scotland, but in 1947 a survey showed that of 64,000 agricultural units only 58,000 were full-, part-, or spare-time farms. Of these only 51 % provided a reasonable outlet for not less than 1800 hours' work a year. These statistics are indicative of the substantial attractions which farming holds for many people.

Such concentration of land use by farmers as does exist is admittedly somewhat greater than the basic statistics suggest; but it is still of minor importance. The special survey during 1941–3 indicated that only 24,000 out of the total 290,600 holdings of over 5 acres in England and Wales were managed in groups of two or more, and the firms concerned numbered 10,000. During 1947 in Scotland, 3300 out of the total 30,400 full-time farms were not managed entirely separately.

The number of private and public companies concerned with agricultural production is not clear but the number of companies and local authorities assessed for income-tax under Schedule D in the United Kingdom was only 3800 in 1952–3. Of these probably some 3600 were companies. The total assessed income for the whole group was only £4·3 million, so that companies and local authorities together accounted for less than 2 % of the number of firms and of the total income in farming. Partnerships are probably a little more important. But by far the commonest type of firm is the individual farmer. His life-span closely determines the length of life of the firm, and thus, to a large extent, the financial problems of the industry.

(b) The markets for production factors

(i) *Capital.* These financial problems are all the greater because the amount of capital required is large in relation to the gross output. Indeed, in few industries with similarly sized firms is the capital requirement so high and the turnover so slow. At 1955 prices, agricultural land and buildings in the United Kingdom were worth £1700 million, or even more if vacant possession values were taken fully into account. The medium- and short-term capital might be valued at £1400 million. But in relation to a total of, say, £3100 million the annual gross output was only £1300 million valued at the farm gate.

Not all the £3100 million has to be re-financed each generation. Much of it is handed down from father to son, and many farmers are tenants able to rely on landlords for the capital in land and buildings. In 1941–3, some 67 % of the total area of crops and grass in holdings of 5 acres or more in England and Wales was on lease to tenants.

Even so, finance is difficult. The industry is subject to a serious drain of capital through the bequests of individual farmers to the sons, daughters and others who do not take over control of farms. Death duties are at preferentially low rates, but they are still substantial. Moreover, the capital required for economic production has markedly increased with (a) rising labour costs and continuing development of new machinery and labour-saving methods; (b) opportunities to intensify systems of livestock husbandry, and (c) the mounting importance of owner-occupancy as against landlord-tenant arrangements (see p. 9.)

As against the £1700 million or so of capital in land and buildings the total loans in 1955 have been estimated as £384 million[1] of which some £250 million were from private mortgages, £95 million from

---

[1] See S. G. Hooper, *The Finance of Farming in Great Britain* (London, Europa Publications, 1956), pp. 60, 65.

commercial banks, £10 million from insurance companies and building societies and £29 million from the Agricultural Mortgage Corporation and other State-fostered institutions for agricultural credit. The total of £384 million was 23 % of the £1700 million 'landlord's' or long-term capital.

The proportion of the 'tenants'' or medium- and short-term capital borrowed is only about 16 %—£218 million out of some £1400 million. Of this, commercial banks provided £110 million; auctioneers and merchants, £84 million; hire-purchase companies, £18 million; and landlords and miscellaneous lenders, £6 million.[1]

The selection of new entrants to the industry and the extent to which established farmers are able and willing to expand the scale of their businesses are naturally affected by this heavy reliance on private family finance, but they are determined largely also by the working of land tenure arrangements and of the markets for farms and farm leases.

(ii) *Farm land and leases.* The 'supply' of farm vacancies in any one year is comparatively small. Control of farms has normally been obtained at an average age of about thirty-two years, and exercised for an average period of some thirty-one years. Farmers' sons who have obtained control of most of the larger holdings have tended to do so at somewhat less than the average age, and once in control they have seldom changed their location. Farmers' sons have also been the commonest occupiers of smaller holdings, but a considerable number of farm workers and others have taken over such holdings, at a somewhat older age. These smaller holdings have also been used to some extent as rungs in the agricultural ladder leading to larger farms. They have changed occupiers rather more frequently than large farms.[2] A reasonable assumption is that somewhat less than 4 % of the holdings of 5 to 25 acres have usually changed occupiers each year, whereas holdings of over 700 acres have changed occupiers at an average annual rate of somewhat less than 3 %.

On the demand side, bids are curtailed by aversion from borrowing more capital, and by restriction of the credit granted to some of the younger farmers until they are 'better established'—and, incidentally, may have passed their years of greatest physical energy and initiative. Thus, the 'mobility' of land-use rights among agricultural users,

---

[1] S. G. Hooper, *The Finance of Farming in Great Britain*, pp. 60, 65.

[2] University of Cambridge School of Agriculture, *An Economic Survey of Agriculture in the Eastern Counties of England in 1933*, Farm Economics Branch Report no. 22 (Cambridge, 1934).
Ministry of Agriculture, *National Farm Survey of England and Wales* (H.M.S.O. 1946), p. 33.
A. W. Ashby, 'The Farmer in Business', *Journal of Proceedings of the Agricultural Economics Society* (afterwards *Journal of Agricultural Economics*), vol. 10, no. 2, February 1953, p. 91.

present and potential,[1] is usually low, and wide variations in the productivity of land due to differences in managerial ability and intensity of use of medium- and short-term capital can persist throughout the industry.

In the past 'mobility' would have been still lower if farmers had not been able to rely on a comparatively large proportion of the available land and farms being available for renting rather than purchase outright for owner-occupation. In 1912 some 89 % of the total area of crops and grass in England and Wales was reported as rented.[2] Thus use of the large amount of long-term capital required was provided, and at low cost because the landlords derived from their ownership, in addition to net rents and shooting rights, social prestige and other benefits. Tenants could fully stock and equip with less need for loans than if they had been owner-occupiers. They could therefore weather well the year-to-year uncertainties of their individual businesses, and their ability to meet these uncertainties was often further strengthened by their landlords' willingness to allow delays in rent payments when circumstances proved difficult. Agriculture very probably gained more from cheap long-term capital, reduced financial uncertainties, and greater 'mobility' than it lost from the entry of a certain number of inefficient users of land with little capital of their own.

On the other hand there have always been dangers in tenure arrangements that permit a 'mobility' of farms and farmers so rapid as to bear heavily on individual owners or tenants. Some tenants might, particularly during periods of declining prices, 'farm to leave'—that is, deplete soil fertility and otherwise disinvest the capital of their landlords. Some landlords might take advantage of the fact that tenants would often be prepared to pay higher rents rather than have to shift, or of the fact that tenants could be forced to go without full compensation for the investments they left behind in soil fertility and other improvements. Moreover, some landlords might fail to maintain buildings and other permanent equipment in repair and to invest in improvements and extensions desirable in view of, for instance, increases in labour costs or changes in the relative prices of products.

For more than a century, the State has been attempting to avoid these disadvantages through a long series of acts of which the last are the Agriculture Act of 1947 and the Agricultural Holdings Act of 1948. The main results have been to strengthen the position of tenants through security of tenure, freedom of cropping and stocking, full compensation

[1] During the 1930's Marketing Boards imposed restrictions on the production of potatoes and hops, but such controls over entry into and expansion of agricultural production have never been important in the farming industry as a whole.

[2] *The Land*, Report of the Land Inquiry Committee, vol. 1: *Rural*, 3rd ed. (London, Hodder and Stoughton, 1913), p. 344. The true figures may have been somewhat lower.

for improvements, slow bureaucratic adjustment of rents, and the right to require maintenance and extension of landlord's capital to the level necessary for 'good estate management'. In return the State has taken the right to dislodge tenants (and owner-occupiers) of agricultural land who do not maintain 'a reasonable standard of efficient production as respects both the kind of produce and the quantity and quality thereof while keeping the [land] in a condition to enable such a standard to be maintained in the future', regard being had 'to the character and situation of the unit, the standard of management thereof by the owner and other relevant circumstances'. In practice, however, this right of the State has probably seriously affected fewer than 2 % of tenants and other occupiers, while the landlord's ability to induce or compel inefficient users of land to make way for efficient users is now weaker than it ever was.

In benefiting the great majority of sitting tenants, State intervention has undoubtedly restricted entry into the industry and 'mobility' of land-use rights among farmers. The ownership of agricultural land leased to tenant farmers has been made less and less attractive. Not only have landlords' rights to control farm management been curbed, and State controls over landlords' estate management increased, but by arbitration procedures gross rents have been kept very low in relation to costs of maintenance and administration. Net rents have not reflected the demand for land-use rights, which during the 1939–45 War and after has reached unprecedented levels. In 1949–50 average gross rents in England and Wales would have had to be increased by some 240 % to yield net rents equivalent to a 4 % return on the vacant possession values of farms.[1] On the death or retiral of a tenant, prospective new tenants might be prepared to offer such increased rents but they would be entitled to seek reductions through arbitration after only three years. Thus when vacancies have occurred, landlords have had strong inducements either to take farms under their own management or to sell, so increasing the supply of land for owner-occupation and reducing that for renting. Sitting tenants have had especially strong inducements to continue their tenancies longer than usual, thus further reducing the current supply of land for renting. Also, some tenants have had inducements to purchase the farms they occupy so as to obtain opportunities for their sons. Others have bought with the intention of profiting by sale later at the much higher prices for farms with vacant possession. In general, tenants' behaviour has reduced the supply of farms available for renting and kept the supply of farms available for

[1] S. G. Sturmey, 'Owner-Farming and the 1947 and 1948 Acts', *Journal of Agricultural Economics* (formerly *Journal of Proceedings of the Agricultural Economics Society*), vol. 11, no. 3, June 1955, p. 305.

purchase by other than sitting tenants below what it otherwise would
have been.

Increases in owner-occupation as compared with tenancy have also
been induced by forces other than those related to Holdings Acts and
the Agriculture Act of 1947. For several decades now much land has
had to be sold from large and medium-sized estates to pay death-duties,
and the social prestige of landownership has dwindled.

Of the total area of agricultural land in England and Wales the proportion let to tenants has now fallen to some 62 %. It would probably
have fallen still further but for two types of change: the increase in
tenanted land held by the Forestry Commission and other public bodies,
and purchases of land by corporations and individuals as a long-term
hedge against inflation and to gain the advantages of the lower rates of
death-duty fixed for agricultural land in contrast to most other assets.[1]

(iii) *Labour.* Perhaps even more important than land tenure arrangements in determining the structure and efficiency of agriculture are the
supply and pricing of farm labour.

A fundamental reason for the small-scale structure is the large supply
of farmers anxious to remain self-employed, and of wives, sons, and other
near relatives prepared to provide closely interested and willing labour.
In 1951, of the total of some 1,200,000 people reported as occupied in
agriculture and horticulture in Great Britain, probably fully 400 thous-
and were farmers and their near relatives, and, as already indicated,
many farms are worked with no other labour.

The small-scale structure of the industry and the heavy reliance on
family labour result in close contact between individual hired labourers
and management. This fosters good labour relations, and efficiency at
least in so far as it can arise from good timing of operations and from
manual dexterity. But it is to be noted that one skilled regular worker
is a unit large in relation to the total labour requirements of most firms
and the 'indivisibility' of labour poses a real problem which is not
always fully solved. Casual labour, much of it skilled in special seasonal
tasks, can be obtained as and when wanted only in certain localities.

The pricing of hired labour has been affected to varying degrees by
the minimum wage rates and conditions of work fixed by the Agricultural
Wages Boards. These have both negotiating and arbitrating functions.
Thus the Board for England and Wales has eight representatives of
employers, eight representatives of employees, and in addition, a

[1] Unfortunately no reliable, comprehensive statistics of the ownership of agricultural land
by type of owner are compiled, but of the State bodies, the Forestry Commission controls
some 730 thousand acres of land not planted with trees, and the Agricultural Land Commission
with its Welsh Sub-Commission controls 227 thousand acres. Most of this land is comparatively infertile. The Commissioners of Crown Lands manage 379 thousand acres; the Church
Commissioners, 217 thousand acres.

chairman and four other members appointed by the Minister of Agriculture. Before the Second World War the functions of the Board were not so fully centralized as they are now but even so wages were kept much higher, and more uniform amongst the counties, than they otherwise would have been. In terms of agricultural produce the minimum wage rate rose by 30 % within the five years from 1928 to 1933. In the United States and other countries without minimum wage controls, agriculture experienced no such increase. During the 1939–45 War, together with restrictions on the movement of labour out of the industry and new supplies of labour including the Women's Land Army and war prisoners, minimum rate fixing somewhat retarded increases in wages. But since 1947 resistance by the farmers' representatives to increased claims has not been very strong. The costs of wage increases have been largely taken into account at corresponding special reviews for the fixing of new product prices guaranteed by the government. Full employment elsewhere has tended to reduce the supply of labour for farms, but a spiral of higher product prices—higher wage claims—higher wages—higher product prices has undoubtedly also been at work, and rendered all the more continuous by the comparatively high level of profits established in 1947 as well as by opportunities for improvements in the productivity of labour.[1]

The pricing of family labour is naturally not closely determined by any minimum rates fixed by the Wages Board. Actual payments for this labour can be flexible, and over much of the industry the money values placed on it by farmers tend to be low. The correspondingly high propensity to save has countered to some extent the tendency to

---

[1] It is noteworthy that the labour force in agriculture apart from that of farmers and their wives is normally comparatively young. Far more youths become farm workers after leaving school than continue after reaching maturity and independence. Thus the occupational census figures for England and Wales show the following numbers of male 'agricultural labourers'.

Ages (years)	1951 census (thousands)	1931 census (thousands)
15–19	86	101 (14–20 years)
20–24	59	53 (21–24 years)
15–24	145	154 (14–24 years)
25–34	92	96
35–44	88	66
45–54	66	65
55–64	46	59
65 and over	22	37
Total	459	477

Thus among the main forces accelerating or retarding the 'drift from the land' are those affecting young men between school-leaving age and about 20 or 21, and, to a lesser degree, before or fairly soon after marriage. It is notable too that the supply of the more highly skilled, experienced men is naturally inelastic even over comparatively long periods, but that during the last decade there has been a significant tendency to earlier retiral.

chronic shortage of capital and further improved the ability to come through financially difficult periods. On the other hand the low valuation of family labour has, except in the more prosperous periods, retarded on many small and medium-sized farms what would otherwise have appeared to be an economic substitution of machinery and other factors for labour.

(iv) *Other factors*. A wide range of conditions prevails in other factor markets. At one extreme is the State monopoly controlling rail transport, and, at the other, full competition in the provision of, for instance, most seeds, non-pedigree livestock, or insurance. Also the State provides free much technical advice, and even some business management advice.

In the important fertilizer markets, conditions of oligopoly prevail, fostered mainly by the economies of large-scale chemical plants for nitrogen and phosphates, and by the concentration of natural deposits of potash in few countries. In 1952, Imperial Chemical Industries had direct control over about three-quarters of the production of nitrogen fertilizers. Sales by Fisons were equal to fully two-fifths of the total purchases of fertilizers by farmers.

Markets for tractors and some of the larger machines are also oligopolistic. Competition in production and distribution of simpler machinery and tools is more nearly perfect, but in the provision of spare parts and in local repair work, which together are of substantial importance, competition has become imperfect with the establishment of agencies by the large manufacturers and the declining number of smithies.

In the market for feeding-stuffs the only considerable tendencies to imperfection are those due to economies by large-scale operation, and opportunities for product differentiation, in flour-milling, oilseed crushing and feeding-stuff compounding. Differentiation between compound feeding-stuffs by advertising may have some effect: but the number of firms concerned is fairly large, some compounding is done by co-operative societies, and some can be done by farmers themselves. In flour-milling the Co-operative Wholesale Societies have a substantial proportion of the total through-put.

The State has had a considerable influence on the markets for feeding-stuffs, fertilizers and seeds by requiring fuller descriptions of quality than would usually be given by private firms or obtainable by simple inspection.

The State has also since 1937 reduced the prices of some factors, notably fertilizers, by subsidies. Of the total civil expenditure for 'agriculture and food' in 1956–7, £73 million were subsidies on factors and operations such as ploughing old grassland and rearing calves.

The State has also invested substantial sums annually in agricultural research and training, of which the economic product is difficult to measure but is obviously very many times its cost. During 1955–6 some £4·0 to 4·5 million of the estimated expenditure by the Ministry of Agriculture, Fisheries and Food and the Department of Agriculture for Scotland could be regarded as for research. In addition, of payments by the University Grants Committee, some £0·3 million was directly for research, and there were smaller payments for the work of the Commonwealth Agricultural Bureaux. State expenditures on the education and training of research workers were also to be taken into account, but in all probability a total of not more than £5 million was spent on research.[1] Expenditures on agricultural training and advisory work were of the order of £4·0 to 4·5 million in 1955–6.

(c) The State's control of management

Through Part II of the Agriculture Act of 1947, the State secured the right to insist on 'good husbandry' and 'good estate management' in return for the guaranteeing of product prices and assurance of markets, in accordance with Part I, and for the greater security of tenure for sitting tenants under Part III. 'Efficiency' was to be required as a twin pillar to 'stability'. But, as was forecast,[2] without itself taking some financial stakes in the firms' affairs, the State has not been able sufficiently to insist on the assumption by individual firms of additional entrepreneurial risks and uncertainties—including those aggravated by a bad executive management. Gross inefficiency in a farm business is not difficult to discern, but to raise the least efficient quarter of the farming industry to par with the next quarter would require intimate study, skilled and careful management, capital, and risk-bearing. Simply as policeman and prodder the State cannot be very effective, for the functions are basically those of entrepreneurs and the State's own efficiency as entrepreneur in farming is not proven.

On an industry-wide scale, none the less, the State has controlled, and to a considerable degree still does control, the volume and composition of output, and combinations of factors. Official advice and propaganda are not without influence, especially when backed by the subsidies on factors and operations and by subsidies on products to provide forward guarantees of returns. In 1956–7 these product subsidies were estimated to amount to £162 million, in addition to subsidies under welfare food schemes. Total estimated subsidies (ex-

---

[1] This compared with at least £17 to 20 million on administration and execution of agricultural policy and a total of £206 million as subsidies on factors, operations and products.

[2] J. P. Maxton, *The Control of Husbandry*, Oxford Institute of Agrarian Affairs (Oxford University Press, 1946).

cluding costs of welfare foods, agricultural research, training and general agricultural policy administration) were £235 million.

This is a sum of the greatest importance to farmers for it is equivalent to about three-quarters of recent annual net farm incomes (returns on short- and medium-term capital, and farmers' labour and management): and the manner in which the sum is distributed, and expectations about future changes in its size or distribution, affect greatly many individual farmers' entrepreneurial decisions.

2. THE STRUCTURE OF MARKETING

(a) The forms of marketing, and price formation

Of the various functions in agricultural marketing most are carried out by numerous small firms. Individual farmers and even co-operative groups have very few opportunities to differentiate their own small shares of the total supplies of produce of comparable qualities. The number of first buyers and wholesalers is also large and entry into the trade is comparatively easy. In some localities, it is true, the number of first buyers of agricultural produce tends to be small, and complaints arise from time to time about the weak bargaining positions of individual farmers. Occasionally collusion between buyers at the smaller livestock markets also causes complaint. But development of rail and road transport and growth of the larger country markets appear to keep competition not far from perfect in the great majority of localities.

Substantial imperfections in competition have, however, developed for three main reasons:[1] (a) the economies of large-scale plants in the processing of certain foodstuffs, and the opportunities for differentiation of some food products through packaging and advertising; (b) the granting of monopoly powers by the State to Marketing Boards; (c) State pricing of farmers' products and control of imports.

The tendencies to oligopoly resulting from the development of machinery and methods for large-scale processing were augmented during the 1914–18 War by the encouragement which the administration of food controls gave to trade associations and, during the late 1920's and early 1930's, by general deflation. The Lucas Committee,

---

[1] In milk marketing it is to be noted that even in the early 1920's imperfections were apparent for other reasons. The demand for milk for direct liquid consumption tended to be segregated from that for milk for manufacture into cheese, butter and other products because, for these, lower standards of hygiene were required and regularity of production between seasons and from day to day was much less important. The expanding demand for milk for liquid consumption as well as joint bargaining arrangements between farmers' representatives on the one hand and milk distributors on the other made this imperfection in the milk market all the more obvious.

reporting in 1947, alleged that 'concentration of control into the hands of a few big concerns had, by 1931, become a feature of such food processing industries as milk processing, flour-milling, brewing, bacon curing and sugar manufacture'.[1] How far concentration of buying power was by 1931 actually reducing farmers' prices and keeping up processors' gross margins is, however, debatable. The local monopsony positions of a comparatively small number of processors, particularly milk product manufacturers and bacon curers, may well have been used against the interests of farmers, but in serious instances new buyers could come forward to compete for supplies or farmers themselves could set up voluntary co-operative societies. Indeed, prior to 1931, farmers' complaints about high margins and imperfect competition amongst processors and other middlemen were seldom supported by sound evidence. These complaints were symptomatic rather than diagnostic. The basic trouble was general deflation together with rigidity in wage rates, both urban and rural.

The Agricultural Marketing Acts of 1931 and 1933 under which the Marketing Boards were set up were due less to recognition of this basic trouble than to the belief that by control of supplies and by 'rationalization' marketing could be made more efficient and agricultural producers' prices raised. The Acts gave producers the right to formulate schemes of organized marketing which could be imposed on all producers provided those in favour at a poll numbered at least two-thirds of the total number voting, and were capable of producing at least two-thirds of the total output of all those voting. Farmers could thus create 'statutory and inviolable monopolies' over home agricultural products. By 1939, boards were in operation for milk and milk products, pigs, bacon, potatoes and hops.

Boards can undertake a wide range of marketing functions, but in practice before the war their most important powers were in fixing the prices at which they would sell the produce of all commercial producers and in segregating demands by discriminating between different types of buyer and user. Full use of these powers was made in milk marketing. Also boards could restrict home produced supplies, and the boards concerned with hops and potatoes did so. Entry into the bacon curing industry and the extension of facilities for bacon curing by established firms was also controlled. The Marketing Board arrangements actual or prospective provided moreover a basis for closer control of imported supplies. The Agricultural Marketing Act of 1933 permitted the Board of Trade to make orders restricting the imports of any products for which 'all such steps as are practicable and

---

[1] Ministry of Agriculture, *Working of the Agricultural Marketing Acts: Report of the Committee* (H.M.S.O. 1947).

necessary for . . . efficient reorganization by means of agricultural marketing schemes' had been or were being taken, provided that without such
orders these schemes could not be brought about or maintained.

In September 1939 the powers of the existing boards were withdrawn
but the Milk Marketing Boards acted as agents of the Ministry of
Food until 1954. These Boards and the Potato Marketing Board are
now fully operative again. Boards for tomatoes and cucumbers and
for wool have been set up post-war and others for apples and pears and
for eggs have been proposed. By the Agricultural Marketing Act of
1949, however, the powers of boards are now somewhat more limited
than they were pre-war: the Agricultural Ministers have more control
over them. They have become State supervised monopolies.

State pricing of products and control of imported supplies became
important during the 1930's. Subsidies were paid not only on sugar
beet (fostered from 1924 onwards as part of an 'infant industry') but
also on wheat, barley, oats, tuberculin tested milk, milk for manufacture, fat cattle, and bacon pigs. Imports of a wide range of products
were restricted by duties and quotas. Much more important now are
the pricing and subsidization arrangements under the Agriculture Act
of 1947.

This Act was largely

for the purpose of promoting and maintaining, by the provision of guaranteed
prices and assured markets . . . a stable and efficient agricultural industry
capable of producing such part of the nation's food and other agricultural
produce as in the national interest it is desirable to produce in the United
Kingdom, and of producing it at minimum prices consistently with proper
remuneration and living conditions for farmers and workers in agriculture
and an adequate return on capital invested in the industry.

Comprehensive annual reviews of the industry, which after 1940 were
a feature of war-time arrangements, were established as a peace-time
procedure. After each review, in February or March, 'guaranteed
prices' have been fixed for fatstock, milk, eggs and wool during the
next twelve months and for grains, potatoes and sugar beet of the next
harvest but one. In addition, every two years, minimum prices for
fatstock, milk and eggs have been fixed for the third and fourth years
ahead. Also, between one annual review and the next, special reviews
could be made, and guarantees adjusted upwards if the costs of any
factors have increased substantially.

As affecting the prices and product subsidies received by farmers
these review arrangements can perhaps most usefully be considered as
those of a fragile bilateral monopoly—the Farmers' Unions of England
and Wales, Scotland, and Northern Ireland acting jointly as monopolist
and the government as monopsonist.

The Unions are sufficiently strong to be treated as spokesmen for all home agriculture and the consultations, which are all that the Agriculture Act requires the Agricultural Ministers to have, seem usually to be little less than negotiations with the unions. Strong claims for high and stable prices and a long-term production plan for home agriculture have been continuously put forward by the unions, and their leaders have been forceful in making use of their strong bargaining positions in the circumstances of continuing balance of payment difficulties and political sensitivity to opinions in the rural constituencies most likely to affect election results.

Even so the position of the unions is fragile. They have not succeeded in obtaining full restoration of the pre-war powers of the Marketing Boards, and it is doubtful whether they could themselves for long directly restrict the supplies offered by their individual members or their individual future production plans. Larger supplies of a few products can seriously undermine the unions' position in relation to the government and to their own members. Thus at the annual review of 1956, prospective supplies of milk, eggs and fat pigs and current rates of subsidy for these products clearly indicated that prices to producers should not be raised further, but the unions were faced on the one hand with heavy claims by their members, particularly the numerous small farmers to whom these three products are most important, and, on the other, with the government's ability to fix prices without their agreement, that is, in the unions' own words, to 'impose a settlement'. Naturally the unions decided to support their own members but the imposed settlement strengthened the resolve of some farmers, particularly in Wales, to break away from the National Farmers' Union of England and Wales.

The government's monopsony position is also peculiar. For most principal products the prices paid are now above those related to freely expressed consumer demands so that the government can bargain all the more strongly by proclaiming the costs of subsidies. They can also influence the multitude of individual members of the unions, coaxing and advising them in a variety of ways in the direction of higher outputs. They still have, too, some control over the levels of demand for certain products through regulation of the volumes of imported supplies. But how far they can use their monopsony position to lower the whole schedule of farm product prices is limited by party political considerations and by fear that lower prices might reduce home production and aggravate international balance of payment problems.

At each price review a large volume of statistics on the economic condition of agriculture is agreed between the government and the unions and this sets limits to the field over which bargaining takes place. But 'there are no figures either of tenants' or landlords' capital sufficiently reliable to be used for the purpose of the review'. Measures of profit—and of 'proper remuneration' and 'adequate return'—are therefore unsatisfactory. 'There is scope for much argument on the extent to which the figures of net income for recent years reflect a justifiable increase due to the higher output and greater efficiency on the part of farmers.'[1] No balance-sheets are presented to disclose financial changes. The range over which prices and subsidies could be negotiated has therefore been wide, and, as in true bilateral monopolies, bargaining has been liable to break down. Neither side was, however, prepared to face any serious breakdown until 1956, and then the disagreement was, apparently, over price relationships amongst products rather than the general level of incomes for farmers.

In an attempt to limit the scope for disagreement in the future, and to provide more effective 'long-term assurances' the government proposed in November 1956 closer restrictions on their right to reduce prices.[2] For each commodity the guaranteed price (adjusted for any change in the basis of the guarantee) would not be reduced by more than 4% after any one annual review, nor, in the case of livestock products, by more than 9% over any period of three years. The total annual value of the guarantees, including production subsidies, *plus* cost increases or *minus* cost decreases, would not be reduced by more than $2\frac{1}{2}$% after any one review (i.e. by more than some £29 million if estimated on the quantities and guaranteed prices of 1956–7). As against these restrictions the government secured a slightly greater flexibility in that, for crops, the guarantees determined after each annual review would apply to the next harvest and not the next but one. Also special reviews would no longer be held unless the cost changes were equal to more than $\frac{3}{4}$% of the total annual value of the guarantees, and even then no adjustment of guaranteed prices would be made 'in respect of that part of the cost change which was equivalent to $\frac{1}{2}$% of the total value of the guarantees'.

While the government thus obtained agreement that circumstances might arise in which the maximum permitted reductions were desirable, and in accordance with the general purposes of the Agriculture Act of 1947, there remained ample scope for differences of opinion with the Farmers' Unions in the future on whether in any one year such circumstances had arisen. Moreover, considering the need for flexibility in

[1] *Annual Review and Fixing of Farm Prices 1951*, Cmd. 8239 (H.M.S.O. 1951), and similar white papers for subsequent annual reviews (published from 1954 onwards as *Annual Review and Determination of Guarantees*).
[2] *Long-Term Assurances for Agriculture*, Cmnd. 23 (H.M.S.O. 1956).

correcting past mistakes in pricing and in meeting changing supply and demand conditions for individual products, it was doubtful whether the wisest price structures for the future could be achieved within the restrictions imposed. (See pp. 37–8 and Table 9.)

(b) Recent trends

The Agriculture Act of 1947 said nothing about efficiency in marketing. This, it implied, was a matter separate from the guaranteeing of prices and assuring of markets which could be handled by Marketing Boards or Commissions or even by a continuation of the Ministry of Food. But care was taken not to require that guarantees and assurances should always be fixed prices for unlimited outputs. 'Guaranteed prices' could mean the provision of direct subsidy payments 'whether by reference to acreage or otherwise' and the 'assurance of markets' could be limited to specific quantities. None the less the fact that subsidies would probably have to be paid was obviously liable to affect marketing structure.

Following the freeing of food markets from the direct controls of war-time, the marketing structure is in many respects little different from that of the late 1930's. Thus the cereal trade is much the same as it was then, market prices being determined freely under competition —somewhat imperfect in flour-milling, malting and brewing. Farmers receive (not now from a special commission but from the Ministry of Agriculture, Fisheries and Food) deficiency payments on each hundred-weight of wheat sold so as to make up their national *average* returns from the crop of any one year to the price guaranteed for it. Similar deficiency payments are made per acre of barley and oats calculated on *average* prices and *average* yields. Potato traders are licensed as they were before the war in substantial numbers, and the Potato Marketing Board's operations are intended mainly to implement the minimum support prices guaranteed by the government rather than to involve widespread trading on the Board's own account. Subject to supervision by the Agricultural Ministers, the Board still has powers of supply restriction. Arrangements for sugar beet and hops are much the same as during the 1930's. Those for fruit and vegetables differ only in that official restrictions on imports are greater, and a Marketing Board has been set up for tomatoes and cucumbers.

The milk trade is also similar except that retail prices and margins for liquid milk are now determined under Treasury supervision and, as an aftermath of war-time rationalization arrangements, the numbers of retail businesses are, in some localities, kept down by the joint action of established firms. The Milk Marketing Boards exercise their pre-war control over prices of milk for manufacture. They also control entry to the milk products manufacturing industry. This industry is, moreover, now more closely organized in the Creamery Proprietors' Association, which exercises considerable influence on margins.

Fatstock marketing has been somewhat affected by the reduced supply of skills in purchase 'on the hoof', resulting from thirteen years of government purchasing, and also by the greater centralization of slaughtering brought about during the war for control and sanitary reasons. The danger that these might aggravate tendencies to imperfect competition between first buyers in particular localities has, however, been avoided by encouragement of larger auction markets and by the establishment of the Fatstock Marketing Corporation by the three main Farmers' Unions. This Corporation offers facilities for the marketing of cattle, sheep and pigs on a deadweight basis and is reputed to have capacity for about a quarter of the total output of fatstock. Whether it will be efficient enough to secure and maintain so much annual business has yet to be proven.

Egg marketing has been greatly affected by the decision to pay the guaranteed support prices only on eggs passing through registered packing stations. Before the war only some 12 % of the total output of eggs was graded and packed by such stations, the remainder being marketed more directly. Packing station operations were economic only in certain areas.

Wool marketing has come under a Marketing Board which employs the pre-war trading firms to buy from farmers at the guaranteed prices and which is itself responsible for selling all home-grown wool. If the realized prices are too low in relation to the guaranteed prices the Treasury makes good the deficiency to the Board.

3. ASSESSMENT OF ECONOMIC EFFICIENCY

(a) The criteria

Having now outlined the structure of agricultural production and marketing, closer consideration can be given to assessing economic efficiency.

Any attempt at such assessment soon discloses very wide variations in farmers' incomes. Thus the Farm Management Survey carried out in England and Wales by ten universities and the Ministry of Agriculture indicated that in 1952–3 returns (net farm incomes) for the labour and management of farmers and their wives and for the use of their medium- and short-term capital ('tenant's' capital) were over £2400 on 12 % of the farms studied but only between £1 and £600 on 34 %.

On 7 % of the farms losses were suffered. Naturally some of this wide variation is due to differences in the land, 'tenant's' capital and other resources used on different farms, and some is due to temporary causes affecting particular systems of farming or particular localities. But allowances for these differences would still leave very wide variations to be explained by other causes, as the data available from Scotland indicate (Table 4). Indeed, these data and much other evidence strongly suggest that many farmers are, by any financial measure, much less efficient than others in the same areas and lines of production, and that although their relative inefficiency persists they remain in the industry, and continue to account for a large part of the resources used in it.

Table 4. *Distribution of farms by net farm income*
(Scotland, 1952–3)

	Percentage of farms studied			
Net income per £100 expenditure*	All farms with rents £100 to 250	Dairy farms	Stock rearing and feeding farms	Arable crop farms with livestock
−£20·1 and over	1	1	Nil	Nil
−£20 to −0·1	4	3	2	4
£0 to 19·9	40	34	38	48
£20 to 39·9	39	42	48	39
£40 to 59·9	13	15	11	9
£60 to 79·9	2	4	1	1
£80 to 99·9	Nil	Nil	†	1
£100 and over	1	Nil	Nil	Nil
Total	100	100	100	100
Net income per 100 acres‡				
−£201 and over	—	7	2	1
−£200 to 0	—	3	2	1
£0 to 200	—	12	17	4
£201 to 400	—	9	28	16
£401 to 600	—	12	24	7
£601 to 800	—	9	10	6
£801 to 1000	—	12	} 17	24
£1001 and over	—	36		41
Total	—	100	100	100

 * Including farms studied by the Agricultural Colleges of the East, West and North of Scotland.
 † Less than 0·5 %.
 ‡ Including only farms studied by the East of Scotland College.
 Sources: D. M. R. Leask and J. D. Rowbottom, *Report on Financial Results of 183 East of Scotland Farms for 1952–53*, University of Edinburgh, Edinburgh and East of Scotland College of Agriculture Economic Department, Bulletin no. 46 (1954). F. Holme, in *Scottish Agricultural Economics* (Edinburgh, H.M.S.O. for the Department of Agriculture for Scotland, 1955), vol. v, p. 14.

Some of the reasons for this persistently wide variation in efficiency have already been touched on but these and other reasons can now best be considered in relation to a set of general criteria by which the efficiency of agriculture as a whole may be judged:

(i) The types and sizes of firm should be such in range and distribution that no further alternations would meantime be profitable.

(ii) For all the factors of production used at least their opportunity costs (or values in an alternative use), appropriately measured, should be paid. And good mobility of factors should be secured within agriculture and between agriculture and other industries.

(iii) The various factors (including new technical knowledge, and credit) should be used in combinations such that no further additions or substitutions would meantime be profitable.

(iv) The prices of the produce of home agriculture should not for long exceed those at which imported produce can be secured, due allowances, up or down, being made for differences in quality, and in season and location of sales.

(v) The output of agriculture should be such in volume and composition that no further changes would meantime be profitable.

(vi) Productive capacity should be maintained at levels that are appropriate in relation to probable future prices of products, costs of factors, and effective interest rates. This is a criterion closely related to (iii) and (v) above.

(vii) The buying of factors and selling of products should be so arranged as to minimize total marketing costs (including processing and retailing) and to avoid marketing charges kept high by imperfect competition.

In addition, the State may have some special requirements arising from matters outside its control or from its own mismanagement of other parts of the economy. Additional production or productive capacity may from time to time be required in agriculture for national security reasons or to meet balance of payment difficulties. The State may also aim to maintain in agriculture certain levels of employment and income. In attempts to meet these special requirements real costs should be minimized.

Each of the criteria may now be applied in turn.

(b) Factors relating to degrees of efficiency

(i) *Changes in sizes and types of farms.* Comparisons of simple measures of the relative efficiencies of firms of different size commonly suggest that 'large' farm businesses are more profitable than 'small' and that, at least within the range of experience studied, farm sizes should be increased. Thus an analysis of the most recent figures available from the Farm Management Survey of England and Wales indicates that returns on medium- and short-term capital, i.e. 'tenant's' capital, were during 1952–3 substantially higher on farms of 300 to 500 acres than on farms of only 50 to 150 acres (Table 5). Per £100 of gross output, the larger firms tend to employ more 'tenant's' capital, and their total machinery use costs are not lower than on the smallest farms, but, they grow more of their own feeding-stuff requirements and, at least in arable crop and in livestock rearing and fattening areas, their labour costs are lower. Their rather better sizes and layouts of field, their somewhat greater opportunities for specialization of labour, their economies in buying feeding-stuffs, fertilizers and other factors, and their opportunities for easier borrowing of capital—all these are substantial advantages. But they have obviously not been enough to alter agriculture's basic structure. The reasons for this are several.

Table 5. *Relation of costs and returns to areas of farms*
(1358 farms, England and Wales, 1952–3)

Total area of farms (acres) Range	Average	Gross output* (£ per farm)	Tenant's capital†	Ferti- lizers, seeds and feeding- stuffs	Machine use and miscel- laneous	Rent	Labour, total manual	Return on 'tenant's' capital and management Percentage of gross output	Percentage of capital
				Dairying areas					
50–99	72	2,947	129	40	22	5	26	7	5·5
100–149	124	4,660	133	36	23	6	25	10	7·8
150–299	202	7,412	139	33	22	6	26	13	9·3
				Livestock areas					
50–99	78	1,921	168	29	24	5	31	11	6·4
100–149	124	2,401	181	23	26	6	31	14	7·6
150–299	213	3,711	192	23	26	6	28	17	8·7
300–499	385	4,648	208	20	26	6	28	20	9·7
500 and over	876	4,763	209	17	26	7	28	22	10·4
				Arable crop areas					
50–99	74	3,408	118	28	25	5	31	11	9·5
100–149	126	5,266	132	26	24	4	29	17	12·7
150–299	220	8,649	130	27	24	4	26	19	14·7
300–499	390	14,099	119	26	23	4	27	20	16·2
500 and over	756	22,623	127	24	24	4	27	21	16·4

* Including small amounts of 'non-farming' income from house and cottage rents, etc. Excluding value of livestock purchased.

† At current market values, estimated by multiplying the written-down book values by 1·7.

Sources: Based on Ministry of Agriculture, *Farm Incomes in England and Wales 1952–53* (H.M.S.O. 1955), various tables.

First, the simple measures of relative efficiency do not take into account the costs of the larger inputs of management required on the larger farms. These inputs are far more difficult to assess than the salary and other costs of higher management in many other industries, but they are no less real. Day-to-day executive management in most of agriculture must be close, discriminating, and flexible because of the biological nature of the processes and products and because among the scarcest of all the factors is favourable weather in due season. The large space required is another difficulty: management of a farm with ten employees might well require close control of operations and results over a whole square mile. Management requirements are all the greater too, because to make optimum use of opportunities most farms must produce at least three quite different products, and many farms several more. Dame Nature grants approval and support more readily to diversified than to closely specialized production. Rotation of crops helps greatly to maintain soil fertility and freedom from the diseases and pests of both crop plants and livestock. The bulky products and by-products of rotations (for example, hay, oat straw, sugar beet tops, low quality potatoes) can be economically used for livestock production and the manure of livestock used to raise soil fertility particularly for the crops most responsive to it. Moreover, different types of crop and stock require labour at somewhat different times of the year. Under diversified systems of farming, therefore, labour requirements can be pieced together so as to secure greater labour efficiency. In some localities, where soil and climate favour one or two products much more than others such diversification is not economic. But even where the products are comparatively few a very wide range of technical and commercial knowledge is required for good farm management. To employ specialists in each subject would seem to permit an increase in farm sizes and a raising of gross outputs, but only at excessive cost. The work and advice of the specialists is especially difficult to co-ordinate in agriculture and most of them are seasonally under-employed as well as expensive. Admittedly, few individual farmers have wholly adequate sets of skills, but any marked disintegration of management functions within a farm commonly has adverse results. Comparatively few hierarchies of control have been maintained for long. Nor have the few large businesses built up by exceptionally able individual farmers attracted managers capable of maintaining them long after the deaths of their founders.

All this implies not only that management in the fullest sense is highly important, but also that it becomes more important, more difficult, and more costly as size of farm business expands. Far more men and their families can manage small and medium-sized farms than

could ably manage large ones. Few indeed can manage, at appropriate
levels of output, farms of a thousand acres or more of average quality
land. And the many expect and receive far lower monetary rewards
than the few. Thus when allowance is made for a basic interest charge
on the short- and medium-term capital invested and for farmers' and
their wives' manual labour, their remaining net returns—those for
management and risk bearing—do not appear, in dairying and livestock rearing areas, to be much more, on large farms as compared with
small, than might be explained as reasonable charges for the additional
management skills and energies required (Table 6). This is not so true
in the arable crop areas, and we are thus brought to the second reason
why simple comparisons of large and small farms are misleading.

Table 6. *Relation of capital investment and returns to areas of farms*
(1358 farms, England and Wales, 1952–3)

Total area of farms (acres)		Number of farms	'Tenant's' capital per farm £	Net returns (£ per farm) to 'tenant' for				'Tenant's' net returns as percentage of gross output
					Own and wife's manual labour	Manage-ment and profit	Total	
Range	Average			Capital at 4%				
				Dairying areas				
50–99	72	145	3,805	152	388	58	598	20
100–149	124	83	6,186	247	391	238	876	19
150–299	202	91	10,331	413	346	550	1,309	18
				Livestock areas				
50–99	78	134	3,235	129	413	78	620	32
100–149	124	106	4,352	174	471	159	804	33
150–299	213	183	7,116	285	472	333	1,090	29
300–499	385	59	9,682	387	473	557	1,417	30
500 and over	876	43	9,940	398	548	637	1,583	33
				Arable crop areas				
50–99	74	143	4,009	160	352	222	734	22
100–149	126	101	6,933	277	337	602	1,216	23
150–299	220	150	11,225	449	328	1,201	1,978	23
300–499	390	90	16,828	673	285	2,059	3,017	21
500 and over	756	30	28,811	1,152	168	3,584	4,904	22

Sources: As for Table 5.

This second reason is that risks and uncertainties are high in agriculture. A decline in the general price level is liable to affect farmers'
incomes much more than their costs for items such as hired labour, for
which minimum wages are fixed, or fertilizers, machinery or transport
services, which are produced largely with trade union labour under

conditions of oligopoly, and for which prices tend to be kept up. Even in the United Kingdom under State price-fixing and supply regulation the general level of agricultural product prices has been unstable, and is regarded by most farmers as likely to continue to be unstable. They realize that their market will continue to be influenced by supplies from overseas varying in quantity and price, and that, since British manufacturing industry must export, what the urban population will pay for food will also vary from time to time. During low price periods farmers of large farms are liable to suffer greater absolute losses because they have more at stake, and because wages make up a larger part of their costs, and feeding-stuffs, which are more flexibly priced, make up a smaller part. The difficulty is recognized as likely to be somewhat greater in arable than on dairying or cattle and sheep rearing areas because crop prices tend to fall farther when the general price level falls.

From year to year on individual farms the risks and uncertainties are also high even in the United Kingdom. Weather, pests, and prices may prove especially unfavourable for the particular products raised. Illness in the labour force may seriously affect seasonal work. Unavoidable breakdowns of machinery may occur during the short seasons when full and flexible working is essential. Such risks and uncertainties are abated to a considerable extent by diversification of production, and by close personal management, but the net outcome of any one year's work—or even that of two or three years taken together—is commonly subject to wide variation. Only some of the causes of such variation would be removed by organization of larger farms, and the gains thereby would probably be offset by the greater difficulties and costs of management. A few joint stock companies are organized for production on a number of farms where day-to-day executive work is entrusted to separate managers, and some of the risks reduced by pooling. But such companies have another type of uncertainty to face —the difficulty of identifying competent and reliable managers prepared to work at relatively low salaries. And as compensation for the shareholders the chance of occasional, very high over-all profits is generally remote.[1] Such companies cannot usually secure for themselves conditions of imperfect competition: they are still too small, and their products insufficiently different from those of thousands of other firms.[2]

The high variability of profits both from farmer to farmer and on the same farm from year to year causes uncertainties for those lending capital to agriculture. Credit tends to be granted more readily on the

[1] Much more remote than for most shareholders in plantation industries, where, too, management functions are simpler.

[2] Some retailing companies have gained from having a part of their supplies produced on farms of their own. Their customers have felt more confident of quality and freshness.

basis of safe proportions of the net worths of borrowers and the tangible securities offered than directly in accordance with the productivities of the additional capital investments to be made by the applicants for credit. Thus comparatively few farmers can, during their thirties and early forties, when they have had good experience and are still physically most active, go boldly forward to secure large farms adequately stocked. Many more enter small or medium-sized farms with inadequate capital and do no more than accumulate a little more before they are too old to want larger places.

Naturally, too, the high risks and uncertainties of farming affect farmers' decisions on the investment of their own assets and on the extents to which they are prepared to borrow. Some older farmers do expand their farms, but many invest substantial portions of their savings at fixed interest or in less risky ventures. Many farmers are averse from borrowing more than a quite small proportion of their total assets even although additional assets would on all rational assumptions very probably result in additional net revenue. Some farmers, particularly some who bought farms with vacant possession about 1950, have borrowed heavily, but as we have seen above, the industry as a whole has not. In this connexion it is significant too that the State has not relied on credit and inducements to borrow to anything like the extent that it has relied on subsidies and capital grants. Aversion from borrowing is thus among the main causes of slowness of change in farm sizes. The structure of the industry has remained one in which the labour and management of the farmer himself and his family, together with the use of his own short- and medium-term capital, are high in relation to other costs and normally equivalent to a large proportion of the value of the gross output (Table 6). This ensures survival of individual firms although not necessarily lowest average long-run costs.

Third among the causes of slow change are the opportunities farmers have had to raise productive efficiency otherwise than by changing farm areas. This history of British farms for almost a century is largely that of changes in the choice of products, of changes in the combination of factors, and of comparatively slow increases in the total volume of output with no great changes in the area of land farmed. To the individual farmer these changes have often seemed more profitable than substantial alterations to his whole scale of business. Faced with rising costs of labour he has been able to adopt new factors and techniques such as the corn binder, the tractor and its equipment, the combine harvester, chemical weed-killers, different crop rotations and so on. The smaller farmers have seen the relative advantages which the larger have gained from the invention of the tractor but they have also recognized that those advantages are not so great as is generally

Table 7. *Comparison of factor combinations on farms with average and above average returns on 'tenant's' capital and management (Six localities and types of farming, West of England, 1953–4)*

Locality, and type of farming	Land (acres)	'Tenant's' capital* (£)	Machine use† (£)	Live-stock (cow units) per 100 acres used for stock	Ferti-lizers and seeds	Total costs‡	Returns on 'tenant's' capital and manage-ment £ per £100 total costs
		Per £100 of manual labour costs			£ per acre overall		
South-West Somerset mixed arable							
Average	9·7	363	51	56	3·2	35	24
Above average	10·2	390	55	67	3·3	45	35
Hereford and Worcestershire mixed arable without milk							
Average	7·9	301	43	56	3·9	35	22
Above average	7·8	332	44	67	4·6	38	35
With milk							
Average	7·8	267	43	43	4·5	38	14
Above average	7·6	258	40	51	4·7	38	29
Cotswold and Wiltshire Downs							
Average	11·4	344	51	36	2·7	28	19
Above average	11·4	372	53	38	3·0	27	39
Somerset, dairy							
Average	9·1	307	42	48	1·4	39	19
Above average	8·5	324	43	56	1·3	42	32
Exmoor 'marginal' farms							
Average	15·2	352	39	40	1·4	18	22
Above average	15·2	402	44	45	1·6	19	36

* As stated in valuations. Underestimates of current market value.

† Excluding costs of work done by contractors, which appear to be about equal between the 'average' and 'above average' groups.

‡ Including rents. Excluding use of 'tenant's' capital and excluding any charges for management.

Source: Based on data collected by the Agricultural Economics Department, University of Bristol: see its *Farm Management Handbook Supplement 1954–5*, part I.

supposed. Excellent small tractors and equipment have been developed that can make it possible to have, on 60 to 80-acre farms, machine use costs per unit of through-put not very much greater than those on large farms. And the use of larger machines can often be bought at reasonable cost from outside contractors, as has long been the practice in threshing grain. Combine harvesters and hay balers are among the very few examples in agriculture of a feasible integration of processes through the use of larger and more complex machinery, and even their use can be bought reasonably cheaply by many small farmers with as little as seven to ten acres of grain or hay. Moreover, many farmers have seen opportunities to increase livestock as compared with grain production and made various other more complex adjustments in their choices of products in response to changing price relationships. In so doing they have secured some levelling out of labour requirements through the year. Many have also found opportunities to increase their *net* returns by allowing the processing of dairy products and the marketing of dairy products, eggs and poultry to be undertaken by middlemen. All these changes have seemed not only easier but more certainly advantageous than large changes in scale.

Fourthly: even if greater difficulties and costs of management, shortage of credit, and aversion from high risks and uncertainties, still leave some net advantages to large farms, and they seem more worth grasping than other opportunities for increasing profits, the difficulties of amalgamation have to be faced. To expand individual farms by absorbing neighbouring farms is not easy. The slow rate of about 3 or 4% a year at which holdings normally change occupiers makes the chance to buy or lease neighbouring farms uncommon, and rare indeed at just the right stage in the life and capital accumulation of the farmer wishing to expand. To induce vacancies at other times is costly because the neighbour's difficulties and losses in changing the location of his farm business would be substantial. His opportunities in alternative occupations are usually unattractive to him since many of his skills are of little value outside agriculture, and he prefers to be self-employed. Also his filial and parental obligations, as well as his upbringing, tend to make him socially immobile, and anxious to maintain his farm home. If he is a tenant, there are also his landlord's views to be considered. Then, too, even if a neighbouring farm can be secured the full advantages of amalgamation cannot be obtained without some re-laying out of field boundaries and roads, and new buildings and building alterations may well be required. All these are costly and require long-term capital. It is therefore not unnatural that amalgamation of neighbouring farms is infrequent.

Despite all this some farmers do expand the areas they farm: they shift from smaller to larger farms and they take over odd fields of nearby holdings. But neither of these changes has affected the structure of the industry much. A more important type of expansion is by taking on two or more holdings at some distance apart, with near relatives as partners, or carefully selected men as managerial assistants. But, again, as already noted, such arrangements have not affected much of the industry, although they have been favoured, especially in arable crop areas since the late 1930's, by high prices for products and, to some degree, by machinery developments.

Fifth and not least among the reasons for only minor changes in farm sizes is the demand for small farms, both for purchase outright and for renting. The psychic incomes which many derive from land and farming and from being self-employed are powerful attractions. And early optimism about material incomes is frequently not countered by sound calculation. For the most part the capital as well as the managerial skill of those wanting farms is strictly limited so that the majority bid for small places, forcing up their prices or rents and out-bidding such established farmers as might be willing and able to expand their businesses.

For all these five reasons, and others of lesser importance, the sizes and layouts of farms appear to have been changed little since they were determined on enclosure during the eighteenth century or earlier.

Some economies could now be achieved by moderate increases in farm sizes, particularly in arable crop areas, provided management skills were better developed and used, financial arrangements made appropriate, and land tenure arrangements altered to secure greater mobility of farms and fields between users.[1] Also, even although non-material returns are valued highly—full allowance made for the strong preferences of many people for farming and self-employment—a considerable

[1] The higher mobility of land between users in the United States is evident from the following table. Between 1930 and 1950 commercial farms which are responsible for about 97 % of the total agricultural output fell in numbers by 30 % although somewhat more land was brought into use as farm pastures, and the area of crop land was little changed. The number of part-time and residential 'farms' increased markedly, but the total number of 'farms' fell 14 %.

Twenty years' changes in numbers of 'farms' and agricultural holdings
(United States and Great Britain)

	United States		
	1930 (thousands)	1950 (thousands)	Change (%)
Commercial farms	5,282	3,706	− 30
Part-time and residential farms	1,007	1,673	+ 66
All farms	6,289	5,379	− 14
	Great Britain		
	1931 (thousands)	1951 (thousands)	Change (%)
Farmers, graziers and crofters	294	317*	+ 7
Agricultural holdings			
1–4·9 acres	100†	98	− 2
5 acres and over	387†	354	− 9

* From 1 % sample of 1951 occupational census results.
† Partly estimated allowing for changes in official statistical classification and coverage in the early 1940's.
Sources: For Great Britain, Ministry of Agriculture, Fisheries and Food, *Agricultura Statistics* series (H.M.S.O.) and occupational census data. For the United States, R. L. Mighell, *American Agriculture: Its Structure and Place in the Economy*, Census Monographs (New York, Wiley; London, Chapman and Hall, 1955), p. 50.

waste of human resources and eventual frustration are to be recognized on many small farms bought or rented more in hope than in reason.

The changing balance between tenancy and owner-occupancy is significant in relation both to mobility and to the problem of financing each generation of farmers. Provided arrangements for agricultural credit can be improved, the advantages of owner-occupancy are considerable, and a further reduction in tenancy may prove economic, but the cheaper long-term capital and greater mobility within the industry which sound landlord–tenant arrangements can secure should not be forgotten. Discouragement of ownership of farms for renting, except as a means for the rich to avoid some death-duties, has probably gone too far.[1]

(ii) *Factor prices and their opportunity costs.* For labour, agriculture appears always to have paid less per week, and still less per hour, than non-agricultural industry. During the whole period from 1850 to 1939 (except perhaps in 1915–18), the wage rate, including allowances in kind, for a full week's work without overtime was never for 'ordinary male farm labourers' more than 53 % of the average rate for fourteen representative predominantly male occupations in non-agricultural industries.[2] Allowances for differences in retail prices in rural as against urban conditions make little difference. By 1946–7, the corresponding percentage was still only 78. In 1953–4, average earnings of men in England and Wales were 146s. 9d. a week on farms, as against some 195s. in the principal industries excluding agriculture, coal and railways: and the hours of work were longer on farms.

The reasons for these differences are several. The higher skills required in some urban industries, the comparative weakness of the agricultural trade unions, the larger supply of new entrants to the labour force in many rural areas—these are contributory. The basic reason appears to be the immobility of many workers between agricultural and other occupations, due to (*a*) the non-material benefits,

---

[1] The efficiency in estate management of some State bodies, particularly the Church Commissioners, is also to be recognized. On the other hand, the State may be too readily led to make unwise investments in land improvements and buildings, as the Agricultural Land Commission has demonstrated (see its *Eighth Report*, for 1954–5 (H.M.S.O. 1955), pars. 8 and 9 and appendices). The same lesson was learnt earlier from experiences in the provision of small-holdings to meet the demands of farm-workers, returned soldiers and others as tenants. Up to 1926 the losses on small-holdings established and administered by County Councils and County Borough Councils in England and Wales were borne by the Exchequer and amounted to more than one-third of the total cost of providing the holdings. Since 1926 the costs have been borne by individual Councils. The total acreage of small-holdings (433 thousand acres) is now not much less than in 1926 but the number has been reduced from 30 thousand to 18 thousand.

[2] J. R. Bellerby, 'Distribution of Farm Income in the United Kingdom 1867–1938', *Journal of Proceedings of the Agricultural Economics Society*, vol. 10, no. 2, February 1953, p. 127; and unpublished data.

including 'whole-life advantages' which they feel they derive from rural life, (*b*) social ties, and (*c*) inadequate knowledge of urban industry and life.

The 'drift from the land' has gone on despite these, and is given prominence in public discussions of agriculture. Higher standards of rural education—which might well be more fully encouraged—closer communications, stronger trade unions, better urban housing and, not least, full employment, are all tending to accelerate the drift. But it has not yet brought about equal material payments for farm and non-farm labour.

For management and risk-bearing, agriculture has also usually paid low material returns. If from 'net farm incomes' to tenant farmers, allowances are deducted for interest on capital (at 1 % above the current yields on consols), the return per man-week of manual-cum-managerial work by farmers and their families was, over the period 1897–1914 in the British Isles as a whole, no greater than farm labourers' weekly earnings. From 1923 to 1932, in the United Kingdom it averaged only 14 % more. Even in recent years of unusual prosperity for farmers, it has been only 62 % more.[1] No valid comparison with material rewards for management in other occupations can be made, but in relation simply to the risks and uncertainties to be faced, the skills required, and hours of work, farmers' long-run returns may well be judged low. The figures do not, however, make any allowance for non-material benefits, and as previously noted these are in fact highly valued by many farmers. Indeed, the supply of farmers has for decades been fully adequate to maintain their numbers, despite low and fluctuating cash returns.

This is not to imply that society should be satisfied with an industry which is not efficient enough to pay good material rewards for enterprise and management. The very wide variations in production and cash profits, found in all localities, indicate rather that substantial improvements could and should be made. But an attempt to make them quickly by use of different sources of enterprise and management might well prove costly for it would not recognize that the low returns to many present farmers are due largely to their own willingness to work at these rates. The supply price of farmers, as of farm labour, is low. And Farmers' Union action is unlikely to alter it much, although it may raise the demand price.

For land, and long-term land improvements, agriculture has been tending to pay less than the alternative use values. State action has kept rents unduly low for most sitting tenants, and subsidies have in recent years been heavy for drainage, water installations, cottages, hill land improvement and so on. The State has also prevented the

---

[1] Based on Bellerby, *loc. cit.*

transfer of considerable areas of land to non-agricultural uses, although such action in favour of agriculture is commonly difficult to justify by any reasonable allowances for differences between the general social interest, and that of individual land users, with their higher effective rates of interest and shorter-term views. The State has very probably under-estimated the extent to which land would be more efficiently used by agriculture if its annual use prices were raised.

For many other factors agriculture pays at least the full opportunity costs. But for nitrogenous and phosphatic fertilizers, costs of establishing good leys, disease controls, and several other factors, the State's subsidies are large.[1] The reasons appear to be not only that the State wants a higher volume of production than, unsubsidized, the industry is prepared to undertake, but also that the State believes many farmers are not operating efficiently, and have to be subsidized into taking rational decisions on the use of factors.

(iii) *Changes in combination of the factors of production.* Continuous changes have been made by farmers in their combination of factors in response to changing price relationships, increasing knowledge of productivities, and new techniques. Thus, for instance, labour has risen in cost relative to machinery; fertilizers and pesticides have fallen relative to the value of the additional products they secure; and farmers have reacted accordingly. Between 1938 and 1953, the total labour force was increased by only 11 %, but the *quantum* of fertilizers, machinery, and miscellaneous services used increased by some 160 %. Through the decades, substantial increases in the productivity of farm labour have been secured, despite the tendency to put low values on family labour and to work with too little capital. Table 8 shows for six counties the average annual increases in the basic task accomplished per man. In

Table 8. *Increase in labour 'task' per man**
(Six selected counties in Great Britain)

Average increase a year (%)

Period	Hampshire	Leicester	Fife	Argyll	Denbigh	Anglesey
1891–1911†	0·4	0·7	0·4	−0·3	0·4	−0·1
1921–31	1·5	2·3	0·9	0·2	1·4	0·9
1931–51	0·6	0·7	0·9	1·6	0·8	0·8

* Acreages of crops and numbers of livestock multiplied by the average number of days' labour each type required about 1951 and divided by a measure of the labour force expressed in terms of adult male workers. No allowances are made for any increased production per acre or head of livestock, nor for any changes in the general maintenance and improvement tasks accomplished.

† No account taken of changes in numbers of poultry.

[1] Total subsidies on factors and operations were estimated as £73 million in 1956–7.

addition, yields per acre of crops and per head of livestock were markedly increased. Significantly, the largest increases in basic task per man were achieved during the late 1920's and early 1930's when product prices were falling but wages were kept up by the Wage Board arrangements. The farmers' response was not to reduce output: increases in numbers of livestock more than offset contractions of acreage of tillage crops. Between 1926 and 1936 in Great Britain the over-all basic task on livestock was increased by 13 % and that on crops reduced by 6 %. The total task rose by 4 %. But the labour force was reduced by 12 %. Thus the task per man increased by 18 % over the ten years.[1]

The increases in yields have been the result not only of much intelligent observation by farmers themselves but also of State-financed research and advisory work on soils, fertilizers, plant and animal improvement, pests of all kinds, animal nutrition and diseases, and of administrative measures to secure good quality in materials and services used. Innovations in agriculture are fostered and spread by the State and the structure of the industry is such that there are always a substantial number of leading farmers prepared to start the process of adoption. In the face of competition from thousands of other farmers at home and overseas they see no gain from delay. Even in the oligopolistic markets for fertilizers and the more complicated machines there can be only limited scope for the holding up of new ideas to keep existing plant profitable. A large amount of useful advisory work and an increasing amount of research and development has in fact been undertaken by some of the suppliers of materials and equipment for agriculture.

But all this does not prove that at any one time optimum factor combinations are achieved by agriculture. Variations in efficiency from farm to farm are indeed so great as to require for explanation not only great differences between farmers in their demands for income and their attitudes to risk and uncertainty but also substantial inadequacies in technical knowledge, managerial abilities, net worths and opportunities to borrow capital. Many farmers do not operate anywhere near their 'optimum profit points' narrowly defined, and, even if full allowance is made for uncertainty and for differences in objectives, it cannot be doubted that a substantial number are not wholly rational in their detailed decisions on use of factors. They follow local leaders, but at various distances.

Statistical proof of these matters is difficult because, in any one set of reasonably uniform conditions of soil, climate and topography, the

---

[1] Hours of labour were also slightly reduced so that per man-hour the task rose about 19 %. The roughly comparable figure for the United States was 20 %. Between 1936 and 1949 the basic task per man-hour increased 13 % in Great Britain—about the same amount as in the United States.

number of farms for which reliable information is available is very
small, and even within such conditions, individual farmers differ
somewhat in their choice of products, so that their factor combinations
vary for that reason. Data from a range of different localities and types
of farming in the West of England can, however, be presented (Table 7)
to give a rough indication of some variations in factor combination
encountered. For each fairly uniform set of conditions various ratios
for the more profitable half of the farms (the 'above average' farms)
can be compared with those for all the farms studied.[1] Farmers on
the 'above average' farms in 1953–4 combined land and labour in
about the same proportions as those on 'average' farms. Their machine
use costs were only slightly higher in relation to the labour used, but
they employed substantially more 'tenant's' capital. They had markedly
more livestock per acre of land used for livestock feeding. They spent
a little more on purchased fertilizers and seeds, and their total annual
inputs per acre tended to be higher. These differences, together with
more careful choice of *qualities* of input, better timing, and other
management decisions served to raise their returns for 'tenant's' capital
and management far above the averages for the same localities (Table 7,
last column).

The ratio of 'landlord's' capital to 'tenant's' capital and to land is
also seriously uneconomic on many farms. The investment of long-term
assets such as modern buildings, water equipment, drainage and fencing
can save much labour and may permit large increases in production.
But in the greater part of the industry, the responsibility for it is that of
land owners rather than land users, and State control over the relations
between these groups has on the whole restricted this investment.
Statutory powers to compel 'good estate management' have had almost
no compensating effect, and there are obvious limits, political and
administrative as well as economic, on the extent to which subsidies
should be used for this purpose.

(iv) *Divergence of home and imported product prices*. The comparatively
perfect competition in the marketing of home agricultural produce and
the absence of subsidies and import restrictions served until the early
1930's to keep the general price levels for home and imported produce
closely similar in their movements, and to ensure that changes in price
relationships between individual products in import markets were
promptly and quite fully reflected in changed relationships in farmers'
markets. Thus the first three columns of Table 9 show that, until after
1929, only minor divergencies of home produce prices from imported
produce prices took place. Variations in qualities were the main causes.
The average price received for milk was an exception, made possible

---

[1] No other comparisons are possible from the published data.

by the difficulties of importing such a perishable product as fresh milk, for which the direct consumption was expanding, and by the segregation within the United Kingdom market already noted. Another exception was the price of sugar beet, from 1924 onwards divorced by a heavy subsidy from the price of imported sugar.

Table 9. *Prices of home agricultural produce in terms of imported**

(Index: 1911–13 = 100)

	1923	1926	1929	1932	1935	1938	1952	1953	1954	1956
Wheat	100	103	101	136	157	138	97	108	126	115
Barley	99	105	97	118	148	134	70	97	116	97
Milk	111	119	120	160	201	169	158	149	143	125
Fat cattle	120	107	87	98	115	114	†	†	110‡	115
Fat lambs	103	102	109	104	104	90	114	108	105	98
Baconers	104	102	98	111	83	88	125	141	129	126
Porkers	101	98	104	91	101	104	93	106	97	117
Eggs	106	95	96	103	119	124	118	120	110	102

* Computed by dividing index numbers of prices (including subsidies) for home agricultural produce in England and Wales by index numbers of average c.i.f. values per unit of imported produce, and multiplying by 100. Milk is compared with the average of imported butter (all sources) and imported New Zealand cheese.

† Not available owing to large change in quality of imports.

‡ July 1954 to June 1955, and based on changes since the 1930's in wholesale prices for English longsides, Australian frozen, and Argentine chilled, hindquarters.

During the 1930's the State's protection and assistance of agriculture raised the general level of home produce prices much above that for imports (fourth to sixth columns of Table 9) and, moreover, the prices of some imports (for example, beef, lamb, bacon and pork) were themselves raised by quantitative restrictions.

In post-war years, the annual price review arrangements have also maintained a substantial divergence of home produce and import price levels (last four columns of Table 9). Percentage-wise this divergence has, for most products except bacon pigs, appeared smaller than during the 1930's, but in absolute terms it has been much greater because the general level of prices has been so much higher. Thus, as already noted, the subsidies required in 1956–7 were estimated at £162 million apart from the welfare subsidies and subsidies on factors and operations.

This picture of substantially higher prices for home agricultural products than for imported, and of State action preventing alterations in price relationships in the import market from being made clear in the prices paid to home producers, would not be significantly different in recent years if detailed allowances were made for unusual differences in quality, or in season of supply, or for temporary subsidies by overseas governments on exports to this country.

(v) *Response of outputs to markets and prices.* The multitude of small firms in agriculture each coming to its own decisions on what and how much to produce makes adjustment of production within the industry as a whole a continuous and highly complex process. State propaganda and action through local committees have had an influence on this process at certain times but usually it is governed largely by changing price and cost relationships as viewed by the individual firms.

Some of the effects of this continuous adjustment may be seen in Table 10. Over the four nine-year periods chosen for study, acreages and livestock numbers were increased and decreased substantially and in a complex way, the amounts and the directions of the changes varying as between the types of crop or stock and as between one period and another. And, from year to year, the changes were quite large.

Table 10. *Changes in crop acreages and livestock numbers*
(Great Britain)

Period	Wheat	Barley	Potatoes	Cows and heifers-in-calf	Cattle under 1 year	Ewes	Sows	Fowls
				Trend (percentage a year)*				
1901–10	+1·1	−1·7	−0·7	+1·1	+0·5	+1·0	−0·5	n.a.
1921–30	−3·4	−4·3	−0·7	+0·9	+0·5	+3·0	−1·0	+6·5
1930–9	+3·8	−1·6	−0·7	+1·4	+0·6	−0·4	+3·1	−0·4
1945–54	+1·0	−0·7	−6·0	+0·6	+2·5	+1·6	+16·1	+7·1
				Mean change from year to year apart from trend (%)†				
1901–10	8·9	1·8	3·4	1·0	2·9	1·4	6·8	n.a.
1921–30	5·7	4·0	6·4	1·1	3·3	2·2	16·1	1·9
1930–9	8·1	8·4	4·6	1·4	4·7	2·7	7·8	4·6
1945–54	10·8	6·7	6·4	1·5	5·6	3·2	19·1	7·2

n.a. = not available.

* Mean rate of increase over whole period expressed as percentage of mean acreages or livestock numbers.

† Percentage changes from year to year, corrected for trend, and averaged without regard to sign.

The extent and complexity of the adjustments are even more evident when those in different localities are compared. Each individual locality tends to have its own particular production conditions determined basically by soils, climate and topography, and also by past capital investments and marketing costs. Therefore the substitution rates between products, and between factors, and the transformation rates between factors and products all differ from locality to locality and the agriculture of each responds somewhat differently to changes in product prices, factor costs or transport charges. A few statistics illustrating this from the standpoint of changing choice of crops in different counties are set out in Table 11.

Table 11. *Acreages of wheat, barley and potatoes*
(Six counties of England)

	Wheat (Thousand acres)	Wheat (Index: 1910 = 100)		Barley (Acres per 100 acres of wheat)			Potatoes (Acres per 100 acres of wheat)		
	1910	1930	1950	1910	1930	1950	1910	1930	1950
Lancashire	20	79	156	22	6	7	215	227	117
Yorkshire									
East Riding	65	109	143	118	73	94	19	16	26
North Riding	24	115	249	318	177	117	48	46	47
West Riding	47	112	187	119	43	86	52	51	53
Lincolnshire	172	104	166	122	79	54	38	54	54
Northamptonshire	45	73	179	82	48	41	6	5	12

Source: Basic data from the Ministry of Agriculture's, series, *Agricultural Statistics, England and Wales* (H.M.S.O.).

Decisions affecting seasonal variations in output of individual products are equally complex and subject to continuous adjustment.

But while it may be claimed that the agricultural industry as a whole has a fairly lively 'sense of the margin', the adjustments made at any one time are probably not as great within the limits of biological conditions, nor as wisely chosen, as full assessments of prospects would suggest. Uncertainties over future prices, lack of capital, and aversion from borrowing, as well as technical uncertainties and poor management on many farms, undoubtedly do dampen and delay adjustments.

Moreover, since the prices paid to farmers have in such large measure been determined by the State the question arises: 'Has State action in control of agricultural prices had advantageous effects on the composition of the home agricultural output?' In that price relationships between home products have been made very different from price relationships between imported products the answer is undoubtedly: 'No, unless import prices are unsound measures of relative costs.' During war-time when shipping space for wheat, feeding-stuffs and other bulky products was short, wheat and other 'ship-saving' products and milk were wisely favoured. And after the war when certain foreign currencies were especially difficult to obtain there was some reason to arrange internal relationships to induce larger outputs of the products most difficult to pay for abroad. But in recent years it is clear that the State maintained too long internal price relationships suited to war-time conditions or unduly influenced by the currency crisis of 1947.

Thus milk, wheat, bacon pig and egg outputs were kept too high relative to beef and lamb production, and home-grown feeding-stuff production, which in war-time had the stimulus of severe shortage of imported supplies, was not given its due proportion of direct subsidies. Of the total subsidies on product prices in 1955–6 three-quarters were for milk, wheat, bacon pigs and eggs.

In the spring of 1956 the government belatedly tried to correct price relationships, particularly by substantially raising the guaranteed price for fat cattle. But by then import prospects for beef had become markedly more favourable and market prices were falling. The subsidy rate on beef therefore became high. The sustained high subsidies on milk and eggs were also increasing to embarrassing levels as a result of the additional home production they had fostered. But as already noted (p. 17) the government then agreed to restrict its right to reduce guaranteed prices and so to secure appropriate adjustments in the choice of products. These restrictions may well result in more serious maladjustments and lead directly to sudden price and market changes. Stability is not to be achieved by near rigidity.

Turning now to the total volume of production of the industry: it too is determined almost entirely by the continuous decisions of the multitude of individual firms in the light of the price and cost conditions each faces. More centralized direct control has been exercised to a substantial extent only by the County Agricultural Committees in war-time.

Groupings of data for individual farm businesses into those with low, medium and high outputs per acre suggest that costs *decrease* as output increases. But since it is improbable that many farmers are wholly irrational in adjusting their outputs the main question such statistical groupings pose becomes: 'What obstacles do many individual firms face in raising their outputs further towards the levels which other firms find more profitable?' Again the answers lie in the industry's structure for production, in finance arrangements, in the market for land, and in technical and price uncertainties. Technical and business management of the numerous small units requires much knowledge and many skills, and these have certainly not been acquired in ideal amounts by all those concerned. Capital requirements are high and turnovers slow on the whole; but finance is largely by individual entrepreneurs, the large technical and price uncertainties causing much aversion from borrowing and considerable limitation of credit facilities. And these difficulties of producing at the optimum intensity are naturally aggravated by the discontinuities of management and finance caused by the ageing and death of individual farmers. Moreover, land is comparatively immobile as between users, and in recent years the price of land and long-term improvements to land has been kept low for many users, so that their incentives to secure increased outputs have been reduced.

Two further points about the total volume of output are noteworthy. First, there is no substantial evidence from past experience to support the opinion that large parts of the agricultural industry tend to reduce production when product prices rise. Rising prices induce larger inputs. Some of these are mainly to ease the labour and management problems of farmers and, admittedly, the large real price increases since 1939 have, together with technical developments, induced an expansion of *net* output by the industry on a tenant-farmer basis (in the sense of net value added) of the order of only 30 % rather than the more commonly quoted 50 to 60 %. The official 'net output' figures take no account of the large increase in use of machinery, fertilizers, and other factors. But the over-all effect of favourable prices has been to raise outputs, not to lower them. Secondly, in periods of declining prices, the total volume of production tends to be maintained for a considerable number of years largely because for the industry as a whole (*a*) prime, avoidable costs are small compared with overhead costs with which must be grouped the costs of family labour because this is, particularly in de-pression periods, highly immobile, with low opportunity costs, (*b*) the production processes are biological, and (*c*) the small-scale structure does not readily permit production restriction.

(vi) *Productive capacity for the future.* Fears are sometimes expressed about the willingness of firms in agriculture to keep up productive capacity for use in the more distant future. The interests of individual firms are not, it is asserted, likely to serve the general interest sufficiently in this respect. Commonly, however, these fears are based on an in-adequate understanding of the complexity of what constitutes produc-tive capacity in agriculture. In order to secure greater gross production in the future at low cost it is not essential that present production should be raised to the same level. Agriculture has shown itself sufficiently flexible to expand production and alter choices of products and com-binations of factors to meet gradual changes in prices of products or costs of factors. And performance since 1938 suggests that, within the limits of the guidance given, adjustment to basic changes that are comparatively sudden can be quite commendable. Criticism is justi-fiable only when there is good reason to believe that the multitude of individual firms have, considered as a composite, (*a*) wrong views about future prices, factor costs, and production possibilities, (*b*) effective rates of interest in mind that are unduly high, or (*c*) irrational production plans. There are some grounds for such beliefs, and opportunities for improvement, but it is highly probable that a single central State view and decisions on the whole complex of future demands, supplies and prices for products and factors, and of production possibilities, would prove to be more mistaken, more inflexible, and, at least in the longer run, more unacceptable both nationally and internationally.

(vii) *Costs of factor purchasing and product selling.* The dispersed location and small-scale structure of agriculture naturally tend to raise its costs of procuring factors and selling products. Dispersion of production is, however, inevitable and no feasible change in the size of the producing units would substantially alter marketing costs. Such economies of scale as exist in marketing must therefore be achieved within the marketing trades themselves. For this purpose reliance has been placed mainly on competition and only in a comparatively few directions has it been imperfect except when prices and margins were fixed, and building severely restricted, in war-time and the post-war years.

Where competition has been most nearly perfect there is little reason to expect that large economies can be achieved quickly. Integrated, centrally controlled arrangements for purchase and slaughter of fat-stock and distribution of meat have been promoted in the expectation of economies of scale, but they are not yet proven. The Milk Marketing Boards have, largely as agents of the Ministry of Food in war-time, been able to secure economies in the assembly of milk, but other marketing boards, and the Ministry of Food in post-war years, have achieved little. Proposals for new marketing boards have been turned down by producers themselves largely because of doubts about their ability to secure economies. Likewise State attempts since 1928 to promote the use of 'national mark' standards of quality have largely failed because, among other reasons, bigger scale marketing organizations requiring such standards have not proven economic. The more centralized organizations for marketing Danish, New Zealand and other countries' exported farm produce are often held forth as examples of efficiency to be copied in a reorganization of marketing in Britain. But the economies of scale in assembly of much produce at a few points for long-distance transport, and in selling at a distance, are substantially different from those in marketing at the nearby towns of a thickly populated country home-produce that need not travel far. This is clear from the experience of the United States. For farm produce transported from the mid-west and west to the east large organizations have tended to out-compete small, and much use is made of Federal and other quality standards: but within the east smaller firms have retained their position, marketing is less centralized and buyers rely more on personal inspection for quality assessment.

Also held out as an indication of inefficiency in British agriculture is the fact that much of the export selling of produce and the buying of feeding-stuffs, fertilizers and other factors is in Denmark and other countries carried out largely by farmers' co-operative societies. Such societies are not, however, lacking in Britain. Indeed, the total memberships in them number over 270 thousand.[1] They handle about 7 % of the produce sold off farms, and about 13 % of the total of feeding-stuffs, fertilizers, and machinery bought by farmers. Some of these societies have grown comparatively large and the tendency appears to be to increase co-operative trading. Societies are a safeguard against imperfect competition and provide farmers with outlets for capital and enterprise which are in several ways complementary to their ordinary outlets. But, in the circumstances of Great Britain, other gains thereby in over-all marketing efficiency cannot be regarded as large.

Where competition in carrying out marketing functions has been most imperfect in the United Kingdom the reason has been State control, or considerable economies of scale, or both. As already noted, some of the processing functions have been the most affected in the product markets—flour-milling, brewing, sugar beet processing, dairy product manufacture, and bacon curing. In the factor markets, economies of scale in the fertilizer, oilseed crushing and tractor industries have been prominent. Considerably more published information and analyses are necessary before sound judgments can be made on the appropriateness of the gross margins of these processing trades and industries. Meantime, safeguards are not entirely lacking, in the co-operative wholesale societies and agricultural co-operatives, and in the competition of imports.

The costs of credit provision for agriculture merit special consideration. By relying on local private sources, merchants and auctioneers, branch banks and the state agricultural mortgage corporations using these banks as agents, such costs have been minimized but the industry's finance is still very largely undertaken by individual farmers themselves and tends to be inadequate. Among other results is the attempt to 'inject' capital into the industry through the costly system of capital grants and subsidies by the State on both products and factors.

(viii) *Impact of State special requirements for balance of payments, security and welfare.* During the inter-war period the State did not try to induce any expansion of agricultural production for security reasons until the late 1930's. But by 1944 agriculture had so changed that, although annual food and feeding-stuff imports were at less than half their pre-war level, the nation was fed. The composition of food imports and a change to more austere diets contributed to the saving of imports but a bigger contribution was due to agriculture's ability greatly to reduce

[1] Some farmers are members of more than one society, since many societies are not multi-purpose.

dependence on imported feeding-stuffs and expand production of wheat, potatoes, milk and vegetables. If during the inter-war years total agricultural production had been kept high, the possibilities of altering and expanding in war-time would have been much smaller and in all probability less shipping would have been available because less would have had peace-time employment importing feeding-stuffs, wheat and other foodstuffs.

In relation to possible future requirements, however, the *promptness* with which home supplies can replace imported may well be crucial. Large peace-time stores of food and of feeding-stuffs, fertilizers and other production factors may be essential. To minimize the amount of expansion of home agriculture required a larger peace-time agriculture may also be necessary. On the other hand recent developments in warfare may well have made reliance on United Kingdom agriculture, at least for a net expansion of output in war-time, wholly inadvisable.

All that can usefully be noted here is that although security requirements are in a vague way still borne in mind in discussions of agricultural policy none of the post-war governments has made any clear statement about them, and they are apparently not defined.

The clearest statement of demands on home agriculture to save imports for balance of payment reasons was that made in August 1947 when the £100 million expansion programme was announced. Figures for production during 1951–2 of the major crops and livestock products were set as 'targets', and the implication was that £100 million a year of expenditure of foreign exchange would be saved by 1951–2 as compared with 1946–7. But the additional inputs to permit such a saving were not brought fully into account, nor was it made clear that the valuation of the saving was at internal United Kingdom prices rather than c.i.f. or f.o.b. prices for imports. After 1951, the 'targets' have been even less well-defined. The general intention now is that the gross output less purchases of feeding-stuffs and imported livestock and seeds— the official 'net output' (see p. 39 above)—should be raised to at least 60 % above the level of the late 1930's. But no time limit has been laid down and no statement of the probable savings of foreign currencies has been published as a basis for discussion and analysis.

Actual results in saving foreign exchange appear to have been worth while in the circumstances of the post-war years, at least up to 1952–3.[1] Increases in annual production between the end of the war and 1952–3 valued at c.i.f. prices in 1953 for the produce normally readily imported and at internal United Kingdom prices for other products such as milk were, after deduction of additional imports of factors valued at 1953

[1] J. R. Raeburn, 'Agricultural Policy: Some Economic Results and Prospects', *Three Banks Review*, no. 20, December 1953, p. 9.

c.i.f. prices, worth £117 million. Internal costs for labour were down by about as much as other internal costs were up and the actual returns of farmers and landowners were not substantially different in 1952–3 than at the end of the war if allowance was made for changes in the general price level.

On the other hand the agriculture of recent years is not to be judged against war-time agriculture, which was geared mainly for 'ship-saving', nor for that matter against the peculiar agricultural situation of the late 1930's. It should be judged against current and prospective demands.

The current contributions to foreign exchange saving are probably not the most appropriate. The subsidies are, as already noted, largely for additional milk used to save imports of cheese and other milk products purchased within the sterling area, bacon pigs and eggs to save imports from Denmark and the Netherlands, and soft wheat saving mainly Australian pounds. Expenditures on feeding-stuffs largely from hard-currency areas tend to be reduced somewhat by subsidies on factors and operations but increased by the heavy requirements for milk, pig and egg production. Net savings of gold or dollar expenditure by the additional products of home agriculture may well be comparatively small. But neither these current contributions nor the government's views on appropriate future contributions are adequately and clearly set out.

Again, as to employment, the State has not been clear about its objectives, nor about the relative efficacies of means to achieve them. Agriculture is not a suitable industry to provide employment for workers laid off by other industries during depressions. Where agriculture was required to do so during the inter-war years the costs were high and the benefits comparatively small. Agriculture's own labour force is not greatly reduced during depressions: farms are not shut down like factories. Moreover, per worker, capital requirements in agriculture are high (p. 27) and much land is required. Not least important, the special skills required are complex.

Measures to secure income distributions more favourable to farmers and farm workers may seem desirable because their cash incomes tend to be comparatively low on average and are unstable. But the protection and assistance of home agriculture cannot rightly be considered in isolation from general monetary, fiscal and trade policies nor from the opportunities to improve choice of products and combinations of factors within agriculture. The pattern of protection developed piecemeal during the depression served to raise farm incomes but its cost was substantial and other measures, with fewer international drawbacks, and better integrated, might well have been thought out.

The Agriculture Act of 1947 was conceived largely to provide well integrated protection in times of falling prices. Since it was passed prices have been rising and some subsidization has been desirable on balance of payment grounds. But several considerations suggest that the assumption by the State of responsibilities for agricultural welfare will almost always lead to large transfers of income from taxpayers and consumers to farmers. There is the concern of governments with the rural vote. Stability of farm incomes may by itself not seem adequate to politicians and they will for this reason continue subsidization into more normal or even prosperous periods. This is all the more likely because the comparatively low long-run incomes of farmers and farm workers are readily looked upon as inequitable and wrong on social grounds, rather than as evidence of the economic fact that the long-run supply prices in cash terms of many of the men concerned is low, supplemented as it is by non-cash benefits which they value highly but seldom discuss.

Moreover, during the next decade, the unusually high level of agricultural incomes established following the currency crisis of 1947 may prove to be the cause of large income transfers to farmers. The political difficulties of returning to a less artificial level are aggravated by the financial difficulties which the ever-increasing proportion of post-war entrants to the industry would face. These entrants may well already feel that post-war attempts to provide 'stability' for the industry have not in practice reduced their own burdens of long-term uncertainties to much less than those borne by previous generations of farmers. The main beneficiaries of the consumer-taxpayer's subsidies may seem to the new entrants to be the older sitting tenants and those with land to sell with vacant possession: the forward guarantees of incomes have already been largely capitalized in vacant possession values and in the prices of breeding and store livestock and of some other production factors.

4. MAIN CONCLUSIONS

This brief review of agriculture suggests three main conclusions. First, there are sound reasons for a basic structure of numerous, small, multi-product firms: the economies of scale and close specialization in farming are not large when management costs and uncertainty bearing are brought into account. Secondly, the managerial skills and the capital in the industry tend to be ill-distributed and inadequate to secure, without State aid, the levels of production and net income that have become State objectives. Thirdly, the State's main methods of achieving these objectives—controls in markets for land and labour, subsidies on factors and operations, forward price guarantees and subsidies for products, Marketing Boards, supply regulation, and even compulsory powers over farm and estate management—these have longer-run economic consequences and difficulties that have been largely ignored.

Perhaps the most important of these, in view of wide variations in managerial abilities and capital resources, is aggravation of the immobility of land between users. The new compulsory powers are, in practice, little or no compensation for this. The annual use values of farms and farm land have come to be incorrectly priced, and many tenants' positions too secure.

Credit arrangements are still not fully appropriate, nor fully used. Injection of capital by subsidies is not a satisfactory long-term substitute, being liable to misdirect resources, costly to taxpayers, and, in all probability, eventually misleading to many new entrants to the industry.

Nor are these subsidies a real assurance of stability for the industry as a whole. The price ratios between products when fixed by the State on the methods so far devised are liable to misguide production. And the general level of subsidies comes under political review at least yearly. Consumers and taxpayers will sooner or later seriously question why farmers should have their basic earnings augmented not simply by the strong natural attractions of their calling but also by heavy subsidies. And the monopoly powers of the Marketing Boards will not inevitably stand the tests of time.

BIBLIOGRAPHY

(a) Books, Pamphlets and Articles

Astor, Viscount and Rowntree, B. Seebohm, *British Agriculture*, London, Longmans, Green, 1938.

Bellerby, J. R., *Agriculture and Industry: Relative Income*, London, Macmillan, 1956.

Cambridge University School of Agriculture, Farm Economics Branch, *Annual Reports on the Economics of Farming in the Eastern Counties*, 1931 to date.

Journal of Agricultural Economics (formerly *Journal of Proceedings of the Agricultural Economics Society*), vols. 1 to 12.

Murray, Sir Keith A. H., *Agriculture*, History of the Second World War, United Kingdom Civil Series, London, H.M.S.O. and Longmans, Green, 1955.

(b) Official Publications

(All published by H.M.S.O.)

Agriculture Act, 1947, 10 & 11 Geo. 6.

Ministry of Agriculture, Fisheries and Food (formerly Ministry of Agriculture and Fisheries), *Farm Incomes in England and Wales 1952–3* and later years, Farm Incomes Series, 1955 onwards.

Long-Term Assurances for Agriculture, Cmnd. 23, 1956.

National Farm Survey of England and Wales 1941–43, 1946.

Report of the Committee on the Working of the Agricultural Marketing Acts (the Lucas Committee), Economics Series, no. 48, 1947.

Report of the Committee appointed to review the Provincial and Local Organization and Procedures of the Ministry of Agriculture, Fisheries and Food, Cmd. 9732, 1956.

Rights and Obligations of Landlords, Tenants and Owner-Occupiers of Agricultural Land, 1949.

Home Office, Ministry of Agriculture and Fisheries and Scottish Home Department, *Annual Review and Determination of Guarantees* (published until 1954 as *Annual Review and Fixing of Farm Prices*), Cmd. 8239, 8556, 8798, 9104, 9406, 9721, 1951 to 1956.

Scotland, Department of Agriculture, *Scottish Agricultural Economics*, vols. I to VI, Edinburgh, 1950 to 1955.

CHAPTER II

THE BUILDING INDUSTRY

By C. F. Carter

1. SCOPE AND SCALE

The industry which comes under review in this chapter is defined in the Standard Industrial Classification as follows:

Establishments engaged in erecting, repairing or decorating houses, shops, factories, etc., including establishments specializing in particular sections of the work, such as plumbing, plastering, roofing or installation of heating and ventilating apparatus....

Establishments undertaking electrical wiring in buildings, etc., and the erection and maintenance of electric signs....

Establishments constructing or repairing roads, bridges, docks, canals, railways, tunnels, airfields, etc.; laying drains, sewers, gas mains and cables; erecting telegraph and telephone lines; open-cast coal mining; laying out sports grounds; and other similar work....[1]

—together with certain similar activities of central and local government.

There is much more here than the elementary activity of enclosing bits of space for the purposes of shelter. The industry is extended, for convenience, to include the installation (and consequently the subsequent repair) of fixtures, for example plumbing, electric wiring, or central heating, which are usually put in position at the time of building. It is also extended to include other structures fixed to the earth's surface, such as bridges, which (though they are not intended for shelter), involve the use of techniques of building. Having thus included the civil engineering industry, the definition is bound for convenience to follow that industry into activities which are only distantly like building— such as open-cast coal mining.

The result is a giant among industries, with a gross output in 1955 of some £1860 million—of which only about a third is accounted for by the typical activity of house-building. The raw materials of the industry cost £850 million, so that the 'net output' or 'value added' in the industry was some £1000 million. This forms the fund from which wages, salaries, profits and taxes must be paid. Wages and salaries took 80%; it is not easy to trace the distribution of the remaining 20%, but about a quarter can be regarded as the 'wages' of working proprietors.

[1] Central Statistical Office, *Standard Industrial Classification* (H.M.S.O. 1948), pp. 23–4.

This leaves 15 % of the value added in the industry, and income and profits taxes probably accounted for about 5 %, interest and dividends for 2 %, and the renewal and extension of the physical capital of the industry for about 5 %, the remainder being available for addition to financial reserves.

Most parts of the building industry have of course been fully employed since the war; but so have most other industries, and there is no evidence that the building industry has been unusual in its prosperity. Thus the rate of profit on turnover (5 to 6 %) and the rate of profit on the total value of the assets employed in the business, as shown in company balance sheets (12 to 15 %), both appear to have been in the recent past somewhat below the average for industry as a whole. But moderate profits are no evidence of efficiency, and the industry has often been criticized for low productivity and high costs. In this chapter those aspects of the industry are considered which are related to its economic efficiency.

The questions to be considered are important, for the industry domi-nates the field of capital formation. Since 1948, building has been between 40 and 50 % of the value of all the so-called 'fixed' capital (i.e. other than stocks and work in progress) which has been created either as replacement or as an addition to the capital stock. Since buildings last longer than plant or machinery, about three-quarters by value of all the fixed capital of the country is probably a product of building or civil engineering. The value of capital formation in the form of new buildings and works in 1955 was £1355 million, of which £642 million was in new housing, £549 million building for industry and trade, and £164 million building for social and public services. This is not the whole value of the work of the industry, since it omits maintenance and repair work; on the other hand, part of the new building work is done, not by employees of the building and civil engineering industry, but by direct employees of the final user classified to other trades. It would seem likely that about £1300 million worth of new buildings and works were produced by the industry, leaving £560 million for repair, maintenance and miscellaneous work.

2. THE TYPES OF FIRM

In order to look further into the structure of the industry, it is necessary to go back to the Census of Production for 1948—the latest which, at the time of writing, gives adequate detail. The gross output of the industry in the United Kingdom was, in that year, about £1200 million, but of this over £100 million is accounted for by the employees of local authorities (whose main work was in the maintenance of roads and buildings), £63 million by civil engineering on the railways, £16 million by work done by government departments, and £11 million by work done by dock and harbour undertakings. Leaving out Northern Ireland (which had no Census in 1948), the gross output of private building and civil engineering firms was about £980 million, of which £800 million was accounted for by the firms employing more than ten people (for which the Census gives full detail).

The output of £980 million was produced by the remarkable number of at least 130,000 different 'firms'. 55,000 or more of these employed no operatives, consisting solely of the proprietor working on his own account. A further 60,000 employed ten operatives or less (with an average of four or five). The small firms are predominantly employed on repair and maintenance work: they have shown a considerable contraction in numbers since 1948. But over 80 % of the 1948 output, and a still higher proportion of new construction, was the product of some 16,000 firms with more than ten employees: and half the output was due to some 1500 firms with 100 or more employees. The multiplicity of small builders and contractors must not, therefore, be allowed to divert attention from the relative importance of the large firms.

The size and varied tasks of the industry result in a great diversity of different types of firm, including the following—

(*a*) Very large contractors, capable of doing a wide range of constructional work anywhere in the world. The strength of such firms lies in their nucleus of trained and experienced technical and administrative staff, and in their command of a great variety of plant.

(*b*) Medium-sized building and civil engineering contractors, doing any but the largest jobs within a local area.

(*c*) Smaller civil engineering contractors, whose scope is limited by the type of plant they own—for example for site preparation, road-making, laying sewers, etc.

(*d*) Specialist contractors mainly employed on subcontracts for new building work—for example, steel-frame erectors, heating and ventilating engineers, electrical installation contractors, stonemasons, plumbers, asphalters and tar sprayers, etc.

(*e*) 'General purpose builders', capable of small-scale housing and similar work, but often employed on alterations, substantial repairs, and subcontracts for larger firms.

(*f*) Jobbing builders, engaged in repairs and maintenance.

(*g*) Small specialist firms engaged in repairs and maintenance—plumbers, electricians, etc.

This structure is of course partly determined by the nature of the industry's work. The jobbing builder and the repair specialist are like the general store; it is convenient to have one close at hand. The largest works of civil engineering are clearly likely to require the resources and experience of a large national firm—advantages which outbalance the difficulty and expense of recruiting a local labour force for the period of the job. But this does not explain everything. In a scattered rural community, it will be sensible enough for each substantial village to have its own jobbing builder, given a natural monopoly by the distance of his competitors. But only a fifth of Britain's population is rural, and in the urban areas large and small builders and contractors can, within a radius much increased by motor transport, compete freely. The free competition of chain stores and small independent shops has led to gains by the larger units. Is there any reason why the same should not happen in building?

One answer is that a large part of building necessarily consists of small jobs, and most of it of jobs which are temporary. The builder does not stay in one place selling his services—he is constantly moving on, as one contract is finished and another begins. As a reason for the existence of many small firms, however, this is not very convincing, for it might be thought that the irregularity of work would give an advantage to the large business, which can buy better organizing ability and which can average fluctuations over a larger volume of work. The true explanation would seem likely to be along the following lines:

(i) It is easy to enter the industry. The craftsman's chances of setting up in business on his own, which in most industries are negligible, are greater in building. Specialized services are easily bought: one does not have to have a full range of crafts within one's own business before tendering for the construction of a house; and suppliers of materials will give credit.

(ii) The numerous tiny firms (say those with 0 to 5 employees) are generally run by a proprietor who himself works on the job. This is an effective means of ensuring that labour is supervised and materials requirements promptly attended to.

(iii) The technical advantages of size (such as the possession of better mechanical equipment) are either not in themselves very great, or are not yet fully exploited. It is possible that in a time of high employment large firms have not troubled to exert their full competitive power.

There are in addition special reasons why numerous tiny firms should appear just after the war, when there were plenty of repairs to be done, returning craftsmen had war-time savings and service gratuities to support them in a new venture, and there was an impression abroad that income-tax bore less hardly on the independent worker or employer. It is not surprising that, as these special factors have become less important, the numbers of the smaller firms have diminished. What may be more significant is that, as compared with 1948, there are fewer firms

at sizes up to 100 employees, and substantially more with over 500.
This suggests that there may already, and despite the factors enumerated
above, be some movement towards the displacement of small firms by
large. In 1948 the net output per person employed was £377 for firms
with 11 to 24 employees, rising to £492 for firms with 1500 employees
or more. This in itself proves nothing, since the small and large firms
do different kinds of work—the large firms naturally undertaking jobs
involving heavy capital equipment, and thus producing a high output per
employee. But the greater part of the rise is accounted for by the fact
that average pay per person is better in the larger firms: in 1948,
£362 against £273. This is no doubt partly due to the employment of
more people in the higher grades—the larger firms have more salaried
employees.

To sum up, therefore—

(*a*) The varied nature of the industry's work requires a great variety
of sizes and types of firm, and the managerial units would have to be
numerous under any scheme of organization.

(*b*) Nevertheless, there are types of work (such as repairs and small-
scale house-building in urban areas) in which small and medium firms
can be in effective competition. Hitherto numerous small firms have
maintained themselves in these fields also: and some reasons for this
have been suggested.

(*c*) But in fact quite a small number of larger firms are responsible
for most of the industry's output: and there are some preliminary signs
that the large firms, besides offering on the average better jobs to their
workers, are gaining at the expense of the small. It is a mistake, therefore, to overstress the economic effects of the 'fragmentation' of the
industry.

3. THE CHAIN OF DECISION IN BUILDING

There is, however, a different kind of 'fragmentation' which has an
important effect on the industry's progress. The production of a building
is broken down into many processes conducted by different business
units. There is nothing which corresponds to Fords of Dagenham, with
an input of iron ore and an output of finished motor-cars. The builder
himself is an assembler of components, and is normally limited to the
range of components on offer from the numerous materials industries.
Even in the work of assembly, he may bring in separate subcontractors:
and his freedom to plan his work is frequently confined to the details
of organization and methods of assembly, the finished product and the
materials to be included in it having been specified in detail by an
architect independent of the builder. The division of labour, though

it may lead to greater technical competence, is by no means an un-
mixed blessing. It gives rise to all sorts of problems in the co-ordination
and smooth planning of work, some of which are further discussed
later in this chapter. It means that progress must often require the
independent decision of several business units to move in the same
direction. One laggard can hold up the whole process, and doing the
same as one did yesterday is vastly easier than change. Why, for instance,
should component manufacturers concentrate on a limited range of
components planned to modular standards when architects continue
to specify other sizes? And why should architects trouble to concentrate
on a limited range of sizes, when a fuller range is still offered to them?
Thus one obtains (as with many consumer goods) a conservative diversity—a great variety of practice, but one in which it is difficult to obtain
the simultaneous agreement of supplier and customer to a fundamental
change. There are of course many exceptions—builders' merchants who
arrange for the manufacture of components to meet customers' requirements, civil engineering firms who both plan and execute their works,
speculative builders who vary the specifications of their houses to take
advantage of better materials or improved components. But the difficulty
of obtaining swift progress where there is no unity of decision influences
many aspects of the industry's development, as will be seen later.

4. RESEARCH AND TECHNICAL PROGRESS

In some British industries, research and development are a substantial
part of the activity of all considerable firms. In others, co-operative
research, organized through a special research association, is the rule.
Building, perhaps because of the special features of its structure discussed
in the preceding paragraphs, follows neither of these patterns. It is
true that a few of the largest contractors maintain their own research
departments: but in general the industry relies on the research activities
either of its suppliers, or of the Building Research Station (which is a
government-financed body, part of the Department of Scientific and
Industrial Research). This division between research and execution,
together with the large number of small units in the industry, means
that (even more than elsewhere) the real problem is not the conduct
of research, but the communication of its results in such a way that
appropriate action is taken.

The Minister of Works appoints an Advisory Council on Building
Research and Development, widely representative of the industry and
its associated professions, whose terms of reference are

(1) To keep under review the whole field of building research and technical
development and the results obtained therefrom:

(2) To suggest from time to time subjects of further research and development, with due regard to their relative importance and urgency:

(3) To advise on the methods of securing the use by industry of the results of research and technical development.[1]

The first and second functions the Council performs by annually reviewing, item by item, the entire known programme of building research in the United Kingdom, and it recommends that attention should be given to subjects which seem to it particularly important. The third function involves the overseeing of the publicity functions of the Ministry of Works. These include the preparation and sale of simple Advisory Leaflets, specially directed to small builders, clerks of works and foremen: the holding of exhibitions, plant demonstrations, and lectures: the showing of technical films: and the appointment of Technical Information Officers in the regional offices of the Ministry. The Council also observes in its 1953 Report[2] that 'architects and consulting engineers can do much to introduce new techniques into building practice, but their interests are largely catered for by the professional institutions and their journals'. The National Federation of Building Trades Employers has set up national and regional research committees, to provide a link between members and the research organization. The Federation also provides an advisory service, open not only to its members but to all in the industry; it distributes research bulletins to its members, and organizes exhibitions; and it co-operates with the Building Research Station in arranging for research on actual building sites.

In building, as in agriculture, the elaborate government provision of research facilities and technical assistance has undoubtedly led to results. The Building Research Station was responsible for introducing the tower crane, which can pick up substantial prefabricated units and lift them into place. The idea for this crane came from France and Germany, and the Building Research Station demonstrated its possibilities in a house-building scheme at Norwich in 1952. It is a key development, since the economical use of tower cranes requires careful planning of the flow of work—planning which may yield other economies. The Building Research Station is also responsible for the powered barrow, which makes it possible to convey concrete at double the speed and half the cost of the previous manual method. The mobile mechanical hoist and the articulated conveyor have been much developed since the war. Prefabrication has not fulfilled the high hopes of 1945, but it has retained a considerable place in the building programme. Research on the properties of pre-stressed concrete has increased the

---

[1] Ministry of Works, Advisory Council on Building Research and Development, *Second Report* (H.M.S.O. 1953), p. 5.　　　　[2] *Ibid.* p. 15.

use of this form of construction, which makes it possible to build structures which are lighter and more economical of both steel and concrete. Numerous new building materials, from pre-cast concrete cavity blocks to plastic tiles, have come into general use. The shifting and levelling of earth, the excavation of trenches, the construction of roads, the laying of railway lines—all these have become more speedy and effective because of the development of new kinds of capital equipment. Some of the advances mentioned have been pioneered by civil engineering, machinery or materials firms, but the general pace of advance has been much increased by government research and publicity.

5. OBSTACLES TO TECHNICAL PROGRESS

The examples given in the last paragraph are only a few leading instances out of many; they suggest that the impression which some people retain, that building is a hopelessly traditional and backward industry, may be far from the truth. But it is of course true that many out-of-date and inefficient practices linger too long. What are the obstacles in the way of a still more rapid progress?

One has undoubtedly been the framework of regulations governing building practice. The special restrictions of the post-war years, caused by shortage of materials, can now perhaps be forgotten; but the confining effect of obsolete building by-laws, and accepted, but out-of-date, codes of practice, remains. New model building by-laws were published for England and Wales in 1952, and for Scotland in 1954, and these have been accepted by a large number of local authorities. But, of course, desirable as it is to protect the public by by-laws against the careless and shoddy builder, any such system of regulation is only as good as the best practice of the time when it is established. It is liable to impede unexpected, but desirable, changes in the future; it is said, for instance, that the development of cheaper and more efficient plumbing systems has been held back by local authority regulations.

Another obstacle is the difficulty of persuading the smaller builder to meet the initial costs of a new method or a new type of equipment. A number of specialist firms exist which hire out plant; and the Eastern Federation of Building Trades Employers has a far-seeing scheme for the loan of plant, and the exchange of technical knowledge, between its members. But it is probable that a good deal more could be done to produce simpler mechanical aids, which would be within the means of smaller builders. This would be easier if it were normal practice to bring electric power to a building site early in the construction work (and at a reasonable cost) so that small power tools could more easily be used. The smaller the scale of work, the greater the importance of versatility in tools and appliances; a small builder cannot afford to have a park of equipment which he only uses on a few days a year.

But the obstacles of regulation or lack of finance are probably of little importance compared with the obstacles of ignorance and conservatism. Too much can be made of the ignorance of good modern practice of numerous small builders: partly because (as we have seen) the majority of the output of the industry comes from quite large firms, and partly because every industry has its 'tail' of less competent firms. The way to encourage progress in those businesses which have small resources in finance and technical competence is for those with greater competence to show an example. What, then, sets the pace of progress of the medium and larger firms?

It is not reasonable to look for the answer to this question wholly within the building industry itself. A considerable part of its work is the assembly of components produced in other industries to the orders of an owner or architect. The power of a builder to improve his methods, say in the building of an estate of local authority houses, is narrowly limited. But the power of the architect (or the professional civil engineer) to prescribe an improved practice, or to leave scope for the application of a better technique, is very considerable.

There seems to be a frequent tendency among builders to put blame for any lack of progress in their industry on the inefficiency and folly of architects. This is in part a natural result of the independent responsibility of architect and builder, which is enforced by the rules of the Royal Institute of British Architects. Yet it is impossible not to be impressed by the great and growing difficulty of the architectural profession. The designer of a building has to fulfil three functions, each requiring for its fulfilment a different type of mind. He must be an artist, able to produce a structure aesthetically pleasing and suitable for its surroundings. He must be a business man, skilled in getting the best product within the financial resources of his employer. He must be a scientist, with an extensive knowledge of the properties of materials, structures and components. The third function, with the increasing scope of technical knowledge, becomes more difficult, and some of it is often subcontracted to specialist advisers; but many of the main decisions on materials and construction must be made by the principal architect of the scheme.

It is unlikely that so formidable a combination of aptitudes will often be found in one man, or that any system of architectural education could produce it. In a large office specialization by the members may provide adequate attention to each aspect of the work. But there is clearly a danger that, especially in the smaller offices, brilliance in design will not be matched by business ability or grasp of the latest in scientific and technical knowledge. The Report[1] of the Productivity Team on Building which visited the United States in 1949 calls attention to 'the vital contribution to productivity in the industry to be made by the architect', and to the fact that the American architect is more conscious than the British of the need to be a business man, 'compelled by the all-pervading urge to efficiency to concentrate upon the task of ensuring that any building project for which he is responsible shall be a financial as well as an artistic success'.

The business relations between client, architect and builder are examined later. In the present context, the important point is that the architect can quite unwittingly impede the technical progress of the industry by prescribing out-of-date materials or practices, or by designing buildings in such a way that modern and economical processes cannot be followed. He is especially likely to do this, because he must often make his designs without knowing which contractor will ultimately be engaged on the work. When the contract is let, amendments to the design to make use of the technical experience of the contractor, or to give better employment to his plant, are liable to be troublesome and expensive variations. Some attempts to bring architect and builder together at an earlier stage are mentioned below.

It would be unfair, however, to put all the blame for backwardness on the architect—he is merely the key man who is most likely to be able to set the pace. Conservatism of practice is bound to occur in all parts of the industry, and is difficult to remove. But the example of agriculture, another industry of many business units, is interesting. It has often been regarded as a backward industry; yet it has progressed very rapidly in technique and equipment during the past twenty years. There appears to have been a change in the farming community, from a situation in which most farmers were proud of being traditional to one in which many are proud of being in advance in technique. A similar change in attitude is needed, and may already be coming, in building and its associated industries.

But will a progressive attitude on the part of architects or building employers be frustrated by an unwillingness on the part of labour to depart from the traditional methods of its crafts? This is not a matter on which much help can be obtained by looking at the technical progressiveness of the United States; for that country has to contend with a craft organization which is far more subdivided than ours, and labour is organized in numerous unions between which demarcation disputes are common. The building industry of the United Kingdom has a

[1] Anglo-American Council on Productivity (succeeded by the British Productivity Council), *Building*, Productivity Team Report (London, 1950).

much better record of industrial peace, and the lesser subdivision of the crafts gives a greater scope for the variation of methods without causing inter-union difficulties. Nevertheless it is reasonable to expect that changes of method which threaten the livelihood of a craft—for instance, the displacement of bricks by other forms of walling, the prefabrication of plumbing units, the use of substitutes for wood—would come up against serious union resistance. On the other hand, changes which make life easier for the worker—those involving a greater use of power —are not likely to be resisted unless they involve the use of labour with a different type of technical knowledge.

On the whole, the verdict must be that the fears of trouble with the unions have been largely unfounded. Demarcation disputes are, of course, not unknown; but it has been noticed in other industries that such disputes, or other resistance by labour to technical change, are often a symptom of a general weakness of labour relations in the particular firm concerned, rather than a disease in their own right. This appears to be true in building also; and a remarkable variety of changes in materials and methods have in fact occurred, to fit the varying circumstances of the past ten years. It would no doubt be convenient to have a labour force of adaptable super-craftsmen, all in the same union and all ready to turn their hands to any new process which the builder wished to try. But it is useful also to have some demarcation between specialists, if only to ensure that proper standards of craftsmanship are observed. It is fortunate that this has not led to a greater conservatism.

6. THE PRODUCTIVITY OF LABOUR

The progress of the industry depends not merely on its use of improved machines and materials, but on its efficiency in employing those which it already has. This efficiency is commonly (though not always rightly) assumed to be shown by the productivity of labour. In building and civil engineering generally, this is exceedingly difficult to measure, because of the great variety of product and of site conditions; most estimates are therefore limited to house-building, though it is believed that a similar movement of productivity has taken place in some types of repair and maintenance. The productivity of labour in house-building was, in 1947, about one-third lower than in 1939: in 1949 and 1951 it was 20 % below 1939, the improvement between 1947 and 1949 being plausibly associated with the development of incentive bonus schemes. Since 1951 there has been a further improvement, probably attributable mainly to improved supplies of materials. Taking a longer view, however, it appears that productivity in the traditional forms of building cannot have risen very much in the last century. G. T. Jones found[1] (in 1928) that the real cost of an imaginary standard building in London fell by 15% between 1850 and 1910, an improvement mainly due to the introduction of machinery in the joiner's shop. Until the recent developments of mechanical handling and fabrication off the site, there were no other large changes in the techniques of building; and such scraps of evidence as exist about labour productivity in the traditional crafts do not suggest that there has been any great improvement.

This judgment, however, must be applied with care. It does not apply to many of the types of civil engineering; it is evident, for instance, that labour productivity in road-making is better than in the days of the steam-roller, and that the whole business of muck-shifting has been greatly changed by the advent of bulldozers and mechanical excavators. Furthermore, no criticism of labour is necessarily implied in a failure to improve productivity: it may be that the work does not lend itself to the changes in technique or organization which can lead to a higher product from the worker. No one is surprised because barbers can cut no more heads of hair per hour than they could a century ago.

But the decline in productivity since 1939 remains interesting, because it indicates a failure to maintain a standard known from past experience to be reasonable. Is this failure merely due to transient post-war difficulties, or does it indicate a permanent change in the attitude of labour, or faults in the organization of the industry? It is too soon to give a confident answer to this question, but some light is thrown on the matter by recent work at the Building Research Station on productivity in local authority house-building.

This work[2] confirms other studies in showing an extraordinary range in the number of man-hours required by different contractors in performing a given task. Even if we take out (in order to be sure of excluding freak cases) the top and bottom one-sixth of the contracts, arranged in order of labour expenditure in man-hours, the range for the remainder is still of the order of two to one. Thus, after exclusion of the top and bottom one-sixth, the ranges for plumbing of similar dwellings in England and Wales, 1948–50, were:

If carried out by a main contractor: 234 to 107 man-hours per dwelling.
If carried out by a subcontractor: 182 to 90 man-hours per dwelling.

It would be natural to attribute these differences to special difficulties at particular sites; but in fact the variation appears to arise between

[1] G. T. Jones, *Increasing Return* (Cambridge University Press, 1933), p. 97.
[2] Summarized in P. A. Stone and W. J. Reiners, 'Organization and Efficiency of the House-Building Industry in England and Wales', *Journal of Industrial Economics*, vol. 2, no. 2, April 1954, p. 118.

firms, rather than between sites. Further analysis yields the following results:

(a) Subcontractors carried out a given task with (on the average) about 15 or 20 % fewer man-hours than a main contractor doing the same work. The extent of subcontracting varies widely between trades and between areas: it is usual for roof-tiling and electrical work, but rare for 'site works', bricklaying and carpentry except in Scotland and in London.

(b) Incentive schemes, and especially target bonus schemes, reduced man-hours substantially, and in general (despite the incentive payments) reduced the money cost of labour also. The saving in man-hours from a target bonus scheme run by a main contractor was of the order of 15 %.

(c) The size of contract affected the man-hours required for a unit of work for main contractors, but not (to any marked extent) for sub-contractors. The reduction in man-hours, as between a 4-house and an 80-house contract, was about 15 % for all the work of a main contractor, but 29 % for bricklaying. This reduction may be related to the size of firm, but it would appear likely that the ability to plan a continuous flow of work is important.

(d) For comparable contracts, without incentive bonus, the main contractor saved on an average about 15 % in man-hours if he super-vised the work himself, instead of leaving the supervision to a salaried foreman or agent. There were similar savings in subcontract work where the principal worked with his labour on the site.

(e) Firms experienced in house-building required, on an average, about 8 % fewer man-hours than firms with little experience.

(f) Main contractors in Northern England required about 10 % fewer man-hours than those in Southern England. On the other hand, subcontractors appeared to achieve their best labour productivity in the Midlands.

The various savings in labour shown in this list do not, of course, all operate together: for instance, personal supervision is inconsistent with large contracts, and incentive schemes are often an effective alternative to personal supervision. But it will be noted that the conjuncture of two or three of the factors in the list could produce very large changes in productivity. It is therefore possible that the fall in building pro-ductivity since 1939 (in so far as it is not accounted for by shortages of materials) may reflect a shift in the nature and organization of the work, as well as in the attitude of labour. In the 1930's the predominant form of house-building activity in England (though not in Scotland) was the building of 'surburban villas' for sale to private owners. In such work the builder is frequently building to his own orders: the modifications he is prepared to make for individual purchasers are marginal only. He therefore has unusually good opportunities to plan the size of estate, the flow of work, the nature of the operations and the use of subcontractors to fit in with his own capabilities of organization. In the post-war period there has been little 'speculative' building: the builder has been working to the orders of an outside owner and architect, and that owner has often been a local authority which has had difficulty in keeping a consistent policy under pressure from government directives, ratepayers and actual or would-be housing tenants. It would not seem at all surprising that it should have been easier to obtain high labour productivity with the pre-war than with the post-war type of organization.

It must be kept firmly in mind that the facts, and therefore the arguments, relate to house-building: there is only fragmentary information about labour productivity in other forms of building and civil engineering work. Further, the argument that some part of the change in labour productivity is due to changes in organization does not mean that post-war labour can be acquitted of the charge of idleness made easy by full employment. The fall in productivity reported by the Laidlaw Committee[1] for Scotland, where pre-war as well as post-war housing has been predominantly on local authority account, suggests at least that factors other than organization have been at work.

The Building Research Station's studies are not only of help in explaining the past: they offer some obvious lessons for the future. They suggest that labour productivity would be increased by continuity and homogeneity of work, and by scientific management—the latter including both proper supervision, and the use of well-planned systems of incentive payment. This emphasizes once again the need for planning building operations as a whole, so that owner, architect and builder co-operate in providing the conditions for high productivity.

7. RESTRICTIVE PRACTICES AMONG FIRMS

So far we have been considering for the most part what conditions make technical progress and productivity possible in the industry. But there are many critics who consider that the industry has plenty of unexploited opportunities of advance, which it does not take because the spur of competition is lacking. It is frequently supposed that builders in an area are organized in a 'ring' and that they consult together before submitting tenders, so that they are able to protect themselves from the inconvenience of having to progress.

[1] Department of Health for Scotland, *Report of the Committee on Scottish Building Costs* (H.M.S.O. 1948).

These beliefs are usually vague, and the evidence for them imprecise: in order to judge the importance of restrictive practices, we must look deeper. First of all, so large and complex an industry is bound to contain many examples of natural, though limited, monopoly. There is, for instance, the rural contractor with no rivals in his area, or the specialist firm developing a patented process. The first of these can afford to stagnate, provided his prices do not become so high as to attract competitors from a distance; but this protection is in fact a slight one in a crowded country. The second may indeed be able to enjoy monopoly profits for a period, but the variety of alternative materials and methods in building is so great that there can be few opportunities for exceptional profit, free from challenge by substitutes.

At the other extreme it is certain that there is a large section of the industry in which there cannot possibly be any effective monopoly power at all. Thus in the field of small repairs, maintenance and alterations the number of possible firms is usually too great, even within a single town, to allow of an effective and permanent agreement between them; and even if such an agreement were entered into, it would speedily be broken by the competition of employed craftsmen setting up to work on their own account. There are many building operations which (if they become expensive) the building owner will do himself, or hire his own direct labour to do. The competition of the 'home handyman', assisted by a great range of specially designed tools and materials, has made large inroads on the business of house maintenance in the United States; there are signs that it may be doing the same here. If a factory owner finds trade charges for small building work excessive, he will get the work done by his own maintenance staff; similarly a local authority will if necessary use direct labour for road repairs or housing estate maintenance.

The opportunities for restrictive practices are therefore limited to work too complex to be directed by the building owner himself, and where the number of contractors in the area who might be concerned is small enough to make collusion possible. Under these circumstances a restrictive agreement can exist and be stable. Such an agreement may prescribe minimum prices or regulate trade terms; it may share out the market or arrange which firm shall get a particular contract; it may provide for the compensation of unsuccessful by successful firms. A restrictive agreement may be harmful even though no exceptional profits are made, for it may secure an inefficient firm against the danger of loss, and thereby perpetuate it in its inefficiency.

Agreements of such kinds are certainly extremely widespread in British industry and trade, though they are often not effective in achieving their objects. It is not therefore surprising that they should exist in building, especially where the builders concerned are few and on friendly terms with each other. Collusion is indeed encouraged by two features of the tendering system adopted for building contracts. One of these is the belief, which seems to have some foundation in fact, that architects will strike from their list of firms who will be asked to tender in the future those who fail to respond to an invitation to tender for a particular job. In consequence a contractor who does not want to take the job preserves his position on the list, an important element in his goodwill, by submitting a dummy or 'cover' price. If he is genuinely unable to take the contract concerned, it is essential that his cover price should be well above the level of other tenders, since it would be disastrous to be awarded a contract which he is unable to fulfil. On the other hand, a cover price must not be so high as to be obviously ridiculous, since this would also harm the contractor's good-will with the architect. In consequence he must contact his competitors, to find a price which will be high enough but yet not too high; and although this does not *necessarily* involve the disclosure of prices by one firm to another (since the firms contacted can merely indicate a safe minimum for the cover price), it is clear that a system which involves contact between competitors before they tender gives a convenient starting-point for more extensive collusion.

The other feature is the practice of some owners of securing tenders by open competition. This means that a great number of contractors may be put to the considerable expense of a detailed pricing of bills of quantities, when only one can hope to recover this expense from his profits on the contract. There is therefore much attraction in a scheme whereby the successful contractor compensates the unsuccessful ones for their tendering costs, the amount of the compensation being added to all the tenders. Such a scheme makes it necessary for the intention to tender to be notified to a central office, so that the necessary addition can be calculated. If in addition the amounts of the proposed tenders are notified, the central office can take action to raise the tenders if the lowest one seems 'unreasonably' low. The word 'unreasonably' does not necessarily carry a sinister implication, that only high and protected profits will be considered reasonable. It is believed that in periods of keen competition builders will sometimes gain a contract at a price which should yield no profit, and try to recoup themselves by skimping the work. The owner is therefore protected by the elimination of an 'uneconomic' tender. Furthermore, builders may sometimes (perhaps to save in tendering costs) be careless in the pricing of a bill of quantities, and put in a figure which by comparison with other tenders is clearly too low. It is in the interests of both builder and owner that such accidental errors should be eliminated.

But even if a group of contractors were determined to rig the market in their favour, their power to do so is limited. If the contract is relatively small, there will frequently be small contractors outside the 'ring' who can be induced to compete. If it is large, it may be worth while to bring in a national contractor or one from a neighbouring area. The larger building owners will usually have enough specialist advice from architects, engineers and quantity surveyors to have a shrewd idea of a 'fair price' in advance. In consequence, scandalous profiteering would require, not simply an agreement between builders, but collusion between a builder and the representatives of the owner. Cases involving bribery of local authority officers are not infrequent in the United States; in Britain they are not unknown, but are happily exceedingly rare.

The Monopolies Commission has recently investigated[1] the activities of the London Builders' Conference, which has applied since 1935 a variety of schemes for increasing 'unreasonable' tender prices and recovering the costs of tendering. Similar conferences exist, or have existed, in other parts of the country, but their activities have never been brought under review. It is probable that informal arrangements with the same effect exist in many towns. But attempts at the exercise of monopoly power do not necessarily succeed; and in fact, over the post-war period, the London Builders' Conference appears to have been singularly ineffective. The Monopolies Commission report states (p. 71): 'We conclude, therefore, that there is nothing either in the evidence or in reason to show that the L.B.C.'s arrangements achieve their avowed purposes.' Nor were they on a sufficient scale to make a major difference to prices. In the three years 1949–51, 6903 competitions were held within the London Builders' Conference's area, of which the London Builders' Conference members won 1687. There were only ninety-five of these in which preliminary prices and submitted tender prices had been reported to the Conference; and the total adjustments made (mostly to cover tendering costs) amounted to £527,000 in a total value of contracts won of £80 million—that is, less than 1 % on the value of less than a quarter of the contracts. The Commission's most weighty objection to the London Builders' Conference's arrangements appears to be that by their secrecy they intensified the ill-feeling between builders and owners or architects, and thus obstructed the co-operation which is needed for efficient working.

This last factor, to which we shall return, may indeed have a substantial effect on technical progress and productivity. It will be seen, however, that there is little evidence that restrictive practices impede progress directly, by enabling contractors to rest upon a guaranteed

[1] Monopolies Commission, *Report on the Supply of Buildings in the Greater London Area* (H.M.S.O. 1954).

feather-bed. In particular areas and trades, or for particular types of work, it may still be true that sharper competition would assist progress; it may be that the facts are not known. But so far the case against restrictive practices as a major and direct cause of backwardness must be considered unproved.

Restrictive practices have so far been considered as they may occur among the main contractors of the building and civil engineering industry itself. There are also, however, possible repercussions on progress of restrictive practices among specialist subcontractors, or in the manufacture and supply of building materials. Certain aspects of these practices are mentioned in a technical paper of the Central Council for Works and Buildings, printed in its Report on The Placing and Management of Building Contracts.[1] The following extracts are taken from this paper:

> Reports published in 1919 by the Committee on Trusts (Cmd. 9236) showed the wide extent of price fixing associations in building materials at that time...there can be little doubt that the general tendency...during the last twenty years has led to more and stronger forms of combination in this, as in other fields. We must also refer to associations of specialist sub-contractors which cover many of the building processes. While we have no evidence of the extent to which associations in this field limit competition and fix costs to the builder, it is well known that these things are done; for instance, in the manufacture, delivery to site, and erection of structural steel competition is almost entirely eliminated....Though we have not attempted to examine in detail the working of trade associations which attempt to regulate the prices of building materials and specialists' work, we are of opinion that in the post-war sellers' market these trade associations will together exercise far more influence over the cost of building than an association of builders such as the London Builders' Conference.

The Report of the Committee on the Distribution of Building Materials and Components[2] drew attention to the widespread fixing of prices by manufacturers, and stated (p. 21):

> Our examination of the field has revealed no industry producing building materials or components in which we can state with confidence that there is free competition in prices.

This Committee further found (p. 50):

> ...that restrictive arrangements affecting the distribution of building materials and components exist on a wide scale: indeed, it may fairly be said that in this field monopoly, quasi monopoly, and restrictive practices have reigned

[1] Ministry of Works, *The Placing and Management of Building Contracts: Report of the Central Council for Works and Buildings* (H.M.S.O. 1944), pp. 69–70.
[2] Ministry of Works, *The Distribution of Building Materials and Components* (H.M.S.O. 1948).

almost unchallenged for many years.... These practices are profitable to the associated manufacturers and also to the majority of merchants. In our view they are not in the national interest. In particular, they have tended to lead to a higher level of prices than would have obtained in their absence; to an inflation of gross and net distributive margins; to the consumer being deprived of improvements, actual or potential, in the efficiency of distribution; to an over-elaboration of services provided in the field of distribution and therefore to waste of manpower and other resources; to there being too many merchants; and to consumers being unable to obtain the precise materials they want from whatever source they prefer.

Since 1948 the continued unpopularity of monopolies, and the marginal effects of the Monopolies Commission and of the Restrictive Trade Practices Act, have trimmed slightly the growth of the practices referred to in the above extracts; but there is no evidence that a major change has occurred.

The effect of monopoly on the efficiency of the building materials industries or the merchants is outside the scope of this chapter (see ch. VIII). What are the repercussions of their practices on efficiency in building itself? It will be noted first of all that restrictive practices may exist among specialist subcontractors dealing in a particular material— the infection spreading, so to speak, from the materials industry into the building industry. Here the direct effects of feather-bedding inefficient and high-cost contractors, and of reducing the incentives to improvement, might appear. More generally, the absence of free competition in materials and their distribution might be expected to give rise to distortions of prices and to the continuance of an excessive variety of lines of production. The distortion of prices could mean, for instance, that a component which ought to be gaining acceptance is held back because inferior or out-of-date components are on sale at an artificially attractive price. The excessive variety of types is likely to occur, because where price competition is inhibited the competitive urge is spent on the attachment of a market by emphasizing minor differences between brands.

But these harmful effects are inferred from theory or from experience in other industries: the plain fact is that there is little firm knowledge about the economic or technical effects of restrictive practices in supplying industries. Again it may be the psychological effect which is really the important one—the suspicion that price-rings exist, often exaggerated because of their secrecy, destroys the confidence and co-operation necessary for the rapid progress of an industry.

8. THE MEMBERS OF THE BUILDING TEAM

This study has now several times drawn attention to the need for co-operation between different members of the building 'team', if the work of the industry is to be planned and carried out efficiently. The first party concerned is the owner—including not only private individuals or companies, but local authorities, the national government or nationalized industries. The contribution of the owner is to know his requirements and his maximum financial commitment precisely in advance, to give his orders, and not to interfere with their execution. Such owners are unfortunately rare; it is much more usual for a large number of minor variations to be proposed while the work is in progress, and it is not unknown for the framework of a building to be erected before the owner has any precise idea of how he wants to arrange the interior. This infirmity of purpose is natural enough, because the owner's requirements may change during the period of building; and, even if they do not, it is difficult to resist the temptation to embody one's latest good idea in a structure which will last a long time, and be expensive to change once erected.

Nevertheless, it is quite impossible to arrange for the proper progressing of work, and to ensure that the right materials reach the site at the right moments, if the owner is going to change his mind while the work is in progress. Such variations may be expensive, but it would be well if they were made more expensive still, so that the owner is fully and painfully aware of the cost imposed by an absence of pre-planning. It is also important that the owner should give the architect or engineer adequate time for the preparation of plans in full detail, and should not expect the work to be begun before it is planned. The Productivity Team Report on Building[1] remarks (p. 21):

The American building owner is as anxious as his counterpart in Britain to see his building begun and finished, so that it may become revenue-producing. The American architect has been able to convince him, however, by practical experience, that thoroughness and completeness in the preparatory stages result in savings both in time and in cost. It would be unthinkable in America for a contractor to be instructed to send half-a-dozen labourers to a site to start excavating, at a time when the final designs were no more than half sketched out in the architect's office, merely to satisfy the owner's desire to see work in progress.

For small work, especially minor repairs, building owners commonly instruct a contractor direct; but for major work they will have recourse to an architect or an engineer, or to a group of architects and engineers.

[1] Anglo-American Council on Productivity, *Building* (1950).

The architect or engineer may be in the owner's employment, or in independent professional practice. An architect is fully responsible for design, for the selection of materials and for deciding the methods of construction. He may call in specialist consultants to assist him in his work. He assists in the obtaining of tenders, and advises on the selection of a contractor to do the work. He may nominate specific subcontractors to undertake specialist services. He supervises the work as it progresses, and is responsible for certifying the payments to be made to the contractor. The work and status of a civil engineer, in relation to building work, is similar.

The architect, once appointed, prepares preliminary and final plans; but he brings in a quantity surveyor, a member of an independent profession, to give a preliminary estimate of cost and to draw up the bills of quantities, which set out in full detail all work required for the execution of the contract. The quantity surveyor is also responsible for assessing the work for the purposes of payment, and for measuring variations—i.e. determining the cost of the changes in plan which the owner through the architect, or the architect himself, may have introduced as the work proceeds. The American system is very different. There the architect normally prepares working drawings in great detail, and these are sent direct to the contractor, who takes off his own schedule of quantities, and prices such items as he considers important, putting in a broad estimate for the remainder. Variations are commonly valued by special negotiation with the contractor before they are undertaken; in consequence the contractor can if he wishes load them with a charge for the inconvenience which they are causing in the general progress of the work. In the British system variations are in effect valued at cost plus a conventional profit, which (as we have remarked above) may give too low a price to reflect their full harm to the efficiency of the whole building operation.

The effect of the American system is that the contractor acts as his own quantity surveyor, and (since many contractors may be doing the work independently before submitting tenders) there is liable to be a waste of effort and added expense in tendering—and we have noted that even in Britain the costs of tendering are considered burdensome. The British system involves a further stage of specialization and ought in principle to be superior; it means that all contractors, small and large, can use a precise list of the work to be done, which should facilitate accurate tendering. But the balance of advantage in practice is not so clear. The American architect draws up and sends to every contractor tendering detailed working drawings—that is to say, the work *must* have been thought out to the last detail before tenders are invited. The British practice is apparently to obtain bills of quantities on much less detailed plans, leaving uncertainties to be dealt with by later variations. Thus the convenient existence of the profession of quantity surveyor makes possible slipshod pre-planning, with its natural results of inefficient use of labour and machinery in the progress of the work.

The bills of quantities having been prepared, the question of who should be invited to tender has to be faced. On this there is a division of view. The weightiest opinion is on the side of *selective tendering*: that is to say, the invitation to tender would go to a limited number of firms, believed to be capable of doing the work and likely to do it to an acceptable standard. The Report on the Placing and Management of Building Contracts[1] argues as follows (p. 16):

> Any system of tendering which does not suitably limit the number of firms invited to compete throws upon the industry an unnecessary burden of time, effort and expense in the preparation of tenders. The more serious consequence, however, is that it gives an advantage to those firms which work to the lowest standards and seek opportunities to avoid their responsibilities. We have already shown that very low prices resulting from indiscriminate tendering lead to bad building; this system is bad for the owner, unfair to the honest builder, encourages unscrupulous methods by the builder, and lowers the standards of honesty and craftsmanship in the industry.

The Joint Committee on Tendering Procedure (a Committee of the Royal Institute of British Architects, the Royal Institution of Chartered Surveyors, and the National Federation of Building Trades Employers, under the Chairmanship of Mr (now Sir) Howard Robertson, Past-President of the Royal Institute of British Architects) reported in 1954[2] (pp. 5–7):

> ...we can find nothing to say in favour of indiscriminate tendering....It is the normal practice of the private owner and of the contracting Government Departments to invite selected firms to tender and the latter have informed us that in no circumstances will they revert to the pre-war practice of indiscriminate tendering....It is, therefore, a matter of surprise and regret that the majority of local authorities still persist in asking for tenders from all and sundry....We regret that the Ministry of Housing and Local Government have not yet seen their way to encourage local authorities in respect of contracts for which they sanction loans and in many cases pay subsidies, to change their practice....

But how is the selection to be done? Some owners advertise an intention to invite tenders, and contractors can then apply to have their names included on the list from which the selection is made. More usually, however, the architect maintains a private list of firms found, on past

---

[1] Ministry of Works, *The Placing and Management of Building Contracts* (H.M.S.O. 1944).
[2] *Report of the Joint Committee on Tendering Procedure* (London, The Joint Committee, 1954).

experience or by inquiry, to be satisfactory both in technique and financial stability. Thus the London County Council Architect's Department maintains a list classified according to the maximum value of work which the firm is considered capable of undertaking. The number of firms to be invited depends on the value of the work: it must (for instance) be at least eight for work of £10,000 to £50,000 estimated value, and at least twelve for work of over £200,000 value (except for 'value cost' contracts: see below). In fact preliminary inquiries are sent to a greater number, so that the minimum number of actual tenders are obtained. The tenders and bills of quantities are submitted in separate sealed envelopes: the tenders are opened by the chairman of the appropriate committee, and the bills of quantities of the lowest tenderer only are opened, checked for arithmetical accuracy, and thoroughly examined by the quantity surveyor. The firms having been pre-selected, it is usually possible to pass the lowest tender as in order, and the remaining bills of quantities are then returned unopened.

But the alternative system of *open tendering* still finds supporters. Thus, the Girdwood Committee on the Cost of House-building, in its first report,[1] said (p. 45):

The keenest tendering is likely to be secured by open competition, and we have had no evidence that in the case of housing work this method of selecting contractors has in fact given rise to the abuses to which the Committee on the Placing and Management of Building Contracts called attention in 1944. It is probable that the potential objections to open competitive tendering apply with less force to house construction than to other forms of building since the work is relatively straightforward and offers scope to many different types of contractor. The alternative of inviting tenders from selected contractors would limit the scope of competition and would tend to prevent the entry of new firms into the housing field.

How in fact is a new firm to obtain a place on the list of approved contractors, to do work of a type or scale which it has not attempted before? There is obviously a very grave danger that, unless there are careful safeguards, the system of selective tendering will operate to protect existing contractors against the competition of newcomers. Where a public body is the building owner, it is important that justice and economy should not only be secured, but be seen to have been secured; and this is not easy if the selection of firms is made from a private list. The case for selective tendering is indeed strong if the owner is a government department or a great local authority such as the London County Council, which can make rules protecting the system against its possible

[1] Ministry of Health, *The Cost of House-Building: First Report of the Committee of Inquiry* (H.M.S.O. 1948).

abuse. But one cannot help feeling that the Howard Robertson Committee was over-anxious to make the system universal, and gave insufficient attention to the need for smaller local authorities and public
bodies to protect themselves against accusations of partiality or corrup-
tion. It is possible also that the firms on the selected list might all be
members of a price-ring, and that the exclusion of outsiders might serve
as a useful support to restrictive practices. Selective tendering is the
usual American practice, the list being commonly obtained by a preliminary advertisement, but experience in the United States shows that
the dangers mentioned are not imaginary.

There are those who consider that it is worth while running greater
dangers of the same kind, for the sake of an advantage which is not
secured by either open or selective tendering. This is the participation
of the contractor in the early stages of planning of the work, which is
possible only if he is nominated by the architect without a competition.
The architect, engineer, quantity surveyor and contractor can then
discuss together the application of new techniques, and the best use of the
contractor's plant, labour force and experience, before the designs are
made final and the bills of quantities drawn up. In view of the importance of team work in securing rapid technical progress, many times
emphasized in this study, this seems a most valuable development.
But the advantages can only be secured by throwing away one of the
conventional safeguards against excessive prices, the competition of
tenderers. The London County Council is experimenting with the early
nomination of contractors, but it will be some years before a fair
judgment of the advantages can be made.

So far only the selection of main contractors has been considered. The
selection of subcontractors unfortunately provides a further occasion for
friction between achitects and main contractors. The main contractors
claim that architects are far too ready to nominate specific subcontractors,
or to specify a material or fitting which can only be installed by one
firm. It should here be observed that in Scotland the contracts for the
various trades are usually let separately by the owner, the work being
co-ordinated by the architect; but the general practice elsewhere in the
United Kingdom is for the main contractor to let subcontracts and to
direct and co-ordinate the work of the subcontractors. The nomination
of subcontractors by the architect is therefore in a sense a limitation of
the rights of the main contractor in carrying on his business. Some
nomination by the architect is certainly necessary. The architect may
be bound by the wishes of the owner to install a particular pattern of
fitting or to employ a particular group of craftsmen. More generally,
the final designs may depend on the choice of a component—for example, the type of heating, ventilation, or lift equipment. Only if the

main contractor is himself nominated and brought into the early planning is it possible to take his choice into account; otherwise the decision must be made before the bills of quantities are drawn up.

There seems, however, to be ground for the belief that some architects nominate subcontractors who might have been left for selection by the main contractor. The whole progress of the contract can be seriously upset if there is lack of co-operation between a subcontractor and the main contractor—with consequent expense and delay for the owner. Furthermore, specialization is growing in building, and there are sound reasons for encouraging it; but to encourage it by whittling away the managerial responsibilities of the main contractor is hardly likely to improve the direction of the work. The nomination of subcontractors is practically unknown in America, the nearest approach to it being a legal requirement in certain states that parts of the work (if public) must be the subject of separate contracts. This may apply, for instance, to plumbing, heating and ventilation, and electrical work; it is part way to the Scottish system, under which there is in effect no main contractor at all. There are few, however, who think that the Scottish system should be exported; it places an additional managerial load on the architect, who is (as we have seen) already expected to have a superhuman combination of qualities.

The relations between owner, architect and contractor are embodied in the contract, and the form taken by this legal document may clearly influence the harmonious and efficient working of the team. Standard forms of contract (such as the Royal Institute of British Architects form) are widely used; standardization of the terms is considered desirable because it helps to build confidence between builder and owner—the builder knows from past experience what his rights and obligations are. The principal types of contract[1] are:

(a) The lump sum contract: for example, so much per house. This was often used in the inter-war period, and is the common form of contract in America (where, however, the detailed drawings and specifications form part of the contract). It is now again used on some small contracts in Britain.

(b) The bill of quantities contract, in which the builder has put a price to each item on the bill, and the total of the prices forms the contract sum. The detailed prices give a basis for the calculation of the cost of variations from the original plan.

(c) The bill of quantities contract with fluctuations clauses for changes in costs of labour and materials. This is the most common form of contract at the present time.

[1] See Ministry of Works, *The Placing and Management of Building Contracts* (H.M.S.O. 1944), ch. II.

(*d*) The standard priced schedule contract, in which the bill of quantities is already priced, and the tenderer quotes a percentage on or off the standard prices.

(*e*) The 'cost plus' contract, in which the contractor's profit is a percentage of the final cost. This is obviously an encouragement to extravagance, and the system has not been generally used except in war-time.

(*f*) The 'cost and fixed fee' contract, in which a fixed fee is agreed in advance, and the remainder of the contract sum consists of the actual cost of the works as they are determined at the end of the contract. This method is in occasional use in America.

(*g*) The 'value cost' contract, used by the London County Council. This is an adaptation of the 'cost and fixed fee' contract, in which the contractor's fee is increased if the cost proves to be less than a previously determined 'value' of the work. Thus the London County Council determines in advance (subject to later application of fluctuations clauses) the 'value' of the work, in the form of a schedule of prices on the bill of quantities; the tenders consist of quotations of percentage increases or decreases on the schedule; the tender price then becomes an agreed estimate of 'value', on which a 'normal fee' of 3 % is paid. If, however, the actual cost exceeds or falls short of the agreed value, a proportion of the difference (initially 25 %) is deducted from or added to the normal fee.

It is not easy to determine the form of contract best suited to encourage at the same time satisfactory work and the progress of the industry in efficiency and technique. Is it right, for instance, to protect contractors against loss arising from fluctuations in wages and prices, thus removing most of the incentive to buy early and buy shrewdly? A contractor undertaking work prescribed in detail by an architect or engineer, and protected by a fluctuations clause, can exercise his business ability only in a narrow field of organization. The Howard Robertson Committee hoped that fluctuations clauses would be dispensed with as soon as possible; but this form of protection is not easily dispensed with, once adopted. An opposite point of view is that building wages and material prices are now for the most part nationally determined or standardized, and that the competition of contractors is therefore rightly limited to their fee for organization. This view would seem to favour types (*f*) and (*g*) above; type (*f*) in particular greatly limits the contractor's financial risk, and therefore makes it easier for men of no great financial substance to rise in the trade—which is desirable, for new men may bring new ideas. The 'value cost' contract is only possible to an owner whose resources enable him to obtain accurate estimates of value in advance, and who can supervise the work with great care so that the contractor cannot increase his fee by shoddy practice. These difficulties explain why this form of contract, apparently so attractive to both parties, has not come into wider use.

Another consideration is the extent to which the work is capable of being planned in advance. If no such planning is possible—for example in the repair of an ancient monument, where the scope of the work may only become apparent when it is begun—a 'cost reimbursement' contract (type (e), (f) or (g)) will be necessary. But starting without knowing where one is going is not in general a recipe for efficient work; and the 'fixed price' contracts, (a) to (d), have the advantage that it is usually necessary for plans to be complete before the contract is drawn up. Even so, as has been shown, the use of bills of quantities makes it all too easy to introduce later variations. If one wants to encourage pre-planning the lump sum contract should be the choice—provided, again, that the work is carefully supervised to prevent skimping.

This long discussion of the relationships between the members of the building team shows, as one might expect, that there is no easy way to encourage efficiency and progress. If the owner, the architect, the engineer and the quantity surveyor can have at hand trustworthy and adaptable contractors, who can be chosen on their quality and brought into consultation long before the plans are finalized: if the plans are detailed and realistic, and the owner does not seek to vary them: if main contractor and subcontractors work harmoniously together: if there are no sudden disturbances in the supply of materials and labour—then indeed the whole operation can be scientifically planned and carried through, and there is fair opportunity for trying new techniques. But if these happy conditions are not present team work becomes far more difficult. The problem is partly one of educating the members of the team to appreciate each others' difficulties; in this, the national and local consultative committees of architects, quantity surveyors and builders, set up in response to a recommendation of the Howard Robertson Committee, have an important part to play. A conference called by the National Joint Consultative Committee in January 1956 recommended interrelated training for the three professions—a proposal which might go a long way to create the necessary team spirit.

9. CONCLUSION

What, in conclusion, can be said about this giant industry? It proves to be an untidy and shambling giant, with some difficulty in co-ordinating the movements of its limbs so that it may move forward. But this analysis does not lend support to the idea that there is any one simple thing which, once put right, will free the industry to progress. There is no simple way out by smashing price-rings, or abolishing small firms, or protecting existing builders from harmful competition. Many proposals for reform seem to involve an uncertain balance of gain and loss. The difficulties of the industry lie deep in its structure and habits, which are the growth of centuries and not quickly to be changed.

One of the main dilemmas is that competition, while a spur to efficiency, makes its attainment more difficult because it prevents co-operation in the planning of the work: while planning, the means to efficiency, is half-brother to restriction and complacency. There are those who are able to resolve this dilemma to their own satisfaction. Thus Mr Kenneth Albert, in his Fabian pamphlet *Policy for the Building Industry*[1] proposes that a public corporation, working (like British Road Services) through a large number of local units, should take over all new work costing £5000 or more. Such a corporation could give good conditions and continuous employment to its workers, it could foster and apply research on a great scale, it could buy materials in bulk and break the power of the manufacturers' rings, and it could undertake universal and complete pre-planning. 'It is conservatively estimated' says Mr Albert 'that this saving [from pre-planning] would be not less than $12\frac{1}{2}$ per cent on any job.'

It is likely, however, that Utopia is not so easily attained. This is not to deny that a public monopoly would be able to achieve certain economies, and offer more satisfactory conditions to its staff. But it would have a monopoly more complete than any other nationalized industry, except perhaps the Coal Board; there would be no alternative which the building owner could choose, if one of its local units proved expensive or inefficient. It is surely premature to suppose that the problem of securing efficiency in public monopolies has been solved. Nor has it been solved for private monopolies; it is no answer to protect the trade of existing substantial contractors, so that they may no longer have to worry about the 'wastes' of competition. Yet these wastes are very real; unrestricted competition is inconsistent with proper team work from the start of the project.

There does not seem to be any tidy solution. Yet the spirit of an industry is not entirely dependent on its organization; even within the present framework there is room for great advance by the growth of habits of co-operation, and of the progressive mind. The need is recognized: the advance of the last ten years is considerable. The present period may lift the building industry to a high place among the leaders of industrial progress.

[1] Fabian Research Series, no. 170 (London, Fabian Society, 1955).

BIBLIOGRAPHY

(a) Books, Pamphlets and Articles

Albert, Kenneth, *Policy for the Building Industry*, Fabian Research Series, no. 170, London, Fabian Society, 1955.

Anglo-American Council on Productivity, *Building*, Productivity Team Report, London, 1950.

British Productivity Council, *A Review of Productivity in the Building Industry*, London, undated.

Report of the Joint Committee on Tendering Procedure, Royal Institute of British Architects, Royal Institution of Chartered Surveyors, National Federation of Building Trades Employers, London, 1954.

Royal Institute of British Architects and The National Federation of Building Trades Employers, *The Building Owner and Planning in Advance*, London, 1951.

Royal Institution of Chartered Surveyors, *The Planning of Building Operations*, London, 1953.

Stone, P. A. and Reiners, W. J., 'Organization and Efficiency of the House-Building Industry in England and Wales', *Journal of Industrial Economics*, vol. 2, no. 2, April 1954, p. 118.

(b) Official Publications

(All published by H.M.S.O. except where otherwise stated)

(i) *United Kingdom*

Ministry of Health, *The Cost of House-Building* (reports of the Girdwood Committee), 1948, 1950, 1952.

Monopolies and Restrictive Practices Commission, *Report on the Supply of Buildings in the Greater London Area*, 1954.

Scotland, Department of Health, *Report of the Committee on Scottish Building Costs* (the Laidlaw Committee), 1948.

Board of Trade, *Building*, Working Party Report, 1950.

Ministry of Works, *The Distribution of Building Materials and Components: Report of the Committee of Inquiry*, 1948.

The Placing and Management of Building Contracts: Report of the Central Council for Works and Buildings, 1944.

Productivity in House-Building, National Building Studies, Special Report no. 18, 1950.

(ii) *International organizations*

O.E.E.C., *Cost Savings through Standardization, Simplification, Specialization in the Building Industry*, Paris, O.E.E.C., 1954.

CHAPTER III

INLAND CARRIAGE BY ROAD AND RAIL

By GILBERT WALKER and C. I. SAVAGE

1. COMPETITION IN TRANSPORT BEFORE 1939

Public transport, whether of passengers or freight, has been (and is) a closely regulated business. Promoters wanting to construct a railway have had to ask, in Great Britain at least, for the right of eminent domain before they could acquire the land over which their rails were to be laid. Gladstone's Act of 1844 gave Parliament powers to modify maximum charges if railways' profits exceeded 10% and also created the Victorian 'Parliamentary Train'.[1] The Railway Clauses Act of 1845 contained the 'equality clause' and the Railway and Canal Traffic Acts of 1854 and 1888 obliged railway companies to afford 'reasonable facilities' and prohibited 'undue preference' both of passengers and freight, though their importance in relation to passengers was not really great. The Regulation of Railways Act of 1868 required companies to provide information about fares and time-tables, and to keep their rate books open to public inspection. The Cheap Trains Act, 1883, imposed on the companies an obligation to grant workmen's fares at specially cheap rates. The Railway Rates and Charges (Order Confirmation) Acts of 1892 and 1894 determined the maximum rates which the companies might reasonably charge. The Railways Act, 1921, provided for the amalgamation of the existing companies into the four main line companies so familiar between the wars. It also laid down principles of classification of merchandise, prescribed the rates and fares which might be charged, the revenue which could be earned and much else besides. The Transport Act of 1947 vested the properties of railway companies (and of other public carriers) in the hands of a British Transport Commission and empowered that Commission to adopt such a system for the determination of charges 'as may appear desirable', subject always to review by a Transport Tribunal. The Tribunal is competent to hear objections from the Commission, from interested users and from their representatives.

The motor carrier appeared three-quarters of a century after the first railways and developed steadily in the decade before 1914. The First World War demonstrated the possibilities of road motor transport. It produced the trained drivers and mechanics, and, when war ended,

---

[1] To be run at least once a day on each line at fares not exceeding 1d. per mile.

a surplus of vehicles. Technical developments during the 1920's such as the pneumatic tyre and improvements in vehicle design helped to popularize bus travel and greatly cheapened the carriage of freight by road. By 1927, the success of the bus had checked the growth of electric tramways, which from then on began to decline, and the growth of rural, inter-urban and long distance travel by bus and coach began to threaten railway passenger traffics and receipts. The rural bus and motor-coach penetrated into districts which the railways had not reached and stimulated travel on cross-country routes where rail services were notoriously roundabout and slow. No statistics of traffic were then being assembled. But the number of motor vehicles rose by four times in the decade from 1921 to 1931 and the growth in freight going by road must have been no less steady and sure than the increase of passengers.

Railway traffics and revenues failed after the War of 1914–18 to fulfil the expectations of a net revenue broadly equivalent to the sum of the earnings of the constituent and subsidiary companies in 1913, itself a good railway year. Railways were caught between falling traffics and after 1930 by the rise in working expenditure. Part of the failure of railway traffic to respond to the improvement can be put down to general causes affecting the whole of the British economy. But the new competitor by road was being cast for the villain of the piece. Public support could be and was enlisted, since, as was all too clear, contributions from the Road Fund (and indeed, the whole proceeds of motor taxation) fell short of the current expenditure on roads until at least the middle 1930's[1]. Fuel tax, reimposed at 4*d*. a gallon in 1928, was raised to 8*d*. in 1931. Registration duty upon the larger and heavier vehicles was increased in 1933; but not quite in the proportions which the Conference on Rail and Road Transport[2] had hoped. The regulation of buses and of passengers carried by bus was undertaken by the Road Traffic Act of 1930; and of the carriage of merchandise by road by the Road and Rail Traffic Act of 1933. Both Acts prohibited vehicles from carrying passengers or goods by road for hire or reward except under licence. That licence could be granted or refused at their discretion by the licensing authorities set up by the two Acts. The Chairmen of the Area Traffic Commissioners, appointed under the Act of 1930, were constituted by the Road and Rail Traffic Act of 1933 as the licensing authority for lorries and vans. Both measures were an attempt to avoid duplication of facilities at a time when supply seemed

---

[1] Gilbert Walker, 'Highway Finance', *Journal of Industrial Economics*, vol. 4, no. 3, June 1956, p. 161.

[2] Ministry of Transport, *Report of the Conference on Rail and Road Transport* (the Salter Report), H.M.S.O. 1932.

everywhere to exceed demand and to eliminate that condition known, but never precisely described, as 'wasteful' competition.

The railway companies in their competition with the road operator made extensive use of the powers they enjoyed under the Act of 1921 to charge sub-standard passenger fares and exceptional rates for freight. They were prevented from making this competition effective, not so much by Part III of that Act, as by the prohibition of undue preference, by their size and above all by their respect for the canons of behaviour which had been enforced by law in the days of their supposed monopoly.[1]

Rates and fares for each class of traffic by rail were fixed according to principles prescribed by statute.[2] The charges themselves were determined after prolonged inquiry by a public tribunal. Licensing authorities were required by the Act of 1930 to secure that passenger fares by road should be 'not unreasonable', a provision interpreted in relation to the costs of carriage by road; and they could attach as a condition of the (passenger) licence a requirement to provide unremunerative services if the needs of the area so demanded. But they had no such powers over road goods transport. Rates for the carriage of merchandise by road were ignored in the decisions of the licensing authorities and of the Road and Rail Traffic Appeal Tribunal to grant or refuse the licence to carry. Operators by road successfully creamed the traffic, as it was said at the time; and the railways were left as the unwilling monopolists of the unprofitable and relatively unremunerative traffics for which the actual costs of carriage were higher than the average of all the (rail) transits on which the railway charge had been computed. There is unhappily no way of testing this conclusion. But it was certainly the impression formed by one of the authors, then making some study of inland transport. Something like it has been the burden of complaint in the annual reports of the British Transport Commission and it has now been explicitly recognized before the Transport Tribunal in the evidence supporting the Commission's application for a scheme of maximum charges for merchandise under Clause 20 of the Transport Act, 1953. The law, and the administration which depended upon it, was able to avoid the appearance of 'excess' in the competition between road carriers. But it did not prevent an obvious deterioration in the fortunes of the railway companies and it was certainly unable to ensure that resources sunk in the transport business were being put to the best advantage— even during that period between the wars of general unemployment.

---

[1] See particularly the evidence of Mr J. R. Pike, the Chief Commercial Officer of the British Railways, before the Transport Tribunal: *Transport Tribunal: In the matter of the application of the British Transport Commission (1955 No. 2): To confirm the British Transport Commission (Railway Merchandise) Charges Scheme.*

[2] Section 29(2) of the Act of 1921.

2. REGULATION OF ROAD CARRIERS OF PASSENGERS
AND GOODS BETWEEN THE WARS

The bus and coach business before 1930 was mainly competitive—sometimes fiercely so, especially between the many small operators engaged in it. Among the larger road carriers of passengers, combination appeared early and, after obtaining the necessary powers under the Railway (Road Transport) Acts, 1928, the railways themselves acquired considerable interests in existing road passenger transport concerns. Combination and railway acquisition did little to protect the larger bus companies from the smaller firms or to reduce competition among the smaller firms themselves. The structure of the industry at this time and the unstable competition that prevailed were partly the result of the economic and technical characteristics of bus operation,[1] but also of the system by which vehicles were licensed to ply for hire. Bus *services* as such were not licensed, but under the Town Police (Clauses) Acts, 1847 and 1889, many urban (though not rural) authorities had powers to license *vehicles* to ply for hire without restriction within a specified area. In most rural districts, anybody could start a service without formality and, in urban areas, the power to prohibit except under licence was exercised neither impartially nor uniformly.[2] All this helps to explain why bus operators in some places enjoyed almost a monopoly from the start, whilst in others fierce competition among many small operators and practices such as 'tail chasing' and 'leap-frogging' were common. Some local authorities contrived to administer their powers so that their own municipal undertaking—or perhaps some favoured private firm—was given the monopoly over a considerable area. Elsewhere, the power to license did not exist or was only loosely exercised. Many small undertakings sprang up and competed vigorously with each other—often for the same traffic over the same route.[3] The grossly imperfect competition which prevailed in bus and coach operation before 1930 is vividly described in the evidence given before the Royal Commission on Transport in 1929.[4] It will be enough to say here that by the end of the 1920's, there was a widespread belief among operators and the travelling public alike that unrestricted

---

[1] On regular services these were manifest in the difficulty of meeting a fluctuating demand and working to a time-table with a number of operators actively competing for traffic on the same route.

[2] Ministry of Transport and Civil Aviation, *Report of the Committee on the Licensing of Road Passenger Services* (the Thesiger Report), H.M.S.O. 1953, pp. 5–6.

[3] In parts of Shropshire and the Potteries, for example, in the 1920's, it was not unknown for as many as twenty operators to compete on the same route.

[4] See also Ministry of Transport, *Annual Reports of the Area Traffic Commissioners*, 1931–7 (H.M.S.O.) and the Thesiger Report, 1953.

competition in road passenger transport did not work to the public advantage and that some system of regulating its development was needed.

The outcome was the scheme of regulation embodied in the Road Traffic Act, 1930. The Act, though slightly modified by subsequent legislation,[1] remains the basis of public regulation of road passenger transport today. The country is divided into eleven Traffic Areas, each administered by three persons, now known as the Licensing Authority for Public Service Vehicles.[2] The Chairman is a full-time paid official. These licensing authorities grant three kinds of licence: public service vehicle licences, drivers' and conductors' licences and road service licences for stage and express services. It is through their decisions on applications for road service licences that entry to the bus and coach business is controlled. Applications for licences are heard at public sittings, where competent objectors may appear. Appeals may be made to the Minister of Transport against the granting or refusal of a road service licence.[3] Neither the decision on appeal nor the arguments are published; but the parties (and the public on special application) can obtain cyclostyled summaries of the proceedings.

The Road Traffic Act, 1930, did not state specifically how the licensing authorities and the Minister were to regulate road passenger transport. The Act specified certain broad objectives. Services were to be 'adequate, suitable and efficient' and those deemed unnecessary were to be eliminated. 'Wasteful competition' was to be avoided, passenger transport co-ordinated, and fares were not to be 'unreasonable'. (None of these terms were precisely defined.) The licensing authority, in considering whether an application shall be granted or refused, is directed by Section 72 of the Act to consider the suitability of the routes on which the services are to be provided, whether the proposed routes are already adequately served, how far the proposed service is necessary or desirable in the public interest, and the needs of the area as a whole in relation to the traffic, including the provision of un-remunerative services and the co-ordination of all forms of passenger transport. The framework of control has followed certain broad, identifiable principles. These were described in 1936[4] as the principles of priority, protection and public need. Their relative importance has changed since then but the principles still hold good. It is still exceedingly difficult for a newcomer to break into the stage or express section of the industry. Where new services are needed, old-established, reliable

---

[1] The Road Traffic Acts, 1934 and 1937, and the Transport Acts, 1947 and 1953.
[2] Formerly the Area Traffic Commissioners.
[3] For a description of the licensing system see D. N. Chester, *Public Control of Road Passenger Transport* (Manchester University Press, 1936), and the Thesiger Report.
[4] Chester, *op. cit.*

operators tend to be preferred by the licensing authority to newcomers.[1] Restrictions protect certain services—usually local bus services and railway services—from outsiders. Evidence of public need must be provided by an operator before he is granted a licence. One significant extension has been the application of 'public need' to un-remunerative services—non-paying services of a 'very desirable or even necessary' kind subsidized out of the profits of an operator's better paying services. It has almost become a principle of the licensing system to expect the larger operators to provide some such services in return for the protection they enjoy under the Act.[2]

The Road and Rail Traffic Act, 1933, following the final report of the Royal Commission on Transport of 1931 and the (Salter) Conference on Rail and Road Transport of 1932, prohibited the use of motor lorries for the carriage of goods except under licence. The Royal Commission had been influenced, they said, 'by two main considerations. First...that it would be greatly to the advantage of the road haulage industry itself if it were placed on an organized basis. Second...the organization of the industry is an essential precedent to any attempt at general co-ordination with other forms of transport.' The Salter Conference considered 'that some regulation of goods motor vehicles was necessary...that it [could] be enforced only through a licensing system...[and] that it would be to the great benefit of all concerned if...the different sections of the transport industry...were less concerned with mutual competition than with the organization of complementary function.' The Act divided licences into four classes.[3] The 'A' public carriers' licence entitled the licensee to carry anywhere, for hire or reward, freight other than his own. The holder of an 'A' licence was prohibited from carrying his own goods except those needed in his trade as a carrier. The contract 'A' licence was issued to public carriers and entitled them to hire vehicles for the exclusive use of persons and firms specified in the contract. The 'B' limited carriers' licence entitled the holder to carry both his own goods and, subject to any conditions which might be attached to the licence, the goods of others for hire and reward. The holder of a 'C' private carriers' licence was entitled to carry for himself alone—none, that is, but his own goods. Application for a licence of the appropriate class was made to the licensing authority. Appeal lay to a Road and Rail Traffic Tribunal, and not to the Minister. Persons seeking only to carry their own goods in their own vans, the 'C' licensees, obtained licences on application. But those who wanted to carry for hire and

---

[1] The Northern Roadways case (1951) provides an exception to this general rule.

[2] *The Village Bus*, Ministry of Transport and Civil Aviation (1956), p. 6.

[3] Royal Commission on Transport, *Final Report*, Cmd. 3751 (1931), par. 332. *Report of the Conference on Rail and Road Transport* (1932), pars. 99, 109.

reward had to prove a need for their services, generally against the opposition of those authorized to object, a category which could and did include both the railways and rival operators by road. New licences could be (and were) refused to prevent wasteful competition if the licensing authority was satisfied that suitable transport facilities were, or would be, in excess of requirements.[1]

The public carriers' 'A' licence was quite general. It could not be confined by conditions attaching to its issue. But there was no right to renewal and the transfer of a vehicle from its usual route or routes might very well prejudice a future application if there was raised in the mind of the licensing authority a doubt as to whether a vehicle really was required in a job from which it could so easily be dispensed! There were of course combinations among hauliers and some in which control was successfully concentrated with no apparent change in the ownership of each constituent. There were also attempts, mainly unsuccessful it must be admitted, particularly among the larger hauliers (and in some of these the railways were joined), to agree upon certain minimum rates —upon a 'rates structure' as it was called.[2] But no convincing evidence had appeared before the war, of anything in the nature of a conference or other form of stable arrangement to preserve a minimum scale of rates. These hauliers competed and competed vigorously between themselves and with the railways. Each not only appeared independent of any other haulier but generally was so. The complaint indeed, preferred against the industry both by its well-wishers and its detractors, was never of too little competition but always of too much.

One half of all public 'A' carriers' licences current in 1936, according to a return issued by the Ministry of Transport, were held by operators who owned four vehicles or less; and operators owning twenty-four vehicles or less, not in itself a large enterprise, made up four-fifths of the whole body of licensees. Vehicles held on all classes of licence rose steadily before the war from 370,000 in 1933 to 495,000 in 1938 (there are well over a million now); and the railways were driven in 1938 to ask for a square deal by which they sought relief, such as became theirs finally in 1953, from the weight of restrictions inherited from the days when they had held the effective monopoly of inland transport.

3. WAR AND NATIONALIZATION

The government, from the outbreak of war in 1939, exercised control over the railways through a Railway Executive Committee, consisting of the general managers of the four main-line companies and the

---

[1] Walker, *Road and Rail*, 2nd ed. (London, Allen and Unwin, 1947), ch. vii.
[2] Walker, *Road and Rail*, ch xi, section 3.

deputy chairman of the London Passenger Transport Board (hereafter referred to as the L.P.T.B.). The first war-time financial agreement between the government and the railways in 1940 was intended to buttress this control by providing an incentive to efficiency. The railways were guaranteed a minimum annual net revenue of £40 million (the average net revenue of 1935, 1936 and 1937 plus the revenue of the L.P.T.B. for the year ended June 1939). If the railways should earn more than this, they would keep all the excess up to £43½ million and share with the Exchequer one-half of any further excess up to £56 million.[1] This agreement, which was criticized at the time as being too generous to the railways, was replaced in 1941 by the guarantee to the companies and the L.P.T.B. of a fixed revenue of £43 million. The government took any surplus. It agreed to meet any deficit[2] and government traffic had to be paid for. Government control of the railways was also strengthened in August 1941 by the appointment of a Controller of the Railways in the Ministry of War Transport, who also took over the Chairmanship of the Railway Executive Committee.[3] The government did well financially out of the second railway agreement. In each year from 1941 to 1945 a substantial surplus was earned above the fixed guaranteed sum.[4]

Government, upon the outbreak of war, did not immediately assume the same responsibility for road transport. There were, for one thing, too many operators each too accustomed to running his own business in his own way. Control instead was combined with and exercised through the rationing of fuel. The licensing authorities (the Chairmen of the peace-time Area Traffic Commissioners) became Regional Transport Commissioners empowered under authority of the Minister of War Transport to determine the use of road vehicles and to administer the fuel rationing scheme for commercial vehicles.

The licensing system for road goods transport under the Road and Rail Traffic Act, 1933, was suspended. War-time control took the form of an elaborate 'grouping' system. Goods vehicle operators organized themselves into groups of 25 to 100 vehicles, the operators in each appointing their own group organizer. The groups, joined with others, formed sub-districts; sub-districts were co-ordinated into districts under district transport officers. The district transport officers were civil

---

[1] Cmd. 6168 (1940), *Government Control of Railways: Outline of Financial Arrangements.* C. I. Savage, *Inland Transport,* History of the Second World War, United Kingdom Civil Series (H.M.S.O. and Longmans, Green, 1957), ch. III, especially pp. 123–9.

[2] Cmd. 6314 (1941), *Government Control of Railways: Outline of Revised Financial Arrangements,* and Savage, *Inland Transport,* ch. VII, especially pp. 290–2.

[3] Savage, *Inland Transport,* ch. VII, especially pp. 292–4.

[4] *Government Control of Railways: Estimates,* Cmd. 6349, 6436, 6512, 6619, 6797 (H.M.S.O. 1942–6).

servants responsible to the Regional Transport Commissioner for their region. As the war progressed the government found it necessary to exercise its power more directly. After lengthy negotiations, the Ministry of War Transport in 1943 decided to set up its own Road Haulage Organization. A number of long-distance road haulage undertakings were taken over in their entirety—the 'controlled undertakings'. In addition, other vehicles normally engaged on long-distance work were hired by the Ministry of War Transport—the 'hired operators'. The Organization thus controlled 34,000 vehicles. The twelve standard areas were each in charge of a divisional road haulage officer supervising the work of fifty-two area road haulage officers and 367 unit centres. The Organization covered only a proportion of the total road goods transport fleet. It did not replace the grouping system, but was complementary to it. Its main advantage apart from economy in the use of scarce fuel, tyres and vehicles was to put long-distance lorries under a direct government control where they could be the more easily mobilized to meet urgent war-time needs.

Procedure for the licensing of buses and coaches was suspended during the war together with the business of public sittings before the Commissioners and appeals to the Minister. Defence permits instead, issued by the Regional Transport Commissioners, took the place of the normal road service licences. No grouping was necessary, owing to the relatively small numbers of vehicles and firms in this branch of the industry.

Traffic passing in Britain by inland transport increased considerably during the war. Railway freight traffic rose from 16,226 million ton-miles in 1938 to 22,023 million ton-miles in 1945—mainly because of longer war-time hauls. General merchandise increased by 77 %, minerals by 35 % and coal class traffic by 9 %. Estimated passenger miles were nearly doubled from 18,993 million in 1938 to 35,248 million in 1945. This was partly owing to an increase in the number of passenger journeys, but mainly again to the longer journeys being undertaken in war-time.[1]

The railways had to carry this heavy load in the face of severe war-time scarcities, particularly, of course, of man-power. The immediate post-war years found the railways severely strained, with heavy arrears of repairs and replacements to be made good. There are no complete statistics of road goods transport activity in the war years. But the policy deliberately undertaken of conserving fuel and tyres suggests that road hauliers were covering a much smaller annual mileage than in peace-time, although average loads were almost certainly much larger.

[1] Central Statistical Office, *Statistical Digest of the War*, History of the Second World War, United Kingdom Civil Series (H.M.S.O. and Longmans, Green, 1951), Table 165.

Road passenger transport operators were also restricted by scarcities of fuel, tyres and vehicles, but many were carrying very large increases in traffic during the war, with consequent over-crowding of vehicles and heavy wear and tear of capital equipment.

Railways and public carriers of goods by road were nationalized after the war before the former owners had been freed from the pressure of war-time shortages. The Transport Bill was introduced in December 1946. It passed through all its stages, assisted by guillotine, by the middle of the following year and received the Royal Assent in August as the Transport Act, 1947. The Act established a British Transport Commission empowered to carry goods and passengers by rail, road and inland waterway within Great Britain, with the exclusive right to carry for the public, passengers and goods by rail and goods by road. Private carriage, whether of persons in private cars or of goods in private traders' vans (vehicles on 'C' licences), was not limited in any way.

Table 1. *Users' expenditure on transport and travelling (Great Britain)*

(£ million)

	1949	1950
Road goods transport	470	540
Road passenger travel	550	640
The use of road vehicles in the public service	40	40
Total road transport and travel	1,060	1,220
Rail goods transport	200	230
Rail passenger travel	130	120
Total rail transport and travel	330	350
Other means of transport and travel	30	30
All transport and travel	1,420	1,600

Source: E. Rudd, 'Estimates of Expenditure on Road Transport in Great Britain', *Journal of the Royal Statistical Society*, Series A (General), vol. 115, part 2, 1952, p. 190.

The Commission began its operations on 1 January 1948, when it entered upon the ownership of the four main-line railways and the properties of the London Passenger Transport Board. The public part of the goods carrying business was acquired during 1949, 1950 and 1951. Petrol was freed from rationing in 1950. Vehicles soon became more readily available. The number of cars and privately owned lorries has since grown immensely. Rudd, estimating in 1952 the value of the output of all transport services, put the whole of users' expenditure on transport at £1420 million in 1949 and £1600 million in 1950. Walters in 1956 calculated that £2133 million might have been spent by users on transport in 1953. The gross national product at factor cost (less tax plus subsidies) for each of those years was estimated at the time to be £10,100 million, £10,600 million and £14,450 million respectively. The proportion of total output produced by transport services has thus remained at a fairly constant proportion, about one-seventh of the whole.

Table 2. *Gross expenditure in Great Britain on road and rail*
at factor cost and net of duplication in 1953

	Freight	%	Passenger	%	Total	%
(1) Transport industries						
Rail	299*	26	130†	13	429	20
Road	176‡	15	273§	28	449	21
Total	475‖	41	403	41	878	41
(2) Private transport						
Road	676	59	579¶	59	1,255	59
Grand total	1,151	100	982	100	2,133	100

(£ million)

* Including collection and delivery by road. Excludes miscellaneous receipts such as demurrage, fees for customs clearance certificates, lavatory takings, etc. *Source:* British Transport Commission, *Sixth Annual Report and Accounts 1953* (H.M.S.O. 1954).

† Including London Transport (Rail). Excludes shipping services such as cross-Channel passenger ships, etc. *Source:* British Transport Commission, *Report and Accounts 1953.*

‡ British Road Services. Gross revenue from carrying operations *plus* an estimate of the expenditure on carriage of goods by 'A' licence, 'A' contract and 60% of 'B' licence vehicles. *Source:* British Transport Commission, *Report and Accounts 1953.*

§ Includes taxi-cabs, tramways and trolley-buses.

‖ 'C' licence, 40% of 'B' licence operation and goods-carrying vehicles operated by government departments, including Post Office.

¶ Excludes pedal cycles and hackneys.

Source: The Advancement of Science, vol. 13, no. 50, September 1956, p. 69 and *The Economic Journal,* vol. 66, no. 263, September 1956, p. 413. The authors are indebted to Mr A. A. Walters, Lecturer in Statistics, Faculty of Commerce and Social Science in the University of Birmingham, for permission to reproduce this table.

4. CARRIAGE BY ROAD SINCE 1947

A striking characteristic of the bus and coach business is the diversity of the forms of organization encountered among the different undertakings. There are one-man businesses, partnerships, private and public joint-stock companies, groups of companies with close financial links controlled by a single holding company, municipal operators, joint boards and nationalized undertakings owned or operated by the British Transport Commission. There were in Great Britain at the end of 1955, 74,572 buses and coaches.[1] 3438 operators owned only five vehicles or

[1] *Public Road Passenger Transport Statistics, Great Britain, 1955–56.* For earlier figures see the issues for previous years.

less. Another 932 owned between six and fourteen vehicles. At the other extreme, fifty large operators (fifty-one with London Transport) each owned over 249 vehicles, and forty-three more owned between 100 and 249 vehicles. 7983 stage buses and road passenger coaches were owned by the London Transport Executive and the underground worked 4032 rail coaches. The following table shows road motor vehicle ownership according to the main types of operator.

Table 3. *Passenger vehicles owned by the several classes of operator*

	1952	1955
British Transport Commission		
London Transport Executive	8,992	7,983
Provincial (Tilling) Group	9,974	} 14,388
Scottish Group	4,368	
Local authorities (93 in 1952; 94 in 1955)	14,375	14,963
Other operators*	38,439	37,238
Total	76,148	74,572

* This includes the privately owned British Electric Traction Group which, in 1949, operated approximately 13,000 buses and coaches.

Just about one-half of the buses and coaches in Britain are owned by public authorities. London Transport Executive own about 11 %, the Tilling and Scottish Omnibus Groups (themselves wholly owned subsidiaries of the British Transport Commission)[1] about 19 %, and 20 % are owned by local authorities. The remaining half of the public service vehicles belong either to the numerous independent operators or to the 'associated' companies, notably the British Electric Traction Group, comprising seventeen large omnibus undertakings. In some of them the British Transport Commission has inherited considerable financial interests, but not the control.[2]

A total of 18,000 million passenger journeys were taken on the British public transport system in 1952. 91 % of these were by road (including tramways and trolley-buses) and 9 % by rail. The average journey by road is considerably shorter than the average rail journey—a few miles as against thirty. Passenger miles for all forms of public inland transport probably amounted to 70,000 millions in 1952. Road passenger transport (including trams and trolley-buses) contributed about two-thirds of this passenger mileage, and the railways (including London Transport lines) about one-third. Buses and coaches, measured either by passenger journeys or passenger miles, thus appear as the most important means

[1] Tilling Group, 13 %; Scottish Group, 6 %. The Tilling Group comprises some thirty-three undertakings and the Scottish Group, seven. See British Transport Commission, *Eighth Annual Report and Accounts 1955*, vol II (H.M.S.O. 1956), Table V-7, p. 37.
[2] British Transport Commission, *Report and Accounts for 1952*, Table V-5, p. 178; and *Report and Accounts 1955*, vol. II, Table V-5, p. 34.

Table 4. *Passenger transport, 1952* *

	(1) Passenger journeys (millions)	(2) Length of journey (miles)	(3) Estimated passenger miles (thousand millions)
Buses and coaches			
British Transport Commission, Tilling buses (a)	1,554	4·5	7·0
British Transport Commission, Scottish buses (b)	794	4·9	3·9
London Transport buses (c)	2,918	2·3	6·7
Local authorities (d)	4,565	(1·7)	(7·8)
Other operators (e)	3,515	(4·6)	(16·2)
Total (f)	13,346	(3·12)	(41·6)
Trolley-buses			
British Transport Commission, London Transport (g)	764	n.a.	n.a.
British Transport Commission, Provincial (h)	20	n.a.	n.a.
Other (j)	999	n.a.	n.a.
Total (k)	1,783	(1·6)	(2·9)
Tramways			
British Transport Commission, London Transport (l)	29	n.a.	n.a.
Other (m)	1,178	n.a.	n.a.
Total (n)	1,207	(1·5)	(1·8)
Railways			
London Transport Executive Railways (o)	584	5·7	3·4
British Railways (London lines) (p)	456	10·2 ⎫ 20·92	4·6
British Railways (outside London) (q)	533	30·1 ⎭	16·1
Total (r)	1,573	(15·33)	24·1
Grand total (s)	17,909	(3·93)	(70·4)

n.a. = not available.

* Gaps in the published statistics have had to be filled in by the authors' rough estimates, shown below in brackets.

Notes:

Col. 1. All figures taken from Ministry of Transport, *Public Road Passenger Transport Statistics, 1952* and British Transport Commission, *Report and Accounts for 1952.*

Col. 2. (a), (b) and (c) from British Transport Commission, *Report and Accounts for 1952.* The London Transport figure is for all road transport.

Col. 2. (d) Estimated from statistics of average takings a passenger journey in *Public Road Passenger Transport Statistics, 1951* and table of typical fares mile in British Transport Commission, *Report for 1951*, p. 26. Average receipts a passenger journey (local authorities 1951–2) 2·34d. 2·34d. divided by 1·4d. (typical short-distance fare, large city, 1951) equals 1·7d. approximately.

Col. 2. (e) Estimated from statistics of average receipt a passenger journey, 1952–3 (all operators other than local authorities and London Transport Executive 5·15d. Table 13 of *Public Road Passenger Transport Statistics, 1952*). The British Transport Commission (Tilling) average receipt is known to be 4·90d. and British Transport Commission (Scottish) 4·70d. for 1952 (Tables IX–1 and IX–2 of British Transport Commission *Report and Accounts for 1952.*) A rough calculation for the remaining operators is therefore possible after weighting in proportion to the number of passenger journeys. It works out at 5·6*d.* a journey for 1952. Since no statistics of fares are available, 1·2*d.* a mile has been assumed (slightly higher than the average Tilling fare). The average length of journey then works out at 4·6 miles. This is slightly higher than the Tilling and lower than the Scottish figure, which is what one might expect.

Col. 2. (*k*) and (*n*) are approximations only. No adequate statistics are available. The authors have been guided mainly by statistics of average takings a journey for trams and trolley-buses, from the *Public Road Passenger Transport Statistics.*

Col. 2. (*o*), (*p*) and (*q*) are taken from British Transport Commission, *Report and Accounts for 1952,* p. 20.

Col. 3. These figures are obtained from those in columns 1 and 2.

of public[1] passenger transport in Britain, accounting for 75 % of all passenger journeys and 60 % of all passenger miles.

Services provided by buses and coaches are customarily classified into stage, express, excursion and contract—the categories used for licensing purposes under the Road Traffic Acts. Stage services are by far the largest category, accounting for about 97 % of all passenger journeys and about 79 % of all passenger receipts on buses and coaches other than those operated by London Transport. They include all regular local, town, inter-urban and country services. Express services are the regular long-distance services run throughout the year and seasonally.[2] Excursions and tours cater for casual traffic, such as day tours, and are not obliged to run regularly. Contract services cover all kinds of private hire. While all classes of operator provide all types of services, municipal undertakings supply almost exclusively stage services. Long-distance services, excursions and tours and contract services are mainly the province of the publicly or privately owned groups of companies or independent operators and some independent operators concentrate entirely on contracts, taking workers to the factories by day, for example, and private parties of an evening for country trips or to the pantomime according to the season.

The number of bus and coach operators declined from 6486 in 1931 to 5242 in 1953. The number of public service vehicles increased over the same time from 46,476 to 74,745.[3] The average vehicle holding thus doubled from 7·1 in 1931 to 14·3 in 1953. All operators, large and small, enjoy a degree of monopoly on their own licensed routes, and although new entry is possible in law, in practice it is rare.[4] Safety,

---

[1] Excluding, that is, the private car.

[2] The legal distinction between a stage carriage and an express service depends on the fare. None of the fares charged on an express service must be less than one shilling.

[3] Based on returns of Licensing Authorities for Public Service Vehicles. These relate to 31 March each year and are not therefore comparable with statistics derived from *Public Road Passenger Transport Statistics.*

[4] The Thesiger Report takes the view that 'if licences are freely given to anyone who applies in the hope of reaping a profit from a remunerative route, it is clear that the consequence might be serious in the public interest' (pp. 36–7). The Report does not, unfortunately, state its reasons for this opinion.

reliability and the quality of service have undoubtedly improved since 1930. Regular services working to a time-table have replaced the irregular, unreliable services which formerly flourished. But this transformation has been achieved at the cost of protecting existing operators in their quasi-monopolies. The intensification of monopoly has been accompanied by stricter public supervision of fares, time-tables and services. Evidence of public need must precede the granting of a road service licence, which means that temporary inconvenience may exist and potential demands remain unsatisfied. The peculiar kind of competitive struggle among the small oligopolists which characterized bus and coach operation in some areas before 1930 was probably not conducive to maximum economic welfare, and the greater stability given to the industry by regulation under the Act may indeed have been desirable. It would be dangerous consequently to assume that the travelling public is necessarily worse off now than under the haphazard and unreliable competition of the 1920's. But stability obtained at the cost of enterprise may always run against the interests of the public and no one can be certain that the right balance between stability and enterprise has yet been struck.

The Transport Act of 1947 nationalized the railways but left the licensing system for road passenger transport more or less intact. The Commission was empowered to acquire road passenger transport undertakings. It could also prepare, and the Minister of Transport might approve, area schemes, by which road passenger transport undertakings within a specified area might be brought into public ownership and be operated by Area Boards or other authorities under the Commission. A beginning was made in 1948 with the task of selecting areas suitable for the schemes which were proposed. By 1949 a Road Passenger Executive of the Commission had been established to act principally as an advisory and planning body for this purpose. Some progress was made with the preparation of a scheme for the Northern Area (comprising the counties of Northumberland, Durham and the North Riding of Yorkshire.[1] Schemes were also proposed and investigated for East Anglia and South-Western England. None had got beyond the stage of discussion before the Act of 1953. The intention presumably was to eliminate competition from a large part of the passenger transport industry and to substitute that thorough-going co-ordination which the 1930 Act had failed to achieve and which the licensing authorities, however apt to encourage amalgamation, were certainly not empowered to enforce.

Meanwhile, and as a result of the nationalization of the railways, the

---

[1] A. M. Milne, 'Passenger Road Transport and the Transport Act 1947', *Economic Journal*, vol. 61, no. 242, June 1951, p. 310.

British Transport Commission had automatically acquired substantial interests in road passenger transport undertakings in the form of shareholdings owned by the former railway companies in the larger bus companies, mainly in the groups managed by Thomas Tilling, the British Electric Traction Company and the Scottish Motor Traction Company. These interests had, in all cases, stopped short of control by majority shareholding and while the railways before the war had been represented on the boards of the omnibus companies, they had 'no executive nor managerial concern' in them. The British Transport Commission, however, 'not unmindful of the provisions relating to area passenger road transport schemes contained in Part IV of the Act', exercised its powers under Section 2 of the Transport Act, 1947, and acquired by agreement in 1948 all the road passenger transport interests of Thomas Tilling (which owned shares in sixteen omnibus companies operating between them 8000 vehicles). By a similar purchase in 1949 the Commission acquired the road passenger transport undertaking of the Scottish Motor Traction Company, owning 3800 vehicles. A number of other purchases built up the Commission's controlling interests to 14,500 buses and coaches by 1953.

More than one-fifth of the buses and coaches in the country (other than those of London Transport Executive) are now controlled by the Commission. The Transport Act of 1953 has subsequently prevented the Commission from acquiring by purchase further interests in road passenger services except by consent of the Minister and the Act also empowers him to require the Commission, if he sees fit, to dispose of its present holdings. This power has not yet been exercised and it is reasonable to doubt that it ever will be.

Part III of the Transport Act, 1947, required the Commission to acquire wholly the undertakings of those professional hauliers of merchandise who worked road goods vehicles under public carriers' 'A' and 'B' licences, when satisfied that such undertakings consisted to a predominant extent of ordinary long-distance carriage for hire and reward. 'Predominant' was interpreted as 50% of gross takings or more, and 'long-distance' as forty miles and over. Certain classes of carriers were exempt, such as furniture removers, haulers of large indivisible loads and so on; and others were left in business by permit issued by the Commission. All road haulage businesses which otherwise fell within the conditions of the Act were acquired by the Commission during 1949, 1950 and 1951.

The whole of the long-distance general haulage trade thus defined, except for the exempted undertakings, had consisted apparently of 3700 or so concerns. 400 of these, among them the largest in the trade, had each owned on the average no more than twenty vehicles apiece.

The remaining 3300 acquired under the compulsory procedure had owned, again on the average, no more than ten vehicles each.[1]

Hauliers had been forced to work together during the war under the official Road Haulage Organization and there had not been time from August 1946, when the public carriers were returned to the control of their private owners, to the date of acquisition after 1948 for the former habits of vigorous competition to be entirely recovered. There was certainly more evidence of combination between hauliers and of other less obvious working arrangements than there had been before the war. The evidence is flimsy but there was certainly a case for supposing that, when the public part of the road carrying trade was nationalized under the Transport Act, 1947, road haulage was still predominantly the preserve of the small owner.

The British Road Services, however, when they acquired the general long-distance haulage business, organized the trade on the large scale. In place of the independent haulier with ten or twenty vehicles they put depots, groups and divisions. The depot superintendents were responsible for the good order and proper running of the vehicles entrusted to their care. The group managers stood before the public in place of the former private hauliers (they were often the same people). But they now had 100, 200 and sometimes 300 vehicles in their control and divisional managers correspondingly more. The private haulier had his own group of customers and did only the work which lay within his own small competence. The British Road Services organized in their place a country-wide network of services and each group accepted traffic for all others. The general haulage section, to judge at least from the evidence of traders, had taken on increasingly in the process something of the rigidity which size had forced on the railways and something too of that inability to cope with the special circumstances of the individual which had earlier been reckoned one of the railway's principal disabilities in competition with the small road carrier. But the wide scale on which general haulage could be organized by the British Road Services also gave to the business of carrying by road something which it had lacked before—a clearing house for traffic capable of covering the entire country.

The British Transport Commission became possessed under the Act of a great deal besides the lorries of the former carriers. Besides vehicles

---

[1] G. W. Quick Smith, 'Growth and Development of Road Haulage Executive', read before the Institute of Transport Southern Section, 8 October 1952, quoted by Walker, 'Transport Policy Before and After 1953', *Oxford Economic Papers* (New Series), vol. 5, no. 1, March 1953, p. 99. There were, of course, some very large firms among those which had been acquired (though not all were predominantly long-distance haulage) and the railways had bought into others such as Carter Paterson, Hay's Wharf and Pickfords, three firms which in any case were not wholly independent of each other.

used in long-distance haulage there often went, too, all the other parts of their undertakings. British Road Services thus found themselves operating, for example, a large fleet of tippers and hiring out on contract, for the exclusive use of customers, about 2000 vehicles, driven by the customers' employees and often finished off in liveries of the customers' own choice.[1]

The Transport Act, 1953, made provision for the return of the public road haulage trade to private hands. The limit of twenty-five miles from the usual base within which the (privately owned) public carriers had been confined by the Act of 1947, except with the permission of the British Transport Commission, was removed from 1 January 1955. British Railways were allowed to retain the lorries and vans needed for collection and delivery of rail-borne traffic; and the Commission, by a later Act,[2] was empowered to withhold from sale the vehicles required to keep in being its main trunk network. The fabric of its road services will thus be preserved and the British Road Services will not, as it at one time appeared likely, be limited to working as a clearing house on the grand scale, accepting freight from customers to any destination in the British Isles to which they could provide a service by hiring either railway wagons[3] or, on the roads, the vans of privately owned contractors.[4]

The British Transport Commission in 1952, just before the passing of the Act of 1953, owned 42,000 vehicles for the carriage of freight, primarily for long distances by road, and another 15,000 motors and tractors,

[1] Known also as the 'C' hiring margin.
[2] Transport (Disposal of Road Haulage Property) Act, 1956.
[3] This possibility seems to have been pushed to advantage during the fuel crisis which followed the closing of the Suez Canal in the autumn of 1956. British Road Services, when the railway time-table served, loaded their traffic into wagons which British Railways had placed at their disposal. Knowing the numbers of these wagons and the times of departure of the trains to which they were attached, British Road Services were able to send advice of their arrival by teletype to the destination. The wagons were met by officers of the British Road Services, and the goods unloaded and delivered to their consignees with the dispatch which the trader has come to expect from road hauliers. British Road Services in all this were acting the part of freight forwarders. The rates asked by the B.R.S. were no more than the charges they were accustomed to make, and were frequently less than the rate for the same class of goods when sent by rail.
[4] The parcels service, with the exception of purely local carriers, is and always has been the field of the large or at least the co-operatively inclined enterprise. A great many separate lots go to making up a van-load of parcels, each consigned to its own destination. The haulier who wanted to make a success of this sort of trade had to be able to reach most of the points to which traffic might be consigned. Few carriers had an organization large enough and some degree of through working was characteristic of the parcels service even when privately owned before the war. The parcels division, now consisting of 4,000 vehicles, has not been sold. The Minister of Transport has ruled that, for the present, to sell would not be in the public interest. For the time being therefore, the carriage of parcels (and of meat) will be organized as a limited company under the British Road Services. (British Transport Commission, *Report and Accounts 1956*, vol. I, pars. 11, 12.)

together with 23,000 trailers used for the collection and delivery services of its railways. 21,000 vehicles out of the 37,000 which constituted their fleet at the beginning of the sales were sold before the Road Haulage Disposals Board was wound up in 1956. All vehicles retained by the British Road Services in the future will have to be authorized on an 'A' licence, granted or refused in their discretions by the licensing authority under the Act of 1933 as amended; and this will be the case in particular of those 7000 vehicles or so which the Commission has been allowed to keep back by the Transport (Disposal of Road Property) Act, 1956. The government was (understandably) unwilling to introduce and provide time for this Bill until it had become perfectly clear that sales to private interests of vehicles belonging to the Commission which had formed so large a part of the scheme of denationalization provided for under the Act of 1953 had come virtually to an end.

It was the expressed opinion of the Minister that by July 1955 the main objects of the Act of 1953 had been achieved. The limit of twenty-five miles on the operations of those 'A' licensees who escaped acquisition under the Act of 1947 had gone. The small man had had his chance to come back into the trade. The road services of the Commission had been placed under the licensing system and competition had been reintroduced.[1] Each purchaser, as an inducement to buy, was given a public carrier's 'A' licence valid for five years with each vehicle bought. These 'A' licences are transferable and can be assigned from one purchaser of vehicles from the B.R.S. to another. A number of lorries seem to have been taken up deliberately for re-sale piecemeal and some sold in the smaller units were certainly absorbed not by the returning small hauliers but by the larger firms wanting to round out their fleets. The statistics of disposals are no guide consequently to the size of the privately owned fleets into which the British Road Services were being broken up. These may be large or small; but the number of vehicles disposed of in each lot is no indication.[2]

There are now (1956) well over one million lorries all told. These are worked by over half a million or so licence holders. 470,000 licensees are returned as private traders. They run 950,000 lorries and vans and as 'C' licensees are debarred by the terms of their licence from carrying any goods but their own. 26,000 licence holders appear as professional carriers (including the British Transport Commission, both as a public haulier—the British Road Services—and as the British Railways). They work 110,000 vehicles on 'A' and 'A' contract licences. The remainder of the 1,119,894 trucks are worked by the 32,168 traders who carry their own goods and those of others on terms limited by the conditions of their

[1] *House of Commons Debates*, 11 July 1955, col. 1702; 21 July 1955, col. 574.
[2] First to Seventh Reports of the Road Haulage Disposals Board, 1953 to 1956 (H.M.S.O.)

'B' licences. The average number of vehicles owned is small. But licences, it should be remembered, are not grouped according to the independence of hauliers from each other and it is always possible for the same firm to obtain licences (though for different vehicles) in different areas. The one firm might in this case be recorded in the statistics as two (or more) licensees and the number of vehicles in possession of each licence holder should be correspondingly increased.

Table 5. *Goods vehicle licensing in Great Britain*

| | Vehicles authorized and in possession | | | | | Licence holders | | | |
	'A' licences	'A' contract	'B' licences	'C' licences	Total	'A' licences	'A' contract	'B' licences	'C' licences
December									
1946	81,056	9,627	58,386	383,738	532,807	17,513	3,853	29,542	197,779
1947	83,933	13,944	64,418	487,151	649,446	17,600	5,437	32,508	253,548
1948	74,210	16,311	65,573	590,516	746,610	17,120	6,610	32,390	311,811
1949	50,666	15,376	63,418	672,301	801,761	14,840	6,423	32,341	351,230
1950	42,878	13,359	63,123	733,044	852,404	13,154	5,489	31,616	378,664
1951	40,499	12,943	62,518	796,343	912,303	12,496	5,263	31,288	403,544
1952	40,381	12,947	62,947	833,936	950,238	12,353	5,134	31,088	416,683
1953	90,813	13,280	63,622	866,322*	1,034,037	12,431	5,193	31,163	432,028
1954	90,635	14,504	64,649	899,773	1,069,561	14,857	5,671	29,190	455,013
1955	90,352	18,860	66,488	944,194	1,119,894	17,295	6,826	32,168	470,864

* Of about 97,000 goods vehicles exceeding 3 tons unladen weight licensed at 31 March 1954, about 7,000 (59 %) were authorized under 'C' licences. *H.C. Deb.*, 28 July 1954, *Written Answers*, col. 68.
Sources: British Road Federation, *Basic Road Statistics* (annual), quoting from *Annual Reports of the Licensing Authorities for Goods Vehicles*, except as follows: December 1946: *The Motor Industry of Great Britain, 1947* (published by the Society of Motor Manufacturers and Traders). December 1947: *H.C. Deb.* 1 March 1948, col. 13; 8 March 1948, *Written Answers*, col. 110; 22 March 1948, *Written Answers*, col. 290.

The increase in 'A' licences between 1952 and 1953 follows from the disposals under the Act of 1953 of the lorries then owned by the British Road Services. The trade was opened to the privately owned professional haulier and the British Transport Commission required to furnish themselves with 'A' licences for all the vehicles they employed in public haulage.

No statistics of the freight road-borne had been collected before the war—one of the first acts indeed of the licensing authorities when they entered upon their duties in 1934 had been to relieve operators from the liability which might have been imposed under Section 16 (*b*) of the Road and Rail Traffic Act of 1933 to require returns of journeys and of the weights, description and destination of the merchandise being carried. It is, of course, not necessarily to be supposed that this information, had it then been collected, would have been of a value to repay the cost of collection; but it is worth remark that the licensing of goods vehicles by road and the changes in the organization of the trade contemplated by the Act of 1947 have all been carried through in happy ignorance of the tons and ton-mileage being run by road. The Ministry of Transport in 1946 may have had some indications of the dimensions of an industry about to be nationalized. But they did not share their knowledge with the voters nor with their elected represen-tatives. One of the authors making his own estimate, guessed that, by 1935, road operators taken as a whole might have been responsible for the diversion from the railway of a quantity of freight at least equal to the tonnage of general merchandise then being carried by rail.[1]

Messrs Glover and Miller, in 1954, reported upon an official survey made in 1952 into the dimensions and distribution of tonnage and ton-mileage hauled by road. This was the first official inquiry which has been undertaken into the goods-carrying trade. (The date of the study alone is worth notice.) The authors' final conclusions (this was before the sale of the vehicles then worked by British Road Services had begun) are summarized in Tables 6 and 7. 1250 million tons of freight was carried by inland surface transport (including coastal shipping) for 51,000 million ton-miles. Road carriers of all sorts handled 900 million tons for 19,000 million ton-miles, 70% and 37% respectively of the total. The difference between the two figures is an indication of the shorter dis-tance for which, on the average, each consignment was hauled by road and of the large number of lorries used mainly for local work. Messrs Glover and Miller could not distinguish in their figures that freight which was carried by road in competition with the railway. But they were able to divide the tonnage and ton-mileage by road between the several classes of licence; and they drew attention to the fact that lorries worked on 'C' licences, the owners of which were precluded by the terms of their licence from carrying any but their own goods, were being run for 75% of the total of vehicle miles, hauling 50% of the total ton-mileage road-borne and carrying 60% of all freight sent by road.

---

[1] Walker, *Road and Rail*, ch. v. The Leader of the House (Mr Herbert Morrison), defending in the Commons proposals for nationalizing the public part of the carrying trade in 1946 rejected the suggestion for a public inquiry as a waste of time, on the ground that, 'possessing as we do, among us, the facts about this matter...the matter should be dealt with directly by legislation'. In 1952 the Ministry of Transport assembled for the first time official estimates of traffic road-borne and the use to which road vehicles were being put during one week in September by inquiry among owners of a 1% sample of all trucks licensed. The British Trans-port Commission, in 1956, was moved to complain of the 'absence of even the simplest annual statistics of freight traffic carried by road vehicles other than for the British Road Services', and one of the authors, writing on inland transport during the Second World War, has des-cribed the problems of attempting without these data, to arrange for the movement of goods when plans were being discussed to meet the threat of war in the late 1930's. *H.C. Deb.* 18 December 1946, col. 2077; British Transport Commission, *Report for 1956*, par. 236; Savage, *Inland Transport*, ch. II, section 1; Walker, 'New Thinking in Transport', *Journal of the Institute of Transport*, vol. 26, no. 5, July 1955, p. 162.

Transport by road was 'long distance' for the purposes of the Act of 1947 when the distance travelled exceeded 40 miles. Of the traffic road-borne, 95 million tons was carried this distance and more and worked for 8000 million ton-miles. 55 % of the former (about 50 million tons) and half of the latter, 4000 million ton-miles, were carried by vehicles operated on 'C' licences.[1] The two authors, asked in discussion which among the results of the survey had surprised them the most, remarked that one among others had certainly been the amount of work done by road vehicles for long hauls, particularly by those owners carrying by private lorry on their own account.

Table 6. *British domestic freight transport, 1952*

| | Tons carried (millions) | Ton-mileage (thousand millions) | Proportions | |
			Tons carried (%)	Ton-mileage (%)
Road	900	19	72	37
Rail	300*	22	24	43
Inland waterways	10*	†	1	—
Coastal shipping	40	10‡	3	20
Total	1,250	51	100	100

* Tons originating including free hauled traffic.
† 0·2 thousand millions.
‡ The 'inland equivalent', that is the ton-mileage by inland transport which would result if the coastwise traffics passed by inland means of carriage.
Source: Glover and Miller, 'The Outlines of the Road Goods Transport Industry', *Journal of the Royal Statistical Society*, Series A, vol. 117, part 3, 1954, Table 23, p. 318.

A large proportion of the vehicles on 'C' licences are small—less than 30 cwt. and 2 tons in weight unladen—and probably used for nothing farther than a local round. A 'surprisingly large number' which must of course include some of the heavier vehicles, according to Messrs Glover and Miller, are used by builders, brewers and others who neither fetch and carry nor deliver outside their immediate area. There was room too, in the design of the survey itself, for errors to accumulate, the sum of which if they were serious, might have increased the apparent tonnages carried long distances in vehicles held on 'C' licences. Licence holders were asked to account for the tonnage and ton-mileage hauled in a sample of vehicles specified by registration number. A particular lorry might at the time have been carrying a varying tonnage for a somewhat indefinite mileage, quantities not easily reduced to the tons and ton-miles in terms of which the work of carriage is usually expressed. The

[1] K. F. Glover and D. N. Miller, 'The Outlines of the Road Goods Transport Industry', *Journal of the Royal Statistical Society*, Series A (General), vol. 117, part 3, 1954, Tables 22 and 23 and pp. 313–14, 317.

respondent could certainly save himself trouble, though at the cost of disturbing the accuracy of the sample, by substituting from his fleet another similar vehicle, but one engaged on a business more easily measured.

Table 7. *Estimated annual aggregates, all goods vehicles, 1952**

	Vehicle miles (millions)	Tonnage (millions)	Ton-miles (thousand millions)
'A' licence	671	86	1·7
Contract 'A' licence	224	44	0·7
'B' licence	834	146	1·9
'C' licence	8,347	540	10·4
Total	10,076	816	14·7
British Transport Commission			
Road Haulage Executive	799	58	4·0
Railway Executive	94	30	0·1
Total	893	88	4·1
Grand total	10,969	904	18·8

* Including petroleum tankers but excluding vehicles licensed by farmers at special rates.
Source: Glover and Miller, 'The Outlines of the Road Goods Transport Industry', *Journal of the Royal Statistical Society*, Series A, vol. 117, part 3, 1954, Table 22, p. 317.

The railways in 1952 carried 285 million tons of freight and 22,000 million ton-miles.[1] The total carried by road, according to the estimates of Messrs Glover and Miller, was divided about equally between British Road Services, then the only public carrier, and the mass of 'C' licensees who worked vehicles for 40 miles and over. The railway statistics and the figures of Messrs Glover and Miller unhappily are not comparable. The first include all freight for all distances; the second only that freight carried 40 miles and more. But if it can be fairly assumed that coal, minerals and heavy merchandise go by road only in the exceptional case[2] and that railway goods traffic is predominantly long-distance (and the statistics of the average length of haul support this conclusion),[3] then the returns of traffic in general merchandise by railway can fairly be set alongside Messrs Glover's and Miller's estimates for freight hauled by road. This has already been done by one of the authors of this chapter in the *Journal of the Institute of Transport* for July 1955; the results are sufficiently startling to be repeated here. Annual estimates of road traffic derived from replies to questions asked of owners of a 1% sample of trucks about work done during one week in September 1952 are particularly liable to error: but if these figures are to be relied upon (there are

[1] British Transport Commission, *Report and Accounts for 1952*, Tables X-2 and X-7.
[2] The British Transport Commission in its *Report for 1955* conveys a contrary opinion (in par. 20).
[3] British Transport Commission, *Financial and Statistical Accounts*.

no others), then British Railways, the public carrier by road, whether publicly or privately owned, and the private carrier using a 'C' licence appear to be sharing about equally between them the total traffic in general merchandise. Each is carrying a round 50 million tons, the railways on the average for the longer distance—126 miles by rail against 85 miles by road.[1]

Ministers in 1947, although they subsequently withdrew from the Bill the clauses[2] confining the operations of 'C' licensees, were deeply apprehensive about the use to which the trader might put the freedom to carry, even privately, his own goods.[3] The Commission has returned more than once to the theme in its annual reports.[4] Mr Herbert Morrison has said in debate that 'there is a prima facie case for dealing with them' (the 'C' licences)[5] and the Commission now sees in the increasing competition from the 'C' licensee 'the main reason for the fall in railway merchandise carryings'.[6] Traders operating on 'C' licences choose their own freight, carry in their own time and at their own convenience. But traders working their own transport may not carry for others and it has been said on no less an authority than that of the British Transport Commission that 180,000 of the million or so vehicles owned by traders and held on 'C' licences, all of them of $2\frac{1}{2}$ tons in weight unladen or over, 'are running empty or less than half loaded for half of the time they are on the road'.[7] Firms which do in fact carry for themselves may do so, not for reasons of cheapness, but because they hope to get the better service, looking to their transport departments to provide some secondary function as salesmen, bill collectors, display and so on, or because they are attracted by 'the prestige and convenience of this type of operation'.[8] But it is surely unusual for the private trader to get, regularly, loads of his own traffic in both directions sufficient to keep a substantial number of vehicles fully employed. The protection offered by the opportunity still open to the trader of carrying his own goods in his own vans is thus conditional, conditional upon the circum-

[1] The large quantity of freight being carried in Western Europe by traders for themselves has been noticed by the Economic Commission for Europe in their *Economic Survey of Europe in 1956*, ch. v, pp. 4, 5. Walker, 'New Patterns of Transport', *Manual of the Association of British Chambers of Commerce*, 1957.

[2] *Transport Bill, 1946*, Clauses 56, 57 and 58.

[3] *H.C. Deb.* 16 December 1946, col. 1631.

[4] British Transport Commission, *Report and Accounts for 1948*, par. 39; *Report for 1951*, par. 64; *Report and Accounts 1954*, vol. i, par. 7; *Report and Accounts 1956*, vol. i, pars. 240, 245.

[5] *H.C. Deb.* 3 February 1955, col. 1324.

[6] British Transport Commission, *Report and Accounts 1955*, vol. i, par 20.

[7] Relief from the consequences of the shortage of motor fuel caused by the closing of Suez and the blowing up of the pipe line in Syria was sought in December 1956, by a general authority permitting holders of 'C' licences to carry for others in all cases in which the goods would in any case have gone by road.

[8] British Transport Commission, *Report for 1955*, par. 175.

stances being such that the trader escapes, or at least need not charge to his transport undertaking, the whole of the costs for provision of vehicle, garage, maintenance, administration and the like, all of which fall normally on the public carrier. Public carriers, being organized for the express purpose of handling traffic, must surely have access to economies not open to traders to whom transport is only an auxiliary? They could of course be protected from the competition of the 'C' licensee by further restraints upon the liberty of private persons to carry their own goods as they see fit. But carriers for hire and reward, if it is a fact that they can reach lower costs than private carriers, should be able to charge correspondingly less. It is thus in their charges schemes that professional carriers should find their principal defence against the private trader and not in a protection designed in effect to prevent the private trader from carrying his own goods in his own way. The results of such a system of transport charges, it must be confessed, may at first be somewhat surprising![1]

5. THE FUTURE OF COMPETITION IN TRANSPORT

The Act of 1930 transformed the road passenger branch of the industry in which competition was already highly imperfect into 'one organized into a series of sheltered quasi-monopolies'.[2] Management and control of public road passenger carriers are in the hands of the British Transport Commission, the local authorities, the relatively few associated bus companies, and the independent concerns. The Commission under the Act of 1953, in common with other operators, must obtain licences for its road passenger vehicles. In pursuit of the obligation laid on it by Clause 3, Section 4 of the Transport Act, 1947, to make both ends meet over its businesses taken as a whole, the Commission has abandoned branch lines and stations, and withdrawn services which do not pay. Licensing authorities have followed the directions of the Act of 1930, to consider, in exercising their discretion to grant or refuse road service licences, 'the needs of the area...including the provision of unremunerative services'. Where it controls the bus companies, the Commission has argued that 'there is an effective means of assuring the provision of suitable alternative road passenger services. But where such branch lines lie within the territory served by independent omnibus companies, no such means

---

[1] Walker, 'Competition in Transport as an Instrument of Policy'. Address before the British Association for the Advancement of Science, September 1956, reported in *The Economic Journal*, vol. 66, no. 263, September 1956, p. 409, and *British Transport Review*, vol. 4, no. 3, December 1956, p. 217.

[2] British Transport Commission, *Report for 1951*, p. 21. It has been alleged, indeed, that 'virtual road-rail monopolies' have been established in certain areas, especially Scotland and East Anglia (Thesiger Report, pp. 51–2).

exist. The licensing authorities have no power to compel an [independent] operator to run a particular service.' That of course is true and the prospect now opened out that some areas may be deprived entirely of a public means of transport has been debated in the House and drawn a statement from the Minister.[1]

Licensing authorities were also required, again by the Act of 1930, to see that the fares asked on buses were 'not unreasonable'. This phrase has been interpreted generally in relation to the carriers' costs and has been designed to prevent the emergence of large profits. Railway fares prescribed by the Acts of 1947 and 1953 are subject to the jurisdiction of the Transport Tribunal. The scheme adopted in 1952 provided for a standard ordinary fare of $1.75d.$ a mile. Over half the passengers by rail are classed as 'ordinary'. The remaining fares are early morning and workmen's and season tickets. There are wide variations in the average distance travelled by rail. Passengers on ordinary tickets travel on the average the longest distance: but that certainly does not exceed 30 miles.[2] Fares of course had been, and are being raised as the value of money falls. But it still remains the case, until the Commission take advantage of their powers under Clause 20 of the Act of 1953, that fares by rail are assessed at the same rate a mile over the railway network as a whole, while the bus fares are those which, in the opinion of the licensing authority, would be considered 'not unreasonable' given the costs of the particular operation.

The conflict between the policy of the Commission and the duties of the licensing authority has become most obvious in the fares being charged on the express coaches. The British Transport Commission has rightly taken the view that long-distance coach services ought not to be expanded to the detriment of the railways, which, on economic grounds, should carry the bulk of long-distance passenger travel. Express buses compete directly with the railway. They are normally run full. Empty seats would be regarded as evidence of excess facilities and wasteful competition. The application for a licence might be jeopardized. Full loading makes for low cost per passenger mile.[3] Duplication is stopped by withholding the licence. Fares by bus, 'not unreasonable' given the costs of the service, are consequently less than the passenger fares for the railway determined by the Transport Tribunal, and passengers not pressed for time stand in line to take advantage of the facility.

[1] *H.C. Deb.* 24 April 1956, col. 1672.
[2] British Transport Commission, *Report and Accounts 1953*, vol. II, Table X-1, p. 184. The average distance a passenger journey (ordinary category) is stated to be 28·96 miles. Later Reports omit this statistic, though the average British Railways journey (outside London) was stated to be 30·8 miles in 1955, *Report and Accounts 1955*, vol. I, par. 169.
[3] British Transport Commission, *Report for 1955*, par. 165; *Report for 1956*, par. 233.

The demand for passenger transport is characterized by fluctuations, which make it difficult to match demand and supply precisely and tend to make competitive working unstable. Seasonal fluctuations principally affect long-distance rail and coach services, since holiday and tourist traffic increases in the summer months. Weekly fluctuations arise because traffic on local market days and at week-ends usually follows a different pattern from ordinary weekday traffic. Most serious of all, however, are the violent daily fluctuations and the peak-hour problem, which affect local services, particularly in large cities. The problem is most acute on the London transport system. The sharpness of the daily traffic peaks not only adds to the cost of providing a service, but creates a periodic surplus of capacity.[1] Passenger services must be produced and consumed simultaneously and the transport apparatus must be large enough to meet traffic at the highest peak.

There are in effect not one but many markets for passenger transport. The public wants services of many kinds: local country services, suburban and inter-city services, long-distance express services, excursions, private hire, contract and so forth. Demands for road and rail services exist and must be met in thousands of different places and on thousands of different routes throughout the country. Effective competition can only exist where many different operators compete in the same market— i.e. on the same or adjacent routes. This is impossible for technical reasons in rail transport; it no longer exists in a large part of road passenger transport owing to legal restriction. Moreover, the times at which competing services are provided are important matters for the consumer. For the services of different operators to be properly 'competitive' they must be provided at approximately the same time. The economic history of passenger transport shows that rigid adherence to a time-table is not readily compatible with free competition—implying choice for the consumer and free entry into the industry—at least in the provision of local bus services.

The Transport Act of 1953 provided that rates and charges for carriage by railway be fixed at a maximum except, and this was contrary to all precedent, 'in cases where it appears not to be reasonably practicable or undesirable to do so'. The actual charges, 'save as aforesaid', are left to the Commission's discretion, with neither condition nor limitation.[2] The maximum rates for which the Commission asked were assessed on the loadability of merchandise. They represented as nearly as possible the estimated costs of carrying consignments by railway in the general run of adverse circumstances. The Tribunal held a prolonged public inquiry. In an interim decision they agreed with the principles

[1] British Transport Commission, *Report for 1955*, par. 171.
[2] *Transport Act, 1953*, clause 20.

on which the Commission had based its claims. But they did not accept the scales proposed. No maxima were fixed for traffic in owners' tank wagons, owners' wagons and road-rail tank wagons, or for consignments of 100 tons and over. The Commission was left to charge reasonable rates, subject of course to a review on the objection of the trader. Traders who allege successfully that the railway is the only practical means of mechanical transport for their goods may claim the protection of the Tribunal under Clause 22. All merchandise sent otherwise by railway is subject to the maximum charge; but the schedules authorized by the Tribunal differ in material particulars from the maxima proposed by the Commission and the Tribunal confirmed not the one scale of maximum charges for which the Commission had applied but two sets of scales each divided into three, or six in all. From 1 July 1957, the day appointed by the Transport Tribunal from which these schedules become effective, the British Transport Commission has been free under the Act to charge for merchandise subject to these maxima, in their discretion, with neither condition nor limitation. The British Transport Commission, toward the end of June 1957, was obliged by the state of its accounts to make use of the powers granted under Clause 23 of the Act of 1953 to propose a rise of 10% in its charges. The coincidence of the introduction of the new system of charging and the announcement of an emergency increase was distinctly unfortunate.

The issue of the public 'A' and limited 'B' carriers' licence has been such as to confer something of a monopoly, as the Minister of the day remarked when moving in 1946 the second reading of the bill which in due course became the Transport Act, 1947. That monopoly is limited by the costs and convenience of the trader who works, or who may work his own vans. Special 'A' licences valid for five years were allowed with each vehicle bought from the British Transport Commission under the scheme of disposals announced by the Act of 1953. These licences could not be refused unless, under the First Schedule to that Act, the licensing authority was satisfied that the vehicles were not being used from their new owners' base in substantially the same areas as those which could conveniently be served from the base or centre last used by the Commission before the tenders were invited. The sales are now closed. In seven cases only has a licence been refused under this provision.

The sale of lorries from the fleets of the British Road Services increases no doubt the number engaged as professional carriers. But it does not enlarge in gross the carrying capacity of the combined fleet. Competition in transport, rather than the regulation of a supposed monopoly, is now being relied upon to give the better service. But that competition is subject to conditions of entry to the trade of professional carrier so severe that the licence to carry for hire and reward has been made

into a property, the value of which can be estimated from the price to
be paid for the special 'A' licence, free for five years from the discretion
of the licensing authority; and it is limited by the terms of the 'C'
licence, which prevent the private trader from carrying for others if he
should so desire.[1] Licensing authorities, on the applications before
them, are empowered by the Act of 1933 to decide whether or not the
case has been made for adding to public facilities for the transport of
merchandise. They had already been enjoined by a ruling of the Transport Tribunal in a case decided in 1948 not to disregard a complaint
that the rates for existing transport facilities were excessive. They are
now required, by Clause 9 of the Act of 1953, 'to have regard...to such
an extent as may in all the circumstances appear proper [to] the charges
made and to be made in respect of the facilities asked for or objected
to'. They could already by Clause 13 of the Act of 1933 and by Clause 9,
Section 4, of the Act of 1953, suspend or revoke the licence to carry on
the grounds that any of the conditions of the licence, including presumably all those relating to drivers and their hours of work, had not
been complied with and that any statement of intention made for the
purpose of getting the licence had not been fulfilled. They can now,
by Clause 44 of the Road Traffic Act, 1956, suspend or revoke an 'A'
or 'B' licence should the licensee by persistently charging for carriage by
road 'sums insufficient to meet the costs of rendering those services' thereby place other holders of licences 'at an undue or unfair disadvantage
in competing with him as respects the carriage of goods by road'.[2] It will
be interesting to see how licensing authorities resolve administratively
the awkward question, which in the past has so plagued practical transport men and theoretical economists, of what constitutes the cost of any
particular service of transport. Should that quantity include for example
just the elements laid out in furnishing the service in question or all the
items of expense, past and present, incurred by the carrier? The two
quantities are by no means the same. Either, depending upon the direction from which the transaction is viewed, can be alleged to be the

---

[1] 'Convictions', we have been told by the Ministry of Transport, 'for using "C" licenced
vehicles for hire and reward continue to increase.' One is sorry to read that 'the extensive
inquiries' involved in the pursuit of these cases add so much to the demands upon the already
over-burdened staffs of the licensing authorities, but happy nevertheless to learn that the
drivers (and, one hopes, the owners) of lorries held on a 'C' licence are showing so much
enterprise! (*Summary of Annual Reports of Licensing Authorities for Goods Vehicles*, 1953–4, p. 9.)
See above, p. 99 n. 7.

[2] A variant of this clause was first included in the Transport (Disposal of Road Haulage
Property) Bill introduced by the Parliamentary Secretary in March 1956. Aimed specifically
at the British Transport Commission, Clause 5 of that Bill was intended to remove the fear,
then present to Conservative minds, that the Commission might abuse their size by using
some of the profits earned elsewhere in their undertaking to finance the carriage of certain
traffics by road—cross-subsidizing in fact their road haulage enterprise. The clause was removed from the Bill in Committee, only to reappear in its present form in the Road Traffic Act.

'cost' of transport. The first is likely to be the choice of the buyer, since he considers the rate for the consignment or the fare for the journey. But the purveyor of transport has to reckon with all the expenses to which he is put in providing the service which the customer has been accustomed to expect. That quantity is usually the larger and it is always open to be undercut by operators not responsible to the public for the regularity of the service. Clause 44, if the administrators should prefer, as well they may, the full allocated cost of the accountant to the marginal cost of the economist, might limit, only too readily, the opportunities now open to carriers by road to enlarge their businesses by reducing their rates!

British Railways are embarking upon a programme of modernization intended to bring their (railway) equipment up to date even at the cost of a heavy deficit which is to be borne by the Exchequer.[1] The improvements forecast should enable the railways of the Commission to reach those low levels of cost which are their surest protection against the depredations of the private trader and the private motorist. The construction of motorways and large (and expensive) improvements may and probably will reduce the costs of carriage by road. Much of course depends upon the nature of the works and where they are undertaken. In the present condition of the Queen's highway, almost any work on the road increases the convenience brought by a motor vehicle. An expenditure on highways can thus be undertaken with profit to the community, even though no reduction can be expected in the cost of carriage by road, particularly when there is reckoned in the account, as there certainly should be, a credit for the greater satisfaction of motor owners generally, including of course the owners and drivers of those $3\frac{1}{2}$ million private cars and the 1 million motor-cyclists. But it might equally be worth while preventing too great an increase in the freight and passengers road-borne even if costs can be shown to be lower, in order, for example, to preserve the railways and canals for time of war, to control an incipient inflation, or to economize on oil. Officials of the Ministry of Transport appeared satisfied in 1952 if expenditure upon highways was kept down to 60 or 70 % in sum of the money spent before the war.[2] Real resources being sunk in roads had by then fallen to one-half or less of the rate current in 1938. A much greater expenditure on roads is now contemplated, rising to some hundreds of millions if the interested parties get their way. Knowledgeable opinion has arrived at the happy conclusion that the money sunk in a motorway or other considerable improvement by public authorities would be well repaid

[1] British Transport Commission, *Proposals for the Railways*, Cmd. 9880 (H.M.S.O. 1956).
[2] *Fifth Report* of the Select Committee on Estimates, Session 1956–7 (H.M.S.O.). M. Beesley and A. A. Walters, 'Investment in British Railways', *Westminster Bank Review*, May 1955, p. 4.

in the savings of time by the users and in the reduced expenses of running their vehicles. Private motorists gain and so do traders carrying on their own account. The first get there faster and with less fatigue and frustration. The second have their goods delivered more cheaply and with greater punctuality. But this reduction in the cost of transport will only be followed by a lowering of the price by professional carriers, provided that licensing authorities exercise their discretion to grant licences permitting a greater capacity for goods and passengers on the road should application be made, and provided that railway rates and fares for the future reflect that 'very great variety of operating conditions' to which the Chief Commercial Officer of British Railways has referred in his evidence before the Transport Tribunal. It is thus on the law, on the response of the public to proposals for large schemes of expenditure to be undertaken on their behalf and on the attitude of legislators and administrators to current economic problems as much as (or more than) on technical improvement in the arts of carriage and on the structure of the industry that the future efficiency of British transport will depend.

BIBLIOGRAPHY

(a) Books, Pamphlets and Articles

British Road Federation, *Basic Road Statistics, Great Britain and Northern Ireland*, annual.

Chester, D. N., *Public Control of Road Passenger Transport*, Manchester University Press, 1936.

Milne, A. M., 'Passenger Road Transport and the Transport Act 1947, with Particular Reference to the North-East of England', *Economic Journal*, vol. 61, no. 242, June 1951, p. 310.

Milne, A. M. and Laing, A. *The Obligation to Carry*, London, Institute of Transport, 1956.

Savage, C. I., *Inland Transport*, History of the Second World War, United Kingdom Civil Series, H.M.S.O. and Longmans, Green, 1957.

Walker, Gilbert, 'Price—and Competition—in Transport as an Instrument of Policy', *The Advancement of Science*, vol. 13, no. 50, September 1956, p. 67. 'Competition in Transport as an Instrument of Policy', *British Transport Review*, vol. 4, no. 3, December 1956, p. 217.

Road and Rail: an Inquiry into the Economics of Competition and State Control, 2nd ed. London, Allen and Unwin, 1947.

'Transport Policy Before and After 1953', *Oxford Economic Papers* (New Series), vol. 5, no. 1, March 1953, p. 99.

(b) Official Publications
(All published by H.M.S.O.)

British Transport Commission, *Proposals for the Railways*, Cmd. 9880, 1956.

Report and Accounts, annual, 1948 to 1955.

Royal Commission on Transport, *Second Report*, Cmd. 3416, *The Licensing and Regulation of Public Service Vehicles*, 1929; *Final Report*, Cmd. 3751, *The Co-ordination and Development of Transport*, 1931.

Ministry of Transport and Civil Aviation (formerly Ministry of Transport), *Annual Reports [and Summaries] of Licensing Authorities for Goods Vehicles*.

Annual Reports of the Area Traffic Commissioners, 1931 to 1937, and *Summaries of Annual Reports of the Licensing Authorities for Public Service Vehicles*, 1947–8 to 1954–5.

Public Road Passenger Transport Statistics, Great Britain, annual, 1951 to 1955–6.

Railways Reorganization Scheme, Cmd. 9191, 1954.

Report of the Committee on the Licensing of Road Passenger Services (the Thesiger Report), 1953.

Report of the Conference on Rail and Road Transport (the Salter Report), 1932.

Reports of Railway Capital, Revenue and Working Expenditure, annual up to 1947.

CHAPTER IV

THE COAL INDUSTRY

By A. Beacham

The purpose of this short survey of the coal industry is to give a brief description of its organization and economic structure and a critical account of its present problems. It is arranged in three parts. Sections 1–4 are mainly descriptive and are concerned with the nature of the product, technique, location, organization and the recent history of the industry. Section 5 is concerned with supply, demand and price relationships. Sections 6 and 7 deal with various critical factors affecting efficiency including technical change and capital investment, size of plant, industrial relations and administrative arrangements.

I. NATURE AND CLASSIFICATION OF COALS

There can be little real understanding of the economics of the coal industry without some knowledge of the product itself. It is not sufficient to say that coal is not a simple homogeneous substance—this would be true of the products of most industries and in itself gives rise to no great difficulties. The important point to emphasize is that there is no single quality or associated group of qualities according to which coal can be graded from 'low' to 'high' quality. To give only a very simple example, coals which are of similar calorific value (on a dry ash-free basis) may have very different ash contents and therefore will be valued very differently by the consumer. Moreover, the word 'quality' has to be viewed not only in relation to the physical characteristics of the coal but also to the use which is to be made of the coal in question. Anthracite may be highly prized as a source of space heating in the home and in this use may compete with 'house coal'. In other (for example horticultural) uses it may be highly prized because it is the only suitable coal. A very 'high quality' coal from a heat-giving point of view may be quite useless for the manufacture of metallurgical coke.

The qualities for which different consumers will value different coals will include ash and moisture content, chemical composition (proportions of volatile matter and carbon, hydrogen, oxygen and sulphur content, etc.), caking qualities, mode of preparation (whether sized, washed, etc.) and friability. Consumers will attach different weights to these qualities according to their needs and the various qualities do not necessarily go together. A coal with a high calorific value may have a high ash content and poor caking qualities.

It is inevitable, however, that some attempt should be made to classify coals in some formal way. In the past coal was sold under many thousands of different names which combined in various degrees place of origin (pit, district or seam), chemical characteristics (for example anthracite), use (for example house or gas coal), and mode of preparation (for example washed smalls). Coals which were identical in all important respects might be sold in different parts of the country under very different names. Since nationalization of the industry in 1947 steps have been taken to systematize the classification of coal. This was done partly as a preliminary to the evolution of a more 'rational' price structure and partly in order that consumers should be better informed of the qualities of the coal they were buying and more willing to take supplies from the most economical source.

In this classification coals are ranked in order of merit according to their calorific value (on a dry ash-free basis) which in turn depends mainly on carbon content. The top-ranking coal is anthracite with 9·5 % or less of volatile matter and a very high carbon content. Anthracite burns almost smokelessly, does not cake and is mined almost exclusively in South Wales. Next in rank are the low volatile steam coals (semi-anthracites) with 9·5 to 20 % volatile matter. These also occur mainly in South Wales. Some types are strongly caking and suitable for blending for coke making. Other types (the famous Admiralty steam coals) containing rather less hydrogen and volatile matter are more suitable for high grade steam raising. Next come the bituminous coals, led by the medium and high volatile coals containing over 20 % volatile matter with strong caking qualities, most generally used for coke and gas making and which occur mainly in South Wales and Durham. The lower ranks of coal are also high volatile coals which are graded downwards as the percentage of oxygen increases and the caking properties of the coal diminish. The major part of the remaining coal reserves are of this type. These coals are generally employed in domestic and general industrial uses and cover grades of very varied properties. The highest ranking of these coals occur most generally in Yorkshire, Durham, North Derbyshire, Nottinghamshire and Lancashire and the remainder are found very extensively in Great Britain. Strictly speaking the classification should be continued downwards to include lignite, a semi-coal of very high moisture content, or even peat, but neither of these fuels are important in Great Britain, nor do they come within the scope of the coal industry.

This classification may be briefly related to the principal uses of coal.

Coals used for steam raising and general industrial use should be free burning (non-caking), of high calorific value and of low sulphur and ash content. Coking coals must produce, when carbonized, a strong hard coke suitable for metallurgical purposes while the proportion of volatile matter is less important. For gas coals a high percentage of volatile matter is important in order to ensure a high yield of gas whilst caking qualities, though important, are less essential. The best types of house coal are free burning and of fairly high calorific value. In most if not all of these uses a wide range of coals at different steps of the formal ranking are more or less suitable and the final choice of the consumer in a free market will depend upon the qualities of the coal in relation to his particular needs and in relation to relative prices. The relative price structure will in its turn be modified by the pressure of demand as consumers adapt to particular uses coals previously considered unsuitable (and which are relatively low priced) and vice versa.

Generally speaking then, coal is nowadays ranked according to calorific value which declines with a rise in the percentage of volatile matter and, except for the non-caking anthracite and semi-anthracites, a decline in its caking qualities. Also throughout the bituminous coals moisture content generally increases as calorific value declines, but it is extremely difficult to generalize about ash content. If within each rank of coal appropriate adjustments are made for ash content, size, mode of preparation, sulphur content, hardness, etc., this classification of coal can be regarded as a very rough indication of the value of the coal to the consumer, since coal is generally purchased for its heat value. It does not follow that relative prices (on a pit-head basis) will or should be in step with such a classification since supply considerations have to be taken into account and these are particularly complex in the coal industry. There is, of course, nothing to prevent a complete monopolist (as the National Coal Board now is) from fixing relative prices on such a basis and allowing the supply side of the equation to adjust itself to this. Meanwhile, whether or not anthracite is the most highly priced coal because it is the top ranking coal or because it is (in some sense) the most expensive and difficult to mine must be left as an open question.[1]

2. WORKING METHODS

During and since the Second World War about 5 % of the current output of coal in Great Britain has been extracted by open-cast working

[1] In the early days of the industry, when anthracite was more easily and cheaply mined, its price was very little more than the price of other coals. Though great efforts were made it failed to push very far into the house and steam coal markets. In America however, where anthracite was more plentiful and easily mined, it was extensively adapted to domestic heating and steam raising.

—that is, the digging out of coal from the surface after removal of the overburden. Otherwise, coal is deep-mined. That is to say, the coal is mined underground and raised to the surface through vertical shafts or (more rarely) hauled up drifts or inclines. From the shaft, roadways radiate and except in a few modern mines, follow the inclination of the coal seams. The traditional method of working coal in Great Britain was the room and pillar system by which headings were driven into the seam parallel to each other and connected by cross headings so as to form pillars of coal which were extracted completely or partially according to geological conditions. When the best seams at shallow depths had been worked, however, this system showed certain disadvantages and the room and pillar method has now been generally replaced by longwall advancing—the method now employed at about three-quarters of the mines in Great Britain, and responsible for nearly 90 % of total output. By this method the coal seam is worked on a broad front, the roadway advancing as the face recedes, with the remaining area of extraction being packed with stone and waste material to support the roof.

At the face the usual method of extracting the coal is by coal-cutting machine; this undercuts the coal which is then blasted out of the seam.[1] But about 6 % of the national output is still being got by hand pick, though the use of the pneumatic pick (a mechanized version of the hand pick) has been increasing until recent years and accounts for about 11 % of the national output.[2] The coal is then loaded into tubs or on to mechanical conveyors (generally by hand) which take it away from the face. The proportion of total output which is face conveyed has been rising steeply and in 1955 was about 91 %. One of the most revolutionary developments in British mining practice since the last war has been the introduction of power loaders of various kinds (that is, machines which simultaneously cut and load). About 15 % of the total deep-mined output of coal was power loaded in 1956.[3]

Face conveyors generally deliver the coal to gate conveyors and thence into tubs or cars which are used to carry the coal along the main haulage roads to the pit-bottom. The general method of main haulage is by endless rope which, although slow, has the advantage of adaptability to varying conditions including the curves and gradients common in many mines. Locomotive haulage is almost entirely confined to relatively few new and reconstructed pits. At the pit-bottom the tubs are generally transferred to cages which are wound up the shaft to the

[1] About 84 % of the total output of deep-mined coal was cut by this machine in 1954.
[2] Excluding picks used with coal-cutting machines.
[3] This output is of course included in that obtained by coal-cutting machine as quoted above.

surface. In a few pits the more modern method of skip winding is employed. The tubs discharge into a bunker at the pit-bottom from which a special container (or skip) is filled automatically. The skip is then hoisted up the shaft and its contents are automatically discharged at the surface. On the surface the coal may be further treated by screening into sizes and cleaned by hand-picking or washing before being despatched. About 79 % of total output was cleaned in 1956.

British methods of coal mining were described and strongly criticized by the Reid Committee in 1945.[1] Partly as a result of this the industry is now undergoing an extensive technical reorganization which is following the main lines of the Committee's recommendations. Further review of these matters must await later discussion of the efficiency of the industry but the importance of current technical changes can hardly be grasped without some understanding of present practice.

3. THE COALFIELDS

The map on p. 113 shows the principal coalfields of Great Britain together with the boundaries of the divisions into which they are at present grouped by the National Coal Board.[2] These divisions do not correspond to the 'districts' into which the industry was broken down for statistical purposes prior to nationalization. These districts generally represented regional groupings for which separate owners' and miners' associations existed, and for wage-fixing and other purposes it was convenient to present coalfield statistics on this basis. The equivalence of National Coal Board divisions and the old districts is as follows:

National Coal Board division	Districts combined
Scottish	Scotland
Northern (N. and C.)	Northumberland, Cumberland and Westmorland
Durham	Durham
North-Eastern	South Yorkshire, West Yorkshire
North-Western	Lancashire and Cheshire, North Wales
East Midlands	Nottinghamshire, North Derbyshire, South Derbyshire, Leicestershire
West Midlands	North Staffordshire, Cannock Chase, South Staffordshire, Shropshire, Warwickshire
South-Western	South Wales, Forest of Dean, Somerset, Bristol
South-Eastern	Kent

[1] Ministry of Fuel and Power, *Coal Mining: Report of the Technical Advisory Committee,* Cmd. 6610 (H.M.S.O. 1945).

[2] The body responsible for the management of the industry since its nationalization in 1947.

Boundaries of National Coal Board divisions.

The changing balance of production between the coalfields is illustrated by Table 1.

Table 1. *Coal output by district**

Coalfield	Percentage of national output of saleable coal produced in							
	1875		1913		1937		1955	
Scotland	14·0	(18·6)	14·8	(42·5)	13·4	(32·2)	10·5	(22·0)
Durham	19·2	(25·6)	14·4	(41·5)	13·9	(33·5)	12·3	(25·9)
Yorkshire	11·9	(15·9)	15·2	(43·7)	18·8	(45·1)	20·9	(43·9)
Northumberland	5·1	(6·8)	5·2	(14·8)	5·9	(14·2)	5·8	(12·3)
Lancashire, Cheshire and North Wales	15·8	(21·0)	9·7	(28·1)	7·4	(17·9)	7·4	(15·6)
Derbyshire, Nottinghamshire and Leicestershire	8·8	(11·6)	11·7	(33·7)	14·1	(33·9)	21·9	(46·0)
Staffordshire, Shropshire and Warwickshire†	12·4	(16·5)	7·3	(20·8)	8·4	(20·2)	8·4	(17·7)
South Wales	10·7	(14·1)	19·8	(56·8)	15·7	(37·8)	11·0	(23·1)
Other districts‡	2·3	(3·1)	1·9	(5·3)	2·3	(5·5)	1·8	(3·8)
Total	100·2	(133·2)	100·0	(287·2)	99·9	(240·3)	100·1	(210·3)

* Figures in brackets represent outputs in million tons.
† Including Cannock Chase.
‡ Kent, Cumberland, Forest of Dean, Bristol and Somerset.

The oldest important centres of coal production are Durham, Lancashire and Scotland, which in 1875 were responsible for nearly half the national output. All have since declined in proportional importance, particularly Lancashire. Between 1875 and 1913 South Wales made spectacular progress both on a tonnage basis and in proportional importance, but has since declined in equally dramatic fashion. In the period between the two World Wars the Yorkshire coalfield was rapidly developed and by 1937 was producing nearly one-fifth of the national output. Since 1937 the most important feature has been the very rapid increase in output from the newer and rapidly developing coalfields of the East Midlands, which now produce over a fifth of the total output of coal mined in Great Britain. Since 1875, therefore, the general trend has been one of fairly rapid decline of the older coalfields, a decline mitigated by the successive opening up and rapid development of South Wales, Yorkshire and the East Midlands. If this process is to continue it is difficult to see which coalfield will succeed the East Midlands.[1] One other important point worth noting is that although tonnages produced continue to decline in the older coalfields the rate of decline in relative importance tends to slacken after a time, probably because

[1] 'The scope for developing areas of coal as yet untouched is strictly limited' (National Coal Board, *Report and Accounts for 1950* (H.M.S.O. 1951), p. 14).

of the increasing degree of protection which it enjoys in local markets and the technical excellence of some of its coals.[1]

With such a large number of coalfields at different stages of development, with very different natural conditions and mining very different categories of coal, it is to be expected that very different working results will be found. Some of the more important differences are summed up in Table 2 but the reader should be warned that divisional averages conceal great differences between pits in the same division.[2]

Table 2. *Differences in regional characteristics**

Division	Number of producing mines	Average output per mine in thousand tons	Output per man-shift overall in tons	Costs per ton s. d.	Proceeds per ton s. d.	Percentage of coal cut by machinery†	Percentage of coal mechanically conveyed†	Estimated resources of recoverable coals in million tons‡	Total exports including foreign bunkers in million tons
Scottish	263	87	1·06	65·2	61·7	86	79	7,700	1·4
Northern (N. and C.)	97	138	1·14	64·7	62·1	97	76	2,700	1·9
Durham	159	164	1·00	67·8	66·5	58	67	600	2·8
North-Eastern	146	308	1·33	54·3	59·5	89	94	6,800	3·5
North-Western	113	138	1·04	67·0	64·7	95	93	2,900	0·5
East Midlands	104	429	1·81	46·0	53·2	98	99	7,400	2·3
West Midlands	126	144	1·32	54·9	58·11	94	95	3,800	n.a.
South-Western	322	78	0·91	72·7	71·0	48	87	8,400	4·2
South-Eastern	4	429	1·12	70·1	70·1	47	96	2,200	n.a.
Great Britain	1,334	159	1·21	59·2	61·2	82	88	42,500	16·6

n.a. = not available.

* Figures are for 1953 except where otherwise stated.
† Figures are for 1952.
‡ These figures have been taken from the Regional Survey Reports of the Ministry of Fuel and Power, 1945. The basis of estimation appears to vary. They generally cover workable reserves in process of extraction and substantially unproved reserves (except in West Midlands and Leicestershire). See also PEP (Political and Economic Planning), *The British Fuel and Power Industries* (London, 1947), pp. 59–61.

[1] There have also of course been important changes in the location of production within coalfields. The most important example of this has occurred in Scotland where coal production has been falling rapidly in the central field of Lanark and has been rising in Fife.

[2] The main characteristics of the various coalfields are described in the Regional Survey Reports of the Ministry of Fuel and Power published at intervals by H.M.S.O. after 1945 and the report on the *Scottish Coalfields* issued by the Scottish Home Department, Cmd. 6575 (Edinburgh, H.M.S.O. 1944). Technical Appendix I of the *Plan for Coal* (National Coal Board, 1950) contains some excellent tables showing the types and characteristics of coal produced in each area.

4. RECENT HISTORY

Table 3 summarizes the main economic trends in the industry since 1920.

The industry reached its peak production in 1913. Its subsequent history down to 1939 is sufficiently well known and need not be summarized here. It is mainly a story of declining production, general depression, embittered relations between owners and men and of attempts to salvage the industry by compulsory cartelization and amalgamation.[1]

On the outbreak of war in 1939 an increase in the demand for coal was anticipated and a Coal Production Council was set up in 1940 to promote an increase in output. The fall of France and the Low Countries led to a substantial loss of export markets and for a time there was an excess of output and unemployment in the exporting districts. Many men were allowed to leave the industry. As the war effort got under way more coal was needed and desperate efforts were made to increase output, but a sadly deficient and unbalanced labour force made this extremely difficult. Steps were taken to direct men back to the industry and attract others. Improved welfare facilities and better training of juvenile entrants were introduced and higher wages sometimes took the form of output and attendance bonuses. Wage negotiations were again placed on a national basis, a guaranteed weekly wage was conceded by the Essential Wages Order and a national minimum wage instituted. Nevertheless the total labour force never increased by more than 10,000 men between 1941 and 1945. Absenteeism increased in spite of sterner measures to check it and output per man-shift had fallen to one ton by 1945. Although no general strike developed there was considerable unrest and indiscipline in the coalfields and in an effort to lessen output losses on account of sporadic small-scale strikes, a new conciliation scheme was adopted in 1943.[2] Direct methods to increase output included concentration of output in fewer mines and speeding up of mechanization but national output of deep-mined coal continued to fall steadily throughout the war and was only 174·8 million tons in 1945. In the central coalfields of England, however, output and productivity declined very little and in some cases increased. Meanwhile open-cast coal production had been started and by 1945 was contributing about 8 million tons of coal. A vigorous fuel economy campaign continued throughout most of the war years and after 1942 domestic coal consumption was rationed. The price of coal was con-

---

[1] By the Coal Mines Act of 1930.

[2] With minor modifications after the nationalization of the industry in 1946, the scheme has continued in operation.

Table 3. *Production, exports, employment and financial results, 1913–56*

Year	Output of saleable coal in million tons	Exports including coke and manufactured fuel and foreign bunkers in million tons	Number of mines at work	Number of wage-earners above and below ground in thousands*	Output per man-shift overall in tons†	Percentage of output mechanically cut	Percentage of output mechanically conveyed	Average number of shifts worked per week	Total costs per ton‡ s. d.	Proceeds per ton‡ s. d.	Profits per ton‡ s. d.
1913	287·4	98·3	3,024	1,107	0·98§	8·5	—	n.a.	8·8	10·2	1·6
1920	229·5	43·7	2,571	1,227	0·72§	13·2	—	n.a.	30·8	34·7	3·11
1925	243·2	70·5	2,479	1,087	0·90	20·0	—	4·81	16·10	17·1	0·3
1929	257·9	80·6	2,146	932	1·08	28·0	14·0	4·92	13·7	13·11	0·4
1933	207·1	56·7	1,782	772	1·12	42·4	30·0	4·63	13·4	13·7	0·3
1937	240·4	56·3	1,807	778	1·17	57·0	47·9	5·18	14·8	15·11	1·3
1941	206·3	9·1	1,737	698	1·07	65·7	63·7	5·37	22·4	24·1	1·9
1945	174·7‖	6·4¶	1,570	709	1·00	72·2	71·0	4·73	36·7	38·2	1·7
1949	202·7‖	19·0	1,366**	720	1·16	77·5	82·0	4·67	45·0	47·11	2·11
1953	212·5‖	16·8	1,337**	717	1·21	82·3††	88·2††	4·70	59·2	61·2	2·0
1954	214·0‖	16·3	1,327**	707**	1·23	84·4	90·4	4·67	61·11	63·6	1·7
1955	210·2‖	14·3	1,297**	704**	1·23	86·0	91·4	4·64	67·3	68·0	0·9
1956	210·0‖	10·1	—	703‡‡	1·23	—	—	4·61	74·5	77·0	2·7

n.a. = not available.

* Prior to 1922 a small number of clerks (about 24,000 in that year) are included. Revised bases of calculation were adopted in 1943 and 1946 but the comparability of the figures is not seriously affected thereby.

† Maximum hours of labour per shift were 8 hours (1913–22), 7 hours (1922–6), 8 hours in some districts and 7½ hours elsewhere (1927–31) and 7½ hours since 1931.

‡ Figures are not strictly comparable. The major factor affecting comparability is that prior to 1946 the figures are calculated per ton disposable commercially (except 1913) and afterwards per ton of saleable coal (i.e. including miners' concessionary coal and mines consumption). The main effect is to deflate costs and proceeds by a few pence per ton after 1946. N.B. Interest on compensation stock and treasury advances as well as taxation must be met from profits as shown here after nationalization.

§ Estimates not strictly comparable with later years. The PEP *Report on the British Coal Industry* (1936), gives 1·07 tons for 1913.

‖ Excluding open-cast coal, the outputs of which were (in million tons) 8·1 (1945), 12·5 (1949), 11·7 (1953), 10·31 (1954), 11·4 (1955) and 12·1 (1956).   ¶ Excluding shipments to the armed forces.   ** Not strictly comparable with previous years.   †† Estimate.   ‡‡ Estimate.

trolled by the government, increases being sanctioned from time to time, generally as flat-rates on all grades. By 1945 the price of coal was double that of 1938.

In 1940 the owners began to operate a scheme whereby a levy per ton was paid into a central fund from which mines that had suffered from enemy action were compensated and redundant collieries placed on a care and maintenance basis. A further levy was introduced in 1941 to spread over the unequal incidence of the guaranteed wage. In 1942 the government took over the administration of both levies and instituted the Coal Charges Account. It was becoming clear that flat-rate national wage increases and the national minimum wage were raising the costs of different districts and collieries unequally and that price increases sufficient to compensate the less productive would provide handsome profits for others. The levy payable to the Coal Charges Account was therefore increased roughly *pari passu* with price increases and the owners were reimbursed from the Account the actual cost of wage increases. In addition the districts were subsidized from the Account sufficiently to maintain a 'standard credit balance'. The results were startling. By 1945 some coalfields (for example Durham and South Wales) were being substantially subsidized through the Account partly by the more prosperous coalfields and partly by the tax payers.[1]

For some time after the outbreak of war the organization of the industry was substantially unchanged. The selling schemes instituted by the 1930 Act continued to operate though the chief officers became Coal Supplies Officers responsible to the government for the allocation and supply of coal. In 1942, however, the government assumed control of the mines. A Minister of Fuel and Power[2] was appointed and for the purposes of control was assisted by a Controller-General and production, financial and labour experts. In each region controllers were appointed with expert staffs and power to give directions to managements and if necessary assume full control of colliery undertakings. A National Board was also set up (representative of producers, distributors and consumers) to advise the Minister on planning production, procurement of supplies, increasing efficiency and increasing manpower. But except for the very few pits completely taken over, the government did not assume responsibility for day-to-day management, which was left in the hands of the colliery companies. This war-time

---

[1] The Account showed a net deficiency owing to the Treasury of over £25 million by 31 December 1944. In 1944 the net result of transactions with the Coal Charges Account was a credit of 3s. 9d. per ton for Durham and 7s. 11d. for South Wales. For full details see Ministry of Fuel and Power, *Financial Position of Coalmining Industry: Coal Charges Account*, Cmd. 6617 (H.M.S.O. 1945).   [2] Now the Minister of Power.

control appeared to have little effect though some progress was made with the grouping of pits, concentration of output and mechanization. A façade of private enterprise remained, but it was obviously going to be extremely difficult to return to the pre-war position. In particular, the finances of the industry were now so much affected by the Coal Charges Account that the future operation of the industry on some nationally unified basis appeared to be inevitable.

In 1946, the mines were taken into national ownership.[1] Compensation of £164·6 million was paid for the 'coal assets' (i.e. the mines and their immediate equipment) and approximately £130 million has been paid for various ancillary assets. Management of the industry was entrusted to a National Coal Board (appointed by the Minister) which was instructed to promote not only the efficient mining of coal but also the safety, health and welfare of persons employed. An instruction to benefit from the practical knowledge and experience of their employees has been interpreted as an obligation to practice the best techniques of joint consultation. The industry was to be so conducted that its revenue would suffice to meet current outgoings on an average of good and bad years.[2] The Minister of Fuel and Power was empowered (after consultation with the Board) to give it directions on matters appearing to him to affect the national interest. Ownership of the coal deposits was transferred from the Coal Mines Reorganization Commission to the Board which also took over the commercial supply of coal from the selling schemes set up under the 1930 Act. Domestic and Industrial Coal Consumers' Councils were also established by the Act to consider representations from the consumers concerning the supply and sale of coal.

The post-war years of the nationalized industry have been chiefly marked by slowly rising output and productivity, though both have consistently fallen short of the hopes and expectations of the National Coal Board. By 1956 the output of deep-mined coal was 210 million tons and output per man-shift had reached 1·23 tons. (The corresponding annual averages 1951–6 were 211·6 million tons and 1·22 tons respectively.) Man-power increased sharply after 1945 but from 1953 to 1956 has been slowly declining. Both costs and prices have risen steadily and gross profits per ton (before capital charges and taxes), though varying from year to year (the average credit balance from 1947–56 was 1s. 6d. per ton), have exceeded the average of the four immediately pre-war years and are very little below the average of the

---

[1] Coal Mines (Nationalization) Act, 1946.
[2] As pointed out below, this has been taken to mean that prices should reflect average costs. This is implied and was almost certainly intended but it is not clearly stated. It may be argued that the clause does not rule out the possibility of revenue exceeding outgoings.

war years.[1] But interest on the compensation stock and on capital advanced by the Treasury is a compulsory charge on the industry and by the end of 1956 it showed an accumulated loss of £23·8 million.[2] Throughout the period under review the Board has pursued a vigorous and enlightened welfare, education and promotion policy and has done its utmost to make a success of joint consultation. The conciliation scheme has worked well but industrial relations in the industry are still far from satisfactory. No major stoppages have occurred but losses due to unofficial strikes, 'go-slow' and other restrictive practices are reckoned by the National Coal Board at about $1\frac{1}{2}$ to $2\frac{1}{2}$ million tons per annum since 1947.

The National Coal Board was originally a functional board, each member being executive head of a major department—production, marketing, finance, welfare, labour relations and scientific research. Following the Burrows Committee Report of 1948 some additional non-functional members of the Board were appointed.[3] The coalfields were divided up into Divisions and placed in the charge of divisional boards which were mainly replicas of the National Coal Board itself and appointed by it. Each division was divided up into areas (in the charge of an area general manager), these being the main operational units of the industry. The administrative structure of the industry has been subject to much criticism mainly on the ground of over-centralization, overlapping and indistinct areas of authority and lack of a clear chain of command.[4] The stated policy of the Board since 1947 has been to decentralize routine administration and to emphasize the responsibilities of area managements.

[1] As a percentage of total costs, however, gross profits have fallen from 7% (1935–8) to under 3% (1947–55).

[2] This figure covers collieries and ancillary activities such as coke ovens and open-cast working. It includes losses on imported coal (sold below cost on the home market) which are borne by the National Coal Board and had amounted to £59·8 million by 1956. The accumulated real profit was therefore £36 million. This real profit is arrived at after interest on compensation stock and capital advanced by the Treasury have been paid. These are charges on revenue—unlike dividends on the equity of a limited company. Before 1939 an average credit balance of 1s. 6d. per ton was taken as evidence of reasonable profitability. During the war a credit balance of 1s. 9d. per ton was accepted by the owners as giving a reasonable profit. (See Ministry of Fuel and Power, *Coal Charges Account*, Cmd. 6617, 1945.) Account must, however, be taken of changes in the value of money since 1945.

[3] The Fleck Committee favoured a functional board. All full-time members of the Board except the Chairman and Deputy Chairman now (1957) have departmental responsibilities.

[4] The Burrows Committee reported on the organization of the Board in 1948 (*Coal Mining Industry: Committee on Organization, Statement by the National Coal Board*) and a further Committee, the Fleck Committee, was set up in 1953 and reported in 1955 (National Coal Board, *Report of the Advisory Committee on Organization*). A new directive on management was issued by the National Coal Board in July 1955 and is reprinted in its *Report and Accounts for 1955*, vol. I, p. 55.

In matters of price the Board has so far followed the convention of advancing prices only with the knowledge and consent of the Minister. Throughout its existence the Board has been much concerned with price policy and the structure of coal prices[1] as distinct from the general level of coal prices. During the war flat-rate price increases had made good quality coal too cheap relative to poor quality coals and immediate action was taken to rectify the worst anomalies. Work was then started on the classification of coals[2] to reflect consumer preferences, and the Board slowly began to work its way towards a zone delivered price structure. Distribution is still controlled by Coal Supplies Officers of the Ministry of Power who are also marketing officers of the Board, and domestic supplies in particular are still strictly controlled. Some progress has been made in setting up selling regions under regional sales officers who will ultimately be responsible for controlling the distribution of all coal sold in the region irrespective of its origin.

The other main facet of the Board's policy has been technical re-organization and reconstruction.[3] The main outlines of the Board's programme for the future of the industry were published in 1950 as the *Plan for Coal*.[4] This related estimates of demand to production possibilities for the period 1949 to 1965 and a detailed programme of mine reconstructions and new sinkings was drawn up on this basis. Much progress has been made though it has been slower than expected when the Plan was drawn up. In addition much progress has been made, apart from major reconstructions and new sinkings, in mechanization of coal getting, underground transport, coal washing, safety measures and the like. Many small and unprofitable mines have been closed and production concentrated elsewhere. The Board has had some success in securing the voluntary transfer of labour to more productive pits in the immediate neighbourhood but inter-divisional transfers have not succeeded or even been attempted on any considerable scale. All these aspects of the Board's policy will be discussed in more detail below.

5. SUPPLY, DEMAND AND PRICE RELATIONS

The nature of the demand for coal is a matter for surmise but the evidence suggests that home demand is more sensitive to the general level of business activity than to price.[5] Export demand for British coal on

---

[1] Further discussed below.   [2] See above, p. 109.   [3] See below, p. 138.

[4] See 'Planned Investment in the Coal Industry' by A. Beacham, *Oxford Economic Papers* (New Series), vol. 3, no. 2, June 1951, p. 125. The Plan was revised in April 1956. See *Investing in Coal* (National Coal Board, 1956).

[5] See K. S. Lomax, 'The Demand for Coal in Great Britain', *Oxford Economic Papers* (New Series), vol. 4, no. 1, February 1952, p. 50.

the other hand is in normal times much affected by price, except perhaps
for special coals in particular markets. It should, however, be borne in
mind that even in the home market the demand for particular grades
of coal is normally sensitive to changes in the price of other grades
which are close substitutes, though the degree of elasticity varies as
between different classes and different uses. The demand for anthracite
from consumers with special combustion appliances or for good coking
coal from steel-makers will not be much affected by price changes in
other ranks of coal. As between different classes of general industrial
coals, on the other hand, a higher degree of price elasticity probably
prevails. This, together with the tendency for output to be maintained
in a falling market and the presence of excess capacity, partly explains
the virulence of price competition in the 1920's and the strong incentive
to cartelization which has always prevailed in the industry. Even before
1900 the miners and many coal-owners had been well aware of the
advantages which might be derived by them from some form of output
restriction and price maintenance.

The consumption of coal in Great Britain varied very little between
the cyclical peak years 1913, 1929 and 1937.[1] It rose sharply after 1945
and is still rising, but this has probably been owing to expansion of the
employed population rather than to any increase in energy requirements
per head which have increased very little in the present century.[2]
It is generally reckoned that at present prices the demand for coal in
Great Britain is not being met but there is little concrete evidence for
this except possibly in the field of domestic consumption. A small
volume of imports[3] is necessary from time to time and some industries
are not getting the qualities of coal they would like to have. It is
difficult to guess at the sort of price rise which would be necessary to
equate home demand and supply, but in view of the probable in-
elasticity of over-all demand under present conditions it might have to
be considerable—a point which has to be borne in mind in considering
current controversy about the price of coal.[4] It is much more certain
that a larger volume of British exports could be sold abroad at current
prices, if supplies were available, but the market is a very changeable
one and it would be futile to try to estimate the extent of the excess
demand.

[1] World production of hard coal (which roughly reflects consumption) moved from
1220 million metric tons in 1913 to 1210 in 1938 and 1486 in 1953. The increase 1913–53
is mainly accounted for by the expansion in Russian coal production.

[2] Apart from fuel oil which now makes a modest contribution (about 12 %), coal is practically the sole source of energy in Great Britain. See *The Economist*, 22 January 1955, p. 302.
(Cf. Ministry of Fuel and Power, *Statistical Digest 1955*, p. 20.)

[3] Imports during 1955 were exceptionally heavy at 11·6 million tons. In 1956 they
dropped back to 5·2 million tons.   [4] See below, p. 129.

The position in 1956 was that 210 million tons of saleable coal were produced by deep-mining, 12·4 million tons by open-cast methods, and 5·3 million tons were imported. Total available coal was therefore about 228 million tons of which exports and bunkers took 9·7 million tons. Inland consumption was 218 million tons, changes in stocks being negligible. Consumption of coal has been rising by about 1·7 million tons per annum during the period 1951–6. Total energy consumption was rising more rapidly, the difference being made up mainly by oil.

Since no estimate can be made of the extent to which conversion to oil was 'forced' by coal shortage no reliable figure of British coal 'requirements' emerges. If we take such conversion for granted, the demand for coal can hardly have much exceeded 218 million tons in 1956 in view of the stability of stocks. What of the future? Expectations of a rising demand for coal are based on estimates of rising energy requirements of $1\frac{1}{2}$ to 3 % per annum.[1] Taking the National Coal Board estimate of 2 % per annum we arrive at a figure of about 300 million tons (coal equivalent) in 1965 and perhaps 350 million tons in 1975 compared with about 254 million tons in 1956. Even if we accept these figures we cannot closely estimate future coal requirements because of uncertainties about the future use of oil and atomic energy. Britain's atomic power programme[2] reckoned that stations to be completed by 1965 would produce 6 million tons of coal equivalent in 1965 and 40 million tons in 1975. Late in 1956 it was stated that the pre-1965 stations would have treble the capacity previously estimated and an additional power station building programme was being forecast. Energy outputs of 100 million tons (coal equivalent) are being forecast by responsible authorities for 1975. The general assumption is that atomic power is now cost-competitive with power generated from coal and will be cheapened still further in the near future. When such revolutionary developments in energy production are upon us and when plans and estimates are being so frequently and drastically revised one must be very cautious in guessing about the future demand for coal. With the possible exceptions of coke ovens and gas-works, the only important consumer of raw coal which is expected to increase its demand is the Central Electricity Authority and it is here that the impact of oil and nuclear power will be most felt. This expectation is very much borne out by recent trends in coal consumption.

[1] National Coal Board *Report and Accounts for 1955*, vol. i, p. 51. Cf. 'Energy for Success', Supplement to *The Economist*, 27 November 1954.
[2] See the White Paper on atomic energy presented by the Lord President of the Council and the Ministry of Fuel and Power, *A Programme of Nuclear Power*, Cmd. 9389 (H.M.S.O. 1955). This programme was drastically revised in March 1957. See below, p. 124 n. 2.

Let us assume that 'assumptions of rapid and continuous economic growth and continued progress in fuel efficiency'[1] are borne out and that energy requirements are of the order of 300 million tons in 1965. It seems not unreasonable to attribute 18 million tons of coal equivalent to atomic power by 1965[2] and 15 million tons to increased use of oil.[3] Thus the maximum increase in home demand for raw coal which it seems reasonable to expect during the next decade would be 13 million tons, that is, a total home demand of 231 million tons.[4] If the revised output target of the National Coal Board[5] is reached (240 million tons including open-cast by 1965) there will then be an exportable margin of 9 million tons compared with present exports of 9·7 million tons. To estimate foreign demand for British coal ten years hence would be sheerest conjecture. More could undoubtedly be sold abroad at present but the general trend of overseas demand over the next ten years is likely to be downward. All in all it seems likely that there will be little if any excess demand for British coal by 1965.

This, however, is to take the planned supply very much for granted. Here the governing factor is the gradual exhaustion of the best and most accessible seams and an apparent lack of further virgin fields which could be developed at low cost. Where (as in South Wales) large reserves of high ranking coal are known to exist the cost of extraction is likely to be high because of difficult natural conditions. The natural and inevitable wastage of output capacity is now estimated at about 4 million tons per annum and this has to be more than replaced by new capacity if output is to be raised. The average cost per ton of raising coal has increased nearly seven times since 1913 as against a general price rise of three to four times. This has been partly owing to higher relative wages of mining labour but it also reflects the increased effort (in men and machines) which is now necessary to win a ton of coal. The impressive programme of technical reconstruction on which the National Coal Board has embarked had by 1956 raised productivity

[1] *Investing in Coal* (National Coal Board, 1956), p. 13. On 13 February 1956 the Minister of Fuel committed himself to this estimate of 300 million tons of coal equivalent.

[2] Assuming a nuclear power station capacity of about 5000 megawatts instead of 1500 to 2000 in the original plan. Cf. 'Atomic Power Arrives', *The Economist*, 20 October 1956. Announcing the revised atom power station programme in the House of Commons on 5 March 1957, the Minister of Power estimated a nuclear power output equivalent to 18 million tons of coal by 1965.

[3] The Central Electricity Authority has already concluded agreements to step up the use of oil for power generation by 9 million tons of coal equivalent'. See its *Seventh Report and Accounts, 1954–5*, p. 11.

[4] Projection of recent coal consumption trends (which are *unaffected by nuclear power*) suggests a broadly similar increase in demand by 1965. The view of the present writer is that the estimates given here are likely to overstate the future increase in demand but where so much is uncertain it seems best to guess on the basis of official assumptions about rising energy requirements.   [5] *Investing in Coal* (National Coal Board, 1956), p. 14.

by less than 5 % above the pre-war record level of 1936. The programme
is enormously expensive and the National Coal Board now appears to
have abandoned its earlier assumption that increases in productivity
will lower costs of production.[1] Also the average quality of coal
produced is falling. Altogether, this represents a serious situation for
an industry facing strong competition from alternative sources of
energy in the near future.

The National Coal Board has now (1956) revised its planned deep-
mined output from 240 million tons per annum in the period 1961–5 as
envisaged in the 1950 *Plan for Coal* to 230 million tons in 1965.[2] With this
estimate of probabilities the present writer has no serious quarrel since
nearly all the capital expenditure on major colliery schemes is still 'in the
pipeline'[3] and present evidence suggests considerable advances still to
be reaped from new techniques—particularly power-loading. Whether
the massive capital expenditure involved can be justified is another
matter. The original *Plan for Coal* envisaged capital expenditure between 1950 and 1965 of £635 million (at mid-1949 prices)—perhaps
£850 million at end-1955 prices. The capital expenditure now envisaged over the same period to reach a lower output target is £1350
million at end-1955 prices.[4] Much of the expenditure is necessary
to maintain present output and to ward off a steeper rate of capacity
wastage in the future. But the cost of raising deep-mined output by
20 million tons over the next ten years must be very high. Without
necessarily condemning the revised 'Plan' more thought might be
given to boosting open-cast capacity (which is relatively cheap and easy
but short-lived) to meet the rising demand for coal (which may continue
but at a slackening rate until 1965) and to a further expansion of the
atomic power programme. Investment plans for coal implicitly based
on an almost indefinite and rapidly rising demand for coal should be
very closely scrutinized.

Since it takes on an average ten years to complete a new sinking and
over eight to carry through a big reconstruction scheme[5] the National
Coal Board must take long views. Looking further ahead than 1965
the Board appears to be thinking in terms of an output of 250 million
tons by 1970.[6] Its estimate of inland energy requirements for 1975 is
350 million tons coal equivalent. An output of 100 million tons coal
equivalent from atomic power by 1975 is now forecast. Of the remain-

---

[1] See *Investing in Coal*, p. 14.   [2] Plus 10 million tons open-cast coal.

[3] Major schemes are those costing more than £250,000. Up to the end of 1956, £171
million had been spent on major schemes but only £25 million was represented by present
working capacity.

[4] This includes £353 million already spent in the period 1950–5. The figures include
expenditure on ancillaries as well as collieries and associated activities.

[5] *Investing in Coal*, p. 10.   [6] *Ibid.* p. 18.

ing 250 million tons oil seems to be expected to supply the equivalent of 50 million tons.[1] This would appear to leave, in round figures, something like 50 million tons of coal to be exported and few would expect overseas demand to reach anything like this level. It must be admitted that such long-term guesses at the shape of things to come are not worth very much and that the old bogy of over-production and excess capacity is distant—but it is there. Such a situation may be less likely because the problems of increasing supply may prove to be more intractable than even now they are reckoned to be. But the optimistic assumptions about the rate of expansion of energy requirements on which all current forecasting is based may also be falsified in the event.

In referring to the tendency of costs to rise over time it must be remarked that the level of costs at any particular time are much affected by total output. As has been seen, there is an enormous disparity of productivity, costs and proceeds per ton between pits and between entire coalfields. This is mainly due to variation of natural conditions, age of coalfields, and the age of individual pits. Unprofitable[2] pits will be found even in comparatively new coalfields where conditions are good. It has been estimated that the elimination of pits producing the least profitable 30 million tons in 1953 would have reduced the national average cost of coal by nearly 3s. per ton.[3] Some of these pits are approaching the end of their useful lives and have only been kept in production because of the pressure brought to bear on the National Coal Board to maintain output at the highest possible level during a time of shortage. But the figures sufficiently illustrate the extent to which average cost is a function of output. If demand fell away and output was contracted by elimination of unproductive pits the competitive position of the industry would be strengthened by the resulting lowering of costs. But the converse need not be true. We cannot say that, if the National Coal Board fails to expand output over the next ten years to the extent it has planned to do, then we can take comfort from the fact that costs will be that much lower. Such a failure of supply would be mainly due to inability to bring into production new and reconstructed units as quickly as had been hoped—and these are expected to raise average productivity.

The National Coal Board has certain advantages in that it is able to regulate total supply. In the past the tendency has been for output

---

[1] Cf. *Report and Accounts* of the National Coal Board for 1955, vol. i, p. 51.

[2] High-cost pits are not necessarily unprofitable because the quality and price of the coal have to be taken into account.

[3] It does not follow that this would be a wise thing to do. Some of the pits concerned may be only temporarily unprofitable or there may be special social reasons for not eliminating them.

to be maintained even on a falling market because of the high cost of keeping pits open without producing and the finality of complete abandonment. During the 1920's most coal-owners would have said that the main problem of the industry was excess capacity, over-production, high-cost under-capacity working and weak selling. Resulting lack of profits made impossible a level of new investment which was necessary to reduce costs and so things went round in a vicious circle. The 1930 Act controlled output and restored some measure of profitability but did little to curtail excess capacity.

The fact that these are things of the past is not only due to the fact that the industry is under single ownership and management but also because of the radical change in market conditions. If market conditions should change in the near future the past might have important lessons for the National Coal Board. New sinkings and pit reconstructions will add substantially to the capacity of the industry and the rate at which unproductive pits can be eliminated cannot be very rapid, if only because so many of them are concentrated in a few areas and severe social dislocation might result. The vicious circle might begin to manifest itself again though not quite in the same way as in the days of private enterprise.

It follows from the nature of the industry that the price of any particular lot of coal from a particular pit cannot be and has never been very closely connected with the cost of mining it. The quality of the coal will partly determine its price and this has little bearing on the cost of getting it, except in the remote sense that the best qualities are generally most intensively exploited at first and their average cost rises accordingly. In the more or less free market which prevailed before 1930 prices were left to sort themselves out. The typical situation was that of a mine-owner producing different grades from different seams (and probably different pits) at different levels of cost and disposing of them in different markets under a wide variety of names. Price was determined by the haggling of the market and was taken for granted by most sellers. In the light of these prices and costs the working of different pits and seams was adjusted to maximize profits and prices responded to these adjustments. Consumers also faced with this complex structure of prices tried to buy economically by buying coals more or less well adapted to their purposes if their prices justified it. They in turn modified the price structure. There was, of course, a great deal of im-perfection in the market—traditional attachments of buyers to sellers and particular grades of coal, much ignorance on the part of buyers about the technical properties of coals, much acceptance of uneconomic prices by sellers to keep pits working or to build up spheres of influence in distant markets where heavy transport costs had to be borne, much acceptance of price differentials which had become traditional and so on. But in the main, similar classes of coal sold at the same price to the same class of user in the same market which meant very unequal pit prices for the same grades. Also, coal-owners would not indefinitely keep pits in production which consistently showed an over-all loss, though there might be some balancing of pit profits and losses between different pits belonging to a single company.

After 1930[1] this market structure crystallized to some extent. The minimum price schedules were based on prevailing prices and classes of coal plus some uniform addition. There was little attempt to reduce the enormous number of categories and names under which coal was sold. Also producers began to enjoy an increasing degree of protection in their traditional markets. Prices hardened as the monopoly organization became more effective, but the basic market structure remained very much as it was. During the war, however, flat-rate price increases seriously upset relative prices and diversions of coal supplies 'in the national interest' produced some dislocation of traditional markets.

The National Coal Board felt that it could not accept a situation where consumers were not necessarily encouraged to take coal from the least costly source of supply, where high quality coals were relatively underpriced, where some categories of coal were sold at different prices to different classes of users in the same area, and where the same class of coal was often sold under different names. To carry out its duty of promoting the economical production and supply of coal, the Board has had to do a great deal of thinking about price policy. In some respects it had a great opportunity. It completely monopolized supply to the home market and the fact that at current prices demand exceeded supply gave it scope for experiment without fear of unpleasant consequences. On the other hand, this deprived it to some extent of the opportunity of gauging the correctness of its own answers. The Board certainly underestimated the difficulty of making price perform its normal function in a free market by a deliberative policy which merely required the application of a few elementary principles. Also, it did not have a free hand since it felt bound by the Nationalization Act to charge prices which would roughly cover its costs. Also it felt unable to adopt any pricing policy which would have the appearance of undermining the traditional position of particular districts in particular markets. In the sense that they were now parts of one large concern pit and district losses and profits were irrelevant so long as the accounts

[1] Part I of the 1930 Act provided for regulation of output and price maintenance. The schemes were later extended to provide for complete central (or controlled) selling in each district with inter-district co-ordination of marketing arrangements. Part II set up the Coal Mines Reorganization Commission to further reorganization by preparing schemes of amalgamation and, if necessary, enforcing them.

were in over-all balance, but the Board felt that they should provide valid indicators of the best direction for future development policy. In the event the Board's pricing policy has been confused and somewhat contradictory.

There are two inter-connected problems here. First, what principle should govern the general level of coal prices? Secondly, what principles should govern the relative market prices for different classes of coal?

Discussion of the first question has largely resolved itself into a difference of opinion as to whether price should be based on average or marginal cost.[1] The National Coal Board has apparently interpreted the Nationalization Act as an injunction to base price on average cost. As previously pointed out, demand has tended to exceed supply at such a price, though to what extent it is difficult to say. In the coal industry, since average cost is commonly reckoned to be rising, marginal cost will exceed average cost. In a free market, it is argued, the price of coal would tend to cover the costs of the least productive unit (marginal cost) and all better placed producers would make profits (rents). The underlying theme of those advocating marginal cost pricing is that it is the business of the National Coal Board to reproduce the results which would obtain in a free market, since these alone will promote the most efficient allocation of resources between alternative uses. More precisely, it is said that average cost pricing results in many consumers getting coal at much less than it costs to produce and this encourages un-economical use. If prices were raised to cover marginal cost it would also help to equate demand and supply (making rationing and allocation of supplies unnecessary) and stimulate supply. These are powerful arguments.

There are, however, arguments against the proposal. The Ridley Committee cited the possibilities that it would increase the risk of inflation, weaken the competitive position of British exports and result in large profits to the National Coal Board of which the miners would promptly claim a share and which would lessen incentives to efficiency. Some of these arguments carry little weight. It might be argued for example that by selling coal below the free market price, the Board is promoting inflation. Other arguments are more difficult to assess. Large profits might very easily undermine the already weakened

---

[1] The theoretical pros and cons of this question, on which there has been an extensive literature in recent years, cannot be reproduced here. For its bearing on coal, see Ministry of Fuel and Power, *Report of the Committee on National Policy for the Use of Fuel and Power Resources* (Ridley Committee), Cmd. 8647 (H.M.S.O. 1952) and I. M. D. Little, *The Price of Fuel* (Oxford, Clarendon Press, 1953). On other aspects of price policy in the coal industry see 'The Price Policy of the National Coal Board' by S. R. Dennison, *Lloyds Bank Review*, no. 26, October 1952, p. 17, and 'Price Policy in the Coal Industry' by A. Beacham, *Journal of Industrial Economics*, vol. 1, no. 2, April 1953, p. 140.

incentives to efficiency in the industry. But on the other hand coal would not be so easily sold at the higher prices and this might keep the seller 'on his toes'.

It might be argued that nationalization makes a difference. The National Coal Board is expected to bear costs which would not be borne by private enterprise, for example the cost of taking long views in working a valuable wasting asset, of an enlightened welfare policy, of avoiding social dislocation through indiscriminate closures, and so on. The price charged by the National Coal Board based on average cost may not be very different from a free market price based on marginal cost—the rents which would have been earned by private owners being used in effect by the National Coal Board to meet social costs.

Moreover, the impossibility of calculating even an approximation to marginal cost has to be reckoned with. Strictly speaking it is the addition to total cost involved in expanding output by one unit. The Ridley Committee took the least profitable 7 million tons (making an average loss of 15s. per ton) as indicating the excess of marginal cost over average cost for all practical purposes. (It would have been much higher if they had taken the least profitable million tons and lower if they had taken the least profitable 10 million tons!) This figure almost certainly refers to the output and losses of the most unprofitable pits since the National Coal Board has never tried to cost individual tons of coal. These pits, however, may not be marginal in any relevant sense.[1] They may be pits undergoing reconstruction or even new pits just coming into production. Certainly this unprofitable output is not altogether the output which would be given up if output were contracted by 7 million tons.[2]

There are many other objections. We are not told whether short-run or long-run marginal cost is being referred to. This involves the question of what costs should be included—whether, for example, capital charges are to be included.[3] As we have previously noted, the Board has consistently charged above average prime cost and made a gross profit. Also output expansion can be achieved on very different terms in different places and for different categories of coal. The Ridley Committee estimate, for example, reflects (in so far as it reflects anything) the

---

[1] W. H. Sales in 'Changing Patterns of Pit Performance', *Journal of Industrial Economics*, vol. 3, no. 3, July 1955, p. 184, has shown that the group of least productive pits is fairly stable in total number but not in membership. It is also noteworthy that there is no close correlation of changes in total output, productivity, costs, and profits for individual pits.

[2] I. M. D. Little, in *The Price of Fuel*, 1953, also criticizes this calculation of the Ridley Committee. He argues very strongly for a rise in the price of coal to equate demand and supply and that the price should be brought into equality with marginal cost as soon as possible thereafter.

[3] I. M. D. Little, *op. cit.* p. 1, appears to include them. Elsewhere he appears to exclude them.

high marginal cost of special coals such as gas coal and anthracite which form a very low proportion of total output.

The advocates of marginal cost pricing have obviously been much impressed by the present excess demand for coal and expectations of its continuance. If, as might happen, the demand for coal starts to decline by about 1965, a rise in price now may affect the future stability of the industry. Suppose price is raised by (say) £1 per ton to equal marginal cost and (which does not necessarily follow) present supply and demand are equated at this price. The rise in price would then have been that necessary to choke off the present excess demand. Any subsequent change in demand would then immediately make itself felt through excess capacity, pressure on prices, and on wages which would almost certainly have risen with the initial rise in the price of coal. The extent and the rate of readjustment will be less if prices are not raised now.

It is difficult to sum up the merits of the controversy. It is easy to defend the present practice of the Board by arguments of a practical kind, for example, that the Act appears to enjoin average cost pricing and that it cannot accept from the marginalists a principle without more precise guidance as to how it is to be implemented. But this does not dispose of the matter. It may still be asked what is the 'right' policy (the Act notwithstanding) and the impossibility of basing price on marginal cost does not dispose of the case for a substantial rise in price.

The proper function of price is to promote the most economical use of coal and to ensure that resources are not used to produce coal which would be better used elsewhere. Also it should have the right effect on the location and investment decisions of coal-consuming industries. An increase in the price of coal so that it more nearly reflects marginal cost would undoubtedly be the right policy to pursue from these points of view. Average cost pricing has encouraged the use of coal for purposes less valuable than the resources used in its production and has put an insufficient premium on fuel-saving devices. Also it has been responsible for a sense of chronic shortage which has been a powerful political stimulant to possibly over-ambitious capital investment schemes, and for a feeling that more coal must be produced at almost any price.

The fact and form of nationalization have immensely complicated the application of a rational pricing policy. Some intelligible and practical pricing rule would appear to be a political necessity under present arrangements. The Board might be instructed to raise price until demand and (present?) supply balanced, but as the industry is organized at present, supply is centrally controlled and this might be construed as an invitation to maximize monopoly profits. A more attractive solution would be to give the areas a wider degree of autonomy and allow them to sell in competition with each other, each being instructed that it must pay its way in the long run and make profits where it can. But some would consider this a retreat from the principles which inspired nationalization.

To produce a workable alternative to average cost pricing would require sweeping changes in the present organization of the industry and in the statute which governs it, and to many people the political drawbacks of such action would outweigh any economic advantage. But the most powerful argument against an arbitrary and substantial increase in the price of coal is not related to any theoretical attraction of average cost pricing. If we are right in our estimate of the future demand for coal such action will, as indicated above, accentuate the problems of readjustment to a changed market situation. The losses involved might be far greater than any immediate advantage derived from the adoption of the 'right' pricing policy now. But this is very much a matter of opinion.

Turning to the second question: the Board has tried very hard to produce a price structure which would reflect real differences in quality, encourage consumers to take coal which could be most cheaply supplied in relation to their needs, and which would give the Board the right pointers to development policy through pressure of consumers and pit profits and losses. Whereas the controversy about marginal cost pricing appears to have gone over the heads of the Board, the problem of classifying coals, the relative merits of pit and delivered prices, etc., have been treated as matters of great urgency.

The present price structure appears to have been worked out as follows. All coals are ranked and classified as previously described[1] and when adjusted for ash content are reckoned to reflect their quality or worth to the consumer. These classes are then grouped roughly into house, industrial and carbonization coals. House coals are arranged in eight groups according to quality and provisionally priced at their national average cost of production. The country is divided into sixty zones and a uniform delivered price fixed in each zone for each grade to reflect the provisional price plus the average cost of transport to that zone. The scheme for industrial and carbonization coals was more elaborate. A datum coal is taken and given a points value equal to its calorific value (less ash adjustment) divided by 100. This coal is then given a pit-head price roughly equal to the national average cost of production which enables a cash value per point to be established. All other coals are then priced by multiplying this by their points value. These prices are subject to adjustment for size, mode of preparation, sulphur content or, in the case of carbonization coals, caking qualities and the like. These are, of course, pit-head prices and the bulk of

---

[1] See p. 109.

industrial and carbonization coals are still sold on this basis. The objective of the Board is a zone delivered price, but until this can be worked out, and to achieve some co-ordination of prices of the same grades at the point of delivery (and to avoid apparent penalization or districts with high transport costs), a coalfield adjustment figure is added to the pit-head prices.[1]

The Board has taken as its basic principles that prices should reflect the average cost of producing and transporting coal to the consumer, that relative prices should reflect 'quality' and that coal of the same grade in the same market should sell at the same price, irrespective of the pit of origin or the type of consumer. But there are many puzzling features in the detailed application of these principles and one suspects that they are only crudely applied. For example, there is no reason to suppose that if prices of each grade reflect quality,[2] they can also be made to reflect its average cost, except over a long period as supplies from different pits are adjusted. Also if price equals average cost by grade how is it that the anthracite-producing areas are making very heavy average losses per ton?

By what criterion should such a price structure be judged? If we assume that the Board sees to it that each zone is supplied in such a way that no rearrangement of supplies will reduce total costs, then the main tests would appear to be (a) whether consumers pay roughly what it costs to get and carry the coal to them, and (b) whether pit profit and losses will indicate where output should be expanded or contracted.

The answer to (a) will depend partly on whether or not the zones are made sufficiently small for transport costs within them to be ignored. But a more serious criticism raised against the policy is that since prices are based on average costs some consumers will be paying less than the coal costs to get and others more. On the other hand, to differentiate pit-head prices according to pit costs would result in different consumers paying different prices for the same class of coal. So long as the Board feels bound to base its prices on average cost the present policy follows inevitably. For, provided the zones are not too large and our basic assumption is borne out, there can be little valid criticism of a delivered price system. But in a free market the probability is that the price of each grade would accommodate itself to the marginal prime cost and no consumer would get coal at less than it cost to produce.

[1] For example, the East Midlands and Kent both have a stake in the London market. In Kent production costs are high and transport costs low. In the East Midlands the opposite is true. An average pit-head price for both districts would show Kent making losses, and East Midland prices (including transport costs) much above those of Kent in London. The Kent coalfield adjustment figure is +13s. and East Midlands nil.

[2] Even this is a large assumption. Quality in the sense of utility to the consumer depends not only on calorific value, etc. but also on the type of equipment available. Quality is in fact a very unstable and probably immeasurable concept.

The answer to (*b*) also revolves around the merits of average cost pricing for with such a system pit profits and losses lose some of their significance. There must be some losing pits whereas when price approximates to marginal cost a loss would be prima facie evidence for curtailment of output or closure. On the other hand, even with average cost pricing the relative magnitude of profits and losses would tell the Board a great deal. The question also arises as to whether the price structure will be sufficiently responsive to changes in demand to encourage appropriate adjustments of supply. Changes will hardly be forced upon the Board so long as demand exceeds supply.

The National Coal Board has tried to make its prices perform the same functions as in a free private enterprise economy. The 'marginalists' are undoubtedly right in arguing that this can only be done if prices are made to approximate to marginal prime cost. The difficulties of reproducing in detail the results of a competitive pricing system by any deliberative process are enormous. If this is what the National Coal Board had wanted it might have been better, as suggested previously, to allow each area to dispose of its coal on a competitive basis and allow the market to sort things out. Consumers could then weigh their assessments of quality against prices which reflect cost and by their demands so modify the structure that the Board would be given the right sort of pointers for future development policy. In the event it is difficult to see what the Board has achieved by its pricing policy except some removal of ignorance and the appearance of order and rationality.

6. ORGANIZATION AND EFFICIENCY

The coal industry is threatened by two major factors—the emergence of competitive sources of energy and the long-term tendency of real costs to rise. Rising energy requirements may be expected to offset these factors of decline to some extent. Taking a very long-term point of view it is perhaps not unrealistic to regard coal as a declining industry but the rate of decline will probably depend very much on the extent to which increased efficiency can check, or reverse, rising costs.

From some points of view the prospects are not too hopeful. The incentive toward cartelization which is inherent in its structure was checked by rising demand prior to 1913 but quickly got the upper hand after 1918. The normal incentives to maximize efficiency were weakened[1] and nationalization has in some ways had a similar effect. Both miners and management are aware that a good margin exists by which prices can be advanced to cover rising costs without affecting the ability to

---

[1] See below, pp. 136 ff.

dispose of all that can be produced. Whatever makes the industry 'tick' it is certainly not the price/profit indicator and the forces of competition. Prices and proceeds credited to individual units are accounting symbols of uncertain meaning and the over-all price level crudely reflects the average of whatever costs happen to be. The probability is that the main motive force is the desire of the National Coal Board and its officials to do a good job for its own sake and this has probably resulted in a higher level of efficiency than might have been expected from mere consideration of the facts of the case. Another factor has been the desire of the Board to avoid public and parliamentary criticism by keeping the supply of coal at the maximum level physically possible. This has inevitably led to a certain disregard of costs and has been reinforced by the Board's determination to shoulder its ill-defined social responsibilities. The latter include not only the promotion of healthier industrial relations (by expensive welfare, education and promotion schemes and fostering of joint consultation) which might raise efficiency, but also consideration of the social costs of abandoning workable coal, dumping refuse on the surface, closure of poor pits, and so on. The fact that efficiency is to be interpreted less strictly than under conditions of private enterprise may result in it becoming such a nebulous concept that it would seem not to matter.

On the other hand, there is undoubtedly some awareness that if market conditions change, the level of operating costs and prices may matter a great deal. Any tendency for output to fall may help to stabilize the industry through cost reduction, but this will be minimized if the National Coal Board feels that for social reasons the impact of falling production must be spread by permitting under-capacity working of pits. It is difficult to believe that such reasoning counts for much at the moment. For some time past, and probably for some little time to come, the structure, organization and market position of the industry have militated against efficiency.

It is impossible to measure the efficiency of the industry. Even in the narrow technical sense it is not properly measured by output per man-shift (O.M.S.) in an industry dominated by natural conditions. For what it is worth, the Reid Committee found that O.M.S. had advanced much less rapidly in Great Britain before the war than in continental areas such as the Ruhr and Holland where natural conditions are broadly similar.[1] It does not follow that Great Britain was relatively inefficient since capital expenditure involved in raising O.M.S. has to be

---

[1] Between 1913 and 1938 O.M.S. in Great Britain increased by 13 %, the lowest percentage increase of any country. Post-war comparisons are very dangerous in view of the uneven effects of the war. In 1953 O.M.S. (underground) in Germany was 75 % of the 1938 figure; in Holland, 66 %; in Belgium, 100 %; in France, 115 %; and in Great Britain, 106%.

reckoned with. But few observers would dissent from the conclusion that more vigorous technical reorganization before the war would have resulted in a lowering of total costs per ton. Total costs per ton varied in almost exactly inverse proportion to o.m.s. in Great Britain before the war, which is not surprising since wages costs represent 60 to 70 % of total costs in the coal industry. Any technical reorganization which raises o.m.s. is, therefore, likely to raise efficiency, and the fact that the rate of increase of o.m.s. in the Ruhr and Holland between 1925 and 1936 was roughly seven times that of Great Britain must rank as fairly conclusive evidence of the latter's technical inefficiency in coal production prior to 1939.

The reasons for this are extremely complex. No reliable pre-war figures for capital investment in the industry are available. It would appear, however, that during the prosperous years following the 1914–18 War, fairly rapid technical development took place.[1] After 1926, however, lack of profits is generally reckoned to have impeded further progress. Mechanization at the coal-face proceeded rapidly but there was little radical reconstruction of pits[2] and the number of new sinkings fell. How far this state of affairs was attributable to the 1930 Act it is difficult to say. Output restriction probably did not reduce total output much below the level which would have prevailed in a free market.[3] Allocations generally exceeded output by from 2 to 6 % and Great Britain improved her share of world output between 1929 and 1933 whilst her share was only 0·8 % less in 1937 than it had been in 1929. It was, however, true that output control tended to follow rather than anticipate market conditions with the result that temporary shortages were often produced on a rising market and vice versa. Also restriction bore heavily from time to time on the more productive inland coalfields and on productive developing mines within particular coalfields. District allocations were based on production in some past period whilst the decline in demand was unevenly spread. Pit standard tonnages were also based on past output and were slowly and insufficiently revised as

[1] Mr W. A. Lee (*Thirty Years in Coal, 1917–1947*, London, Mining Association of Great Britain, 1954) states (p. 23) that the owners spent £53 million on improved methods of production, chiefly in the way of underground mechanization, between November 1918 and October 1925, i.e. less than £8 million per annum or say £16 to 20 million at present prices. The capital expenditures of the National Coal Board have averaged over £56 million per annum from 1947 to 1954.

[2] Along the lines later suggested by the Reid Committee (see below, p. 138).

[3] After 1930 prices fluctuated much less and output fluctuated more than previously (Leeds University Coal Industry Research Memorandum, 1935). This suggests that price control did reduce demand and output. But the probability is that in the abnormal conditions of the world economic crisis a very sharp decline in output was inevitable. In the absence of the 1930 Act output might have been a little higher but prices would have fallen very sharply in the early 1930's and would have recovered less quickly after 1935. It is significant that prices were well maintained during the slight recession of 1938–9.

different pits developed or declined. The general effect was to guarantee a share in the market to all producers, and efficient pits could only develop rapidly by purchase of quota rights from elsewhere.[1] After central and controlled selling was introduced in 1936 the trade share principle operated in much the same way since penalties were payable on all coal supplied above the 'share'. The retirement from production of the least profitable pits was, therefore, retarded, and general under-capacity working raised the level of costs. It was noticeable that the decline in the number of pits at work was much slower from 1930 to 1939 than from 1913 to 1929 though other factors partly accounted for this. The sinking of new modern pits became a much less attractive proposition after 1930 and such figures as are available bear this out. Between 1921 and 1929, 1340 small pits and drifts were opened and 311 large new shafts sunk[2] whereas during the period 1930–8 the corresponding figures were 1020 and 83.

As against all this, prices were raised by the Act and increased profitability meant that more money was available for modernization.[3] Some progress was undoubtedly made in raising efficiency by concentrating production on fewer pits within the same undertaking and within pits on fewer faces as mechanization proceeded.[4] The lowering of costs which attracted favourable comment at the time was probably more due to mechanization and the concentration of mining operations which went with it than to anything else. Much had been hoped for from the building up of larger undertakings by Part II of the 1930 Act and Part I seemed to provide some incentive in that quota rights were interchangeable between pits in the same ownership. But Part II would hardly have been such a complete failure if this incentive to concentration had been strong. It failed, mainly because of faults in the Act itself. But its failure must also be partly attributed to Part I. The bargaining power of weak concerns was strengthened and incentives to increased efficiency were weakened.

It seems almost certain, therefore, that the general inefficiency of the industry in 1939 was partly the outcome of the 1930 Act. But the

[1] Large undertakings had the advantage that quota rights could be freely exchanged between pits in the same ownership and district.

[2] 226 out of the 311 large new shafts were sunk before 1926.

[3] But the raising of proceeds and the market protection afforded by the schemes may have made cost reduction seem less urgent.

[4] It is difficult to prove anything about concentration of output as between pits during the 1930's. Average output per mine rose but this was partly owing to the number of very small mines taken out of production. The figures are indeed compatible with the possibility that remaining mines were producing lower outputs. That some concentration did take place is suggested by the rise in the average number of shifts worked per person and the fact that (on a crude estimate) output capacity declined by 31 million tons from 1929 to 1937 whereas output declined by 17·5 million tons. But the progress made was probably slight.

alternative of free competition also had little to commend it. The structural features of the industry were such that in the face of declining demand price-competition was likely to be extremely debilitating in its effects and any adjustment to changed market conditions long delayed. Except in the very long run and at the price of considerable dislocation and labour unrest a more efficient industry was not likely to emerge from this process.

The nationalized industry was in fact presented with a great opportunity. Conditions had further deteriorated during the war in spite of the efforts of the government.[1] But with an excess demand for coal and the assurance of adequate funds for new capital development from the Treasury the prospects for a considerable raising of efficiency on the technical side seemed bright. Moreover the Reid Committee had recommended sweeping changes in current technical practice. Its report[2] advocated further extension of the use of pneumatic picks, mechanical and power loaders, steel supports at the face, underground man-riding facilities, skip winding, double shift working and improved standards of lighting. These suggestions have been accepted by the National Coal Board and are being introduced where conditions permit and particularly in new and reconstructed mines. The Reid Committee also suggested an extension of room and pillar working with a high degree of mechanization along American lines. The Coal Board, however, has taken the view that because of difficult natural conditions opportunities for such developments will be very limited and experimental mechanization of some existing workings with American equipment has been a failure.[3]

The most emphatic and far-reaching technical recommendation of the Committee was that traditional British haulage practice should be changed by the introduction of locomotive haulage on the main roads. This would require a drastic reorganization of the layout of most British mines since reasonably level roads would be required, whereas at present the main haulage generally follows the seams which are often steeply inclined. This recommendation was therefore coupled with an advocacy of 'horizon' mining.[4] The initial outlay is, however, very great and it is hardly surprising that the Reid Committee pleaded

[1] See above, pp. 118-19.

[2] Ministry of Fuel and Power, *Coal Mining*, Cmd. 6610 (H.M.S.O. 1945). See also 'Efficiency and Organization of the British Coal Industry' by A Beacham, *Economic Journal*, vol. 55, no. 218-19, June–September 1945, p. 20.

[3] National Coal Board, *Plan for Coal* (1950), Technical Appendix II, p. 62.

[4] 'Under the horizon mining system the main roads are driven horizontally through the strata at different levels and intersect the sloping seams of coal. When the coal is being worked some way above the main haulage road, the workings are connected with the main road by a vertical [staple] shaft...through which the coal descends by a spiral chute...' (National Coal Board, *Report and Accounts for 1949*, p. 60, par. 221).

for larger mines (where the coal reserves justify it) than is usual in Great Britain. In the *Plan for Coal* (p. 60) the National Coal Board accepts these recommendations but with some reservations. It is agreed that new pits will require to be larger than in the past but it is thought that very large units such as are often found in Europe are not likely to be economic in Great Britain because the density of coal in the strata is low and natural conditions set severe problems. To get very large outputs would mean working a very wide area from one pit, excessive capital costs and excessive travelling time underground. The Board accepts the case for horizon mining and with new and reconstructed pits where the coal measures are steeply inclined this will probably become general. Locomotive haulage is also likely to become general practice though this will not necessitate 'horizon' mining where the coal measures are fairly flat.

The application of the latest mining techniques is not easy therefore in the difficult and varied mining conditions found in this country and much experiment and modification are necessary. Also, many of our present difficulties are the consequence not only of natural conditions but also of comparative old age and unsystematic exploitation before 1914. If any great progress is to be made there will need to be capital investment on a very large scale and an extensive programme of new sinkings. Many existing pits will require such drastic reconstruction that they will need to be taken out of production for a fairly long time. The important point is that technical reconstruction is no longer mainly a question of increasing mechanization at the face, which was the chief direction taken before 1939.[1] The time and energy devoted to systematic planning of future production will far exceed anything previously known and will make heavy demands on the limited supply of technically trained man-power available.

The Reid Committee followed many earlier committees and commissions in advocating the merger of the conflicting interests of individual colliery companies into compact and unified commands of manageable size and the establishment of an authority to see that this was carried through. Its report was, of course, written against the background of private enterprise, but when nationalization quickly followed, the grouping of pits into areas was done with the case for larger administrative units very much in mind. Most observers were agreed that considerable economies would accrue from this[2] although very few would have accepted all the arguments and statistical 'proofs' put

---

[1] Except perhaps that the full possibilities of power loading have yet to be reaped. In 1956, 36 million tons were power loaded at the face. Output per man-shift for all face-workers was 67 cwt. compared with 114 cwt. on power loaded faces.

[2] Particularly since the mineral rights were also vested in the National Coal Board.

forward.[1] To what extent they have been realized is doubtful. So far they have probably been offset by the temporary dislocation caused by nationalization and administrative reorganization but there can be no reasonable doubt of the greater long-term efficiency of the present structure.

Equally it may be said that the case for larger mines is not capable of statistical proof. Here again the Samuel Commission had produced statistics to show that generally speaking the larger mines were the most productive. A detailed breakdown of the figures showed, however, that large mines were more common in the newer developing coalfields so that it became doubtful if the figures proved very much about the relation of plant size to efficiency. There is, however, no real reason for doubting the opinion of most experts that under given conditions and provided that a certain density of coal in the strata obtains, the large mine is more economic.

Table 4 shows what has been happening to the size of mines since 1924.

Table 4. *Size distribution of mines*

Mines employing	1924* (%)		1940† (%)		1952‡ (%)	
Under 50	818	(33)	706	(40)	455	(34)
50–499	848	(34)	469	(27)	351	(26)
500–999	422	(17)	316	(18)	274	(21)
1,000–1,499	198	(8)	134	(8)	138	(10)
1,500–1,999	77	(3)	71	(4)	74	(6)
2,000–2,499	61	(3)	29	(2)	19	(1)
2,500–2,999	31	(1)	10	(1)	20	(2)
3,000 and over	26	(1)	6	(–)	3	(–)
Total	2,481	(100)	1,741	(100)	1,334	(100)

* Taken from the Samuel Commission Report (*Report of the Royal Commission on the Coal Industry (1925)*, vol. I, *Report*, Cmd. 2600 (H.M.S.O. 1926).
† Compiled from *List of Mines, 1940* (Mines Department).
‡ Taken from the Ministry of Fuel and Power *Statistical Digest, 1953* (H.M.S.O. 1954).

The changes have not been pronounced. There has been a proportionate decline in the number of small mines and a proportionate rise in the medium-sized mines employing 500 to 2000 men. A surprising feature is that the number of very large mines has declined both absolutely and proportionately. Size is measured by employment, but the trends would not be much different if measured by output, because changes in productivity have not been sufficient to disturb the picture. Average output per mine (in thousand tons) was 109, 127, and 160 in 1924, 1940 and 1952 respectively. Average employment per mine was

[1] For example, by the Samuel Commission in 1925.

485, 423 and 537 in 1924, 1940 and 1952 respectively. In brief, the growth in average size of mines has been very slow over the period as a whole but has become more pronounced in recent years.

Table 5 relates size of mines to productivity per man in 1952.[1]

Table 5. *Productivity and size of mines*

Output per man-shift over-all	Number of mines	Average number employed
Under 15 cwt.	174	177·2
15 and under 20 cwt.	318	582·1
20 and under 25 cwt.	363	655·6
25 and under 30 cwt.	241	646·3
30 and under 35 cwt.	114	575·1
35 and under 40 cwt.	56	338·1
40 cwt. and over	68	181·5

No clear correlation is discernible. If the table is further broken down some surprising results are obtained. For example, forty-three pits out of 455 employing less than fifty men and only eight pits out of 528 employing over 500 men had an o.m.s. of over 40 cwt. in 1952. Such figures, however, do little more than illustrate the variety of the industry and the dependence of results on natural conditions. They do, however, suggest that the National Coal Board is wise in not regarding the very large mine as a major key to increased efficiency.

Nevertheless under conditions which obtain quite widely in this country and provided certain conditions about the density of coal are satisfied, it is almost certainly true that coal can be mined most economically by the use of methods involving large capital expenditures which in turn require large-scale working if they are to be fully justified. Also, the fact that labour is both scarce and costly further tilts the balance in favour of large mines. One cannot doubt the wisdom of the Board's preference for mines larger than the great majority of those now in production and of conforming whenever possible to the best technical practice. On the other hand one suspects that there has occasionally been a tendency to work to a technical rather than an economic optimum. Costly failures in mechanization should perhaps be written off as the necessary and inevitable price of progress. It is also true that plans for large reconstructions and new sinkings are carefully costed beforehand and will only be adopted if they show an expected clear margin of profit. It is not so certain, however, that less costly, if less modern alternatives, are sufficiently considered.[2]

[1] Ministry of Fuel and Power, *Statistical Digest, 1953*.
[2] The Fleck Committee (see below, p. 149) reported that there should be sterner and keener scrutiny of large capital schemes than obtains at present.

The first capital investment programme of the National Coal Board was set out in the *Plan for Coal*.[1] It provided for a capital expenditure of £635 million (at 1949 prices) of which £484 million was to be spent on collieries. The output planned for 1965 was 240 million tons. 70% of the 1965 output was to be produced by 250 reconstructed pits, 10% by twenty-two new pits and fifty-three new drifts and the remainder by existing pits. Some 350 to 400 pits working in 1950 were to be closed by 1965.

Output per man-year was expected to rise from about 300 to 390 tons by 1965 and man-power requirements to drop by about 80,000. On the assumptions of the Plan the cost of coal was estimated to fall by 7s. per ton at 1949 prices. The increased output was expected to come mainly from Scotland, Yorkshire, the East Midlands and South Wales in roughly equal amounts of 8 to 9 million tons.[2] By 1965 the central coalfields of England from Yorkshire to Kent were to increase their share of the national output by 1%. Output was expected to fall slightly in Lancashire and the share of Scotland and South Wales to rise by from 1 to 2%. Of the projected expenditure of £484 million, South Wales was allocated £102 million, the East Midlands £79 million, Yorkshire £72 million, Scotland £64 million and Durham £54 million. Nine of the new pits were planned for Scotland, seven for South Wales, two for the East Midlands and two for Yorkshire.

The formulation of the Plan started from an estimate of future demand[3] placed at between 230 and 250 million tons in 1965, which was broken down into major categories of coal. For each pit (and by aggregation for each area) estimates of possible output at different levels of average cost were obtained on the assumption that any possibilities of technical reorganization were carried out. These ladders of cost were then matched against the demand estimates and the pits and areas which could most economically meet the demand were identified. The results were then scrutinized and modified in the light of transport costs, social considerations, etc. For example, the Midlands and the Yorkshire coalfields could produce much of the coal needed by Lancashire more cheaply than Lancashire itself could provide it, but transport costs limited the advantage and Lancashire's planned output was scaled up accordingly. Also the first results predicted a sharp fall in the output of West Durham and Cumberland and in view of the social consequences their planned outputs were also scaled upwards.

---

[1] Published by the National Coal Board in 1950. See also 'Planned Investment in the Coal Industry' by A. Beacham, *Oxford Economic Papers*, June 1951, p. 125.

[2] In 1953 the planned outputs of the Midlands and North-Eastern Division were scaled up and those for South Wales adjusted downwards.

[3] It was assumed that up to a point this could be done independently of price.

The Plan was revised in 1956. The Board reported that 'experience during the past five years has shown that both the difficulties and cost of creating a healthy coal industry were much greater than was thought [in 1950]...'.[1] The revisions make interesting reading.

Deep-mined output planned for 1965 is scaled down from 240 to 230 million tons plus an estimated open-cast production of 10 million tons. South Wales, Scotland and Durham show an aggregate reduction of 13 million tons in planned output and the East Midlands' target is scaled up by about 5 million tons. This inter-divisional adjustment is not unexpected and actual outputs in 1965 may show the balance tilted even more in favour of the East Midlands.[2]

Capital expenditure over the period 1960–5 is now reckoned (at constant prices) to be about 50% above the original estimate[3]—an increase explained by previous under-costing and the addition of new projects. Productivity is expected to rise substantially but any consequent saving in costs will be offset by increased capital charges. The proportion of large coal in total output is expected to fall and with the readjustment of output between the coalfields one would expect the proportion of high-ranking coals to diminish compared with the 1950 estimates. In short the coal offered by the revised Plan is less both in quality and quantity, and more expensive, than in the original Plan.

As regards new sinkings and reconstructions the Board was abreast of its original investment plans in money terms (adjusted for price changes) by the end of 1956, but in physical terms the work has been much slower than anticipated. The fact that very little new capacity has so far been brought into use[4] explains the failure of output to rise appreciably since 1950. Balancing one factor against another there seems to be no reason why the present target should not be reached by 1965, provided the Board's assumptions about its ability to redistribute man-power and continued working of the Saturday shift are borne out. One must admit to some anxiety on this score.

No one outside the industry could pretend to judge the revised Plan in detail. It seems a reasonable statement of physical possibilities and an output of 230 (plus 10) million tons by 1965 measures up fairly well to expected demand on the assumptions previously given. But its underlying tone is disquieting. There seems to be an implicit assumption that practically any scale of investment in coal can be economically

---

[1] *Investing in Coal* (National Coal Board, 1956), p. 6.

[2] 'The experience of the last six years has brought a much clearer understanding than before of the severity of the "factor of decline"—the current loss of capacity—particularly in some of the older coalfields.' *Investing in Coal*, p. 17.   [3] See p. 125.

[4] Due mainly to shortages of skilled man-power and the emphasis laid in the early years on short-term plans to raise output (for example, face mechanism) and on overtaking arrears of maintenance.

justified. The Board states flatly that 'even in the longer term the problem of over-production can scarcely arise'. We can hardly agree if the farther target of 250 million tons in 1970[1] is to be taken seriously. If the foundations for this further advance are being laid in the present programme many doubts arise as to its advisability. But it seems unlikely that such outputs will ever be reached with any practicable scale of investment in an industry now encountering such severely diminishing returns.

Up to the end of 1955 about 190 mines (mostly small) had been closed by the National Coal Board. They probably produced about 9 million tons per annum at the time of closure. This can hardly be regarded as anything more than natural and inevitable wastage. Very little has therefore been achieved by way of concentration of output which might have produced considerable economies if the immediate need for output had been less pressing. The decision to sacrifice the long term to the short term has undoubtedly been a major factor in the apparently disappointing record of the British coal industry since nationalization.

Industrial relations are an even more important factor in efficiency than technical achievement, for the record of the industry in this respect is extremely bad. The incidence of industrial unrest varies from year to year, but, speaking generally, over one-third of the losses caused by industrial disputes[2] in Great Britain over the past twenty years were suffered by the coal industry which accounts for less than 4 % of the working population. The annual average loss of output per annum on account of disputes over the ten-year period 1944–53 is about $1\frac{1}{4}$ million tons, excluding losses on account of 'go-slows' and other restrictive practices. Nor can it yet be said with confidence that losses on this account have been much affected by nationalization.[3] The remarkable thing is that such losses are generally most heavy in particular coalfields (South Wales, Yorkshire and Scotland) and even in particular areas within these coalfields. These three coalfields accounted for between 80 % and 90 % of the tonnage lost through disputes in recent years and some ten areas within them accounted for over 50 %. Industrial relations in the anthracite area of South Wales are so bad that reconstruction schemes for the area were only embodied in the 1950 *Plan for Coal* on the express understanding that relations would improve.

Why should worker–management relationships in the coal industry be so difficult? A great deal is often made of the physical strain, dirt

---

[1] *Investing in Coal*, p. 18.

[2] Whether measured by number of disputes, work people involved or working days lost.

[3] The number of days lost per annum is about the same in the first six years of nationalization as in the six immediately pre-war years.

and danger associated with underground work. The suggestion is that 'the worst types' are attracted to it and that the conditions have a brutalizing effect on the man. There can be very little, if anything, in this. Their comparative segregation in mining villages may partly explain some differences between them and other categories of industrial labour and the circumstances of their work may partly explain others. The qualities that most stand out amongst them—physical courage, intense loyalty and political consciousness—are certainly not bad qualities.

Perhaps the best explanation derives from the variability of working conditions to which attention has been previously called. Most disputes are on wage questions—dissatisfaction with existing agreements, allowances, interpretation of price-lists and so on. The latter are necessarily very complex and however carefully drawn are not easy to interpret, nor will they cover all contingencies. Variability of conditions also breeds anomalies in that concessions are more easily made in some places than others and that wages will rarely reflect accurately the skill and effort involved. Some of the most bitter fights have been fought over the question of national negotiation of wages and the principle of a national minimum wage. Also, the fact that wages are a high proportion of total costs has probably helped to make wages an unusually sensitive issue with employers.

But custom and tradition undoubtedly count for a great deal. Memories are long in an industry where father is often followed by son and where mining communities are often set apart and self-contained. The tradition in such areas is one of extreme militancy. A man with a grievance will leave the pit and, without hesitation or knowledge of the merits of the case, the rest of the men will follow. Customary practices and wage differentials which have been fought for at great cost in the past will now be vigorously defended however irrelevant to present working methods and however much a hindrance to efficient management they become. It is not simply that the miner is conservative in his outlook. There have been many bitter episodes in their past relations with the owners and it takes very little to reopen old sores. The greatest obstacle the National Coal Board has to face is the cloud of suspicion and hostility that still hangs over the industry and which is not much related to anything in the recent past. For the moment the determination of the miners to keep and use their traditional weapons and practices —the lightning strike, the 'go-slow', the 'stay down', seniority rules and working stints—cannot easily be shaken.

The miners' Union (the National Union of Mineworkers)[1] is a near approach to a complete industrial union. It was established in 1943

[1] Hereafter referred to as N.U.M.

when it succeeded the Miners' Federation of Great Britain (M.F.G.B.). The growth of mining unionism was chiefly through strong district associations which were exceedingly jealous of their autonomy and were only loosely federated in the M.F.G.B. which possessed little formal power. The N.U.M. is, however, a strongly centralized national union which men join as individuals and which alone can sponsor official strike action. The former district associations function as 'areas' of the N.U.M. through which most of the detailed routine work of the union is transacted, though they retain some autonomy in such matters as friendly society benefits. The N.U.M. claims to organize all workers in and around the mines below management level—a claim which has brought it into conflict with some small craft unions (such as the winding-enginemen) who regard it as mainly a colliers' union and a poor guardian of other interests. Inter-union friction has added its quota to the labour troubles of the industry since 1947. Nationalization of the mines added immensely to the power and prestige of the N.U.M. and at the same time increased the apprehensions of small groups of separately organized workers.

The militancy of the N.U.M. is an outcome partly of its appreciation of structural forces in the industry which were likely to weaken its bargaining position. This could only be combated by discipline, unity and militancy of spirit. The Union has been foremost in the fight for the closed shop and was one of the first to win recognition of the principle from employers. One of the bitterest episodes in the miners' history followed the formation of a rival union in Nottinghamshire where wages and working conditions were better than in most other coalfields. But militancy is also partly the outcome of the democratic structure of the Union which makes its leadership very sensitive to rank and file opinion. Given the usual apathy of the majority of members, rank and file opinion tends to be the expression of vocal and radical minorities.

All this, of course, does not go far to explain why particular spots should be most troublesome. In the main the most troublesome districts are fairly old mining areas, where mining conditions are difficult and a good deal of pressure on wages was to be expected. South Wales (and to some extent Scotland) has in the past depended substantially on the export trade and lacked the protection afforded to the inland districts by the cartelization of the 1930's. Neither of these explanations, however, applies very closely to Yorkshire. The uneven incidence of disputes may be as much a matter of tradition and local personalities as anything else.

Much of the preceding argument refers to the past. What is most difficult to explain is why the position has not been appreciably improved by nationalization. Superficially everything pointed to such an improvement. The miners had achieved their most cherished objective.[1] The 'wicked coal-owners' had gone. With a centralized administration of the industry the objection to national wages settlements could be expected to fall to the ground, and since individual pit profits and losses now mattered much less some greater uniformity of wages and working conditions was to be looked for. Also the Nationalization Act had made it clear that the National Coal Board was to concern itself with the national interest, to encourage joint consultation, and to look to the welfare of the employees. There were in addition a number of other favourable circumstances—coal was in short supply, the N.U.M. was better placed to control disorderly district elements than the M.F.G.B. and so on.

But there was something to be said on the other side. Many of the older workmen had expected[2] a syndicalist solution and were disappointed to see the industry handed over to an organization which contained at different levels many persons whom they regarded as coal-owners. Many miners' leaders were also brought in and whilst this may have mollified the men it seriously weakened leadership in the Union.[3] Also, and perhaps most important, custom and tradition die hard and it may be too soon yet to look for any substantial results from nationalization.

It would certainly be a mistake to say that nothing has been achieved. The published indices of industrial unrest do not indicate any clear reversal of pre-war trends but most people in close contact with the industry would probably say that there is a better atmosphere prevailing in the industry today than at any time in the past.

Various factors have contributed to this. First, there is the record of the National Coal Board as a good employer. It has been most assiduous in its promotion of the health and safety of its employees by provision of baths, canteens, dust suppression, and the like. Also its policies for training, further education and promotion leave little to be desired. Secondly, although joint consultation has not been uniformly successful, it has done something to give the miners the impression that they are partners in the business. Failures in joint consultations have been due rather to failings of men on the spot than to lack of enthusiasm on the part of the Board. Thirdly, there has been the effect of the conciliation scheme first introduced in 1943 and later adapted and adopted by the National Coal Board. It provided for negotiation and settlement at

[1] That is, nationalization. The miners' Union was the only one to write such an objective into its rule-book.
[2] Naturally enough in view of the history of the agitation for nationalization.
[3] The extent to which the National Coal Board has drained the N.U.M. of potential leaders is more serious than might be indicated by this passing reference.

three levels—pit, district and national. Failure to agree at any level results in reference to a higher level or to some form of external arbitration, the results of which both sides are pledged to accept. So long as the agreement is adhered to there can be no official dispute leading to strike action. Nearly all the tonnage losses due to strikes are on account of local action being taken without the consent of union officials.[1] Nearly all disputes arise initially at a particular pit and the great majority are settled at once by direct negotiation at pit level. Comparatively few district questions become the subject of disputes, but even here the majority are settled by direct negotiation. There has been a significant and encouraging tendency for fewer references to be made to pit umpires or district referees for final and binding decisions. A large number of the small disputes resulting in stoppages of work are due to men leaving work before the matter is referred to the manager or before the trade union officials can be called in. It seems likely that tonnage losses on account of trade disputes will become less as experience of the negotiating machinery[2] grows and a new tradition of orderly settlement of industrial disputes develops.

A fourth hopeful sign is that negotiations have been opened up between both sides for a new wages structure, which will cut the number of job descriptions, try to secure that reward is more closely related to skill and effort, and secure greater uniformity of rates. Progress has been very slow but in 1955 agreement was reached (for day-wage men only) and a new wages structure was put into operation.[3] This affects about 400,000 men. Much more remains to be done.

Output losses due to strikes and restrictive practices reflect adversely on the efficiency of the industry but a strike may sometimes be preferable to constant and unconditional surrender. Even the necessity for management always to be conciliating union opinion may become a serious drawback. The right balance for management must be very difficult to achieve. Management is now forced to spend a very great deal of time on labour matters—investigating grievances, settling pit disputes, investigating the complaints and suggestions of the consultative committee and so on. It is now normal practice to put proposals for new sinkings, reconstructions, closure of pits, transfer of labour, etc. to the consultative committees before any final decision is taken.[4] In some districts many managers spend much less time underground than was customary before the war, although they have been trained primarily

---

[1] Though some strikes have received the tacit support of local leaders.
[2] Still comparatively new at pit level.
[3] National Coal Board, *Report and Accounts for 1955*, vol. i, p. 38.
[4] In some districts there is also a great deal of informal consultation between the N.U.M. and the National Coal Board. So much so that some cynics profess to be uncertain as to which organization is running the industry.

as technical production experts—certainly not as experts in industrial relations. Deficiencies of training and temperament on the part of managers (as well as lack of adequate leadership at pit level on the N.U.M. side) have probably been responsible for much avoidable friction in the industry.

But management has had other troubles of its own. Widespread allegations of administrative inefficiency have been common since 1947 and although we are not primarily concerned here with administrative problems some brief reference is necessary and relevant at this point.

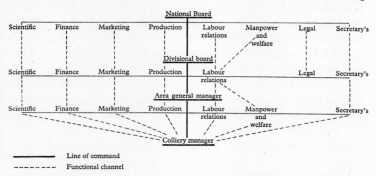

The organizational structure of the industry since nationalization has been briefly referred to in the first part of this essay.[1] The main principle underlying the Board's organization is that of 'line and staff'. This implies a clear line of command and responsibility from the National Coal Board to the coalface. The main authorities in the line are the National Coal Board, the divisional boards (collectively responsible to the National Coal Board), the area general managers (personally responsible to the divisional board) and the colliery managers (personally responsible to the area general manager). Attached to each authority in the line are such staff of functional experts (production, finance, labour relations, etc.) as is necessary. Each authority in the line together with its attached staff is known as a level of management. The simplified diagram above embodies the main features of the organization.

Criticisms of the Board have been easy to make; the magnitude of its task is easily forgotten. As the Fleck Committee pointed out, the effect of nationalization was to deprive the industry of one complete level of management. Most of those who had directed the fortunes of the industry at the level of managing director under private enterprise did

[1] For a full account see the Annual Reports of the National Coal Board and the *Report of the Advisory Committee on Organization* (the Fleck Committee), published by the National Coal Board, 1955.

not enter the service of the National Coal Board. From the outset the Board was desperately short of first-rate top level managerial ability with that experience of large-scale working which was now more than ever necessary. Also, its organizational arrangements have been under constant scrutiny. This was to be expected in view of the fact that coal remained in short supply and everyone was seeking the reason why the industry had failed to deliver the goods. The Board itself has not shirked inquiry. It invited both the Burrows and Fleck Committees[1] to vet its organizational arrangements and to suggest improvements. Very few organizations would have escaped criticism after such searching and constant investigation. The general conclusion of the very frank and thorough report of the Fleck Committee was that the main structure of the Board's organization revealed no big defect which was hindering it from solving its problems.

These investigations have confirmed the view that many of the Board's troubles have been due to factors beyond its control in the short period. Most serious has been the shortage of skilled man-power. The output of mining graduates was seriously deficient before the war and well trained experienced managers are in very short supply. Moreover, until recent years their training has been almost exclusively technical, though much of their work involves the handling of labour problems, the co-ordination of the work of other specialists at pit level, and the provision of information for higher management levels. They were therefore not well fitted by training for many aspects of management. This weakness was felt much more seriously after nationalization when area general managerships were necessarily filled mainly from the ranks of the managers. The Fleck Committee remarked that many area general managers do not measure up to the requirements of the job and proposed that some of these posts in future be filled by men who were not mining engineers. At colliery level it was proposed that managers should be assisted by administrative and personnel officers and that there should be training courses for colliery managers in administration and management.[2]

Other factors, partly beyond the control of the Board, have also been sources of inefficiency on the organizational side. They include the constant changes that have taken place in the personnel of the National Coal Board itself, the fact that they have not always been able to work together as a team, and the number of ex-trade-union officials appointed to fill posts on the personnel side in spite of their unfitness to bear heavy administrative responsibilities. But the Board itself has

[1] It is generally thought, however, that there was some political prompting in both cases.

[2] It is valid criticism of the Board, however, that more might have been done along these lines before the Fleck Committee was set up.

contributed its quota to the inefficiency of the industry. Its chief weakness has been lack of clear and decisive leadership. It has not been sufficiently firm in seeing that its policies are carried out at lower levels, that responsibilities are made clear at all levels of management and that the line of command is kept absolutely clear.[1]

One reason for the Board's lack of firmness may have been fear that it would be accused of over-centralization of authority, of stifling local initiative, and so on, and the charge of over-centralization is one that has been most constantly pressed. Charges of over-centralization have generally referred to excessive interference by the Board in day-to-day management and the need to refer back to higher authority relatively minor matters. Decentralization in this sense is to be welcomed and the Board has consistently encouraged this in recent years. Although the Board must remain responsible for major policy decisions some further decentralization of administrative authority and policy making is probably desirable.

Controversy has also revolved round the functional character of the Board which it is alleged must impart bias to policy decisions by departmental heads and lead to too much routine matter being brought to the top for final decision. As against this it is argued that a policy-making board without departmental responsibilities could not be sufficiently in touch with things to decide policy wisely or to see that policy was carried out. Following the Burrows Committee the number of Board members with departmental responsibilities was reduced and until recently some major departments were not represented on the Board. The Fleck Committee, however, came down heavily in favour of the functional board and recommended that all full-time members[2] should have departmental responsibilities and that all major departments should be represented on the Board. It is agreed that they should be men able to take wide views and that they need not be responsible for the day-to-day management of their departments. They would also be strengthened on the Board by the addition of part-time members free of routine duties.[3] In the face of these recommendations there seems little doubt that the functional character of the Board will be retained and there is little to suggest that during the past eight years it has been a source of weakness.

Another major criticism has been that of indistinct spheres of authority and responsibility. The main point made here is that of divided loyalty.

[1] The new directive on management, July 1955, attempts to remedy this. For this and other action taken to implement the Fleck Committee recommendations see the National Coal Board's *Report and Accounts for 1955*.

[2] Other than the Chairman and Deputy Chairman.

[3] The Committee also recommended that there should be greater continuity and that full-time Board members should be recruited from within the industry.

For example, it is alleged that the production specialist on the staff of an area general manager may not know whether his primary responsibility is to his superior in the functional chain or to the area general manager. Also, it is not clear whether definite instructions can pass down the functional channels and so undermine the authority of those in the direct line of command. What we are concerned with, however, is not the theoretical pros and cons of such an administrative system but the fact that it has led to a great deal of confusion and frustration in practice. Much of this has been due to lack of experience in large-scale organizations which time may smooth away. Meanwhile, the Fleck Committee is undoubtedly right in asking for a clearer statement of how the functional channels should work.

This ties in with the complaints that operational management at the pits has been much impeded and the authority of managers undermined by hordes of functional experts who have descended on the pits. The complaints have probably been exaggerated but managers have certainly felt the impact of nationalization very sharply. This is partly owing to the fact that managers are inadequate and the nature of their job is changing. But it is also partly owing to organizational changes and it would be a step forward if the link between the pit and the area were strengthened by the interpolation of another level of management.[1] The manager must be made to feel assured of his position in the line of command and less cut off from the hierarchy above. No amount of efficiency in the 'higher' management of the industry will compensate for inefficiency of pit management. For as the old miners say, 'Coal comes from the point of the pick'.

7. CONCLUSIONS

To sum up. The most critical aspects of Britain's coal problems are, first, the growing exhaustion of the coalfields and the inevitable tendency of real costs to rise, and secondly, difficulties of labour supply and industrial relations. Whatever form of organization had been adopted and however brilliantly the industry had been administered, Britain would have faced a serious coal situation after the end of the war.

In the event, however, the record of the industry has belied hopes which might reasonably have been entertained for its future. In spite of considerable real advances in wages and working conditions and a very ambitious programme of modernization and new development, deep-mined coal production after a post-war spurt had become virtually stationary by the early 1950's and down to 1956 was showing a slight

[1] This has now been done. The intermediate level of management is called the group. Some 200 groups have been constituted.

tendency to fall. Labour productivity has not much exceeded the best pre-war level. Insufficiency of coal for home consumption and exports has been a major factor impeding Britain's post-war recovery.

For this situation the National Coal Board has only been partly to blame. It has not been entirely master in its own house and has had to work within the framework of the Nationalization Act. The Board may nevertheless be criticized for indecisive leadership and a rather cumbrous over-centralized administration. But its achievements have been considerable, particularly with technical re-organization, improvement of working conditions, and its efforts to win readier co-operation from the miners.

Some form of nationalization was probably inevitable in 1945 because of the temper of the men, the effect of the war on the finances of the industry and the need for larger capital expenditures than private enterprise would have been willing to risk. But the Nationalization Act and the way in which it has been implemented have been a serious contributory factor to our coal difficulties.

How then might present arrangements be modified to the advantage of the industry? The wise man will hesitate to offer more than tentative suggestions as to the probable direction of desirable change. An effort should be made to take coal out of politics. There is an element of truth in the gibe that coal-mining is now more of a political than an economic activity. Even such a minor act of business policy as the closure of a small pit causes more than a ripple at Westminster and this must have its effect on the Board. Appointments to the Board should be determined by ability and not by quasi-political considerations or a desire to preserve some sort of balance of interests. The Board should be given more freedom in the formulation and execution of business policy. It is not desirable that it should be bound to average cost pricing or to seek approval of the Minister before advancing prices. In its turn the Board, whilst giving a firm lead on basic national policy, should give areas more autonomy than they possess at present. Some thought should be given to the possibility of areas competing for business between themselves and determining their own price policies on the basis of doing the best they can for themselves. A more meaningful price structure would emerge which would be flexible and responsive to consumer demand. The present price structure appears to be rigid and artificial and one suspects that it may be 'rigged' in order to preserve the existing balance of production between coalfields and their spheres of interest in traditional markets. The changes proposed would allow financial results to be regarded as more valid indicators for future development policy. Proposals for new development schemes should originate in the areas but would require approval by the Board.

Prices would almost certainly rise though whether they would rise substantially it is impossible to say. Price would not necessarily rise to cover the marginal cost of present output since area losses could be tolerated in the short run to an extent determined by the Board which would have to see to it that prices did not rise sufficiently to imperil the future stability of the industry. Prices should not rise as much as if the National Coal Board acting as a single seller attempted to equate present supply and demand.

How far such changes could be contrived without formal amendment of the Nationalization Act it is difficult to say. They should not arouse the determined hostility of the miners or involve serious political repercussions.

BIBLIOGRAPHY

(a) Books, Pamphlets and Articles

Beacham, A., 'The Coalfields of Britain', *Economic Journal*, vol. 56, no. 222, June 1946, p. 319.

'Efficiency and Organization of the British Coal Industry', *Economic Journal*, vol. 55, no. 218-19, June–September 1945, p. 206.

'Fuel and Power Policy in Great Britain', *Journal of Industrial Economics*, vol. 3, no. 1, December 1954, p. 22.

'Planned Investment in the Coal Industry', *Oxford Economic Papers* (New Series), vol. 3, no. 2, June 1951, p. 125.

'The Present Position of the British Coal Industry', *Economic Journal*, vol. 60, no. 237, March 1950, p. 9.

'Price Policy in the Coal Industry', *Journal of Industrial Economics*, vol. 1, no. 2, April 1953, p. 140.

'The Proposal for a Coal Subsidy', *Review of Economic Studies*, vol. 7, no. 1, October 1939, p. 59.

'Some Notes on the Future Size of the British Coal Industry', *Agenda*, vol. 3, no. 2, May 1944, p. 168.

'Some Observations on the Future Organization of the Coal Industry', *Agenda*, vol. 3, no. 1, February 1944, p. 60.

Browne, E. H., 'Improving Coal Production', *Journal of the Royal Society of Arts*, 26 June 1953, p. 564.

Court, W. H. B., *Coal*, History of the Second World War, United Kingdom Civil Series, H.M.S.O. and Longmans, Green, 1951.

Dennison, S. R., 'The Price Policy of the National Coal Board', *Lloyds Bank Review*, October 1952, p. 17.

Dickie, J. P., *The Coal Problem: a Survey, 1910–1936*, London, Methuen, 1936.

Foot, R., *Coal: the Price Structure*, London, Federation of British Industries, 1952.

A Plan for Coal, London, Mining Association of Great Britain, 1945.

Haynes, W. W., *Nationalization in Practice: the British Coal Industry*, London, Bailey Brothers and Swinfen, 1953.

Houldsworth, Sir Hubert, *The Pits of Britain*, Transactions of the Manchester Statistical Society, 1952-3.

Jones, J. H., Cartwright, G. and Guenault, P. H., *The Coalmining Industry: an International Study in Planning*, London, Pitman, 1939.

Little, I. M. D., *The Price of Fuel*, Oxford, Clarendon Press, 1953.

Lomax, K. S., 'The Demand for Coal in Great Britain', *Oxford Economic Papers* (New Series), vol. 4, no. 1, February 1952, p. 50.

Munby, D. L., 'The Price of Fuel', *Oxford Economic Papers* (New Series), vol. 6, no. 3, September 1954, p. 226.

Neuman, A. M., *Economic Organization of the British Coal Industry*, London, Routledge, 1934.

PEP (Political and Economic Planning), *The British Fuel and Power Industries*, London, 1947.

Report on the British Coal Industry, London, 1936.

Reid, Sir Charles and Reid, William, 'The Reconstruction of the British Mining Industry', *Journal of the Royal Society of Arts*, 20 May 1949, p. 461.

Sales, W. H., 'Changing Patterns of Pit Performance', *Journal of Industrial Economics*, vol. 3, no. 3, July 1955, p. 184.

Wilson, H., *New Deal for Coal*, London, Contact Publications, 1945.

(*b*) *Official Publications*

(All published by H.M.S.O. except where otherwise stated)

Ministry of Fuel and Power (now Ministry of Power), *Coal Mining: Report of the Technical Advisory Committee* (the Reid Committee), Cmd. 6610, 1945.

Regional Coalfield Survey Reports, 1945–6.

Statistical Digest, annual.

Mines Department, *Annual Reports of the Secretary for Mines*.

National Coal Board, *Annual Reports*.

Investing in Coal, N.C.B., 1956.

Plan for Coal, N.C.B., 1950.

Report of the Advisory Committee on Organization (the Fleck Committee), N.C.B., 1955.

Summer School Speeches, N.C.B.

Royal Commission on the Coal Industry, *Report*, 1925.

Scottish Home Department, *Scottish Coalfields*, Report of the Scottish Coalfields Committee, Cmd. 6575, Edinburgh, 1944.

CHAPTER V

THE OIL INDUSTRY

By DUNCAN BURN

I. INTRODUCTION

The petroleum industry—for brevity called hereafter the oil industry—comprises the production of mineral oil which is obtained as 'crude oil' from oil wells or from oil shale, the transport of the crude oil to a refinery, its manufacture there into a range of joint products—fuels, lubricants, bitumens and 'chemicals', and the transport and distribution of these finished oil products or semi-products to their various markets.

This industry is now characterized by an exceptional degree of concentration and vertical integration on an international scale, which is its most distinct economic characteristic and is the source of the most striking economic problems to which it gives rise. Extraction of the crude, refining, and distribution, outside the Russian sphere, are largely though not exclusively in the hands of a small number of large international firms of complex structure. Some have their headquarters in London.

The structure of the oil industry in Britain must therefore be examined as part of this international structure, in a sense which does not apply to any other major British industry. Many British industries use mainly imported raw materials, and firms in these industries in varying degrees set out to ensure the supply of these imports at what they regard as satisfactory prices. But the situation in the oil industry is wholly different. Practically all the raw material used by the industry in Britain is, certainly, imported, which has contributed to the more unique structural development. But the outstanding feature of the industry is that its physical operations in Britain are carried out almost entirely by a few firms, some British or British-Dutch, some foreign (the chief of these all American), whose activities outside Britain are far larger than their activities in Britain, and are not confined to raw material production but extend to processing and marketing.

Oligopoly on an international scale, with the centre of gravity in the United States, and unmatched by political structure of like extent, has naturally prompted perplexing economic questions. What sort of competition exists in these circumstances? Does the international focus militate against the interest of particular areas, and in particular against Britain's interest? How far is the structure sensitive to local needs?

How does it affect conditions of entry, and the position of unintegrated independents? Are prices or profits—or even investments—in any definable sense too high?

Within a single chapter it is impossible to answer these questions thoroughly. The first section of this chapter sketches the development of production, processing and marketing in the industry and the forces, inherent and historic, which have led to the characteristic integrations. The next section deals with the industry in the United Kingdom: first the activities of British firms abroad, secondly the activities of British and foreign firms in the United Kingdom. The third section is on competition and price formation; it is focused on the British situation but necessarily not limited to it.

2. PRODUCTS AND PROCESSES—AND THE IMPULSES TO INTEGRATION

Large-scale operation and vertical integration have been favoured by the nature of the markets for oil products and by the nature of the producing, processing and transporting methods of the industry and the technical developments which have occurred in them—some imposed by the need, which arises with all minerals, to obtain oil progressively from less accessible sources. The degree of international integration reflects basically the influence of the distribution of major crude oil sources and the wide disparities between the political and economic stage of development and the legal systems of the countries in which these sources occur. It is convenient here to trace first in the markets and in successive stages of production the more general factors which have favoured larger-scale units in production, refining, distribution; and to show subsequently the interplay of more complex and specific factors leading to international integration in its present form and degree.

(a) Markets

For most of the products into which crude oils are manufactured there are potentially large markets in most countries, largest naturally in industrial countries. Most of the products, conspicuously the fuels or lubricants, are wanted in fairly uniform qualities so that successive deliveries to consumers give a standard performance; hence the markets tend to demand large quantities of uniform products even when, or particularly when, the final consumer takes small quantities at frequent intervals, as with motor spirit. Consumers of motor spirit, who are for the most part uninformed buyers, want to be able to buy it in any part of a large market 'on call', and this combined with the fact that slight differences of quality can be introduced makes it an ideal product to sell by brand. All the products are, however, marketwise adapted to large-scale production, though not all to the same degree.

(b) Production

Crude oils, the raw materials of the refineries, are almost exclusively now obtained from deep wells. Underground pools are found in many parts of the world, but abundant reserves which can be relatively cheaply extracted are found in a few countries only. Of the world's proven reserves of oil in 1956 the United States had 13·4 %, Venezuela 5·8 %, the Middle East 63·5 % and Russia and associated countries 10·9 %.[1] New reserves, as experience shows, will be found, but this balance is unlikely to be greatly changed quickly.

Crude oils are not a homogeneous commodity. There are differences between oilfields, and within the same oilfield. They differ in gravity and in their content of such impurities as sulphur or vanadium. Some Middle East crudes, those from Kuwait for example, have a lot of sulphur. Some Venezuelan crudes contain an exceptionally high proportion of heavy oil of the fuel-oil category. In the Middle East the heavy oil fraction also varies from place to place but not in the same degree. It appears possible, by blending if need be, to get supplies of crude of fairly homogeneous character from any major oilfield and to supply a large refinery with a feedstock of fairly standard quality. It is also possible if the balance of demand shifts from one kind of product to another within limits to extend the development of the crude oil pools which give crude oil of the more suitable kind.

When the modern oil industry based on mechanically drilled wells was started in Pennsylvania (the traditional date is 1859), drilling for oil, which is the starting-point in making oil products, was a relatively light operation, analogous to the customary drilling of wells for water. Before this, mineral oil had been obtained in small quantities 'from time immemorial' from seepages in many parts of the world. In the 1850's in the United States there were fifty small refineries making lighting oil from oil skimmed off ponds: in Britain oil was obtained (as some still is) by roasting shale mined in the Scottish Lowlands. The market for oil was the stimulus to the development of drilling, the basis of the modern industry.

The first oil well, drilled where oil was already obtained from seepages, 'struck oil' at 69½ ft. Since then prospecting for oil has become progressively—though not uniformly—more difficult and costly. Modern geophysical methods have been added to modern geological

---

[1] Of the other 6·4 % Canada had 1·3, Japan and Indonesia 2·2, India and Pakistan 0·2.

methods, the wells are often over a mile and sometimes three or four miles deep, and some are located off shore in the sea. Thus in 1955 of new exploratory wells in West Texas the average depth was about 7000 ft., and one-quarter were over 10,000 ft. deep. The average depth of the 44,000 wells in operation in the area was over 5000 ft.

The greater cost involved in obtaining oil has encouraged efforts to use more of the oil in the 'pools' that are tapped: the pace of extraction is controlled, a 'maximum efficient recovery rate' is established when a well is started up. This involves more elaborate and expensive processing.[1] As a result as much as 80 % of the available oil is sometimes recovered, compared with 20 % in the early days. Success requires that the number of wells drilled into a pool be limited and policies co-ordinated. Advances in methods of prospecting and in the efficient use of wells have depended much on research which only larger concerns can afford. When the newer methods are employed in a given situation the operation will be cheaper. They cannot make oil from deep wells as cheap as oil from shallow wells of comparable productions, but they can help to keep down the cost of oil from deep wells, as modern methods of mining coal can counteract to a considerable extent the worsening of the natural conditions from which coal must increasingly be mined.

Less accessible oil may be merely on the outskirts of or underneath existing 'fields' and 'pools': but much is in new fields, often remote from all the necessary services—power, transport, water, housing, labour, engineering skill. Where this is so—notably in South America, the Far East, and the Middle East, or under the sea—the costs of starting operations can be extremely high, though the ultimate cost of the oil may be fairly low. Companies operating in these conditions must put in large initial investments and normally first secure exclusive rights to develop vast areas for a long period. This probably leads to the most orderly extraction of the oil: the crowding of the wells is impressively less in such areas (though conservation policies in the United States have reduced the crowding). Here too the normal trend soon sets in—the cost of the oil rises as less accessible oils have to be tapped.[2]

In the early days small operators in America drilled wells in likely places speculatively. Where oil had been struck there was soon a forest

---

[1] The flow of oil from a well is checked at early stages when gas pressures may force it up very fast, and accelerated subsequently by the use of acids and explosives, and later by pumping, pressure maintenance, 'repressuring' (i.e. gases which come out with the oil may be pumped back via a specially drilled bore) or by water flooding (bores are drilled on the edge of an oil pool and water pumped down to drive the oil to the producing wells).

[2] For example in Iraq, Saudi Arabia and Kuwait the more recent wells are deeper. In the largest and first-developed field in Iraq (Kirkuk), for example, wells are from 1500 to 5000 ft. deep, but mainly under 2500 ft. In the Basrah field most of the wells are from 8000 to 11,000 ft. deep. Aramco's deepest drilling—over 14,000 ft.—proved dry (1955).

of derricks, with several wells to an acre. This proved wasteful of reserves as well as of effort and has been eliminated by state conservation policies.[1] Although all exploratory wells are still called 'wildcats' there is relatively little of the early practice: but in parts of American oilfields where there is a good chance that oil will be struck (as in many parts of Texas on the limits of known pools, and where there are labour and transport and other services), and since vast concessions are not given to single companies, some relatively small operators are still found who drill new wells. It is a risky existence: a surprising number of wells drilled prove dry, and others have very small outputs, so that there are probably many failures.[2] So-called small operators are probably

Table 1. *Crude oil outputs and productivities*

	Output 1955 (million tons)	Number of wells working	Output per well (tons per year)	Number of workers*	Output per man (tons per year)	Earnings per man† (£ per year)
United States	352	553,000	635	168,200	2,095	1700
Texas ‡	99	97,500	1,015	—	—	—
Venezuela	113	9,720	11,500	30,000	3,750	—
Iraq	33	—	—	11,000	3,100	420
Iraq P.C.	24	42	576,000	—	—	—
Mosul P.C.	1	7	183,000	—	—	—
Basrah P.C.	7	30	241,000	—	—	—
Qatar P.C.	5	33	163,000	2,200	2,300	—
Iran	17	60	283,000	18,200	934	345
Kuwait	54	211	256,000	6,000	9,000	—
Saudi Arabia	50	157	318,000	20,397	2,450	400

* Coverage is not precisely comparable. All include direct labour at the wells: but the Middle East figures include a far larger component for transport. Refinery workers are not included for Iran or Iraq: but they are at Kuwait and Saudi Arabia where the proportion of oil refined is, however, small. Part of the construction labour providing new capital equipment is included: but the proportion depends on (i) how much outside contracting there is, (ii) how active the company is in a particular year. Thus Aramco employed contractors in 1955 who employed 9000 workers; Kuwait employed 15,000 workers when expansion was at its peak. The total number of workers in the Venezuelan oil industry, in the oilfields and refineries, was 46,000. The figure of 30,000 has been taken for oilfields and pipeline transport, assuming 16,000 for the refineries whose throughput was 28 million tons of oil.

† This includes where possible insurance payments, and staff salaries: it does not include amenities or other benefits. Iran was still recovering from the shut-down.

‡ These figures are for West Texas, North, North Central, and Upper Texas Gulf Coast only.

Sources: Statistics of Oil and Gas Development and Production (American Institution of Mining, Metallurgical and Petroleum Engineers). Kuwait Oil Company, *The Story of Kuwait, 1957. Iranian Oil* [Report of Operating Companies]. Aramco, *Report of Operations for 1955.*

[1] Even now the number of wells in the United States oilfields seems high, and is much higher than elsewhere, as Table 1 shows.

[2] For example in West Texas in 1955, out of 839 wildcat wells drilled 664 were dry. For the United States as a whole out of 12,000 exploratory wells 1800 found oil in commercial quantities, 350 struck gas.

responsible for one-fifth of the American crude oil output: the six largest international companies produced about one-third. The rest is produced by medium-sized independents.

Outside America the situation is quite different. About four-fifths of the oil output in South America, four-fifths of the Far Eastern output (neglecting production in communist controlled areas), and almost the whole of the Middle East output are (1957) produced by seven major companies, directly or in co-operation (to a small extent in co-operation with some other companies).

Costs of producing oil vary greatly both within particular countries and between different countries. No comprehensive data are published. The variations in output per head and per man employed in major producing areas are indicated in Table 1.

The differences between labour costs in the Middle East and the United States are clearly immense: in the former they are a slight cost, in the latter relatively heavy. Material and power costs are probably not very different and relatively low. It is probable that capital costs per ton of output are also much lower in the Middle East than in the United States. As mentioned already all new developments in the Middle East require large initial outlays—thus the expenditure on the Basrah oilfield was £18 million in six years before any oil was produced: and to allow the increase of the output of the Kirkuk field from about 7 million tons to 22 million tons it was necessary to build a pipeline costing £40 million. Sometimes large initial outlays are also needed in the United States—but it is not universal. The 'cost' of Iraq oil, as established in an agreement with the Iraq government in 1951, implies a capital investment of not more than £6 for a capacity of 1 ton per year.[1] The 'average' investment commonly spoken of in the industry is £20 a ton/year. Taxation and payments for concessions, in varying forms, are a major part of Middle East oil costs.

A recent survey of the investments in oil, made by the Chase Manhattan Bank,[2] which may be regarded as a fairly authoritative document, shows very striking variations between different regions which indicate broadly that the expenditure may exceed £20 a ton/year in the United States but is considerably less in Venezuela and much less in the Middle

---

[1] The agreement takes the agreed cost of production (i.e. excluding profit) as 13s. a ton which includes depreciation of all plant in Iraq at 10 % and all other capital investment at 5 %. Labour cost was presumably about 3s. a ton: so that depreciation was below 10s. This would appear to imply a capital cost of at most £6 a ton. This figure, it must be emphasized, is the author's deduction: it has no authority in a published source. The 13s. a ton has probably moved up to nearer 20s., since average wages increased by 50 % between the agreement (1951) and 1955, and costs of equipment rose. The figure includes no profit, and no taxation or royalty. Cf. below, p. 173.

[2] *Investment Patterns in the World Petroleum Industry* (December 1956).

East. The figures cannot be interpreted precisely in the form of £x a ton/year: instead in Table 2 the total capital expenditure for 1946–55 and the estimated net investment at 1955 are divided by the 1955 output.

Table 2. *Capital investment in oil production*

($ million)

	(1) Production	(2) Pipe-lines	(3) Total	(4) Crude oil output 1955 (million tons)	(5) Invest-ment or expendi-ture in $ per ton
United States					
Capital expenditure, 1946–55	26,575	2,235	28,810	350	80
Gross investment, 1955	23,925	3,050	26,975		
Net investment, 1955	11,450	2,000	13,450	350	38
Venezuela					
Capital expenditure, 1946–55	2,491	161	2,652	115	23
Gross investment, 1955	2,650	210	2,860		
Net investment, 1955	985	130	1,115	115	10
Middle East					
Capital expenditure, 1946–55	980	587	1,567	170	9
Gross investment, 1955	950	590	1,540		
Net investment, 1955	575	310	885	170	5

(c) Refining

Crude oil can rarely be used directly: it must be subjected to some treatment if only to avoid smoke and smell. Originally refining was a simple distillation process, and the crude was treated in batches. Under two impulses refining has undergone progressive changes so that now it is carried out more and more in large complex plants where the processing is continuous and initial capital costs extremely high, though if the through-put of crude oil is large enough the cost per ton of oil is relatively small.

One chief object of development has been to reduce costs by taking advantage of the adaptability of oil to continuous automatically controlled processing. Supervision now is exercised at a few control stations where what is happening in the plant is recorded remotely by instruments, and if anything is going wrong it calls attention to itself and if automatic controls are failing human controls can be brought into play. But technical developments have been brought about for another object: to extend the range of products and alter the proportions in which they are obtained. Hence the process of refining has been changed and added to. Simple distillation (which separates the various types of hydrocarbon compounds present in the crude, according to their boiling points) remains the primary process but in a modern refinery a series of processes follow by which it is possible not only to extract unwanted constituents and improve the appearance, odour and stability of the oils, but also to convert selected hydrocarbon molecules to others of different size or internal structure. Thus the larger molecules may be 'cracked' to yield smaller ones, lighter molecules, for example in the gasoline range, may be 'reformed' to improve the quality of the gasoline, while the lightest, for example gaseous hydrocarbons, may be built up into larger ones to give desired end-products. Several processes combine these functions to a varying extent so that depending upon the processing equipment used, the proportions in which the joint products are obtained can be varied within wide limits from refinery to refinery. Even within the individual refinery there is a degree of flexibility in the product pattern which can be produced, although certain plants are highly specialized and inelastic, and a change in the balance of a particular refinery's output may mean that some costly capital is under-employed or unemployed.

Of the joint products made in a refinery, however much the proportions may be adjusted to the markets, there are at any given time one or two which are the most remunerative products. A refiner naturally tries to make his less remunerative products more valuable and to maximize his sales of the remunerative ones. The chief object has been until recently to obtain larger 'fractions' of light spirits (motor spirits) and to make spirits of higher octane ratings. This has been achieved most in the United States where aviation and motor spirits were over 45 % of the refinery output by 1955, whereas in Europe the figure was about 20 %. Recently the object in Europe has been to get more fuel oil. (Even in the United States the market for motor spirit was overstocked by the end of 1956.) Refinery products are sometimes further varied and enriched by additions of chemical 'reinforcements' such as tetraethyl-lead in motor spirit, and various additives in lubricating oils.

The development of refinery design and technique, like that in production, is the result of research. Large refiners can obviously do much more of this research and development than small ones, though manufacturers of equipment have contributed much to it as well. The work of developing special fuels is often done in close association with user industries so that in some respects their designs are adapted to the fuel as well as the fuel to the design of the machine; this again is something which a large oil firm is better able to do.

Competent refinery engineers have said that by increases in the size of a refinery costs of refining can be reduced until a through-put of 10 million tons a year is reached. The capital cost of such a plant would be about £100 million. It is rare for a refinery to start at this size. The rate of cost reduction is not given: it arises partly from the spread of labour costs and overheads over larger outputs, partly from the familiar economies in making larger units of plant.[1] Probably the optimum is reached when the further fall of costs is slight but the managerial burden is as heavy as one manager can effectively carry.

Increases of refinery output may increase the cost of obtaining crude oil and will increase the cost of distributing products, because they will need to be used over a wider area. Only a limited proportion of refineries even in the United States (where most oil is consumed) have reached the 'technical optimum': this is partly no doubt because many were made when the optimum was smaller, but sometimes because market conditions militate against it. In the United States only five refineries had a through-put of over 10 million tons in 1955; and forty from 2·5 million to 10 million tons. The forty-five, with an average of 6 million tons, produced two-thirds of the whole United States output. The large companies have several refineries. Six American companies have about 45 % of American refinery capacity, an average of about 30 million tons each. The combination of several refineries should reduce the cost of research per unit of product, and in practice some interchange of intermediate products occurs. Refineries can specialize to some extent, hence to have several refineries increases the range of a company's products and probably the changeability of its production programme. The extent of these advantages is not enough in the United States to prevent a large number of smaller though often still substantial 'independents' thriving.

The economic problems of refining are far more uniform in different countries than those of producing: since Britain now refines on a large scale, a more detailed treatment of these problems is reserved till later.

(d) Transport, storage and distribution

That cheap and plentiful crude oil occurs in few places while oil products have an almost ubiquitous market means that immense quantities of oil in one form or another, crude and refined, must be transported long distances and much must be stored. As often now remarked, oil provides the largest of the international commodity trades. Transport is an enormous job inside the United States, where great using and producing areas are remote from each other: and

---

[1] For example the amount of metal, and of fabrication, needed for a vessel or pipe will fall in proportion to its volume as the volume increases if the increase is not offset by the use of thicker or a higher quality metal.

internal and coastal transport of oil is a large part of the cost of distribution in all developed countries.

Until the product is near its final market large quantities of homogeneous products are transported, which gives scope for large-scale specialized operations which reduce costs. Pipelines and 'tankers' date from early in the industry's history. Only a substantial firm can lay a pipeline; and though a moderate size firm can run a small tanker fleet there are advantages in running large fleets or getting long-term charters from big firms, and the progressive increase in the size of the tankers, to reduce costs, must raise the minimum scale of economic operation. The transport of a growing quantity of Middle East oil to America stimulated the building of tankers of up to 80,000 tons or more, and the advantage of using such tankers between the Persian Gulf and Europe by way of the Cape, emphasized by the Suez dispute, has given a further fillip to such construction. When the volumes to be transported fall, specialized rail and road tank vehicles of high capacity are used.

Pipelines are necessarily costly installations: no representative figure can be given, as cost varies considerably with diameter. They were used first to transport crude oil from wells to refinery, and their economy remains primarily in this use, where a large uniform load can be organized. Costs rise almost in inverse ratio with a decline of load; and are much lower in large than small diameter pipes, but even with a 30-in. pipeline (with a capacity of 20 million a year) they are appreciably higher than a small size tanker's costs for a comparable mileage.[1] Large tonnages in a regular flow sufficient to keep a pipeline busy between two specific terminals occur much more often for crude oil than for finished products. Companies opening up new areas commonly have to build pipelines, sometimes of considerable length, to bring crude oil to the coast or to a convenient refining point: and in some circumstances products are sent long distances by pipeline, usually of smaller diameter: Shell for example transport twenty products through a 350-mile pipeline in the United States, along which all the pumping stations are unattended.[2] This implies the transport of large quantities of products to one market—and a distribution terminal with large storage capacity.

The world's tanker fleets in 1956 amounted to 43 million tons, representing a capital investment (plus accumulated depreciation and at replacement costs) of some £2000 millions. A relatively small tanker of

[1] An admirable comparison is given by M. E. Hubbard and D. C. Ion, 'Transport Problem to U.K.' (in *The Post-war Expansion of the U.K. Petroleum Industry*, 1954).

[2] Shell *Survey of Activities for 1955*. Finished products can be sent in batches along a pipeline: the flow is so good that no significant mixture of successive products occurs. This would probably not be true if high viscosity fuel oils were being sent.

18,000 tons costs much more than £1 million, one of 32,000 tons (though cheaper per ton) over £2 million. The trend is towards much larger and faster ones, since costs fall greatly as size and speed increase.[1] For much oil, tanker freights are an important part of the cost. Thus the freight on Middle East oil costing £4. 3s. a ton f.o.b. at Kuwait in the beginning of 1956 was approximately £3. 10s. a ton to the United Kingdom, £4. 5s. a ton to the Eastern seaboard of the United States, £2. 10s. a ton to Italy. On fuel oil from Venezuela to the United Kingdom costing £5 a ton the freight was approximately £2. 5s.

The freight market is notoriously liable to violent fluctuations. But in mid-1956 about 40 % of tanker tonnage belonged to oil companies, and of the remainder about half was on long-term time charter, one-quarter on long-term consecutive voyage charter, one-quarter only on short-term charters or on a single voyage basis. The volume for which the fluctuating 'spot' rates were relevant was thus small. Of new tankers then on order 5·8 million tons were for oil companies, 8·3 million tons for independent shipowners.[2]

At all stages in distribution an advantage has been held by those firms most successful in increasing the size of unit of plant, such as storage tanks, tank lorries, even customers' tanks. Storage facilities are important in the distribution of a product which is used quickly in great bulk but though produced continuously is almost always transported intermittently, either in tankers, or by pipeline in batches, or by road or rail vehicles. Seasonal demands also impose a need for storage, though the amount of oil stored is to be measured in terms of a few weeks' supply, not a few months', because the cost is high. The finance of storage is eased because the peak consumptions in different products, for example petrol in summer and fuel oil in winter, are staggered.

The fact that a refinery always produces joint products in bulk in a fairly inflexible pattern adds, however, to the complexity of its distribution problems. It must dispose of all its products at a fairly even pace: it is only possible for a time to take into stock a larger proportion of its less easily marketed products.[3]

(e) International vertical integration

The various factors so far discussed—the scope for brand marketing over wide areas, the rising unit cost of exploration and production, the

---

[1] Hubbard and Ion, *loc. cit.*, pp. 31–7. The authors state that a 32,000 ton tanker costs 8 % per ton deadweight less than a 16,000 tonner, and requires only sixty crew against fifty in the smaller vessel.   [2] *Petroleum Times*, 8 June 1956, p. 446.

[3] There is little published information on capital costs of distributing. Some of the storage is part of the refineries. The Chase Manhattan survey quoted above (p. 161) estimates capital investment in distribution in Western Europe as $855 million from 1946 to 1955: investment in refining and chemical plants as $1672 million.

economies of large refineries, large-scale transport and storage—favour the growth of large units at each stage in the industry; though they do not imply that every expansion until monopolist units exist will progressively bring net cost reductions. They do mean that except in the final retailing and transport stages no very small new entrant can come in: the capital units required are in general substantial, with partial exceptions for minor developments.[1]

A growth in scale in one stage—especially in refining or selling—may stimulate a growth of scale in others, and benefit as a result. A large refinery for example may justify the building of a large pipeline. This would not in itself require vertical integration. The main impulses to vertical integration are essentially commercial, not (in a narrow sense) technical: the desire for security of supply or markets, and in particular for cheap supply and remunerative markets. The nature of the processes, the high cost of stocking, the high fixed capital cost, put a premium on continuity of operation.

The earliest structural development in the industry which 'hit the headlines' in a big way was the growth of the Standard Oil monopoly in the United States. This was a horizontal expansion in refining and marketing: the company in 1900 had 90 % of the refining, transport and distribution, but about 30 % only of the oilfield operation and little interest in oil lands. This near-monopoly in refining and distribution was largely based on the development and ownership of large-scale transport—pipelines and tank wagons—associated with secret rebates on railways (a tribute to size and vigour). In addition rival building of pipelines was hindered, charges to rivals for the use of Standard's pipelines were high, and vigorous local discriminatory price-cutting tactics on a 'staggered' programme were used to eliminate small rivals piecemeal.

The break-up of Standard Oil in 1911 by antitrust action (it was already losing ground as the industry expanded) was followed by a period in which vertical integration became more important. The independent successor companies into which the original Standard Oil was divided up (on a geographical basis) became more interested in securing crude oil supplies, and invested heavily in 'proven' oil-bearing lands. They soon began to enter each other's territories (sometimes by the purchase of other companies) and established rival national brands. The spread of motor-cars in the 1920's brought an immense growth of the market. New oilmen did well, and invested profits from drilling in subsequent operations. No doubt this, combined with the lurking fears about reserves, prompted the established refiners to forge more vertical links back.

[1] A recent estimate gave £10 million as a minimum for a new venture in production £40 million in refining.

In the late 1930's the twenty major American oil companies had 60% of production, 70 to 80% of refining, and 90% of pipeline operation. Smaller 'independents' were also commonly integrated. The position has not greatly changed.

But during the 1930's the general aspect of affairs was abruptly altered by acute depression, and this brought a new facet into the integration problem. Interest in conserving oil resources which was first stirred by the sensational rise in demand and output was now reinforced by the converse experience. On either count too much oil was being exploited: hence the famous Conservation Laws were introduced into various states (including Texas in 1935; but not California) whereby a small elected commission now decide how much oil shall be produced month by month, basing it on the 'maximum efficiency rate' or 'market demand' whichever is the lower. The force of these state laws received Federal support from the Connally 'Hot Oil' Act, which declared contraband any oil produced in excess of State government quotas.[1] Since these laws restricted operations of all wells equally they could strengthen the position of the small 'independents' who remained numerous and were a powerful voting force in states like Texas.

Outside America the industry's development was largely conditioned by the fact that major industrial countries lacked or seemed to lack deposits of crude oil,[2] and the countries outside America who had great accessible supplies of crude oil lacked capital and industrial skill, as most still do. European countries became importers of oil, at first naturally from America (with Standard Oil, which *was* the American industry, blazing the trail and setting up subsidiaries), but the progress and profits of the American industry naturally stimulated efforts to find other sources, whose development was financed largely from London, The Hague, Paris, Berlin and Vienna, and organized and engineered by merchants and contractors from the same countries. That the Dutch played so large a part was owing to the occurrence of oil in the Dutch East Indies: it was also in this area that the Shell group, originally a London Far Eastern trading concern (Marcus Samuel and Company), came into the trade in 1891, selling Russian oil from Baku in competition with Standard Oil. Standard gave free lamps for which Shell provided the kerosine, so it is said. Royal Dutch started refining in Sumatra in 1892, Shell in Borneo in 1896: and by the end of the decade Shell was trading in Texas oil as well. Between 1910 and 1920

[1] Cf., for example, R. Cassady, *Price Making and Price Behavior in the Petroleum Industry* (1954), pp. 111 ff.

[2] Since the war many European sources have been developed and have proved extensive —the oil produced is important in Austria, Holland, Germany, France and Sicily, and may prove so in Italy. But the importance is for balance of payments reasons: the production is dear. It may have some insurance value.

it became strongly entrenched in Venezuela. Firms producing oil in the newer oilfields usually had to refine it and also to organize its distribution in competition with the ubiquitous American oilmen. The newer firms often had the advantage of crude oil which was cheaper because nearer the markets or cheaper to produce.

By 1920, as demand for motor spirit rose, the bigger American firms became anxious not merely to secure home crude oil supplies by integration but to get overseas supplies; domestic reserves were becoming dear to buy and seemed likely to be insufficient, especially for an export business. Firms had tried to get concessions earlier with little effect. In the 1920's the Standard Oil Company (New Jersey) and the Gulf Oil Corporation became principal holders other than Shell of concessions in Venezuela and became predominant in the rest of South America. Five of the largest of the American 'majors'[1] also progressively secured interests in the Middle East. The determination of the American companies led to the diplomatic struggle by the American government for the 'open door' in mandated territory (namely Mesopotamia). Companies of all countries, the argument ran, should be free to seek concessions, but no concession should be so large as to be exclusive. This conflict was the prelude to American participation in the Iraq Petroleum Company in 1925. Thereafter these few United States companies, integrated at home and selling for export, took an increasing part in developing oilfields outside the United States. These companies acted sometimes in association with each other as joint owners to form a producing company, as Aramco in Saudi Arabia, 1933[2] (jointly owned by Standard Oil (New Jersey), Standard Oil Company of California, The Texas Company, and Socony-Vacuum Oil Company) and The Bahrain Petroleum Company, 1940 (owned by Standard Oil of California and the Texas Company); sometimes in association with British or other foreign concerns (the Kuwait Oil Company, 1934, for example, is jointly owned by The British Petroleum Company and Gulf Oil; in the complex structure of the Iraq Petroleum Company referred to above the American part-owners of $23\frac{3}{4}$% are Standard (New Jersey) and Socony-Vacuum.[3] One Middle East enterprise was recently undertaken by a consortium of ten (now reduced to five) United States 'independents'.[4]

---

[1] The Shell Oil Company, though an American company, is not counted since its Middle East interest was essentially Dutch-English in national affiliation.

[2] The dates given are of the concessions, sometimes to a single part or parts of the operating companies. Socony-Vacuum is now Socony Mobil.

[3] The major American companies in the Middle East were also the chief American operators in South America.

[4] American Independent Oil Company—Aminoil (the largest shareholders being Phillips' Petroleum Company)—and the Paul Getty Company. Cf. John Murray, *The Economic Impact of Oil on the Arab Middle East* (1956), pp. 12–16.

Expansion of Middle East oil from new areas was not rapid before the Second World War.

The situation is complicated further by important long-period contracts of international implications for large supplies made between some major companies. Thus Shell, being rather short of Middle East supplies, contracted to buy a large part of the Gulf share of the Kuwait output for a long period; this was a complicated contract which related the prices paid for the crude oil to the profits earned by Shell on its products in certain markets. In 1947 The British Petroleum Company (then Anglo-Iranian Oil Company) made twenty-year contracts to provide Standard (New Jersey) and Socony-Vacuum with oil from Persia and Kuwait, to be sold in specified areas (some for parts of Europe, some for America) at prices based on 'cost-plus'.[1]

If the outputs of international companies are allocated to their parent companies in proportion to their interests, American companies in 1955 had an output more than twice as large as the British in South America, and about 60 % greater output in the Middle East.

The motive behind the American companies' vertical links in foreign oil centres was partly to secure supplies on a competitive basis for some of their foreign distribution, partly to secure cheap supplies for expanding refining and distribution at home. Only the larger United States companies had the resources or, originally, because of their export trade and foreign distributive organizations, sufficient motive to undertake these immensely costly operations.

3. THE INDUSTRY IN THE UNITED KINGDOM

Against the background of Section 1 the survey of the industry in the United Kingdom falls naturally into two parts—the work of United Kingdom companies outside the United Kingdom, and the activities of United Kingdom and foreign companies inside. Several of the companies in both fields are inevitably the same or interrelated.

(a) British companies' operations overseas

Although little crude oil occurs naturally in Britain and there was little domestic refining till after the Second World War, nevertheless the British—perhaps better called the London—oil industry, as has been seen, took an extremely important part before the war in getting the crude oil and refining it for use in the United Kingdom and elsewhere by, so to say, remote control, through a few large companies

---

[1] For the details cf. *Report to the Federal Trade Commission by its Staff on the International Petroleum Cartel* (1952), ch. III–VII (especially pp. 139 and 149).

whose domicile was in London and much of whose capital was owned in Britain. Before 1914 British interests had contributed much capital to the development of United States refining. As early as 1914 (indeed earlier) it had been thought that for strategic reasons oil supplies must be made secure by government action, at first for the Navy and merchant shipping and later for motor transport and aircraft. Hence in 1914 the government took a 51 % share in the Anglo-Persian Oil Company, now The British Petroleum Company. The present scale of this oversea activity, in weight of oil produced or refined, is shown in Table 3.

Table 3. *Oversea production of petroleum by companies largely British or British-Dutch owned in 1955 (excluding their production in the United States and Canada)*

(Million tons)

	Production of crude petroleum	Total of oil refined	Output of refined products
Europe (excluding United Kingdom)	0·7	29·4	27·9
Middle East	56·7	11·4	10·1
India, Pakistan, Burma	0·8	2·0	1·8
Far East and Australia	10·7	14·8	13·6
Caribbean and South America	43·5	37·7	34·5
Total	122·4	95·3	87·9
World output	786·3	—	—

Almost all the products refined abroad are sold abroad: the companies are engaged in distribution in most countries outside the Russian sphere. The principal group—Royal Dutch-Shell—also participates in the American home market; it probably produces most of the oil (6 % of the total United States output in 1939, 4·1 % in 1955) which is produced there by foreign capital.

The Royal Dutch-Shell group is one of the two largest oil company groups in the world. It has an exceptionally complex structure, whose apex is not one but two holding companies; the Royal Dutch Petroleum Company of The Hague, and The 'Shell' Transport and Trading Company of London. These formed three operating subsidiaries in 1907, the Dutch interest in each being 60 %. After a structural simplification in 1955 the three became two: (a) The Shell Petroleum Company, of London, (b) the Bataafsche Petroleum Maatschappij (B.P.M.) of The Hague. In broad terms the London company deals with commercial, The Hague with technical matters, but the line of demarcation cannot be drawn neatly. Both remain in part operating companies—Shell Petroleum for example buys crude and refined products from the companies operating in the producing areas and supplies oil and products to marketing and refining companies elsewhere, and the B.P.M. directly conducts exploration and production in some areas—but they have in turn become holding companies in a big way, providing expert advice, and co-ordinating. Many subsidiaries operating in particular countries are separately registered companies, often with large shareholdings held locally, and some degree of autonomy. For example two-thirds of the shares of Shell Oil U.S. are held by B.P.M., the remainder by Americans. The Shell Group in 1954 included 440 subsidiaries in which Shell had 50 % or more of the shares. It participated in twenty other companies where the Shell interest was less than one-half. These included for example 23¾ % of the shares of the Iraq Petroleum Company, a share in the consortium which operates the Persian industry (Iranian Oil Participants) and participation with the British Petroleum Company in explorations in Africa and Trinidad. The group also is linked in marketing with B.P. (and with the Canadian Eagle Oil Company) for selling in the British Isles and Africa, and with the Burmah Oil Company in India. The turnover of the Shell Group (excluding minority participations) was £2052 million in 1955, arising primarily from the sale of 92 million tons of products.[1] The turnover was larger than that of the Standard Oil Company (New Jersey), and the recent investments of the Shell Group have also been the larger, though the total nominal investment is smaller.

The gross annual capital expenditure of the group rose from £164 million in 1951 to £283 million in 1955 (part of the increase being due to inflation) and was divided among the main activities as shown in Table 4.

Table 4. *Gross investments of Royal Dutch-Shell Group by sector of industry, 1951–5**

	£ million
Exploration and production	519
Oil refineries and chemical plant	311
Marketing facilities	148
Ocean-going fleets	79
Miscellaneous	24
Total	1,081

* From the *Report of Royal Dutch-Shell Group* in 1955. This did not represent in full the comparative capital expenditure required for the different aspects of the company's activities, since it only partly provided its own tanker requirements. Moreover since the company's marketing outlets were large in relation to its supplies of crude, expenditure on exploration and production may have been rather high.

[1] The Shell Group gross production of crude oil in 1955 was 19 million tons in North America (4% of total United States production), 35 million tons (27%) in South America, 1 million tons (8 %) in Europe, 13 million tons (7 %) in the Middle East and 12 million tons (57 %) in the Far East. It also received for processing 22 million tons, largely from the Middle East under special supply contracts.

The other major British oil company operating abroad is British Petroleum (formerly named Anglo-Iranian, and before that Anglo-Persian), which was among the early companies to develop Middle East oil. Their major refinery at Abadan was lost when Persia decided to nationalize her oil industry; now, as referred to above, an international consortium in which British Petroleum have the largest share (though less than 50 %) operates the Persian industry, and its component participants severally undertake the distribution of the oil. B.P. have in addition other refining interests outside the United Kingdom, the largest being at Aden, with others in Australia, France, Germany, Italy, Belgium and Israel. They have a 50 % interest in Kuwait (the remainder belongs to the Gulf Exploration Company, United States) and like Shell they are 23¾ % shareholders in the Iraq Petroleum Company.

The latter in turn counts as a British company, though as seen above only just under one-half of the capital is British owned (by Shell and B.P.), the remainder belonging to two American companies and one French and to the famous Gulbenkian estate. It is thus a jointly owned 'consortium' of other major oil companies. The I.P.C. has pipelines from its oilfields in Iraq to Tripoli and Banias on the Levant coast, and from its more recently developed South Iraq fields to Fao on the Persian Gulf. It is not a distributing company, its output being handled from there on by the refining and marketing parts of the four partner organizations. It is a non-profit-making company. The oil is sold at cost plus 1s. a ton to the shareholders, who 'post' their price for the oil and sell it to third parties or take it and refine it themselves.[1]

Among other, smaller, companies, the Burmah Oil Company (which has considerable shareholdings in Shell and B.P.) produces and refines in Burma and with Shell operates the largest oil company in India (Burmah-Shell Oil Storage and Distributing Companies). On a smaller scale the Lobitos Oilfields operates in Ecuador and Peru and has a small refinery in the United Kingdom.[2]

Such companies are an important source of income both to the

---

[1] The profits of the I.P.C. are divided on a 50:50 basis with the Iraq government. The profit is calculated according to an agreed formula: posted price less 2 % discount (from 1957, 1 %) less operating costs on a basis agreed when the agreement was made, though subject to revision. The calculated profit accruing to I.P.C. interests is equal to the sum paid to the Iraq government, which in 1956 was £72 million.

[2] Lobitos Oilfields markets its heavier fractions in the main directly through subsidiary merchanting companies: its motor spirit is sold partly through its own agencies, partly by some of the major distributing and producing companies. The Trinidad Leaseholds company until 1956 produced crude oil in Trinidad which it refined locally there with other Caribbean oil, and it was joint owner with Caltex of a distributing company, the Regent Oil Company, in the United Kingdom. It also had Canadian interests. In 1956 it was bought by the Texas Company. This possibly was a reflexion of the great cost involved in creating a market for a refinery in the United Kingdom; the Regent Oil Company was doing this. Cf. below, pp. 190-1.

United Kingdom and the producing countries. How much the United Kingdom income is, it is hard to assess; because apart from distributed profits retained in the United Kingdom and United Kingdom taxation there are also net new investments (as a source of larger future income)[1] and the domicile of the companies is a source of exports—the British oil companies buy plant and supplies extensively in the United Kingdom —also they bring professional work here (for managements, contractors, civil engineers, lawyers and bankers). The value of orders for equipment (excluding ships) either at home or abroad placed by oil companies in recent years is shown in Table 5:

Table 5. *Orders for oil company equipment**

(£ million)

1951	84·0	1954	80·4
1952	91·4	1955	125·5
1953	67·1	1956	153·7

* These are collected by the Oil Companies Materials Secretariat and published by the Council of British Manufacturers of Petroleum Equipment.

(b) *British and foreign firms operating in the United Kingdom*

(i) *Statistics of size and shape.* The physical operations in the oil industry in the United Kingdom are limited almost wholly to importing, refining and distributing. A little crude oil is produced in Nottinghamshire and some prospecting goes on: some shale oil is produced in Scotland, some benzole at coke ovens and analogous works, and a little motor spirit from the operation of Imperial Chemical Industries' hydrogenation plant at Billingham.[2] These supply a small fraction only of the raw material of the British industry.

If these activities be omitted, the numbers engaged in the oil industry, excluding the labour-consuming stage of retail distribution, have changed since the war as shown in Table 6.

[1] The dividends distributed by Shell and B.P. for the years 1951–5, which were paid free of income-tax, were:

	'Shell' Transport and Trading (£ million)	British Petroleum (£ million)
1951	6·5	3·2
1952	8·2	3·9
1953	8·2	4·7
1954	9·8	8·8
1955	12·3	15·1

[2] It is marketed by Shell-Mex and B.P. and by the Esso Petroleum Company.

This points to the outstanding transformation in the British industry since the war—the growth of domestic refining. Employment in it remained at the end only one-half of that in wholesale distribution. The slight fall in this from 1951 to 1955 was also, in its way, a striking change, because the volume of business handled was rapidly growing: the tonnage of finished products sold was 14 million tons in 1947, and rose fairly steadily to 27 million tons in 1955. The fall in employment from 1951 to 1955 corresponded with a rise of about 30 % in the volume of sales.

Table 6. *Employment in the oil industry, 1948–55*

	1948	1951	1955
Refining	7,387	12,126	16,700
Wholesale distribution	*	36,692	35,977

* Figures for 1948 are not available, but are not very different from those for 1951.

Those employed in retail distribution fall into two categories. (Or it may be three: because some supplies to ultimate consumers are made by merchants who probably count statistically as wholesalers: but where, as happens, these sell to, say, farmers, it is close to retailing.) There are petrol filling stations, which are basically retailing outlets for petrol but often also do repairs to cars; and shops which sell parafin, as part of a more general retailing business, for household purposes. Only the first can qualify as part of the oil industry, and then only because in fact the links with producing and refining are intimate. The numbers employed can only be guessed. There are (end-1956) about 30,000 filling stations.[1] The average number of persons employed per station, when the Census of Distribution was taken in 1950, was three for filling stations which did no repair work, six for filling stations which did repair work. The enumeration in the Census was not complete enough to give a total of persons employed in all stations. The number of stations doing repairs considerably exceeded the number which did not. Since 1950 filling stations have become larger and more numerous, but there are no comprehensive statistics. If the average size of a 'pure' filling station is used as a notional average for all stations it could be argued that the number employed in retailing rose from, say, 85,000 in 1951 to 95,000 in 1955. But filling stations in reality employed far more people, and had a considerable net output beyond the sale of petrol. The full employment in petrol stations must be around 150,000.

To return to Table 6, employment in refineries in 1951 was in fifteen

[1] Stations with more than one pump. Sites with one pump only are normally adjuncts to some other major activity, as for example hotels.

establishments. The number tends to be static. Employment in wholesale distribution in 1950[1] was by 157 firms, whose total sales were
£577 million. Of these eighteen accounted for £500 million, and eight
of these for £399 million. No subdivision for a later date is available,
but the picture which emerges is a simple one. The main forces in
wholesale distribution comprise a small group of large oil companies
(the major British and American international companies) who are
also the main force in refining: but the number of smaller merchants
and the size of their business is considerable.

Because of vagaries in the relations of prices of crude and refined oil
respectively which will be discussed later the net output of the oil
industry in Britain is not satisfactorily measured in published statistics.
Between 1951 and 1955, for example, the gross output of oil refineries
rose from £181 million to £303 million; the net output from £3·7
million to £43·1 million. The first net output at least is a flukish result,
and it is not possible rationally to assess the industry's relative importance on such figures.

(ii) *The United Kingdom market for oil.* The development of consumption of oil for different uses in the United Kingdom is shown in
Table 7.

The most striking change, since before the war, but also since 1947,
is the decline in the relative importance of motor spirit. This is only
slightly counterbalanced by a large increase in use of diesel engine road
vehicle fuel (from which the name 'derv' fuel has been derived). The two
combined accounted for nearly three-fifths of total use (by weight) in
1938 but only just over a third in 1955. (In terms of value, before tax,
their importance was greater: two-thirds of the total value in 1938, and
nearly one-half in 1955.) The main large increases in consumption were
in shipping, industrial steam raising, various industrial furnace processes, gas-works, and for oil refining itself. Use for mobile diesel engines
(for example compressors in road work and contracting) expanded
seven-fold over 1938 but the total used remains relatively modest. The
principal consumption in manufacturing industry is in metallurgical,
glass and ceramic furnaces: the steel industry used over 1·5 million
tons in 1955.

The change in proportionate importance reflects in part the indirect restriction on the supply of motor-cars to the home market by purchase tax
and until 1953 by steel allocations related to exports, the low expenditure
on roads, limited licensing of road haulage vehicles and buses, and the
impact of taxes on motor fuel. Demand for motor spirit and diesel fuel
for road vehicles is determined primarily by the number of vehicles in

---

[1] These figures are based on the Census of Distribution. They do not absolutely match
with the table, but they refer to an employment of just over 34,000.

Table 7. *Use of petroleum products*

(Thousand tons)

	1938	1947	1950	1955	1956
Transport					
Motor spirit (A)	4,831	4,594	5,195	6,240	6,324
Aviation fuels (A and D)	113	283	468	1,698	1,754
Diesel oil for road vehicles (B)	387	701	1,034	1,601	1,797
Bunkers (B and C)	1,333	1,957	2,228	4,074	4,436
Marine craft (inland, fishing, coastal) (B and C)	65	171	430	701	790
Railways (a) Public ⎱ (B and C)	7	35	10	16	18
(b) Industrial ⎰		9	12	21	22
Total	6,736	7,550	7,377	14,351	15,141
Power					
Stationary diesel engines (B and C)	219	299	347	639	748
Mobile diesels (B and C)	43	137	219	316	346
Steam raising (industrial) (B and C)	103	633	982	1,580	2,185
Vaporizing oil (for tractors) (D)	178	843	801	689	574
Total	543	1,912	2,349	3,224	3,853
Heating (B and C)					
Industrial furnaces	336	1,034	1,535	2,657	2,856
Central heating (a) Private homes	20	17	30	62	94
(b) Other	225	184	335	786	1,081
Total	778	1,235	1,899	3,505	4,031
Gas-works (for gas making)	130	684	540	536	463
Oil refining—own use	183	343	650	2,060	2,157
Lubricants	560	665	749	887	895
Domestic lighting, heating and cooking (D) (except central heating)	407	457	408	558	711
Feedstock for chemicals	—	12	215	566	666
Bitumen	607	424	621	865	941
Miscellaneous	373	601	706	756	802
Grand total	10,320	14,083	17,505	27,308	29,660
Exports	592	644	1,198	6,283	7,700

Note: A = light spirits; B = diesel or gas oils; C = fuel oils; D = kerosine.

use; and while this number could become closely dependent on relatively small variations in the price of fuel it has not so far. The relative costs of motor spirit and 'derv' fuel, however, are likely to affect the choice of car or lorry markedly when taxation is high. A diesel engine involves higher capital outlay but gives more miles to the gallon: as fuel prices rise it becomes more attractive. Since motor spirit is dearer in the United Kingdom than in the United States the development of cars with low petrol consumption per mile is more encouraged. High rates of taxation are thought to have increased demand for premier petrols, which give more miles to the gallon.[1]

[1] A. L. King, 'The Effect of Taxation on Consumption of Petroleum' in *The Post-War Expansion of the U.K. Petroleum Industry.*

The other uses of oil almost all involve a more direct competition with alternative sources of heat or power (apart from lubricating oil, where the demand must be largely a function of the use of machinery) so that except in conditions of scarcity demand would be likely to be more elastic in the short period. For furnaces and boiler heating and the provision of static power, users have a choice between oil, coal, gas and electricity when installing new plant, and sometimes can adapt existing plant to or from oil. For some uses oil has technical advantages over other fuels: thus the use of oil for open hearth steel furnaces in place of producer gas allows continuous working since the flues do not have to be cleaned at week-ends, and provides a more luminous flame with better heat transfer.[1] The gains through the use of oil have to be measured against the higher cost of the fuel: in several British works they have, at various dates, not been thought sufficient. The major gain has been more steel from a furnace.

This is one typical situation. The substitution of oil- for coal-firing of boilers presents a somewhat simpler problem. The end result (i.e. the quantity of steam raised) is the same. The substitution may require no more than the installation of oil burners in place of the normal grate, and of storage tanks: boilers can be built to use both coal and oil. A boiler specially designed to use oil only will probably have dimensions adjusted to the character of flame produced by the fuel and be more efficient in the use of oil. The use of oil for an increasing range of industrial purposes has required a considerable design effort, to which oil companies have contributed much in extending their markets.

For some uses—as already remarked—the price of oil is loaded with heavy taxation. This is notably so for motor fuels. Here the tax was imposed as a payment for the roads: but with vehicle licence fees it now much exceeds the current expenditure on road maintenance and development. It can be argued that the extra is payment for the acquisition and development of roads in the past: but it is not a serious calculation, and the alteration of the tax for budgetary convenience shows the readiness of governments to depart from the rigours of a rational price economy when convenient. This is illustrated more forcibly by the high taxes maintained on light hydrocarbons used for industrial purposes, for the manufacture, for example, of plastics, rubber compounds, rubber adhesives, paint, polishes, varnishes, linoleum and wallpaper, and for dry cleaning and weed killing. Imported spirits are taxed 2s. 6d. a gallon, home produced spirit 1s. 3d. a gallon. With an

---

[1] Oil had largely replaced producer gas in America before the war: it has advanced in the United Kingdom since the war. Meantime in the United States natural gas has largely displaced oil in open hearth furnaces, and electric furnaces have gained a little at the expense of open hearth.

odd inconsequence heavy oils (diesel and fuel oils) are specifically free from tax if not used for automotive purposes.

Though the relative advance of industrial uses of oil fuels must be attributed primarily to the advantages offered by them in relation to their comparative cost, and to their greater availability with the spread of domestic refining, it has also gained something and is likely to gain more from the unexpectedly slow recovery of the coal industry, while increases in demand for fuel and power have been higher than was expected by the more influential prophets. The coal position was a greater force throughout the post-war years in countries deprived of coal imports—like Sweden—and its force in Britain was lessened by the policy of keeping coal prices low. From 1946 onwards the use of oil was often advocated as a means of meeting what was treated as a temporary scarcity of coal, gas and electricity; after 1953 (when Europe seemed for a brief period on the verge of a coal surplus) the attitude rapidly changed, and oil came to be regarded as the fuel to fill the 'energy gap' expected in the two or three decades before nuclear power could become a major source of energy.[1]

The conviction became more widespread that rapid economic expansion was not merely or mainly a reflex of reconstruction and re-armament but a durable outcome of population growth, technical advance and fuller employment and 'Point Four' policies. There was a spate of estimates of world fuel consumption in terms of coal equivalent till 1975 or 2000, with upper and lower levels. All assumed a faster rate of growth than from 1900 to 1950, and the net result for oil seemed that Europe would need to double supplies within ten years. 'Probable consumption' glided into a 'requirement', and private enterprisers talked like planners.

What happened in Britain over this happened also in Europe, though not in the United States. This was largely because in most of Europe fuel oil played a part as a supplement to or replacement of coal which in the United States was played by natural gas. Refining policy in the United States concentrated on raising the yield of motor spirit. The immense growth in use of motor spirit in the United States brought with it a great growth of industrial oil supplies while the proportion of motor spirit refined from crude went on increasing. Natural gas was an immense additional source of power: and in general Americans, now regularly exporting coal to Europe, felt no pressure to fill an 'energy gap' of their own whether by diverting more oil to industry or by

---

[1] It was possible to import coal from the United States, and there have been large imports. Since the B.Th.U. content of a ton of oil appreciably exceeds that of coal, and also because it is easier to handle, oil is a 'better' import when freights are a large item in the cost. But coal may be needed for existing equipment. Coal prospects looked better by 1957.

introducing nuclear plants for practical ends before, as they thought, the economic way of doing so had been evolved.[1] They were concerned to make their supplies of oil secure (which meant strengthening their position in the Middle East) because domestic use increasingly exceeded home production and larger imports were needed—but the requirement was largely determined by the prospective demand for motor and aviation spirit.

In Britain the problem in 1955–6 was seen differently. When policy was being discussed fuel oil was no longer treated as a residual product for which it was desirable to find an outlet: it was a product whose supply should be increased for its own sake. This was part of the fuel policy advocated by the Ministry of Fuel and Power, who intervened, for example, to persuade the Central Electricity Authority to use more oil.[2] It is questionable whether such intervention would have been needed if coal prices had been allowed to 'find their market value'.

The 'imperfections' of the market on the demand side have already been pointed out. Government policy weighed heavily on the supply of motor-cars and lorries, by steel allocation policies until 1953, by purchase-tax policies more continuously, and by road haulage licensing regulations always; and the influence of price was distorted by taxes on motor fuel and light hydrocarbons and by government pressure to keep coal gas and electricity prices down (much lower than a 'competitive' money economy required). Possibly largely as an outcome of nationalization the government tended to rely on direct action and persuasion to encourage the greater use of fuel oil: though no doubt when it finally decided to push the use of oil almost to take the pressure off the coal industry it became more ready to accept higher prices for coal.

(iii) *United Kingdom imports of oil.* Until the end of the Second World War the physical operations of the oil industry in Britain were restricted almost wholly to importing and distribution. Some lubricating oil was blended, and practically all the bitumen used (some 600,000 tons) was

---

[1] In discussions of oil policy in 1944–5 Americans referred vigorously to the prospect that atomic energy would take the place of other fuels—including fuel oil—as a source of heat, for example for electric power generation. (Cf. *Petroleum in War and Peace*, papers presented by the Petroleum Administration for War to the Special Senate Committee to investigate Petroleum Resources, Washington, 28–30 November 1945, for example pp. 187–8, 'Residual fuel oil is a product of which the oil industry will probably be making a smaller and smaller percentage. The industry's lowest priced product, the trend is towards cracking and hydrogenating it out of existence. By the time atomic energy enters the power plant it may find little or no residual fuel oil to oust' (R. K. Davis). The author is informed, however, that no oil company allowed its refinery building policy to be influenced by the prospect of nuclear energy.

[2] Some oil company spokesmen still felt, however, in 1956—before Suez—that the government was insufficiently committed to a permanent policy of coal to oil conversion, and to a price policy consistent with it. The Suez experience introduced new undertones into the discussion.

produced in the United Kingdom (mainly for road asphalt), but production of the main bulk product, motor spirit, was trivial, about 6% of the total used in 1938.

During the Second World War dependence on imports was even greater; there was less home refining, and at the close a much larger consumption than before the war, the increase being mainly for service use. After the Second World War the dependence on oversea refining was rapidly reduced. Consumption, it has been seen, remained higher after the war than before, and grew faster, a growing proportion being for uses other than as motor spirit. This involved a large further growth in imports, but after 1947 there was a rapid rise in crude imports and from 1948 a fall, rapid though with interruptions, in imports of refined products. One major distributor (Regent) still relied solely on imports in 1956, but was planning to build a refinery. The trends are shown in Table 8.

Table 8. *Imports of oil into the United Kingdom, 1946–56*

(Yearly or annual averages, in million tons)

	Crude*	Refined		Crude*	Refined
1920–4	0·9	3·8	1949	6·0	11·5
1925–9	2·2	5·2	1950	9·2	9·9
1930–4	1·6	7·4	1951	16·7	9·8
1934–9	2·1	8·9	1952	22·8	6·0
1946	2·2	12·2	1953	25·6	6·1
1947	2·5	10·6	1954	28·2	6·6
1948	4·6	13·2	1955	28·0	8·6
			1956	28·6	9·4

* Includes process oils for further refining.

This change was accompanied by another, the progressive growth in importance of imports from the Middle East and the diminution of imports from the Western hemisphere. This was partly determined by the desire to reduce dollar expenditure: but it would have been imposed in large degree by the growing trend in the United States to import oil—partly to conserve their own reserves, which were far inferior to those of the Middle East—and by the low costs of Middle East oil. The United States drew imports first from the Caribbean, and then increasingly from the Middle East. The increased imports of crude oil since the war to Europe in general, and Britain in particular, have been almost exclusively from the Middle East (until the pattern was interfered with by the Suez affair). Imports of some finished products continued to come into Britain from the Western hemisphere, partly as noted above because one major distributor relied on imports, partly because European refineries have not produced certain products either at all or in sufficient quantities. Thus marketing companies with British refineries have chosen to import some refined products (and export others) and the Middle East refineries could not supply what was needed.[1]

Table 9. *Imports of oil by origin*

	Crude			Refined		
	1947	1955	1956	1947	1955	1956
Origin	(million gallons)*			(million gallons)*		
United States	11	16	142	823	330	355
Venezuela	101	616	714	98	232	209
Netherlands Antilles	222	247	232	1,024	493	413
Trinidad	—	7	3	234	367	431
Iran	155	376†	846†	422	n.a.	32
Kuwait	}44	4,202	3,785	—	—	—
Bahrain, Qatar		429	554	54	144	197
Iraq	—	1,006	710	—	—	—
Saudi Arabia	61	90	152	—	—	—
Netherlands	—	—	—	neg.	331	404
All sources	616	6,834	7,045	2,636	2,259	2,496

n.a. = not available.   neg. = negligible.

* 1 ton of crude oil = 250 gallons; of heavy fuel oil, 240 gallons; of diesel and gas oil, 267 gallons; of kerosine, 276 gallons; of motor spirit, 310 gallons.
† Other foreign countries—but mainly Iran.

(iv) *Oil refining in the United Kingdom.* The most dramatic aspect of the oil industry within the United Kingdom since the war has been the expansion of oil refining. This has been illustrated in the change in imports. The increase in the 'through-put' of crude and process oil in British refineries is set out in Table 10.

Table 10. *Crude and process oils (including shale) refined in the United Kingdom, 1938 and 1946–56*

(Thousand tons)

1938	2,427	1950	9,314
1945	1,488	1951	16,481
1946	2,527	1952	22,518
1947	2,625	1953	25,425
1948	4,490	1954	28,077
1949	6,194	1955	27,597
		1956	28,681

The output of the refineries after the expansion followed an entirely different pattern from the pre-war pattern—because pre-war refining was mainly directed to production of a few special products, though since the process always yields joint products the range of products actually made was fairly wide.

[1] This was accentuated by nationalization in Iran.

Table 11. *Output of finished products, 1938, 1955, 1956*

(Thousand tons)

	1938	1955	1956
Aviation and motor spirit	316	6,875	6,771
Kerosine	127	803	869
Gas/diesel oils	378	4,584	5,189
Fuel oils	644	12,355	12,526
Lubricants	158	706	776
Bitumen	613	851	933
Liquefied gases	2	58	66
Industrial and white spirits	30	137	136
Waxes	12	18	19
Miscellaneous and loss	112	1,211	1,394
Total	2,392	27,599	28,681

This expansion of refining has been carried out mainly by the largest United Kingdom and leading United States oil companies. It required a complete change in their policies, and as late as 1944 the proposal to extend domestic refining was highly controversial. The companies regarded the pre-war pattern as having been essentially right. Oil, they argued, is normally best refined where it is extracted; refining uses up part of the crude as fuel (6 to 7 %) and there are wastes (1 to 2 %); it is better not to transport needlessly the 7 to 9 % of crude oil: and location at the oilfield gives the advantage of flexibility in distribution of finished products. For example, Abadan could send more motor spirit to Australia and more fuel oil to Norway according to demand.

In some forms refined oil or processed oil was much more costly to transport than crude—lubricating oil, for instance, carried in cans not tankers, and bitumen. These would often best be processed near the consuming market. Before the war these were the principal products of refining in the United Kingdom. They were made usually not from full crudes, but from oil already partly refined. Among the factors which deterred oil companies from refining in Britain before the war was the fact that taxation was lower elsewhere: but it was probably a minor factor.

The British government, along with most European governments, thought of domestic refining after the Second World War as a means of saving dollars and foreign exchange. Apart from this, as the British (and European) markets for oil grew rapidly and the supply had to be based largely on Middle East crudes, the advantages of domestic refining rapidly increased. The argument that transport costs were unfavourable had always probably been somewhat overplayed. Since the demand for oil was rapidly expanding companies did not now have to think of finding an outlet for spare capacity. Many more refineries were needed —somewhere—most of them to refine Middle East crudes. New refineries in Britain would not mean surplus refining capacity in the oilfields, and the companies would have found it hard to expand refining quickly enough in the Middle East fields, where it was necessary to build houses and other amenities as well as refineries and where it is difficult quickly to increase the supply of technicians. These difficulties are acute too in Venezuela. To build refineries in Britain therefore saved time and, on one estimate, halved the capital cost in the first post-war decade. Politically the refineries were more secure.[1]

More general considerations probably favoured the location of refining in the United Kingdom. The components into which crude oil is manufactured are not all in forms which are required, or used, or can be carried, in tanker loads.[2] This applied not merely to bitumen and lubricating oil but, for example, to some of the white spirits, to wax products, to raw materials in general for the chemical industry (for plastics, solvents, glycerine, etc.) and to refinery gases—which were likely to have a higher value away from the oilfield unless the oilfield had a large industrial hinterland. There was no simple presumption in favour of refining on the oilfield when the receiving market was large enough to permit the building of refineries of efficient size located so that distribution costs were not excessive. The centre of gravity of refining moved into consuming centres in the United States before the war. The British market for all the products has been large enough since the war to allow the building of several fairly large refineries fairly widely scattered. The list given in Table 12 includes new and old refineries: but most are new or greatly expanded.

In discussions since 1944 it has been accepted that 1 million tons is a minimum for efficient working, and clearly production costs are lower in plants whose capacity is above that size, the savings being probably more significant in respect of capital costs than in processing costs. In the United States several refineries have a through-put of over 10 million tons capacity. A balance must be struck between higher distribution costs (these will be larger in any circumstances for a larger refinery which, other things being equal, including the location of rivals, must distribute farther afield if it has more to sell) and lower production costs.[3]

---

[1] Politics have affected refinery programmes in various ways. Thus decisions to build refineries in Ceylon and in Ireland in the later 1950's both probably reflect concessions to government pressure: the size of market would hardly justify it economically.

[2] Larger tankers with lowest freights would bring in too much of any finished product.

[3] The suggestion has been made that a refinery with a crude oil through-put of 300,000 tons only could be economical if it was designed to provide fuel oil for an adjacent power station. It would market most of its other products (e.g. its motor spirit) through other large distributing organizations, and would do no research or development. It is half analogous to, for example, a pharmaceutical firm that may tablet aspirin but develops no new products. However, it is not generally accepted that this would 'pay'. This theory assumes simple distillation only, and the existence of the more broadly based industry doing the research and development and distribution.

Table 12. *Oil refineries in Britain, 1956*

Areas	Company	Capacity per annum (thousand tons)
Thames Estuary		
Isle of Grain	British Petroleum	4,600
Shell Haven	Shell	3,750
Coryton	Mobil Oil	1,750
Kingsnorth	Berry Wiggins	100
Ellesmere Port and Manchester Ship Canal		
Stanlow	Shell	5,150
Ellesmere Port	Lobitos	190
Barton	Manchester Oil Refinery	150
Weaste	Berry Wiggins	80
Southampton		
Fawley	Esso	8,000
South Wales		
Llandarcy	British Petroleum	3,000
North-West Coast		
Heysham	Shell	1,800
Scotland		
Grangemouth	British Petroleum	2,200
Dundee	William Briggs	35
Ardrossan	Shell	160
Pumpherston	Scottish Oils (B.P.)	180

Note: The Regent Oil Company has plans to build a refinery at Hook, close to the Solent; and Esso has a project for building at Milford Haven.

The choice of refinery sites in the United Kingdom was influenced by the pattern of pre-war distribution, when the major ports were naturally the main centres of distribution; the use of readily available sites adjacent or close to existing importing facilities, with some storage capacity, some dock facilities, and power supplies, made it easier to get off the mark quickly. When the locations were chosen the standard tankers were still relatively small; the fast increase in the size of tankers was not foreseen. The choice of Southampton for Esso's Fawley refinery, which was not among the first to be built after the war, gave scope for the use of very large tankers.

How far the ports selected are ideally located in relation to the centres of gravity of consumption no published data show. For fuel oil alone in 1955 nearly 40 % of consumption was in regions (the North-East, Northern, North Midland and Midland regions of the Ministry of Fuel and Power) not directly served by any of the major ports where the refineries are located. Parts of these regions could be effectively reached by coastal tanker: but where they have to be reached by road tanker, or rail or sea and road, then it might be expected that transport costs were rather high. Refineries on deep water at Hull or Immingham and on

Tyne and Tees would partly compensate for this, though the tanker freights would be slightly dearer than to London, Southampton or the Welsh ports. Recent plans for building an oil port and refinery at Milford Haven reflect the new recognition of the value of very deep water. The location looks remote as a distributing centre; pipelines to Llandarcy and Birmingham are visualized.

It is sometimes argued that the correct way of supplying the heart of the Midlands would be to pipe crude oil to inland refineries. The decision to pipe oil from Milford Haven to the Llandarcy refinery, in order to benefit from the use of the largest tankers, lends support indirectly to this view. While there are no published cost data[1] the preference of some oil companies for coastal and inland water transport when it is available points forcibly to the burdensomeness of road transport, though this is, of course, very flexible.

In oil refining capital costs are extremely heavy and processing costs relatively light. The Census of Production provides a record of investment in the industry from 1948 onwards. The figures as published did not include expenditure on unfinished refineries until 1950, when additional data for these were given separately. The following table includes these, and gives the figures in 1955 prices as well as the prices current at the time the work was done.

Table 13. *Capital investment in oil refining, 1948–55*

	In prices then current (£ million)	In 1955 prices (£ million)
1948	6	9
1949	18	25
1950	32	42
1951	35	41
1952	40	42
1953	34	36
1954	16	16
1955	13	13
Total	194	225

This investment corresponded with an increase in the through-put of crude oil from 4·5 million tons to 28 million tons. This suggests that roughly speaking the cost of investment in refining is approximately £10 per ton of average finished product per year. (The average value of the finished product was about £11 a ton in 1954, ranging from £7 for fuel oil to £10 for diesel oil, £13 for gas oil, £17 for motor spirit, £21 for lubricating oils, to over £30 for some special products.) But

[1] For pipeline economics cf. above, p. 165.

obviously this is of limited significance; refineries are of different types, and it is necessary to differentiate between the investment needed for, for example, catalytic cracking or platforming or hydroforming, and to be able to isolate the added cost of making higher octane spirits and special products. However, taking 15 % as a reasonable estimate for depreciation, obsolescence, interest or profit, the average capital expenditure would imply a capital 'cost' in 1954 prices for fixed capital only of 30s. a ton of 'average oil': more, obviously, for motor spirit, less for fuel oil—but how much less or more is obscure.[1]

The conversion costs, on whatever basis calculated, are low.[2]

Table 14. *Conversion costs in oil refining*
(United Kingdom)

(£ thousand)

	1952	1953	1954
Processing materials			
(a) Tetraethyl-lead	1,732	2,533	2,478
(b) Chemicals*	2,103	2,398	3,087
(c) Water	418	426	305
Packing materials: drums, etc.	661	721	890
Other purchased materials†	2,475	3,176	5,238
Fuel and electricity (purchased)	1,716	2,233	2,193
Wages	4,684	5,619	6,557
Salaries	1,871	2,195	2,587
National insurance superannuation and pensions schemes	911	1,148	1,340
Total	16,561	20,449	24,675
Tonnage of finished products (thousands)	21,583	24,344	26,915
Average processing costs (per ton)	15s. 3d.	16s. 9d.	18s. 4d.

* Such as sulphuric acid, fuller's earth, various catalysts, etc., chemicals for laboratory work, etc.

† This would presumably include materials for repairs and maintenance, which would be a heavy expense.

The wage and salary bill shows oil refining as an industry which employs few workers, where the output per man in tons is high. The change from 1948 to 1954 shown in Table 15 indicates the growth in 'productivity' in its simple-minded sense with the building of the new large refineries.

[1] The problem of attributing costs between joint products is insoluble: but there are specific additional costs in increasing output of motor spirit or raising its octane rating, which should be calculable, though with difficulty.

[2] Here the assumption is that 'blending materials', as described in the Census of Production, added in refineries are themselves commonly refinery products or their equivalent—benzole from coke ovens, for example. Chemical additions such as tetraethyl-lead fall into a different category, though they should no doubt be treated as a raw material. They are, however, included here as a conversion cost.

Table 15. *Output per man in oil refining*

	1948	1955
Number of operatives	5,890 (£368)*	12,400 (£590)
Number of other workers	1,883 (£418)	4,300 (£698)
All workers	7,773 (£380)	16,700 (£623)
Finished product output per man (tons)	486	1,580

* Figures in brackets give average annual earnings.

Although the rise in output per worker was continuous in this period the movement in 'net output' per worker in the Census of Production sense was erratic, falling from £923 in 1948 to £638 in 1949, £577 in 1950 and £303 in 1951. Thereafter it rose to £932, £1510, £2410 and £2580 from 1952 to 1955. These quite erratic figures are explained mainly by the way in which the values of the input and output of the refining industry are determined, which will be dealt with later, though a contributing factor was the introduction of new plant brought into use throughout this period. (The low figure for 1951 is an average which conceals the fact that for the East, Southern, Welsh and Scottish regions net output was negative!)

The net output provides or should provide the source both for payments of wages and salaries and for depreciation, interest, obsolescence and profits (and other payments too, of course). The following figures show the amount left for covering 'capital costs' after wages and salary costs were covered in the years 1948–54. It will be observed that this amount fell far short of the 30s. a ton calculated above as the 'reasonably low' figure for capital costs.

Table 16. *Margin for capital costs (per ton of crude oil through-put)*

	Net output (a)		Wages and salaries (b)		Outside limit of margin for capital costs (a) − (b)	
	s.	d.	s.	d.	s.	d.
1948	31	6	8	9	22	9
1949	17	0	11	0	6	0
1950	11	6	8	0	3	6
1951	4	8	6	5	−1	9
1952	10	0	6	0	4	0
1953	16	0	6	5	9	7
1954	26	6	6	10	19	8
1955	31	3	7	6	23	9

Despite the nominal profitlessness of this refining relatively little difficulty seems to have been found in providing the necessary capital. As the list of refineries shows, most was provided by the major oil groups: Shell, British Petroleum and Esso. In addition Socony-Vacuum, who in Britain had hitherto imported only stock oils to compound into lubricants (though producers of crude oil in the United States with Middle East participations, and refiners and distributors on a wide international scale) joined with Cory Brothers and Company (who were a coal and oil marketing subsidiary of Powell Duffryn, the former chief coal producer in South Wales) to build a moderate-sized refinery on the Thames. Here part of the capital presumably came from the compensation paid to 'P.D.' for their loss of coal-mining properties. This, like the three major investing groups, was, by virtue of Socony-Vacuum's position in the United States, a vertical integration; and apart from the capital drawn from compensation, in this instance the source of the capital for the refinery was in the profits and accumulated resources of an integrated concern, with a substantial initial contribution from the Finance Corporation for Industry (F.C.I.). The demands on the resources of the joint parents were so heavy that 'P.D.' drew out. The company, now Mobil Oil, though British, is a wholly-owned subsidiary of the American firm which provided capital for the refinery. The Caltex refinery at Hook will presumably be financed by the American parents.

What proportion of the capital for the new refineries came from the United Kingdom, what proportion from the United States, it would be hard to identify. The practice in the international groups is for investment funds to be accumulated at the centre and to be invested without reference to their country of origin. Designs came almost entirely from America, and a great deal of the plant itself was made either by the leading American firms in this field or by British firms using American patents and 'know-how'. A number of American plant makers opened subsidiary design and engineering offices in the United Kingdom. At the end of the major programme the refinery plant-making industry had been considerably built up in the United Kingdom.[1] British ownership of much equipment abroad had, as remarked earlier, brought many orders for plant and supplies to this country: but the most specialized oil industry equipment had been brought from the United States, which was the technical birthplace of the industry. Hence these oversea oilfields always required dollar expenditure, and 'sterling area oil' cost some dollars.

(v) *Marketing oil in the United Kingdom.* Before the expansion of refining, the oil industry in its domestic manifestations mainly imported oil and distributed it. Some companies did both. Some large importing concerns set up separate distributing companies. Some importers sold partly to wholesale merchants, of whom there were a large number scattered round the country; many operated in ports, using their own wharves and storage. Other imports were sold to concerns who applied

[1] See above, p. 174.

finishing processes such as the manufacture of bitumens or the blending of lubricating oils; while still others were sold direct to large users—gas and transport companies, shipping and so forth. The older part of the Stanlow and Fawley refineries were for bitumen manufacture. C. C. Wakefield and Company was the principal company applying finishing processes to produce lubricating oils, and became the largest firm in the world specializing in lubricants, with a considerable business abroad. The lubricating oil business, narrowly specialized but highly profitable, attracted many companies: there were still some 600 of varying sizes, most of course small, in 1956.

Marketing presents diverse problems for different oil products varying according to the scale and frequency of purchases, the precision of specification, the buying skill of consumers, the pressure of demand and its responsiveness to advertisement. Final sales to consumers are often by partially or wholly independent retailers who buy in bulk from the main distributor, or (rarely) from an intermediary.

The nature of the marketing problems and the pattern of the distributing organization have been considerably changed in certain respects by the building of the refineries. First, it is now necessary for the distributing companies associated with the companies who own the refineries to market the whole range of a refinery's products—in the United Kingdom if possible, otherwise in export markets. (Some refining of high value products has possibly been planned for export; and some exports of blending or chemical base materials for use in oversea refineries are also planned by big groups that can specialize in their various refineries on different products and derive advantages of larger-scale operations by inter-plant trading.[2]) Previously it was possible to import according to the size of market for different products: it might be commercially interesting for refiners to try and build up demands for the less easily sold of their refinery products, but it was not so exigent a problem before the products were actually produced in the United Kingdom.

This difficulty has not had to be faced equally by all the distributing groups. One, Regent Oil Company[3], has so far (till 1957) remained

---

[1] Retailing varies in character: thus sales of petrol or domestic paraffin are on a smaller scale than sales of tractor oil for farmers, which is now being organized to an increasing extent through special dealers. Shell-Mex and B.P. sell burning oil, power-paraffin and all products for the agricultural market normally through 'authorized distributors' who are in part wholesalers, in part retailers.

[2] The Shell refineries at Pernis (Holland), Stanlow, Shell Haven, and even Cardon (Venezuela) inter-trade in this way.

[3] See above, p. 173. The Regent Company was formed as a 50:50 subsidiary of Trinidad Leaseholds and Caltex (itself a subsidiary of the Texas Oil Company and Standard Oil of California. Texas Oil bought up Trinidad Oil in 1956. Treasury, *Trinidad Oil Company: Proposed Purchase by the Texas Company*, Cmd. 9790, H.M.S.O. 1956).

outside the refinery business in the United Kingdom, though it has plans to build a refinery. As an importer it has been able to concentrate on building up markets, without having to face the problem of disposing of a balanced assortment of oils on a scale to make a refinery 'pay'. The signs are that the firm will build up vigorously the desirable pattern of outlets so that this will exist when its refinery is built.[1] The reverse procedure was followed by Mobil Oil, who before the war (as Vacuum Oil) sold only lubricating oil, which they imported into the United Kingdom. The new Coryton refinery thus did not have a motor spirit or fuel oil distributing organization to rest on: the company has proceeded to build one up (it has relied on two existing large wholesale coal and oil merchant companies to market fuel oil).

A second repercussion of the refinery programme on the pattern of selling has been to weaken the position of the small wholesalers. Possibly the restriction on dollar purchases has been most potent, as it cut off their free access to independent suppliers from the Gulf. Moreover Middle East oil, handled entirely by the large groups, has become the cheaper oil. Most of the small merchants appear now to have gathered into two groups—the Petrofina group, and the E. A. Gibson group. Though both are importers, both buy largely from British suppliers (mainly from Shell-Mex and B.P.). The Petrofina group is the most conspicuous, because it sells motor spirit. It is also international, having started (in 1920) as a marketing organization selling Roumanian oil in Belgium. It bought its first English company in 1939, but soon lost its oil source. It has grown since in the United Kingdom by progressive amalgamations, and outside the United Kingdom also.[2] In combines the merchants now grouped have proved strong buyers.

The sale of motor spirit is the most familiar sales activity of the oil companies. Part is sold—inconspicuously, though it is a large part—to large users, the government, bus companies, large road hauliers or taxi companies and any concern which runs a lot of cars or lorries from a central garage. Two-thirds or more is distributed through a network of filling stations, with pumps and tanks straddling the whole country. They are essentially a sort of shop: and are commonly associated with garages in the sale of other supplies for motorists. They normally combine the sale of lubricating oil for cars with the sale of motor spirit. The

[1] The Regent Oil Company had 6 % of the total trade in oil in 1955, but much more of the trade in motor spirit (c. 11 %). It was expected to build up its sales of fuel oil in preparation for its refinery.

[2] Known in the U.K. as Fina till October 1957. It produces oil in Canada, the United States, Mexico, and Egypt (possibly on a small scale), and is looking for oil in Portuguese West Africa and the Congo. It has refineries in Belgium and Canada. But it still buys much of the oil which it sells—in most West European countries, in North America and in parts of Africa. It has a few tankers—one of 30,000 tons.

distributing companies supply the stations by road tanker. In the past
the major companies rarely owned petrol stations but this is changing.
They have for long sold petrol by brand and have advertised heavily, to
establish the superiority of their brand; this has taken the form not only
of straightforward advertising but (for example) the development and
preferential supply of special products for aircraft or for motor racing.

Before the war the 'national' companies as they called themselves
formed a group (The Petroleum Distributors' Committee) which
dominated the retail trade and collectively fixed the retail prices.
Dealers who undertook to sell their products exclusively had an 'exclusive buying rebate' which, for example, was $1\frac{1}{2}d.$ a gallon in 1931.
Hence most 'independent' spirit was perforce sold in stations which
did not sell the main brands.[1] The Group got most of the best sites.
Independents who tried to get in were met with price cuts: they were
offered entry to the trade if they maintained Group prices: and they
were allowed a small share. The largest 'outsider' was Russian Oil
Products—which co-ordinated its petrol prices with the Group's in
1929 after two years' conflict, though its products were still not sold
at filling stations which sold exclusively the Group's products. Prices
rose in consequence by $2\frac{1}{4}d.$ a gallon (though by November 1930 they
had fallen again below their former low level).[2] The 'case' put forward
for the Petroleum Distributors' Committee was that 'national' companies distributed to a nation-wide market, hence to sites which were
costly to supply and where the volume of business was small or erratic.
Newcomers always began selling in the concentrated business areas
near ports. The national companies thought it desirable to sustain
a uniform price everywhere, but newcomers could undercut if they
chose the favourable trade only.

These arrangements were not restored after the Second World War.
But to an increasing extent the distributors have individually made
exclusive agreements with filling stations for a period of years whereby
the owner or lessee of a station undertakes to sell one company's or
one group of companies' brands of petrol exclusively and in return has
a special rebate, and also usually a loan for the improvement of facilities.
By financing improvements a company will ensure that the stations which
sell its products are attractive and efficient. (It is widely felt that service
in the United Kingdom is by international standards low.) The
companies have also bought new sites and built new filling stations.
They have become in varying degrees owners of stations.

[1] These were Shell, Anglo-American (at first Pratt's, later Esso), B.P., Dominion, National
Benzole, Power, Cleveland, Redline.
[2] This possibly reflected trends in world prices and world demand, not a more competitive
condition in the domestic market.

The policy obviously aims among other things at giving market security without collusion. It has involved the oil companies in a large aggregate capital outlay,[1] some of which has been provided by insurance companies. The policy is not designed solely to give a secure market, and this may not have been its main *raison d'être*. By concentrating a large company's business in fewer stations, each with a larger turnover and larger tanks, it lowers the cost of distribution. In the United States large superstations with up to twenty-four pumps have greatly reduced distribution costs.[2] Success in increasing average business at stations will depend to some extent on the ability to secure stations which are, in the various ways in which it is possible, strategically well placed; there is thus acute competition alike in persuading existing station proprietors to make exclusive agreements, and in finding new sites and discovering where new building or other developments are going to create new business. Companies have set about this in different ways. Some garages already dealt mainly with one company and this helped the largest groups in the early stages of the new policy: Esso, for example, (which is credited with starting the policy) secured its first 3000 exclusive stations out of a target of 6000 with great ease. Regent had a large interest in two important and widely spread garage groups—Lex and Blue Star. The newcomer may aim largely at skimming some of the cream, though it is costly to get the sites. The competitive process became intense from 1954 onwards when the refinery expansion had raised petrol capacity to a pitch at which it was hard to market all the motor spirit (especially the standard or as some prefer to call them ordinary grades) which could be produced; some plants were not being run at full capacity in 1956 before the Suez crisis.[3] This surplus was helpful to distributors who bought motor spirit from major refiners on long-term contract.

One criticism of the new policy is that it tends to stimulate the building of too many new filling stations. It is a possible danger, obviously. It is one which town planning authorities will tend to hold in check on grounds of amenity if they think there are enough garages, and those who exercise control over capital tend to frown on new garages. The number of stations now is in fact less than before the war. But larger ones (often at new sites) have replaced smaller ones. Expansion in facilities may in fact have been excessive in the short run. Whether in the long run companies are likely to proliferate outlets which have a small business is less certain. There are conflicting influences. It is possible that with tied

---

[1] It has not proved possible to find out how much.

[2] Cassady, *op. cit.* p. 257.

[3] It was sometimes argued that they had been run at over capacity after Abadan went out of action, so that a fall in output did not mean running below capacity. But there were other signs of difficulty in finding outlets—for example, B.P. persuaded the Central Electricity Authority to use, as fuel oil, oil which had a low flash point and required special precautions.

stations smallness of business is consistent with large 'drops' and therefore cheap but infrequent delivery from the refiner's depots. The condition necessary may be that the lessees or owners of small stations are
satisfied with small incomes from petrol sales. Most stations have
additional activities: but the possibility of staff being under-employed
and margins higher than they need be, cannot be ruled out. The
greatest multiplication of small stations tends to occur where wages
are low—in Ireland, for example, and in Italy. The firms' recognition
of their rivals' strength will act in this as in other respects as a moderating
force. But for tactical reasons they may build more ahead of demand
than would be essential to give motorists an adequate supply.

The development of the tied filling station owes much to American
precedent: though the United States position has developed from a
situation in which the majors who sell a 'national' brand owned and
managed most of their selling points, to ensure complete coverage of
the area in which the brand was heavily advertised.[1] For legal or tax
reasons they usually lease stations to dealers who bind themselves to
sell their brands only—for a rebate and possibly other advantages. The
dealers' price policy is largely a company policy, though arrangements
are informal, and there is no national price. Two features distinguish
the American from the British situation. In the United States there are
in all states in varying degree 'independent' suppliers, small refiners, or
jobbers who obtain petrol from 'majors' for rebranding or from small
refiners. These usually have tied dealers, but the ties leave the dealer
freer, for example in fixing prices. Normally non-national brands are
cheaper. There is scope for aggressive price-cutting and price wars,
which occur when motor spirit is plentiful and when local supply
conditions change, for example, if a new refinery or new pipeline should
appear—or a new dealer. The other difference is that stations tied to
national brands of petrol have commonly become tied agencies also for
particular makes of tyres and other accessories: brands of petrol and
tyres, and so forth, become associated.[2] In the United Kingdom this
seems to have made no headway. Some companies have set out in
negotiations over petrol to extend their sales of their own brands of
lubricating oil on their tied stations. They have not, however, made exclusive agreements about motor spirit depend on exclusive terms for selling
lubricating oils, though in some arrangements restrictions[3] on the sale of
lubricating oil have been combined with agreements for the sale of petrol.

---

[1] This account is based mainly on Cassady, op. cit. pp. 236 ff. It was the position therefore
in 1953–4: the arrangements are subject to antitrust pressure.

[2] This is now (1957) the subject of antitrust proceedings.

[3] For example, one contract in exclusive dealing in petrol prescribed that a dealer should
sell only brands of lubricating oils whose sale was agreed to by the petrol supplier, in writing.

Refiners who make motor spirit usually also make lubricating oils, which come from the heavier fractions of the crude, and the 'independent' lubricating oil manufacturers usually buy from the major oil companies lubricating oil base stocks or fully refined oils, and carry out either a finishing or blending process. In the past the margin on lubricating oils—for blending and distribution—appears to have been high: it is not surprising to find the major companies now seeking more of this. They offer special rebates to dealers who undertake to sell minimum quantities of their oil or give it exclusive advertisement or display. Normally, however, other well-known brands, notably Wakefield's, continue to be stocked. Since it is probably advisable to use the same brand of oil in a car engine because the additives vary considerably, if all the major petrol companies linked exclusive sales of oil with exclusive sales of petrol the independent lubricating oil blenders would be in danger. As it is the independents can offer their own terms to all petrol stations. They will not be vulnerable as buyers of base stock from oil companies so long as they can buy these from American independents if price difficulties arise.

The extent to which the process of tying the petrol stations to the exclusive sale of particular brands has gone is illustrated approximately in Table 17. The largest network is that of Shell-Mex and B.P. On the smaller of these stations only the brands of Shell-Mex and B.P. are found, but at the larger stations the dealer can also sell the brands of the Dominion Motor Spirit Company, the Power Petroleum Company, and the National Benzole Company (since January 1957 a wholly-owned subsidiary of Shell-Mex and B.P.), whose products are based on benzole made at coke ovens and gas-works, blended with motor spirit from Shell-Mex and B.P. and are very widely used. Marketing several brands must limit the advantage from specialization. The pattern is now developing of separate Shell, B.P., and National Benzole stations so that in one most striking respect the ties recorded in the table will be radically changed. Esso stations are entirely limited to Esso motor spirit: the Cleveland Petroleum Company, though a subsidiary of Esso, has its own tied stations. The table gives approximately the percentage of the total number of sites with two or more pumps which sold exclusively the motor spirit of one of the main companies or groups of companies, together with the percentage still independent and selling several unassociated brands, early in 1957. The number of stations was about 30,000. Some stations do more business than others, and the average varies appreciably from one company to another.

The large networks would seem to have an important advantage in that they can cover the whole country more intensively; users seeking their particular brand will be more certain to be able to get it, and

Table 17. *Affiliations of petrol stations**

Percentage tied to		Percentage tied to	
Shell-Mex and B.P.	44·5	Fina	3·1
National Benzole	3·4	Mobil	1·5
Esso	20·9	Other smaller companies	0·2
Cleveland	7·3	Independent stations	7·8
Regent	11·3		

* Estimates by a trade body based on a representative sample. A 'poll' of consumer preferences has shown significant deviations from the distribution in this table, the Shell Group and Esso both being stronger. The figures are for late 1956.

persons choosing a brand would prefer one universally available. The smaller networks are pushing out and aim at a more complete coverage: some at the moment cover only parts of the country, and that lightly. There are always people who like to deal with small sellers (who may be more careful to nurse custom) and it may be thought that the less familiar name must provide something special to be in the race. Much more important, many motorists find from experience that the difference between their favourite motor spirit and others is slight: hence just as buyers of the ordinary grade (of which a lot is sold)[1] will have no preference for one make, buyers who judge most premier spirits to be alike will not worry much which brand they get. The fact that competing motor spirits at the same price are broadly similar in users' experience does not prove that competition is having no effect—it is more properly regarded as a proof that it is working.

However, it is bound to weaken the bonds between buyers and brands, though the mystique created by skilful advertising, appealing by

[1] The progress of premier and standard petrols has been as follows:

(All figures in thousand tons)

	Sales to dealers (i.e. filling stations)		Sales to commercial consumers	
	Premier	Standard	Premier	Standard
1953	2,197	1,578	255	1,709
1954	2,533	1,452	289	1,649
1955	2,827	1,455	320	1,638
1956	2,929	1,541	336	1,517

The high proportion of 'standard' taken by commercial buyers no doubt reflects the character of their operations, often local, in town, at low speeds, and that—partly for this reason—they use low compression ratio engines so that there is no economy in using premier grades. It also reflects an interest in costs, and the absence of 'snob' interest. Dealer sales of standard grade are mainly for vans and light lorries: of sales to motorists, below 15 % are of standard grade.

different styles, will have an enduring effect on some buyers.[1] It will not diminish the substantial gains from the new system of distribution, some security of sales volume (based primarily on having the right sites) coupled with a great reduction in distributing costs. The tied stations are part of a considerable process of rationalization in the oil distributing business since the war. The American majors have provided the model. The changes have been both facilitated and prompted by the growing capacity of road tankers. The object of the exercise has been simple enough—to reduce the number of storage depots, increase the size of transactions, carry as much oil as possible in the largest possible tankers (including rail tank wagons and ships or barges from refineries to main depots), reduce the number of discharges per journey, and in the analogous ways to reduce costs (labour costs most obviously but also capital costs) by keeping equipment more fully employed and more on the move, and reducing the number of units and increasing their size. The pattern of storage and wholesale distribution has been very considerably changed as a result of this effort, and 'productivity' of labour greatly increased. For Shell-Mex and B.P., for example, between 1950 and 1956 the tonnage of motor fuel handled rose by 27 %, the number of wholesale distribution points operating (and handling other oil products as well as motor spirit in increasing quantities) fell from 440 to 141. The average capacity of road tankers in use by the firm in 1950 was 1340 tons; by 1956 it was 1970 tons.[2] This resulted in labour savings on a scale larger than the average rate of fall for wholesale distribution which is shown for 1951–5 in the figures on p. 175. These figures cover a period in which some growing organizations were being built up; the established organizations were slimming.[3]

Sales of motor spirit are made to all filling stations on a published price basis, subject to agreed discounts (with special discounts for exclusive dealing), and the price to final consumers, subject to some regional variations to take account of differences of transport costs, is announced by the companies, which effectively fixes a maximum. The firms appear to take no steps to enforce the price, but the prices seem to be almost universally observed. The leading firms tell other firms

[1] For a few thoroughbred cars one premier petrol may be the most suitable. (Few cars at the moment of writing can take advantage of the super grades introduced in 1956. From a purely technical point of view the number was extremely small: though it was stated that in experience a larger number in fact seemed to benefit, and a considerable number of the new 1957 models had a higher compression ratio.)

[2] The average cost of delivering petrol per gallon in a 1000 gallon road tanker was over 0·6d. in 1956; in a 2000 gallon vehicle it was nearly 0·4d., in a 4000 gallon one 0·2d.

[3] Thus Shell-Mex and B.P. reduced their staff from 16,000 to 12,000 while increasing the volume of trade by 70 %: but two-fifths of the saving was achieved by getting contractors to do work hitherto done by company staff.

when they are making a price change: there is no collusion, but a lead is normally followed, when it is a rise as well as when it is a reduction. If it was not, the leader could react strongly: the part that this plays in making decisions is possibly almost unconscious, but the price changes tend to be infrequent and small.

This is not to say that all firms sell all their petrol in exactly the same price grades. There have been a number of patterns in the period since the return of premier grades in 1953. Thus in 1955 Esso had 'Esso Extra' which at 4s. 7d. a gallon was 1d. above what might be called the standard premier grade (4s. 6d.) and it also had 'Esso Mixture' selling at 4s. 4d. A Fina grade sold for slightly less. There was a demand to be tapped at this level; many motorists bought premier and standard grades (then 4s. 1d. a gallon) and other brands to mix, with the same effect.

The dealers' margins varied in 1955 from 4d. a gallon on the ordinary grade to 4½d. and 4¾d. on premier grades: in addition dealers obtained rebates for 'exclusive dealing' long-term contracts which raised the average margin to about 5½d. a gallon in 1956. The average sale of a filling station was about 44,000 gallons a year: so that the gross earnings from sales of petrol averaged little over £1000 a year. Most filling stations sold other products and had other activities. The 'normal' American filling station sold about twice the British average—96,000 to 120,000 gallons a year—and new superstations sold from 96,000 up to (in a rare instance) 500,000 gallons in a month.[1] The normal dealers' margins were very close to the British (they were about 5 cents a gallon in 1953—possibly without allowance for rebates). It is probable that the average size of transactions in the United States was higher than in the United Kingdom which would make for larger turnover and smaller costs. The whole distributors' margin—i.e. wholesale plus retail—is difficult to establish for the United Kingdom, but in 1955 the value of imported motor spirit c.i.f. was £16 a ton: this is used to determine the ex-refinery value, which was thus nearly 12½d. a gallon. The average selling price at the pump, ex-tax, was about 1s. 11d.: giving a margin for wholesaling and retailing of about 10½d. a gallon.[2] The distributing *cost* from refinery to dealer was over 4d. a gallon on an average. The total distribution cost in the United States about 1953 was given as 6 to 7 cents a gallon: reduced in one instance in a superstation outlet to 3 to 4 cents.[3]

---

[1] Cassady, *op. cit.* p. 257.

[2] It would have been less in 1954 when imports cost more: but it is rather a notional figure.

[3] Cassady, *op. cit.* The margin between Oklahoma refinery prices and the retail prices in fifty cities was about 10 cents a gallon in 1955–6: but refinery prices away from crude would have been higher.

The precise significance of such comparisons is difficult to assess because conditions are different. Do the American costs arise from the conditions, or from price competition? At least it must be recognized, in approaching the question 'Do the tied garages keep prices up?', that the changes it is associated with in Britain have been inspired by changes in America. The tied garages are part of the rationalization which has reduced the labour employed in wholesale distributing while the volume of sales has greatly increased. Moreover the dealers' margin of $5\frac{1}{2}d$. a gallon compares with $2\frac{1}{2}d$. before the war: it has risen much less therefore than wages or the price of capital goods, though there has of course been an increase in average sales per filling station.

The price wars of the United States filling stations have not been repeated in Britain. This is probably due to the absence of independent suppliers (including producers of crude, and refiners) who are conspicuous in the United States, and the absence of the variety of natural conditions of supply arising from the location of crude oil, and the distances, which help to account for the status of the American independents.

By and large the evidence that prime costs of distributing are lower in Britain than they would have been without the group of related changes of organization is strong. This is not to say there is no unnecessary duplication of services which a perfect plan would avoid: but the alternative of large multi-company stations—or should one say free houses—whose development would not be so readily linked with developments in the rest of the distributing machine—is not without probable drawbacks and might have required more space and more capital. Moreover, it most likely would not have occurred because there was no adequate coming together of incentives and resources.

The right questions to ask would seem to be, does the system of tied garages prevent the benefits of large-scale distribution being fully passed on to consumers, and is it associated with selling methods which involve other avoidable costs? It could involve restriction in the freedom of sale of other products, but as practised in the United Kingdom it has hardly any such effect. The tied garage is above all a manifestation of the 'brand' system—even when some of the minor brands are, as seen above, 'rebrands' or mixtures based on major makers' products. It involves therefore the usual doubts—whether the costs of advertising the brands and the differentiation of product to establish them more than outweigh economies of scale in manufacture and sale.

There is a risk that in order to take business, rival makers will supply premier grades which have qualities which few cars can utilize: and this has happened to some extent. On the other hand, there has also, it is claimed, been a deliberate avoidance of a publicized 'octane race' over the first group of premier grades of petrol.[1] There has been some restraint. It is probably right to say that in their general character the changes and diversification in the qualities of petrol sold have been improvements in line with changes in car engine design and responsive to the pattern of demand, and that the cost of differentiations introduced mainly for the sake of advertising has been fairly small.[2] These conditions did not start with the tied garage: the branding and the elimination of price competition, it has been seen, have a pre-war history.

In conditions of oligopoly, which are even more fully realized in the United Kingdom than in the United States in the oil business, price competition in petrol at filling stations is naturally avoided because the demand for any one brand is highly elastic: people do transfer readily in response to a small change in the price of well-known brands, which are all by repute good products and (grade for grade) interchangeable. The effect of a price cut for well-known brands with a national coverage cannot be localized (in the United States, independents with little-known brands, and with intermittent coverage, can localize the effects of price cuts in their products). It would be wrong to assume that because price competition is avoided the existence of such competition in filling station prices would in the long run establish a lower price level. The oil industry is one which has shown immense energy in investing in facilities to reduce its costs and improve its products and service, and it has gone out for volume of sales. Its power to increase sales by lowering retail prices of petrol within the practical limits is extremely restricted, since the tax component in price is so high.

There is, however, price competition in other parts of the oil business —on a discriminatory basis. The pattern is again as in the United States, but less vivid. Where sales are made direct to larger users there is some scope for individual negotiation, though how much occurs is necessarily obscure. Motor spirit and derv fuel are sold by contract to large customers—such as corporations, bus companies, 'C' licence holders. At any one time there is a market rate for quantity rebates but there are at least occasional departures from this—it is said they occur only in a few

---

[1] Octane rates were being raised but not publicized. Firms did bring up the standard of their product as rivals got an 'edge' on them.

[2] The discussion of brand selling with price leadership in the United States in the 1930's by A. R. Burns, *The Decline of Competition* (1936), pp. 93 ff., is suggestive. The Federal Trade Commission is quoted as saying that the control existed only 'as long as they follow the general trend of market conditions'—which 'suggests', Burns argues, 'that prices have not departed widely from what might have been expected had competition existed' (p. 103). But he also emphasized that prices gave wide margins which were reflected in rivalry in purchase of oil lands, heavy expenditures on advertising and retail outlets, providing elaborate equipment and securing control (p. 108).

of the largest sales, but the evidence is conflicting.[1] The practice of different firms probably varies at different times, as they have surpluses or deficiencies. Other products sold in large quantities—to gas or electricity companies, the railways, or, say, chemical or rubber companies —are commonly sold by contract, and standard 'announced' prices if there are any are not invariably observed. Sometimes the departure is public—as when the Ministry of Fuel and Power announced in 1955 that the price of fuel oil supplied by the Fawley refinery to the local electricity generating works would be pegged to the price of coal.[2] There are price schedules for fuel oil, but in practice the precise price is commonly 'negotiated', fuel oil having still (before the Suez trouble) a competitive market although its scarcity in Europe was referred to in numberless discussions of the 'energy gap'. Newcomers selling in the market found it necessary to cut prices to get orders, and they did this most for users near their refinery, if they had one, or where delivery costs were lowest. Naturally, when one firm cuts, others tend to follow. 'Cutting' is, however, localized: one informed estimate is that 80 % of fuel oil (1956) was sold at the standard rate less standard rebates.

The products sold fall, it has been seen, roughly into two categories: those like petrol and diesel fuel for cars and lorries, whose demand is dependent on the number of vehicles and on general economic conditions affecting demand for transport, and those like fuel oil and gas oil whose demand depends partly on the cost and availability of alternative supplies of fuel and power. Petroleum chemicals form a third category perhaps—which straddles the first two. Solvents made from oil residues compete with solvents made from other bases—either the same solvents, as, for example, acetone which competes with acetone made from molasses, or different solvents with comparable properties. The competition may be more remote—as, for example, with the raw materials for synthetic rubbers, where there is a margin of competition with natural rubber (the two 'rubbers' are not identical, and 'synthetic rubber' covers a wide range of products with different properties) except when supplies of both are scarce. For many markets selling must be well informed technically, and the sales departments of the major companies (very prominently in Britain, Shell-Mex and B.P., who have as a result of their 'crudes' always had a lot of fuel oil to sell) have done much to encourage the development and use of more efficient oil-burning equipment. Buyers are also informed, and selling is not based on 'brands', though a name may count because of the service it connotes.

[1] It is stated (1956) that it is not unusual for commercial sales of petrol to be at lower prices than sales to garages, though the latter take the larger 'drops'. Hence the question is asked, do the public buying at garages subsidize commercial users or contribute to high profits?

[2] No doubt this sale was very satisfactory to Fawley. The refinery had exported much fuel oil to Denmark: a local market with negligible delivery cost would be attractive.

Selling costs are necessarily less for the larger transactions common to the 'black oils' than for retail sales of petrol, though as a percentage of the lower valued fuel oils they are not necessarily much less.[1] Though the efficiency of selling affects the final price a large component of this price is determined largely by international forces. This is dealt with in the next section.

4. COMPETITION, PRICE FORMATION AND ECONOMIC EFFICIENCY

Because so much of the world oil industry is concentrated in the hands of a small number of large and extremely strong international firms, fears that it may by implicit or explicit restrictions and agreements keep prices up or otherwise distort what would be the 'normal' development of the industry are endemic. In the remote past the American industry provided a classic case of monopoly: in the early 1930's the industry openly adopted restrictions on prices and output. Now there are no such agreements, and there is vigorous competition of certain kinds, including sporadic price-cutting, which have been referred to earlier. Nevertheless disquiet is still often expressed. It is impossible in a short space to do more than describe the shape of the problem.

For British firms operating overseas the prices of the crude and refined products which they sell determine their income, and the profits they bring into the United Kingdom, and the new investments they make abroad. The profitability of oil industry operations inside the United Kingdom depends upon the margin between the cost of imports, especially now of Middle East crude oils, and the prices of the oil products sold either in the home market or for export. When the companies operating abroad and at home are not the same there is room for a conflict of interest: the home operator will want a low import price, the company operating abroad may as a seller like a high crude oil price. In general the companies are integrated and interested in both ends of the trade, and this conflict does not arise. The distinction is none the less important, since it affects the scope for independent refiners in the United Kingdom.

All these oil prices, of crude oil and products, are related, in varying degrees, to United States prices (or more precisely to Western hemisphere prices, because Texan and Venezuelan prices are closely linked, Venezuela selling largely in the United States). Western hemisphere

---

[1] Mr C. T. Brunner, Director of Marketing, states that it costs £50 million a year to run the Shell-Mex and B.P. distributing organization, the turnover being £400 million. That gives an average of 12½% on all products. The cost of getting petrol to dealers' stations is (on figures given earlier) nearer 25% on the distributors' turnover.

finished product prices exert their influence in Europe because the products are exported to Europe: hence they tend to establish a ceiling for prices in Europe (including the United Kingdom). Western hemisphere crude oil prices are related to Middle East prices for the opposite reason, because, that is, the United States import Middle East crude oil. It might be expected that in this case Middle East crude oil prices would tend to determine American crude oil prices. It would, however, for reasons to be discussed later, be wrong so to describe the relation.

This relation has been recently described with no implications of cause and effect, in the following terms: 'Allowing for a fair long-term freight differential, plus United States import duty, Arabian crude is approximately competitive with Texan crude for delivery to the United States Eastern seaboard.' The Middle East crude price, that is, would tend to be below the Texan price by the amount of the import duty (about 80 cents a ton) and by the excess of the freight from the Persian Gulf to, say, New York over the freight from the United States Gulf to New York. This provides at least a useful starting point.

It is sometimes known as the watershed theory of oil price determination; the price of the two crudes must be equated at the point where they meet in competition. When Middle East output was lower the watershed, or 'frontier of competition', was farther East—e.g. midway between the two sources, when the f.o.b. prices in the Middle East and Texas were the same. If the relation of Texan and Middle East crude were established on this basis then the cost of Middle East oil at ports in the United Kingdom would be approximately the same as the cost of American crude in Texas, because the freight from the Persian Gulf to England is close to the 'freight differential' referred to plus the American duty.

Historically, over the years 1949–56, it must be said that the price relation as exhibited in published figures did not fit this pattern. Table 18 shows figures from published sources which come closest to agreement with the doctrine. During the period covered the posted prices for crude oil in the two areas concerned were changed (apart from a few minor changes[1]) once only, in July 1953. From the last quarter of 1949 (i.e. after sterling was devalued) till July 1953 the prices of East Texas crude oil—a high quality low sulphur oil— was $2.65 a barrel in the field, and Arabian oil at Ras Tanura was $1.75 f.o.b. From July 1953 to the third quarter of 1956 inclusive the prices were slightly higher: $2.90 (Texas) and $1.97 (Arabian) respectively. In establishing the differences between the prices for the table

[1] For example, a minor change in the Ras Tanura price occurred in July 1953, when Esso first set the price at $2, whereas Socony put it at $1.97, which Esso followed.

20 cents has been added to make the Texas price a f.o.b. price, and 10 cents subtracted to allow for its better quality.

While the prices were thus rigid for long periods freights varied greatly. For the table, stabilized freight rates are taken which aim at giving a balanced indication of the level for a standard rather small tanker of all the freights actually incurred quarter by quarter for oil being carried under all the various types of charter indicated above[1] and by oil companies' own ships. The amount of oil for which 'spot' rates applied was relatively small (15 to 20 %). Nevertheless the fluctuations of the 'stabilized' figure as calculated were wide, especially in the Korean period.

Table 18. *Crude oil price and freight differentials, 1949–56*

Quarter		Texas price minus Arabian price (s. per ton)*	Nominal freight† differential plus duty (s.)	Quarter		Texas price minus Arabian price (s. per ton)*	Nominal freight† differential plus duty (s.)
1949	4th	54	57	1953	2nd	54	64
1950	1st	54	57		3rd	55	64
	2nd	54	56		4th	55	59
	3rd	54	56	1954	1st	55	59
	4th	54	80		2nd	55	63
1951	1st	54	80		3rd	55	60
	2nd	54	96		4th	55	62
	3rd	54	96	1955	1st	55	63
	4th	54	115		2nd	55	62
1952	1st	54	115		3rd	55	59
	2nd	54	123		4th	55	63
	3rd	54	123	1956	1st	55	75
	4th	54	104		2nd	55	66
1953	1st	54	104		3rd	55	74

* Assuming that 7½ barrels = 1 long ton.

† This is based on freights in the London Market Tanker Nominal Freight Scale (freight Ras Tanura to north of Cape Hatteras but not north or east of New York, minus freight United States Gulf to same), and the L.T.B.P. (London Tanker Brokers' Panel) and A.F.R.A. (Average Freight Rate Assessment) indexes of balanced freight changes. Duty is taken as 7s. a ton.

The implication of these figures is that the c.i.f. value of Middle East oil fluctuated much while the f.o.b. value, and the American crude price, changed once only in six years. This conclusion is compatible with the movements of the c.i.f. values of imports into the United Kingdom recorded in the *Trade and Navigation Accounts*—which rose from £6·64 a ton in 1949 to £8·03 in 1950, £10·39 in 1952 falling back to £7·90 in 1954, rising again in 1956. Some who should know say that these import values, if not to be disregarded, are somewhat theo-

[1] Pp. 165-6.

retical. (They are used in valuing the input into the British refineries, and it will be recalled that the Census of Production 'net output' of the refineries fell conspicuously in the period when the values rose sharply, and vice versa.[1])

How exactly Table 18 should be interpreted is obscure. Selling transactions in crude oil are for large quantities over long periods, and relatively infrequent. Most are either by one part of an international company to another part of the same company (when the price is a transfer price)[2] or to another major company. There is only one small 'independent' seller, and its 'Wafra' crude oil, sold to Italy, is sold at a low price but is of a low quality. The proportion of sales to independent buyers—such as Argentina, for example, whose buying tends to be conspicuous—is not known. Most sales are on long contracts, five years being a common period: there are often price concessions,[3] and sometimes the seller agrees to cover the freight during the currency of the contract either at a uniform figure—which may be low and a form of concession—or according to the A.F.R.A. index.[4] Specially low freights are sometimes reckoned when the use of large tankers is arranged or visualized ('nominal' freights still relate to 12,000 ton tankers).[5] At least one long (twenty years) contract has complex conditions relating the crude oil price to product prices in certain markets. Some sales, but probably not many, are on condition that the price will be reduced if an important competitor gets a lower price.

Against this complex contractual background it has been suggested that the stable United States-Middle East price differential from 1949 to 1956, with one small change in 1953, can be rationalized on these lines: that the freight differential at the end of 1949, although freight levels had then come to their lowest since the war, was likely to prove lasting because though inflation might carry some costs up, and other costs would go up in response to rising living standards and progressive exhaustion of mineral deposits, nevertheless the progressive rise in the size and efficiency of tankers would offset these. Hence since oil prices on long contracts must be related to long-period probabilities—looking five or ten years ahead—the price differential should be reasonably stable, despite violent freight changes, which to a considerable extent

[1] See above, p. 188. The correlation is not complete, but close.
[2] There were sometimes low inter-company sale prices: cf. for example *The International Petroleum Cartel*, pp. 369–70.
[3] While a field 'posted price' for crude in the United States is the price offered by buyers, in the Middle East the posted export price is a price quoted by sellers. This one is therefore subject to negotiation—downwards.
[4] The contracts are not published. Low inter-company freights are recorded in *The International Petroleum Cartel*, p. 369.
[5] The way in which different companies estimate freights for long periods is not known: there is no reason to suppose they use the same measure.

the oil companies avoid because of their ownership and long-term chartering of tankers. The relation of American and Middle East prices is never the result of applying a formula. Every price negotiation starts in the light of existing prices but existing prices are not day-to-day prices. The 'watershed' would exert its force inevitably over time. Thus a company may apply the formula notionally in forecasting the future, though not commercially in the present.

From another (*realpolitik*) angle it was inconceivable that Middle East oil prices should fall in the Korean war and during the Persian shut-down, since demand was acute and Middle East government incomes have grown and depend on oil profits. A wider differential could therefore only have come if the United States price for crude oil had risen at the same time. Since Middle East supplies rose from 71 million to 105 million tons from 1949 to 1952 there must have been plenty of new contracts (however discontinuous the process of contract making is). Hence many freights must have been fixed in periods when freights were and looked like remaining high. Hence, again, much of the oil will have had in fact to bear much higher freights than those ruling in 1949.

The rigidity of the United States crude oil price is as striking as the rigidity of the margin between it and the Middle East price. It is a relatively recent development: up to 1933 there were frequent violent movements,[1] and it is reasonable to date the change from the conservation policies which restrict supplies according to forecasts of demand.[2] Imports into the United States are limited too by acquiescence to political pressure so that total supply is restricted. Proration both raises prices[3] and stabilizes them.[4] While therefore competition in the distribution of products is often acute in the United States, there is little or no competition in sales of domestic crude: the refiners compete for supplies. 'Pure' oil producing companies seem to show (though the samples are meagre) a higher percentage of profit margin than integrated companies making products partly or wholly from their own crude or than mere refiners and marketers.[5]

---

[1] Cassady, *op. cit.* p. 136, has a useful graph.

[2] See above, p. 168.

[3] It is argued that the crude oil price is also raised by the allowance of a percentage of proceeds free of tax for 'depletion'. This could have no effect on price unless there were restraints on outputs and imports.

[4] See for example Cassady, *op. cit.* p. 113.

[5] *Ibid.* p. 326. In 1949 nine companies who were only producers had profits averaging 24·6%: four whose oil production exceeded their refinery requirements made 14·9%: seventeen whose production was less than their refinery requirements 12·3%. Burns, *The Decline of Competition*, p. 435, gives figures from the Federal Trade Commission relating to 1922–5 which show profits on production above those on refining, but equal to those of refining plus marketing.

The situation described is of fundamental importance for the United Kingdom because as seen already the United States product prices provide a ceiling for product prices in the United Kingdom. Finished products are imported into the United Kingdom from the Caribbean or United States; and they come in at the United States 'Gulf' or the Caribbean price (which move closely together) plus freight from the Caribbean (which is lower than from the 'Gulf'). This is called the 'import parity price'. If United Kingdom refinery prices tended to exceed the prices of the imports the imports would tend to increase in volume—though dollar restrictions might check this. The British market is small in comparison with United States-Caribbean supplies, which therefore can exert a strong influence. The import parity price is the basis of the valuation of finished products in the Census of Production. Before the war when there was hardly any domestic refining it was the actual basis of prices, not the ceiling. The ceiling price would not necessarily now be the real price: and as has been seen the real price departs in many competitive transactions from the scheduled price. The scheduled price itself sometimes also falls below the ceiling. However, this appears to be less common in the United Kingdom than in Mediterranean Europe, where it is apparently the rule rather than the exception, especially in Italy. One reason for this is that freights from the Middle East are lower to the Mediterranean ports, hence refineries have cheaper raw materials. Whether for this or other reasons, 'local refinery supplies', according to an expert from the oil industry, Mr Pattman, 'obtain prices diverging considerably from United States Gulf or Caribbean import parity and generally lower'. In part at least this is due to 'competition between the many local refiners': there are independents, there is a state oil company, and 'the trend towards reduction of the refiner's margin to the cost of the marginal refiner, based on supplies of Middle East crude, has proceeded far'.[1]

In the United Kingdom, where the refiners who are not specialized are all integrated, the schedule prices of only a few products appear to have fallen 'through refiners' competition' below the import parity. Fuel oil, despite the known price-cutting, is not among these: standard grade petrol, also subject to some price-cutting, and which 'tends to excess production from local refiners in relation to demand', is; but not premier petrol. Some grades of lubricating oil were sold for a time at £2 a ton below the United States price. Here too there was new competition, not an equilibrium position. An expert assessment of the position was that 'buying crude from the Middle East and freighting it to North-West Europe leaves only comparatively small scope for even an efficient refiner to accept on any product for a sustained period

[1] *Institute of Petroleum Review*, May 1956, p. 122.

a price very substantially below the "Caribbean import parity" ceiling: there is no scope for this on all his products'.[1]

The squeeze of British refining, as thus set out, between Middle East crude prices and Western hemisphere product prices, provides a useful focus for considering how effectively the kind of competition which exists in the industry works. No one seriously contends that competition is 'perfect' or near perfect: the characteristics—few but large sellers in most markets, exceptionally high cost of entry, unhomogeneous raw materials, brand selling, many uninformed buyers, joint production—all rule it out. Nevertheless competition persists. As Mr Pattman put it in the article already quoted, since the main firms are large and mature 'each is individually alive to the virtues of self-discipline and stability in its activities including pricing. Price competition in the international field is thus massive rather than hysterical: nevertheless it is real.' He enlarged on the topic of firms expanding their business 'at the competitive fringe' which 'is going on all the time between companies: there is nibbling away...to get that extra customer, and to do that companies often concede prices that are lower than normal prices, which they would be willing to accept for the whole of their business; and of course a criterion for what they can accept in those marginal cases is their out of pocket "marginal" costs....A good deal of that goes on, which merely shows that we do live in a competitive world.'[2]

There are, however, conflicting opinions of the effectiveness of this in keeping prices down and leading to the best disposition of resources; the production for example of the range of products best suited to the European and more particularly the British market.

The most forceful statement of the 'case against' its effectiveness was in an Economic Commission for Europe report in 1955.[3] Broadly it argued that the appearance of a 'unified world market' given by the links between United States and Middle East crude prices and United States and European product prices was misleading. The pattern of production and trade is not in fact responsive to comparative costs. The Middle East crude oil price was kept too high, and the influence of United States product prices imposed a set of price relations between the various refinery joint products unsuited to Europe's and Britain's pattern of demand.

The first point was on theoretical grounds unassailable. The fact that the United States crude oil price is unresponsive to the price of Middle

---

[1] *Institute of Petroleum Review*, May 1956.   [2] *Ibid.*

[3] *The Price of Oil in Western Europe* (Geneva, 1955). This stimulating analysis owed much to Dr P. H. Frankel, and to *The International Petroleum Cartel* (which also relied heavily, in quotations, on Dr Frankel, who was then with an independent oil company, and is now a consultant).

East imports for as long a period as it has been, and this owing to restrictions on output and import, turns the published price pattern into something of a façade if it is thought of as the outcome of free competition, which of course it is not.[1] Investment in expansion and the development of new oilfields was not the result of free market influences. Whether the geographical distribution of investment would have greatly differed if competition had been free cannot be dogmatically assumed. Development was particularly cheap in the Middle East and much cheaper there than in the United States, but it was also much more risky. This had already been underlined by Persia's nationalization of the oil industry, and has become still more evident in the disputes over pipelines and the Suez Canal. The risks were high; and expansion stimulated increased appetites in the Middle East for revenues from oil.

In any case it seems unrealistic to suppose that, even although competition is not allowed to work out, the price link between Middle East and United States oil can be severed, or that if it were the Middle East price would necessarily drop. So long as the United States uses substantial quantities of Middle East oil—it took one-ninth of the Middle East exports in 1955—the Middle East price must be linked to the United States price. From the British standpoint it would be best if the freight differential did operate sensitively: for in this event the United Kingdom price for crude would always be lower than the United States source price. Since United States products would have to carry the freight cost this raw material price would put British refineries in a strong position. The reason why the United States-Middle East price link ostensibly squeezed the United Kingdom in 1950–3 was precisely because it was less than the freight differential—which was unavoidable if the United States price was rigid. When the price difference came close to the freight difference in 1955, refining in the United Kingdom showed for the first time in Census of Production terms a net output almost high enough to remunerate the capital investment.[2]

The E.C.E. discussions seemed to assume that because the Middle East oil price included a large profit it was possible to negotiate a lower price for a larger output: but this seems to underestimate the bargaining sense of the Middle East—illustrated constantly in the negotiations of new agreements since the war—and to assume that those who possessed cheap oil might shape their price policy to suit the convenience of

---

[1] This would probably be accepted by the most recent American analyst who takes a kindly view of the 'workability' of the competition in refining and marketing. Professor Cassady writes in a footnote: 'As a matter of fact the competitive structure in crudes might not pass muster because freedom of production is curtailed by law' (*op. cit.* p. 336).

[2] See above, p. 188.

Europe when Europe thought of herself as short of fuel.[1] On the contrary, in this situation the United States price may be of value as a ceiling.

The nub of the criticism of the Middle East crude prices was that North-West European refiners are squeezed between these as raw material price and the ceiling imposed by American product prices. The United States prices fall into the pattern appropriate to their market, where—the argument runs—the different oil products are not required with the same relative intensities as in the United Kingdom and Europe. Europe needs 'a pattern of relative prices for the different products which will make most attractive commercially their production in proportions appropriate to the pattern of demand in Western Europe'.

The large American demand for motor spirit and the ample supply of competitors of fuel oil in America—cheap coal, natural gas, water power—will keep the price of fuel oil relatively low in America and the price of motor spirit relatively high; and in these circumstances it will always be attractive to have a refinery programme with as large an output of motor spirit as possible, and as little fuel oil as possible. Since in the United States the proportion of motor spirit in the programmes is 45 % but in the United Kingdom below 25 % naturally the gross returns from sales would be higher for a given through-put of crude at a given price level (but the American refining would be a more costly one). The American price structure, reflected in Europe, would—it was argued—encourage a type of refinery development which Dr Frankel called 'retrograde' in Europe's economic circumstances, that is more cracking.[2]

This line of argument though ostensibly based on the expanding *need* for fuel oil indicated by estimates of future consumption in fact seems to have neglected the recent history of *demand* for fuel oil, because even in Europe the price of fuel oil had been kept low by difficulties in selling it, which had been acute even in 1953—as the E.C.E. well knew. Acute competition in Europe between coal and fuel oil had disturbed the coal industry, and as a result the E.C.E. made a special study: but the basis of competition was a fuel oil price close to the equivalent price of coal. In Britain in 1953–4 the average value of fuel oil c.i.f. was £6. 10s.: the delivered price in Inner Zones was from £9 to £9. 10s. a ton. (The average pit-head price of coal was £3. 2s. a ton: it is convenient to estimate the B.Th.U. content of the oil at 1·5 tons

---

[1] Agreements operate on the margin between posted prices and costs: the governments show a lively interest in the level of posted prices and no disposition to see them fall.

[2] The argument as set out here neglects the middle-range distillates because their required proportionate yield is more nearly similar in both the United States and Europe, though in fact since they are often required where the use of oil has technical attractions their price could become more attractive and could influence the 'refinery economics'. But the problem is simpler and starker without this complexity.

of coal.) The c.i.f. average was lower than that of 'crude and process oils' imported—indeed the fuel oil import value was consistently below the average value of crude oil imports from 1948 to 1955. There was a large net export of fuel oil from the United Kingdom in 1952–5.[1] The plain implication is that at the current price there was no market for all the fuel oil produced in British refineries: while on the continent higher coal prices offered a better outlet. It is useless to expect a large substitution of fuel oil for coal if coal is the cheaper unless there is an actual, not merely a prospective, scarcity or unless there is government pressure exerted where it can be effective. It is equally unrealistic to expect refiners to import more crude oil to supply more fuel oil at prices below that of the crude.[2] From 1951 to 1953 the price of fuel oil fell while coal prices were rising. When coal was imported into the United Kingdom and the continent from the United States, at high costs, the cost was spread over other sales so that the 'marginal cost' of coal supply could not effectively push up the price of fuel oil. The argument which visualized European fuel oil prices as being determined entirely by the American price structure was thus fallacious.

Would the American price provide a discouragingly low ceiling to future fuel oil prices? For motor spirit notionally at any rate the American price could be regarded as a ceiling: in 1955 it became clear that it was not a floor: for as Dr Frankel said, the greater availability of motor spirit had 'driven down the marginal prices for low and medium octane spirit below the world market price'. But would the American price for fuel oil be a ceiling if demand for fuel oil rose in the United Kingdom—and in the rest of Europe?

The price of fuel oil, the residual product, is the oil price most sensitive to market pressures. In the United States it has swung violently. If the market improved in the United Kingdom—and in Europe as a whole, where the fuel problem appears in this aspect fairly uniform—it might be expected that a price rise would attract imports and that in effect the 'world price' would be raised. Only as coal prices move

---

[1] The net exports from 1951 to 1955 were:

	Million tons	Value ($£$ per ton)
1951	−0·1	6·2
1952	2·3	6·8
1953	3·4	6·6
1954	2·7	6·3
1955	0·6	6·6
1956	0·3	7·4

[2] Of course it *was* true that the crude oil price could be lowered to a point at which fuel oil even with its price governed by coal was higher than the crude oil price. But this was only relevant to the argument that the Middle East price should be lowered—not that the United States price pattern distorted refinery planning.

so as to give fuel oil a value higher than that of crude oil could fuel oil be more than a residual product.

The supposition that the relative prices of different products would check the greater supply of fuel oil was probably a misjudgment. The emphasis in public discussions on the prospective demand for fuel oil was new. Some oil companies had been cultivating the market, but the countervailing effort to rely as far as possible on indigenous fuel (coal) had been vigorous. When demand for fuel oil began to reach the point where supply presented an obstacle, interest developed in heavy crudes which naturally gave a lower yield of motor spirit and a higher fuel oil fraction, and because of their quality were cheaper. Cheaper crude was available within the existing price structure. Aramco found it necessary to produce more oil from wells with heavier crudes in 1955.[1] Some Venezuelan crude is almost directly usable as a fuel oil.[2] Imports from Venezuela of fuel oil, which might be diverted from the United States to the United Kingdom by better prices, would raise the 'dollar' question: but since it seemed reasonable to use dollars for coal why not for fuel oil?

In retrospect the discussions of prices in 1955 seem to have under-estimated the flexibility and responsiveness of the oil industry's structure. For British conditions, however, the conclusion that the price arrange-ments kept out independent refining is beyond reasonable doubt. It is clear that for the big integrated international firms the price arrange-ments allowed profits on imports of Middle East oil either into the United States or the United Kingdom. Perhaps most of the profit was on the crude. But independent refiners could in some circumstances thrive—Johnson in Sweden is an outstanding case. He is also a large tanker owner. An independent getting no regular rebate on the Middle East posted price and having to pay for tankers could not make straight-forward refining pay from 1949 to 1956. This could be partly an outcome of geography: the same prices did not have the same effect in the Mediterranean. In some countries independents had price con-cessions on crude: either the posted price was cut or a delivered price agreed which meant the buyer did not pay the whole freight. Some such sales may have been made to Italian buyers; they were certainly made to Argentina. Possibly political circumstances helped in this: but if it depended on temporary chance surpluses the situation was too unstable to have calculable effects.

The same is true of price-cutting in distribution of the kind described

---

[1] These trends did not affect only United Kingdom supplies. Thus Esso, for example, planned in 1956 a refinery near Cologne which would produce a large amount of fuel oil.

[2] Where the refining operation is slight, and the fuel oil import is as dear or nearly as dear as the crude for making into fuel oil, it is hardly material whether the refining is done in the United Kingdom or not.

earlier. Its effects are not foreseeable. It is a normal token of real competition between big integrated groups which are trying to get more of the new business available or more of the business especially convenient for their installations, or to dispose of the least marketable of their joint products if they refine. Inevitably in an industry like oil refining where efficient units are large the building of a new unit will disturb the market even if the market is growing. The competition between big companies in the United Kingdom reflects interest in a growing market—there are signs of still other oversea groups coming in.[1] The growth of Mobil, Regent and Fina shows that the proportions of trade held by firms change in the United Kingdom: there have been changes in the proportions held internationally also (for example, the percentage of crude oil handled by Caltex has risen significantly in recent years). In form the price-cutting competition is discriminatory. The offer of lower prices may tempt some people to convert to oil sooner than they otherwise would, and may hasten the growth of the market: though it is unlikely this would be of great significance. Some concessions may do little more than give users the full benefit of their location in relation to the source of supply.

The practice of making concessions possibly checks the general level of prices—but there are no data to show the difference between realized and list, posted or quoted prices. It no doubt stimulates energy and resource in selling and leads to better service and, as the companies emphasize, to the production of better products.[2] The question arises whether the improvements are always in some sense worth the cost. Advertising, for example, presumably does not sell more petrol, but sells more premier petrol. It is possible that the competitive effort in producing 100 octane spirit, in addition to the other premier brands—now of about 95 octane rating—is unduly costly in relation to the rational demand for such a product (i.e. the demand for users whose cars really need the product to work efficiently). Capacity to supply may greatly exceed demand: demand may be stimulated among people for whom the service is of little or no substantial value.

These problems are in their nature insoluble. But competition is certainly not carried to the point of being destructive: it does not make the industry unprofitable. In the years 1951–4 there was a falling trend of profits and the return on capital invested by the twenty largest

---

[1] For example, the Compagnie Française des Pétroles had leased storage in the United Kingdom in 1956. The venture does not seem to have thrived.

[2] 'Intensification of competition...has made itself felt in higher quality products, for which particularly expensive items of capital expenditure...are necessary, as improved additives, and service advice, behind which are millions spent on research, and on more convenient service stations and other supply equipment.' F. C. Waddams (Shell) in *Institute of Petroleum Review*, November 1955, p. 282.

international companies fell from 15 to 12%.[1] But there was a downward trend in United States profits in most industries: and refining was among those well above the average.[2] (Moreover, though in the United States profits in the oil industry as a percentage of capital employed fell, gross profits, dividends and cash retained all rose significantly each year from 1951 to 1955.) There is no means of identifying profits earned by British companies from operations in the United Kingdom alone.

The oil industry is one in which 'self-finance' has been the principal source of finance, and the volume of investment is immense. It is this probably more than the price structures which presents the most obscure and baffling problems. The large investments in refineries alone in the United Kingdom have been recorded earlier. Gross investment in the oil industry of the United States rose, fairly steadily, from $3600 million in 1951 to $5600 million in 1955: in the rest of the 'free world' from $1675 million to $2600 million. In the American figures rather over 50% represented replacement-depreciation. Of the rest —the net investment—two-thirds was financed from retained earnings, and about 22% was raised on the capital market: the rest, in the years 1953–5, coming from cash deficit. This could not be a stable position —bankers closely associated assumed it meant the price was 'subnormal', since the capital market was only 'geared' to supply the proportion of capital (the 22%) raised in this way.[3] This in one form or another seemed a general oil industry view—so much capital was needed that it must almost all come from undistributed profits. (It may be wondered whether perhaps if profits are in general undistributed this will not 'denude the market of funds for ordinary shares'. The industry's argument is possibly circular?)

The industry outside the United States raised a still lower proportion of its capital from the market, and more came from retained profits. A review of the British position in 1954 showed that only 2½% of the money which came from the 'market' was in the form of stock, the rest being borrowings of which over one-half came from banks and insurance companies. Gross new borrowings were less than 2% of self-generated funds (including 'write-offs').[4]

At the same time dividend payments were far smaller year by year than either gross or net investments. The following is the record for

---

[1] Waddams, *loc. cit.*: he states that return on new investment was 20% a year in 1950–1 and 5% a year from 1952 to 1954. But it is not an easy calculation.

[2] Cf. *Economic Report of the President, January 1955* (Washington, United States Government Printing Office, 1955), pp. 190–1.

[3] J. E. Pogue and K. E. Hill, *Future Growth and Financial Requirements of World Petroleum Industry* (Chase Manhattan Bank, 1956), pp. 34–6.

[4] Waddams, *loc. cit.* p. 283. In 1956-7 the industry came rather more into the market.

the American companies: it is unfortunately not possible to give such comprehensive data for the British companies, but the general situation was identical.

Table 19. *Capital formation in the United States oil industry*

	Dividends paid to owners ($ million)	Retained cash income ($ million)	Capital expenditure ($ million)
1951	875	3,498	3,625
1952	907	3,629	4,400
1953	1,030	4,119	5,025
1954	1,067	4,268	5,350
1955	1,181	4,726	5,600
Total	5,060	20,240	24,000

How do the owners tell whether the enormous part of the earnings returned into the business is well used?

With such large investments the popular tokens of efficiency—newer and bigger machines, bigger tankers, more automation, more research laboratories—abound. The tokens need not be wholly misleading; oil is one of the industries in which, despite its dependence on 'wasting assets', prices have risen less than the average. But they are not a proof of economic efficiency. The big firms invest increasingly, to maintain their position, and to 'compete in strength'.[1] Dividends increase. But there is a risk in 'self-finance' that the return on new capital may be exceptionally small without this becoming apparent. Superficially this may seem a social gain at the expense of the investor, but it can lead to a use of capital which is relatively unproductive. An objection to public issues of stock, it was said in 1955, was that 'they suggest the ability to sustain, if not increase, dividend payments', which 'in view of lower returns in recent times' (on new investment) would be unwise.[2] The danger is thus not wholly imaginary.

Moreover the process leads inevitably to the building up of bigger and bigger industrial empires, powerful and in a sense remote (though conscious of the need for 'good public relations'), and because of their size liable to the difficulties in promoting efficiency which face all large organizations. The companies face it largely by the holding company technique, giving a large degree of autonomy to subsidiaries. But this cannot have the same effect as competition between independents. The oil industry is possibly the supreme example of 'managerial economy'. Those who run it are conscious of competing to earn large profits in

[1] Lord Godber in the 1955 *Report* of 'Shell' Transport and Trading Company.
[2] Waddams, *loc. cit.* p. 283.

order to extend their business, and only subsidiarily to remunerate the shareholders, whose authority is too remote and ill-informed to be effective. Over all and above all is the sense of responsibility to an expanding world. 'Without oil our modern industrial civilization would, for better or worse, perish. It is incumbent upon that civilization to ensure that the machinery exists whereby these products may be supplied smoothly, plentifully and cheaply....Provided these conditions are granted, the oil companies may be depended upon to play their role adequately and satisfactorily in the interests and to the advantage of all concerned.' A typical chairmanlike statement: yet despite these assurances, and their evident sincerity, a sense of uneasiness is often still felt. The E.C.E. report suggested that 'more effective consumer representation in solving the problem of oil pricing might well be regarded as to the long-run advantage of the industry itself', and it recalled the proposals of the unratified Anglo-American Oil Treaty of 1945 for an inter-governmental consultative body. In England the oil industry has close and friendly relations with governments and there is mutual consultation over demand trends which provide part of the background to the industry's investment policies. (In the United States the relations are more difficult, possibly through antitrust; but antitrust will not be so interpreted as to liberate production from restriction for market reasons, or to free imports.) The dangers to which the main firms in the industry would seem exposed are akin to those which beset powerful bureaucracies. Judgment as to whether they fall into the dangers has to be based, as far as it can be, on performance; an analysis of structure is necessarily indeterminate. It cannot be said that in retrospect the criticisms of price and investment policies in their relation to fuel oil supplies have become more cogent with growing experience. Changes in governmental policies over the oil industry seem more likely now to come in response to Middle East political difficulties than in response to economic criticisms.

BIBLIOGRAPHY

(a) Books, Pamphlets and Articles

Brunner, C. T., *The Problem of Oil*, London, Benn, 1930.
Burns, A. R., *The Decline of Competition*, New York, McGraw-Hill, 1936.
Cassady, Ralph, *Price Making and Price Behavior in the Petroleum Industry*, New Haven, Conn., Yale University Press, 1954.
Coqueron, F. G. and Pogue, J. E., *Investment Patterns in the World Petroleum Industry*. New York, Chase Manhattan Bank, December 1956.
Frankel, P. H., *Essentials of Petroleum*, London, Chapman and Hall, 1946.
Institute of Petroleum, *The Post-War Expansion of the U.K. Petroleum Industry* (Papers at Summer Meeting, 1953), London, 1954.

Longrigg, S. H., *Oil in the Middle East*, Oxford University Press, 1954.

McLean, John G. and Haigh, Robert Wm., *The Growth of Integrated Oil Companies*, Boston, Harvard University Graduate School of Business Administration, 1954.

Murray, John, *The Economic Impact of Oil on the Arab Middle East*. (Papers collected from the *Institute of Petroleum Review*, 1956.)

Pattman, R. A., 'The Price of Oil', *Institute of Petroleum Review*, May 1956.

Waddams, F. C., 'Investment in Oil', *Institute of Petroleum Review*, November 1955.

(b) Official Publications

(i) *United States of America*

Federal Trade Commission, *Report to the Federal Trade Commission by its Staff on the International Petroleum Cartel*, Washington, United States Government Printing Office, 1952.

(ii) *International Organizations*

E.C.E., *The Price of Oil in Western Europe*, Geneva, 1955.

  Relationship between Coal and Black Oils in the West European Fuel Market, Geneva, 1954.

O.E.E.C., *Oil: Outlook for Europe*, Paris, 1956.

CHAPTER VI

THE CHEMICAL INDUSTRY

By W. B. Reddaway

I. THE PROBLEM OF DEFINITION

Any discussion of the chemical industry inevitably starts with the problem of definition. This study will, however, be concentrated mainly on certain sections of the industry which lie near its centre, and therefore would be included on any reasonable definition;[1] the problem of where to put the boundary lines is therefore less important here than it is, for example, to the compilers of comprehensive statistics of employment or output. Those readers who wish to study that problem more deeply will find it discussed in the first two books in the bibliography. In so far as the industry is spoken of as a whole, the definition adopted will be largely that used by the Association of British Chemical Manufacturers (A.B.C.M.) for its 1949 and 1953 Reports, because some of its figures will be used. It is as follows: 'Heavy chemicals, industrial gases, fertilizers, dyestuffs, medicinal and other fine chemicals, explosives, plastics and synthetic resins, but not the compounding of chemicals to make such products as paints, insecticides, sheep and cattle dips and pharmaceutical preparations.' In adopting this definition the A.B.C.M. took a relatively narrow view of the industry, confining itself to what might be called 'the chemical industry proper', and leaving out the 'allied' trades, such as are indicated at the end. It omitted coal-tar distillation for administrative reasons, although this would naturally be classified as part of the chemical industry, even on a narrow definition.

What makes the problem of definition so difficult is that the industry produces, literally, many thousands of different products, without taking account of differences of grade and the like; some firms only produce one, but many produce hundreds, and for a single firm to produce a thousand different products is not a source of amazement.

By many economic tests, one product of the industry often seems to have little in common with some of the others. Thus soda ash and dyestuffs are in no sense serving the same market, they are produced in quite different plants and they require different raw materials; only in the most general sense do they require the same sort of expertise or

---

[1] Or so one might think—but the manufacture of plastics materials was classified in the fancy goods industry in pre-war Censuses of Production.

organization, and there is virtually nothing to be gained by combining their production in the same firm.

In such circumstances there is only a very limited sense in which the structure of 'the industry' can be analysed, or its influence on efficiency, etc., considered. Nor can we dodge the difficulty by further subdividing the industry into sub-industries of a more homogeneous character. Chemicals are not produced in standard combinations even by factories, let alone by companies; no matter how they are grouped, it will be found that many companies cannot properly be assigned to any single sub-industry.[1]

In these circumstances the most useful method of analysing 'how the industry works' seemed to be to take certain products, or groups of closely related products, and examine the conditions under which they are supplied. This means abandoning any attempt to apply some of the concepts normally applied to an 'industry' and its 'structure', since the production of the commodity in question may be only a small part of some companies' activities, and it is not possible to cover the whole of the chemical industry. But the analysis relates to a meaningful set of problems, and the products selected give, between them, a reasonable view of the varying conditions found in the industry.

This analysis is attempted in Sections 5 to 8. Before embarking on it the question why it is that individual firms combine the production of so many chemicals, and in such different combinations, is examined in general terms in Section 2; and then in Sections 3 and 4 the varying sizes of companies in the industry are examined briefly, together with certain other of its characteristics, most of which are illustrated by the subsequent sections on particular products.

2. WHY INDIVIDUAL FIRMS PRODUCE MANY DIFFERENT CHEMICALS

Despite Adam Smith's emphasis on the virtues of specialization there have always been sound reasons why many firms should make more than one product. These very often apply to the chemical industry with particular force. Thus many chemical processes yield joint products, or by-products which can best be worked up on the spot (notably gases). The advantages of marketing a *range* of chemicals is often considerable, because users often want small quantities of a large number (for example, dyes, or fine chemicals); research facilities are extremely important, and one way of securing the necessary volume of output to

---

[1] The Association of British Chemical Manufacturers has eight groups covering a rather wide definition of the industry. But even with this very broad classification its 1955 Directory shows only ninety-four out of its 222 members as belonging to one group only.

support a well-equipped laboratory is to add other lines to the firm's production.

The point about research needs some elaboration. The laboratory does not merely solve problems thrown up by the production departments in the course of their activities: it evolves new products, or new techniques which may be applicable to products not made by the firm in question. In principle this need not lead to further diversification of the firm's output: the knowledge might be sold by one means or another to other firms, and indeed there is quite a lot of licensing of patents in the chemical industry. But very often it is more attractive for the original firm to follow up its own research discoveries, especially as the process of development normally throws up further problems which can often best be solved by the people who have worked on the subject from the start. The rapid progress of chemical technology along many different lines makes this point of great importance in explaining the diversity of many firms' production.

An allied point arises where the original discoverer is seeking to license his patent. Almost invariably he will go to an existing firm working in that broad field of technology, which will add the new product to its range—this very commonly happens internationally, the right to use an American process in the United Kingdom, for example, being granted to an existing British firm (or vice versa). A new firm would almost never be considered as a licensee, but even if there were no question of patents—for example, if a new process were made freely available by a government laboratory—the new firm would usually be at an almost hopeless disadvantage owing to lack of trained staff, organization, finance and market contacts.

Historically, the diversification of output inside some of the large chemical firms has on several occasions been carried forward in large strides by amalgamations. It is seldom possible to say precisely why amalgamations take place, or why some subsequently lead to further growth whereas others may even be reversed or end in bankruptcy. Questions of personality, finance and struggles for a good position in markets at home and abroad may all play a big part, as well as the more technical factors which suggest that the grouping would bring advantages. But it would be a mistake to neglect these last and attribute everything to (say) 'the empire-building of Mr X'. In the chemical industry the technical conditions were such that empire-building by able entrepreneurs was likely to lead to enduring success: perhaps the most solid foundations for this are the gains to be secured from large-scale research facilities and a large body of trained staff to turn laboratory results into efficient commercial production.

The considerations which explain why most firms produce more than one product also largely explain why so many different combinations are found, as one moves from firm to firm.

Thus the dynamic nature of the industry and the importance of research lead to firms of very different character deciding to enter a given field, such as plastics: very commonly they will evolve different products, with technologies appropriate to their previous experience, but this need not be true—much the same discovery may be made by research workers starting from very different base-points. When a patent expires a great variety of firms may consider that the product can appropriately be added to their range: some will have experience of similar processes, others will serve the same type of users, yet others will be making one or more of the materials needed to produce it, and so on.

Even the more 'static' reasons for diversification may lead to different combinations. Thus in the case of joint products, the section on alkali below shows how it is necessary to produce caustic soda by two distinct processes—one combining its manufacture with that of chlorine, the other with soda ash. And as regards the working up of by-products, it is clear that the same by-product (e.g. ammonia) may emerge from quite different processes, and so cause a finished chemical (ammonium sulphate) to be produced in conjunction with many different main products (including ordinary town-gas and steel).

Finally, however, this discussion of the merits of diversification must not be allowed to hide the arguments in favour of specialization and sticking to one's last: there are in the industry a good number of firms which concentrate on one product, or a very limited range, which they often produce in what may seem like old-fashioned premises and without any of 'this new-fangled research'. By concentrating on the things they know and keeping down costs in various ways they manage to survive alongside their apparently better-equipped competitors and sometimes to make a good living—thereby revealing another aspect of the industry's diversity, and showing once again that there are more ways of killing a cat than one.

3. THE SIZE OF CHEMICAL FIRMS

The diversity of chemical firms noticed above is reflected in Table 1, taken from the 1949 Report of the Association of British Chemical Manufacturers, which gives some idea of their distribution by size. It is important to remember two things when considering this table.

First, the analysis is by *firms*, not by individual factories: thus Imperial Chemical Industries (I.C.I.) appears as one unit in the bottom row,

covering all its numerous chemical works. Subsidiaries are included
with their parent company.

Secondly, however, the companies were asked to confine their returns
to those activities falling within the chemical industry as defined at the
beginning of this chapter. Substantial parts of the activities of various
large firms were thus excluded, such as the leathercloth and metals
divisions of I.C.I., the whisky production of The Distillers Company,
the compounding work of The British Drug Houses, etc. The forces
which lead firms to combine the production of one chemical with another
do not lose their powers when the boundary of the industry definition
is reached.

Table 1. *Size-distribution of chemical firms, 1948*

Size of firm (number of employees*)	Number of firms	Number of employees* in such firms	Percentage of total	
			By firms	By employees
0–10	31	206	11·5	0·15
11–24	49	861	18·3	0·6
25–99	89	4,748	33·2	3·35
100–499	61	13,711	22·8	9·7
500–999	20	13,832	7·5	9·7
1,000–1,999	12	17,891	4·5	12·6
2,000 and over	6	90,568	2·2	63·9
Total	268	141,817	100	100

* As explained in the text, the returns covered only that part of a firm's activities falling
within the chemical industry as defined on p. 218.

Source: Association of British Chemical Manufacturers, *Report on the Chemical Industry, 1949*
(London, 1949), p. 71.

Note: No later analysis on these lines is available, but the general pattern probably still
holds.

The table makes it clear that the six companies with over 2000 employees accounted for nearly two-thirds of the total labour force, but
that the next three size categories were also important, and that there
were quite a substantial *number* of smaller firms. Indeed well over half
the firms had less than 100 employees.

In an industry as diverse and ever changing as chemicals it is not
perhaps surprising that there should be scope for many different kinds
of firm. Thus medium-sized companies may flourish on a business built
primarily round some particular strong-point—such as expertise in
working up some particular material or group of materials (e.g. by-
products of petroleum refineries), or in carrying out some particular
kind of process (e.g. ones involving great bulk of liquids) or in meeting
some kind of user's requirements; they may well do some 'snowballing'
around this nucleus without turning into giants. Again, small firms
may find a suitable function in meeting some limited demand—for

example, by purifying chemicals to laboratory standards—or in treating some particular kind of raw material which is available only in quantities sufficient for small-scale activity—for example the monazite sand for the separation of rare earth compounds, or seaweed from the Scottish beaches.

It is of some interest to supplement the statistics given in Table 1 by some information about the leading firms in the industry, and the way in which their activities are related to the main sections listed in the definition adopted by the Association of British Chemical Manufacturers' Report. There is no similar source of precise information available, but Table 2, based on trade advice, gives a broad picture of the twelve firms with the largest number of employees covered by Table 1.

Table 2. *Twelve largest* chemical firms in relation to the various sections of the industry*

Firms	Heavy chemicals	Industrial gases	Ferti-lizers	Dye-stuffs	Other fine chemicals (including medicinal)	Explo-sives†	Plastics and synthetic resins
Albright and Wilson	× ×	.	.	.	×	.	.
Bakelite	.	.	.	.	.	.	× ×
British Oxygen Company	.	× ×	.	.	.	.	×
Clayton Aniline Company	.	.	.	× ×	.	.	.
Distillers Company	× ×	×	.	.	.	.	× ×
Fisons	×	.	× ×	.	×	.	.
Glaxo Laboratories	.	.	.	.	× ×	.	.
Imperial Chemical Industries	× ×	×	× ×	× ×	× ×	× ×	× ×
Imperial Smelting Corporation	× ×	.	.	.	.	.	.
Laporte Industries	× ×	.	.	.	.	.	.
May and Baker	.	.	.	.	× ×	.	.
Monsanto Chemicals	× ×	.	.	.	× ×	.	×

Key: × × indicates that the firm is one of the leading producers in the section and × that it a substantial producer, but not a leader.

* In the sense that in 1948 they had the largest number of employees engaged on the activities covered by the A.B.C.M. Report.

† Explosives are also made on a large scale in government establishments.

The table tries to give an idea of the sections in which each firm may be considered a 'leading producer', but the concept is inevitably rather unsatisfactory. Thus a section like 'heavy chemicals' or 'fine chemicals' covers many distinct products, and a firm might be the sole producer of one or more of them without qualifying as a leader for the section as a whole. It seemed more realistic to count a larger number of firms as leaders in big heterogeneous sections than in small ones.

Crude as it is, Table 2 does show that varied combinations of activities are followed, and that different firms occupy the leading positions in each section. Taken by itself, however, it may give a misleading impression of the relationship of I.C.I. to the chemical industry. As there is a mistaken tendency in many quarters to speak of I.C.I. and the chemical industry as though they were almost synonymous, it is important to consider this matter more fully.

First we may consider the over-all measure of 'net output' (i.e. value of goods produced less purchases of materials and fuel), which is probably the best single indicator of a firm's size in relation to the industry.

The Census of Production for 1948 shows the following figures for net output in the trades which together correspond broadly to the Association of British Chemical Manufacturers' definition, plus coal-tar distillation.

Trade	Net output of industry* (£ million)
Dyes and dyestuffs	17·7
Fertilizers, disinfectants, etc.	10·8
Coal-tar products	4·8
Chemicals (general)	
(a) Plastics materials	10·5
(b) Rest of trade	64·4
Explosives and fireworks	11·1
Total	119·3

* Excluding firms with ten or less workers.

The net output of I.C.I. in factories classified within these trades represented just under 40 % of this total. It is not helpful to give the recorded figure for each of the trades separately, because the whole net output of a factory or works has to be classified in the Census to that trade which represents its main activity, and this principle does not work well in some of the complex I.C.I. cases—for example, at Billingham.[1] But broadly one can put the I.C.I. share at zero for coal-tar distillation, 30 % for plastics, 40 % for fertilizers, and two-thirds for dyes. The percentage for explosives would be very high if government establishments were omitted: on the census basis the proportion is about one-half.

A second over-all measure is employment. Here I.C.I. has stated that it employs about one-third of the workers in the industry. The comparison inevitably encounters definitional problems, and it would be wrong to regard the comparison between this proportion and the

[1] Such complex cases tend to be classified to the chemicals (general) trade, and it may be that the over-all figure of 40 % is rather too high, through the inclusion of I.C.I. output which probably belongs outside this group of trades—for example, pharmaceuticals.

40 % for net output as any measure of relative productivity in I.C.I. factories. Both measures give the same broad picture: I.C.I. certainly occupies an outstanding position in the industry, but in no sense does it constitute the industry, or even half the industry.

The same picture also emerges from the Directory issued by the Association of British Chemical Manufacturers. I.C.I. is a member of each of the eight broad groups which this uses, but it is entered as a supplier of under 10 % of the 8000 or so individual products listed. Too much must not be read into this—the products are of very unequal importance, and I.C.I. makes for its own use many for which it is not entered as a supplier. But it is a useful corrective to the mistaken view that I.C.I. is a 'universal supplier'—and *a fortiori* to the still more mistaken view that I.C.I. is the *sole* supplier of all chemicals.

These three global measures are no real substitute for a consideration of the position product by product, on which something is said in the four case-studies below. But they serve as a useful introduction, and the first two do give a general sense of proportion.

It is interesting to note that at least one very large firm, with interests in nearly all the main branches of chemical production, also emerged in other countries with a large chemical industry (notably Germany and the United States). There are good reasons why it should happen, which are largely the logical extension of the analysis in Section 2.

Not only are there physical links between many chemicals—either horizontally through joint production, or vertically through the use of one to produce others—but there is often also a broad similarity of problems to be solved which enables experience in one line to be carried over to others. The wider the field already covered, the more likely it will be that a new product will seem appropriate as an addition—whether because it needs intermediate products which are already produced, or a technique of production in which the company is already expert, or a skilled staff which can be seconded from existing works, or a marketing organization, or general experience in solving the problems of commercial development. Common research facilities and organizational know-how are likely to play a key role in the snowball process, and of course an established company of this kind can afford to take risks and secure the necessary finance more easily than a smaller one. The scope for attractive amalgamation is great.

At the same time it is also understandable that this outstanding combination does not try to produce *every* product, and, perhaps more important, that it does not usually produce 100 % of the output of the chemicals which it does make. In the first place the firm was not born as a giant at the start of chemical production, and other firms had established themselves in various lines before it had reached its great size: there is relatively little to encourage it to invade many of these fields, where it would suffer from lack of experience, and this is one of the reasons why there are many chemicals which I.C.I. has never produced. Secondly, for chemicals which it has always produced its advantages in the various respects noted above will probably make survival easy, but may be at least partially offset by some advantage in other respects enjoyed by other producers, such as a particularly good process, or site, or works manager, or reputation, possibly based on greater specialization; this makes any attempt to capture the whole market unattractive. And finally, in the case of new developments it is again unlikely that a single firm will secure a place in every field, let alone occupy the whole of it, even if it is likely to be in more fields than any other single company and to be amongst the leaders wherever it appears.

4. OTHER CHARACTERISTICS OF THE CHEMICAL INDUSTRY

Despite the heterogeneous character of the chemical industry it is possible to make a number of generalizations about it which apply to most of its branches, though in varying degree and with some exceptions. These may serve as a useful background to the studies of particular products in the next four sections.

We may start with a few general remarks about the nature and extent of competition in the industry. With such a multitude of different chemicals it is almost inevitable that the demand for many of them is very limited and the number of producers extremely small; indeed the Association of British Chemical Manufacturers Directory shows only one producer for about a third of the 8000 products listed, and this proportion would doubtless be even higher if some of the items were more narrowly defined—for example, if 'acid wool colours' were replaced by a vast list of individual dyes. Nevertheless it would be wrong to infer that there is correspondingly little competition in the industry, still less that the single producer can behave as an unrestricted monopolist. In many cases (though not all) other firms could start making the product very easily, and this potential competition is almost as effective a curb on monopolistic exploitation as actual production by a rival would be. A point which is sometimes of special importance here is that some at least of the customers are often in the chemical industry themselves, or in an allied one which gives them some facilities for making their own supplies if they consider it desirable: as we shall see in the case of sulphuric acid there is a considerable amount of self-supply by big users, though in that case the motive is mainly to save transport costs, not to break a monopoly.

Besides this check through potential competitors, however, there is nearly always actual competition from other chemicals, at least for certain uses. Indeed it is fair to say that in the chemical field competition more often than not takes the form of firms making different but rival products, which compete in performance at least as much as in price, though price considerations may of course be very important for those users who do not have a marked preference for one product; it is relatively rare to find a number of producers whose products are so nearly identical that a small price cut by one of them would make all users want to buy from him unless the other producers followed suit. The economist has therefore to analyse the situation in terms of monopolistic competition, not pure price competition: even where he might expect the latter to apply, as with standardized sulphuric acid, other considerations besides price seem to be of importance—for example, regularity of supply or reciprocal loyalty between producer and customer.

This competition between products often constitutes a chain process to link producers who might seem to operate in quite different markets. Thus two chemicals A and C may have no common use, and their makers may have no facilities for switching from one to the other; but if chemical B competes with both of them, then the fortunes of their makers are to some extent linked: a cheapening of A, on the basis of greater efficiency, will spur the makers of B to greater efforts, and drive them to compete more intensively with C.

In this way linkages between products create overlapping spheres of interest for the various firms in the chemical industry, and the overlapping is intensified by the potential expansion of the output of each firm into additional lines for which their know-how and facilities are broadly suitable. This is indeed one of the strongest justifications for grouping together producers who make apparently unrelated products and calling the group an industry.

One further point may be made in regard to the extent and nature of competition in the industry. Sales are, for the most part, to other industrialists, who buy the product regularly and often in substantial quantities. Such buyers may reasonably be expected to be much better informed than many buyers of consumer goods, and better able to compare prices and test performance. All this might be expected to make for keener competition, both in price and in giving the customer what he really wants (instead of persuading him to want what the seller wishes to supply). At the same time, however, a market of this kind is influenced by other factors, some of which dull the edge of price competition. The need for regular supplies and regular outlets fosters the use of long-term contracts, or of looser liaisons between particular buyers and sellers, which break up the unity of the market. The customer may regard the assurance that he will get continued supplies, even in time of shortage, as more important than a small price concession now, and remain loyal to his traditional supplier in consequence even if others might serve him at a slightly lower price; this is particularly likely where the chemical is indispensable to his operations, but only a small part of his costs (as is often the case). Where large tonnages are required every week it may be easier to organize their delivery if they always come from the same source, and continuity of the precise quality may be more important to a manufacturer than to a final consumer. On the seller's side a reciprocal sense of loyalty to his regular customers leads him not to exploit the conditions of a seller's market when this prevails—quite apart from considerations of business ethics and other ties which may exist between the firms or their managers.[1]

In view of all this, and of the fact that for each chemical there are usually only a few producers, each offering a slightly different article, and quoting his own price, it is not surprising that chemicals show marked stability of prices 'in the short period'. This short-term stability is quite compatible with vigorous efforts to secure a long-term downward trend in costs, which is reflected in periodic price revisions; this movement is fostered by rivalry between existing producers, or by potential competition, or simply by the desire of managers to increase the volume of business and of technical experts to do a good job and demonstrate their achievement to the world.

The other broad topic about which some general observations seem useful is that of risk and uncertainty. This is a highly important subject in the chemical industry, for a number of interrelated reasons. Thus

(a) The ratio of capital to labour or to output is usually high in the production of chemicals, where one typically finds complex and expensive plant being tended by a relatively small number of workers. This means that any given annual percentage of obsolescence of capital absorbs a bigger proportion of the selling price than in most other industries, and the need for a high ratio of gross profits to selling price is further enhanced by the high rate of obsolescence to be expected in a developing industry—and by the need to spend large sums on research so as to make it develop.

There are two aspects to this conclusion which need to be distinguished: considering the matter 'ex ante', the level of gross profits which firms estimate as likely to result from a piece of capital expenditure must be

---

[1] This tradition of 'fairness' might lead to an excessively rigid pattern of distribution in times of temporary shortage, but consumers who have an exceptionally powerful reason for wanting supplies can often get them from merchants—though at the cost of paying a 'retail' price.

high enough to make the venture attractive, despite the likelihood of obsolescence; and 'ex post' the actual results should at least keep the firms in a good enough financial position to raise the funds for the further expenditure needed in a rapidly developing industry.[1]

(b) Chemical plant often takes a long time to design, build and get working. Plans for expansion or modernization must therefore be based on estimates of demand several years ahead: in particular, if shortages are to be avoided the growth of demand must be foreseen well in advance.

(c) The changing nature of the industry makes it hard for the makers of an individual chemical to foresee the course of demand for their product, since developments in some other field may on the one hand call for a great increase in supply, or on the other hand introduce a rival product to share the market—or even produce a flood of the chemical in question as a by-product, to be sold almost regardless of cost. From the seller's view-point shocks of this kind have hitherto been mitigated by the general upward trend of demand for chemicals; even if more plant is built than is needed to meet the demand which prevails when it starts working, the demand usually grows sufficiently for it to be fully employed later on and the growth can often be hastened by research into possible new uses for it, or a sales campaign. But the buyer has no corresponding consolation, if demand outruns capacity, except that the construction of more plant will probably be put in hand, and may this time cover both the further growth in demand and the existing deficiency. Since most chemical producers are also buyers of other chemicals, they have a lively interest in the timely erection of sufficient plant to provide their materials.

(d) Since the consequences of the shortage of a key chemical can be serious, it has been suggested that they should be treated like public utility services, and that their development plans should include a certain amount of additional capacity, over and above the 'best estimate' of the future demand, so as to give a safety margin. The strength of this argument should not, however, be exaggerated. In the first place additional plant can only remove one possible cause of trouble; the leading example of a shortage—sulphuric acid in 1951–2—was essentially due to a fall in supplies of sulphur, so that a reserve of plant would only have helped if it had used one of the other materials. But apart from this there is normally some scope for raising production above the planned normal level—for example, through overtime, or diversion of plant

---

[1] For this latter purpose it is not really sufficient that the realized results should be satisfactory when averaged over all firms, with the average made up of some firms doing extremely well and some unlucky ones going bankrupt; an efficient chemical firm is a complex entity which cannot be created overnight. The fact that the bulk of the capital expenditure and the research is done by big firms whose activities are spread over many different lines is an important safeguard against efficient units being paralysed by one unfortunate venture.

from other chemicals, or postponing overhauls, or driving plant above
its rated capacity or the continued use of obsolete plant; some consumers
can normally switch to substitutes, at least in part, and so spread the
pressure over a greater field; and variations of imports and exports
produce the same spreading effect geographically. The problem of
short-term peaks in demand, which is so troublesome for public utilities,
can of course be met by drawing on stocks in a way which is impossible
for electricity or gas. All in all, whilst it is desirable that the introduction
of additional plant should if anything be a little ahead of the growth of
demand, the amount added to the best estimate in planning should be
relatively small, *so long as that estimate assumes a high general level of
economic activity.*

(*e*) If capacity is to be fully sufficient for good years there are almost
bound to be times when it is in excess of demand. Moreover demand
for many chemicals is likely to be rather inelastic to price changes—
at least so long as we consider the whole group of chemicals serving a
broad purpose (for example dyestuffs). Since we have seen that production is normally highly capitalized we have then a combination of
factors which might be expected to produce intense price-cutting—if
there were a large number of truly independent producers: the differentiation of products would mitigate this result, but would not do more
if buyers were anxious to exploit the position. In practice price-cutting
is greatly reduced by the smallness of the number of producers, by tacit
recognition that it does not pay any one of them to start a price war,
and by the acceptance of the situation by the big buyers; sometimes a
price leader in effect calls the tune, and the others recognize that it is
wise to conform.

(*f*) This sort of situation does not lend itself easily to positive state-
ments about the public interest. A doctrinaire attempt to enforce
atomistic price competition would almost certainly fail, but would also
be open to the objection that if producers had to cut one another's
throats whenever demand was short of capacity the level of capacity
would probably be insufficient for any year of good trade—and
perhaps for average years too. On the other hand there is no reason
for the State to use its own powers to organize a price-fixing cartel, as
it did for coal in the 1930's, still less to enter into formal commitments
about allowing price maintenance 'if things go badly' in order to
induce an expansion of capacity.

(*g*) As a practical judgment there is much to be said for leaving the
firms to make their own decisions, subject of course to the Restrictive
Trade Practices Act, whilst retaining the Monopolies Commission and
the Board of Trade as watchdogs over situations which are not affected
by that Act because only one producer is involved. One of the advan-

tages of having production largely in the hands of a few very big firms is that they assume a sense of responsibility to the public interest which is probably more valuable than any formal regulations or agreements could be in such a complex and changing industry. Moreover there are a number of checks and balances in the industry which make unduly restrictive practices hard to maintain—notably the competition of other products, and the ability of big consumers to produce for themselves if they think that the price is being held above a reasonable long-term level under the guise of an arrangement to prevent ruinous price-cutting during a recession. The crucial question is probably the long-term trend of demand: if that is upwards for most products, and periods of serious excess capacity are short, there is little for the State to worry about—it can rely on the natural expansionist instincts of technical experts, on rivalry between research teams, and on the assumption of responsibility to the national interest by those in control of big organizations which results almost automatically from the current socio-political conditions. If, however, there were a long period of excess capacity, because demand had stopped rising or was falling, then positive action to limit restrictive practices might be needed in the public interest. Fortunately this is a situation which has not arisen since the war, and which is likely to be rare; in general the State can be thankful that it need assume no responsibility for doing more than hold a watching brief.

5. SULPHURIC ACID

It is now time to turn to the first 'case-study'—that of sulphuric acid—which may best be started with a brief indication of this product's nature and uses.

As regards its nature, the most important point in this context is that sulphuric acid belongs essentially in the 'cheap, bulky and basic' category of industrial materials. The output in 1954 was some 2 million tons (in terms of 100 % acid) and the average selling price ex-works some £10 per ton. Transport considerations are bound to be important with such a low price per ton—and the price is even lower for weak acid—but their influence is further enhanced by the special precautions which have to be adopted for handling such a corrosive article.

In a broad sense sulphuric acid is a standardized product, sold by reference to objective tests of purity, strength, etc., rather than the reputation of the particular supplier, and branding plays little role; as usual, however, there are some minor quality differences, especially in the case of weak acid which may contain some impurities, and these may lead individual consumers to have at least a limited preference for the output of some particular seller.

(a) Uses of sulphuric acid

Sulphuric acid has a very wide range of uses, and fortunately the National Sulphuric Acid Association (N.S.A.A.) collects very full statistical information on this subject, as well as on many aspects of production. Table 3 gives an abridged version of its figures for 1955, with 1939 for comparison.

Table 3. *Principal uses of sulphuric acid, 1955 and 1939*

(Thousand tons of 100 % acid)

	Tonnage		Percentage of total
Uses	1955	1939	in 1955
Chemical and allied trades			
Superphosphates	491	188	23
Sulphate of ammonia	285	266	13
Titanium oxide	232	negligible	11
Dyestuffs and intermediates	81	53	4
Hydrochloric acid	62	58	3
Oil refining and petroleum products	61	21	3
Other specified products of chemical and allied trades*	254	140	12
Classified non-chemical trades			
Rayon and transparent paper	261	109	12
Iron pickling (including tin-plate)	118	111	5
Textile uses (excluding rayon)	19	32	1
Others*	59	32	3
Dealers and unclassified*	210	110	10
Export	4	negligible	n.a.
Total	2,137	1,080	100

n.a. = not available.

* The unclassified products and sales through dealers are not allocated between 'chemical' and 'other' trades; the split between those three categories for 1939 is guessed. The specified products, in rough order of importance in 1955, are: *Chemical and allied trades*: Soap, glycerine and detergents; plastics; explosives; tar and benzole; sulphates of copper, nickel, etc.; drugs and fine chemicals; lithopone; bichromate and chromic acid; bromine; hydrofluoric acid; vegetable oils; sulphate of magnesium; phosphates (industrial); glue. *Non-chemical trades*: Sewage treatment; clays; accumulators; paper; agriculture; leather; metal extraction; copper pickling; sugar refining.

Source: National Sulphuric Acid Association.

The following points may be noted as of interest:

(i) The range of uses is very wide, and extends to many industries outside the field of chemicals, even if that is taken very broadly to include the 'allied' trades; thus agriculture uses acid for spraying potato tops to facilitate the lifting of the crop, and the steel industry uses large quantities for pickling.

(ii) Nevertheless, the chemical and allied trades took some 70 % of the 1955 total, and this figure would be raised to over 80 % if rayon production were regarded as an allied trade (as logically it might well be); within the chemical field, the consumption for fertilizer manufacture was outstanding.

(iii) Exports were negligible, and the same is true of imports; cost of transport is an obvious explanation.

In most of the uses sulphuric acid is 'essential', using that word in the debased sense which has become traditional in a world of allocations and the like to mean that it is difficult to cut down the consumption of acid without a serious (though not usually proportionate) effect on output, or at least that acid is much cheaper than any substitute. The shortage of 1951–2 showed that the amounts needed were not all quite as rigid as consumers made out—it would indeed be surprising if economies in the use of so cheap a product were not found to be possible when the effective price of marginal supplies threatened to become infinite—but it also showed that a major fall in supplies could not be met without cutting down the output of superphosphates and other heavy users.

(b) Production

On the production side, sulphuric acid presents a lot of interesting features, which would justify a much longer account than can be given here. Briefly, we may note the following points:

(i) The sulphur content of the acid may be obtained from a considerable variety of raw materials, and the very varying proportions in which they have been used at different times are shown in Table 4. The reasons for the changes are discussed below, but we may note here that the supply of the various by-products of other industries depends on the output of those industries, and is nearly all used for acid production; sulphur and pyrites are both imported, so that anhydrite is the only local material of which supplies can be expanded to any great extent.

(ii) The use of anhydrite as raw material involves some complex technical problems, and is only economic if it is done on a substantial scale (at least 50,000 tons of acid per annum); moreover it has to be combined with the production of a similar tonnage of cement from the clinker which emerges as a joint product, and a local market for this is needed. Consequently the minimum capital outlay is measured in millions of pounds, and altogether this process is only suitable for large firms.

(iii) For materials other than anhydrite, however, the technique of production is relatively simple and well known, and can be applied on quite a small scale—for example, a plant producing 10,000 tons of acid per annum and employing perhaps twenty workers (divided between three shifts) would not be at all uneconomic. Table 5 shows the number of producers in various output categories, and the amount

Table 4. *Production of sulphuric acid, 1935–56, analysed by material used*

(Thousand tons of 100 % acid)

		Tonnage of acid produced from			
Year	Total production	Pyrites	Sulphur*	Anhydrite	By-products of other industries*†
1935	897	390	130	53	324
1940	1,181	416	320	78	367
1945	1,168	259	425	88	396
1950	1,803	267	1,000	99	437
1951	1,606	275	760	101	470
1952	1,506	289	630	101	486
1953	1,875	503	700	103	569
1954	2,043	635	716	100	592
1955	2,117	586	758	242	531
1956 (first half)	1,156	287	409	203	257

* In the N.S.A.A. figures, acid produced from hydrogen sulphide (32,000 tons in 1954 and 16,000 in 1955) is grouped with that from sulphur. An estimated amount has been transferred for the other years.

† In order of importance these are spent oxide (from gas-works), smelter gases (from zinc manufacture), and hydrogen sulphide (from various processes).

Source: The National Sulphuric Acid Association.

Table 5. *Output of sulphuric acid in the United Kingdom analysed by size of undertaking*

(All figures relate to 1953–4, and are in thousand tons of 100 % acid)

Range of output of undertaking	Number of undertakings with output in range	Tonnage of acid			Percentage of output used by producer
		Produced	Used by producer	Sold	
Under 15	27	206	123	83	59
15–50	13	326	159	167	49
50–100	4	272	168	104	62
Over 100	5	1,168	506	662	43
All sizes	49	1,972	955	1,017	48

Source: N.S.A.A.

Notes: (1) Where a number of works belong to one firm, or where two or more firms are known to be closely associated, they are grouped together as one undertaking. In deciding whether the acid is 'sold' or 'used by the producer', however, deliveries from one division of Imperial Chemical Industries to another are treated as sales; if the opposite treatment were adopted the proportion used by producers would be rather over half instead of rather under.

(2) No later analysis on these lines is available, but one can say that (a) the importance of large producers has increased somewhat, (b) for the industry as a whole the proportion of acid used by the producer had risen to 52·6 % in 1955–6.

which they produced in 1953–4; it will be seen that the small producers are not only the most numerous, but account for over 10 % of the output.

I.C.I., which is included in the largest category, produced rather less than a quarter of the total output.

(iv) Table 5 also shows that about half the total output of acid is used by the producers, and this proportion does not vary strikingly from one size-category of producer to another, though naturally it varies greatly from firm to firm—some consuming the whole of their output, and others none. The firms which consume the bulk of their output are not, of course, primarily acid-producers—their main business is making fertilizers, or rayon, or some other product, and their production of acid is essentially ancillary to it, even though they may sell a certain amount which is surplus to their needs. I.C.I. is one of the companies which occupies an intermediate position: it has substantial needs itself, but it is also the biggest supplier of the general market, in which it sells about two-thirds of its production. This represents rather over a quarter of the total amount sold by the industry, so that I.C.I.'s position is important but not dominating.

(c) Marketing and competition

The above brief account of production and consumption has already referred to the two points that are crucial for an understanding of the marketing process which links them: the fact that sulphuric acid is expensive to transport, and that although it is cheap it is essential, so that users want to be assured of supplies.

These two facts combine with the relative simplicity of acid production to explain the large extent of self-supply. The force of the second has been increased by the attitude of I.C.I. towards the big consumers: they have explained that they do not regard acid production as a particularly profitable use for their resources of capital and skilled staff, that they regard it as part of their function to help ensure an adequate supply for the 'general' user who cannot be expected to produce for himself, but that they consider that big consumers should look after themselves. Given the rising trend of consumption (reflected in Table 3) it was inevitable that new plants should be installed somewhere, and as the growth largely consisted in the expansion of such consumers as fertilizers, rayon, and titanium dioxide, a substantial proportion of these plants could best be situated in or near the consuming factories: ownership by the consumers was not inevitable, but these were mostly 'chemical' firms to whom acid production presented no real problem; self-supply would give them control over the rate of expansion and amount of reserve capacity, and I.C.I. at any rate were not prepared to 'hew wood and draw water' for them.

In the general market the normal arrangement is for acid to be supplied under standing contracts, and consumers normally deal consistently with the same suppliers. There is indeed a strong tradition that one producer will not solicit business from the customer of another; the customer is free to change his supplier if he wishes, just as he is free to change his banker, but in neither case does this often happen. During the post-war shortages this 'loyalty' was almost inevitable, since suppliers in turn were loyal to their old customers. But even before the war there were advantages in being an old-established customer (see pp. 227–8 above) and transport costs often gave a powerful reason for getting supplies from the nearest producer unless another would quote a much lower price 'ex-works'. When a new plant comes into operation it normally negotiates an 'arrangement' to take over those customers who would naturally buy from it on the basis of its declared price; as most new plants have been erected by consumers the amount of negotiation needed has been relatively small.

The N.S.A.A. has never done any price-fixing, but until 1956 some of its regional sections made arrangements of various kinds, which were generally observed by producers in that region, although there were no sanctions; these might provide, for example, for common prices to be quoted, usually on a *delivered* basis, for certain types of business (especially *new* customers), or for common changes in price. With the passage of the Restrictive Trade Practices Act the sections all discontinued these activities, but it is possible of course that much the same result may be achieved by informal contacts between the firms.

In judging such a situation the important question is how much flexibility there really is for longer-run adjustments. An apparent short-run rigidity matters little if in fact there is sufficient freedom for efficient producers to quote a low enough price to enable them to grow, for new methods to be introduced and reflected in lower prices, and so on. It is not an easy matter for an outsider to assess, for example, how inflexible the tendency for producers to move their prices in harmony really is: but the ever present possibility of more self-supply (coupled with sales of 'surplus' acid at low prices) is a great safeguard against inefficiency or extortionate prices, and the tendency of I.C.I. to regard acid production as an unwelcome duty rather than a source of attractive profits is reassuring. The continued survival of some very small units is not necessarily due to inadequate competition: quite apart from the usual reasons which justify the continued operation of a plant that already exists, transport costs may in some cases provide a double reason for a small unit's existence, for example, to convert the spent oxide arising in local gas-works into acid for local consumption.

(d) Problems of raw materials and plant

The most interesting and important problems in connexion with sulphuric acid supply arise through its raw materials. If an adequate supply of these at stable prices could be taken for granted, we should not have to worry much about the problem which is common to nearly all chemicals, of ensuring the timely construction of additional plant to meet the growth of demand. This is much less formidable for sulphuric acid than for many chemicals, partly because the big users so largely make their own acid, and can be expected to foresee their own demand with fair accuracy, and partly because the time-lag between the decision to build and the plant's operation is not as great as usual (except where anhydrite is to be used). The opposite problem, of not creating a long-run excess of capacity, is unlikely to be really serious so long as demand continues to grow, especially as it is possible to add to capacity in units which are small relative to total output. Decentralized decisions by the individual firms can be expected to lead to an amount of plant construction which will be 'near enough'—or rather they *could* be, if uncertainties about raw materials did not complicate the whole issue.

Very broadly, the expansion of output between 1935 and 1950 rested on an increased use of natural sulphur (see Table 4). The increasing supplies of spent oxide available as a by-product from the gas-works were absorbed—their price was adjusted to ensure that this happened—and the output from I.C.I.'s anhydrite plant was gradually increased as experience was gained. But in the absence of some special reason a producer laying down a new plant in that period would almost automatically choose the 'contact' process, based on natural sulphur: the output from pyrites actually declined. Even though sulphur nearly all comes from the United States, whereas pyrites come mainly from Spain, the dollar expenditure seemed to be well justified by the cheapness of the sulphur and the 'cleanness' and efficiency of the sulphur-using process.

The limitation of supplies of American sulphur, and the danger of its getting worse, then provoked a crisis. Producers who had been using sulphur were urged to instal new pyrites-burning plant, and most of them responded; three large schemes for production from anhydrite were started, which came into operation during 1955; a stimulus was given to the recovery of waste sulphur from various processes (for example, oil refining); and as a short-run measure usage of sulphuric acid was forcibly limited by various devices—notably a differential quota scheme, which particularly affected the production of super-phosphates as the 'big' user whose product could best be partially replaced by imports.

These developments raised considerable organizational problems for the industry and indeed for the nation. Sulphur remained the cheapest material: how should the limited supplies be divided between the acid producers? Should the firms who patriotically erected pyrites plant be rewarded with a higher sulphur allocation, or a guarantee of continued orders at profitable prices even if sulphur supplies recovered (as they did), or a higher price for their acid during the shortage period? If the last, how should it be arranged—for example should their customers be unlucky compared with other buyers of acid by having to pay it? Who was to put up the large amounts of capital needed for the anhydrite plants?

Such problems would have been easier to solve in a neat and tidy way if all production had been carried out by a single monopolist, so that separate financial interests need not be considered. In fact, as we have seen, there are many separate producers of acid, whose interests vary further because some are also—or even primarily—consumers. But the administrative problems were greatly eased by the fact that a relatively small number of big firms accounted for a large part of the total, both for consumption and production, and by the sense of responsibility shown by the bulk of the industry.

Various schemes for levies and the like were considered, but they would have been very hard to operate in the face of continually changing conditions and numerous uncertainties. No levy was in fact introduced, but rough justice was done to those firms which 'responded to the call of duty by installing pyrites plants' through the system of allocating the limited supplies of sulphur in proportion to 1950 usage, more especially as they could sell their quota at a profit if they liked. As the possibility of importing sulphur improved, imports were for a time deliberately held down to the amount needed to meet the total demand for acid, after allowing for the maximum production from other materials; this both ensured a market for acid from the pyrites plants, and gave the sulphur quota a market value.

There were, however, obvious economic objections to using restrictions on imports of sulphur—the cheapest material—as a balancing factor for more than a short period, and the force of these was increased when the new anhydrite plants came into full production. From January 1956 onwards therefore the restrictions on sulphur were removed, and it was left to 'market forces' to determine which plants should be closed or run below capacity. In view of the nature of the market and the many links between producers and consumers this did not mean that the outcome was settled by the blind working of price competition: much was settled by the deliberate decisions of multi-plant firms—for example I.C.I. shut down some old pyrites plants—and other developments were the result of negotiations between firms.

The last line of Table 4 shows some of the big changes which took place between 1954 and the first half of 1956, and also shows how the problems caused by the new anhydrite plants and free imports of sulphur were eased by the growth in total demand (and hence production). Even so production of acid from pyrites and from certain by-products has been significantly reduced.

The arrangements for the anhydrite schemes present features of special interest. Prior to the sulphur crisis I.C.I. had been the only producer, with a plant at Billingham whose output had been worked up from some 50,000 tons in 1935 to 100,000 tons in 1950. The company was prepared to undertake an expansion scheme to increase this to 175,000 tons, but beyond that it adhered to its general policy that large con- sumers should accept a substantial amount of responsibility for ensuring their own supplies. Consequently a company was formed—the United Sulphuric Acid Corporation—by eleven of the leading consumers to erect a new plant at Widnes with a capacity of 150,000 tons; I.C.I. provided technical advice, based on its Billingham experience, and indeed subscribed for shares in its capacity as consumer of acid, but maintained the principle that *consumers* should undertake a development designed primarily to ensure continuity of supplies of acid in face of uncertainty about imports of sulphur and pyrites.

The third scheme—for a plant of 90,000 tons capacity—was under- taken independently by Solway Chemicals, but the acid is mainly for its own use.

Fortunately, it seems that production from anhydrite is not 'an obviously high-cost process, to be justified only on autarchic grounds'. The financial outcome seems to be reasonably satisfactory if a good *local* market is available both for the acid and for the cement, as is the case with all the schemes. An industry which relied wholly on anhydrite plants would not be very efficient, because it would lack the flexibility in meeting changes in the geographical pattern of demand, and the ability to adjust capacity smoothly to meet its growth, which is obtained by having various sizes of sulphur-burning plants; an anhydrite plant needs to be operated continuously at something like full capacity. But if the fine adjustments of this kind are obtained by other processes, a small number of anhydrite plants in key positions can probably be justified on economic grounds, apart from their value as an insurance.

The new anhydrite plants added some 300,000 tons per annum to the industry's potential output within the space of a single year (equal to some 15 % of previous usage); coming on top of the pyrites plant erected in previous years this created a situation of moderate excess capacity despite the spurt in demand. The excess was not, however, big enough to cause serious embarrassment to the industry, especially as some inferior plant was really due for scrapping anyhow, and the secular growth in demand should remove any problem in a few years—indeed Fisons were already erecting a new sulphur burning plant in 1956 to meet their own expanding needs. Meanwhile a modest reserve of capacity has its advantages from the national point of view when supplies of particular materials and the level of demand are both liable to sudden change.

6. ALKALI

The next case-study relates to a commodity group rather than a single chemical, but it contains very few products: it does not cover everything which is chemically alkaline, but only the main commercial products commonly referred to collectively as 'alkali'—sodium carbonate, sodium hydroxide (or caustic soda) and sodium bicarbonate. Sodium carbonate is commonly known in industry as soda ash, a name which survives from earlier processes, and is widely used by many industries; in the household it is used in crystalline form ('washing soda'), but this, like sodium bicarbonate, is a relatively unimportant item.

(a) Uses of alkali

The main reasons for considering soda ash and caustic soda together lie in the field of production, but on the consumption side they have several broad characteristics in common. In brief, both belong to the category of 'bulk' chemicals which are 'essential' to their users—a category which we have already met in the section on sulphuric acid. Soda ash is indeed similar in price to sulphuric acid at about £10 per ton, but transport considerations are not so important as it is despatched to big users in truck-loads without special precautions. Caustic soda is priced about twice as high.

As with sulphuric acid, large quantities of alkali are used in the chemical industry itself, or in its allied trades (notably for soap-making). The proportion taken by outside users is, however, considerably higher than for sulphuric acid, the main consumers being rayon and paper-making (for caustic soda) and glass and paper-making (for soda ash). In addition, the export trade is of considerable importance, whereas it was negligible for sulphuric acid.

Table 6 summarizes the published statistics which are available on the subject, derived from the 1948 Census of Production (no later census gives the information). It is not complete, because many industries did not have to record their purchases of alkali, but it gives the main outline of the picture. In 1948 exports were being restricted, so that the needs of home consumers might be met, and increased by 50% between 1948 and 1951 (see Table 7); but they subsequently

Table 6. *Production and consumption of alkali in 1948*

(Thousand tons)

	Carbonate and bicarbonate	Caustic soda	Total
Production	n.a.	n.a.	1,620
Sales by producers	n.a.	n.a.	1,565
Exports	224	111	335
Purchases recorded in Census			
Total	(704)	(325)	1,029
Of which			
Soap, candles and glycerine trade	88	48	136
Chemicals (general) trade	172	76	248
Other chemical and allied trades	37	36	73
Glass (all trades)	271	n.a.	271
Rayon, nylon, etc., trade	11	83	94
Paper and board trade	47	46	93
Textile finishing trade	n.a.	n.a.	61
Brine pits	45	n.a.	45
Sales not accounted for	n.a.	n.a.	201

Source: Census of Production Reports.

Notes: (1) n.a. = not available.

(2) The difference between 'production' and 'sales by producers' represents consumption at producing works (for example, carbonate converted into silicate of soda) plus any addition to stock (or minus any decrease).

(3) In some of the census trades shown above purchases were not asked for in sufficient detail to give the full picture required for the table—for example, bicarbonate was not included, or 'alkali' was given as a single figure. No allowance has been made for omitted items, but undifferentiated figures have been split equally between the two columns so as to give approximate totals.

(4) No allowance has been made for purchases by firms in the above trades which did not report to the census (having ten workers or less) or for any alkali included in 'unclassified materials' because firms' records were inadequate.

(5) The 'sales not accounted for' include all washing soda used in households, restaurants, etc., industrial uses of alkali in trades not required to report them, and the minor omissions indicated in notes (3) and (4); probably they consisted mainly of carbonate, so that the total sales by producers may have consisted of 30 % caustic and 70 % carbonate, etc.—implying that the *values* were not very different.

Table 7. *United Kingdom exports of alkali*

(Thousand tons)

Year	Carbonate and bicarbonate	Caustic soda	Total
1948	224	111	335
1949	171	114	285
1950	244	177	421
1951	357	151	508
1952	257	161	418
1953	202	143	345
1954	242	188	430
1955	266	198	464
1956	276	268	544

Source: Board of Trade, *Accounts Relating to Trade and Navigation of the United Kingdom* (H.M.S.O., monthly).

declined again, largely owing to import restrictions in such markets as Brazil, so that the table gives a reasonable view of the relative importance of exports.

Soda ash is now all made by one process, the 'ammonia-soda' or 'Solvay' process, and this is only operated by one producer—I.C.I.— and nearly all in a small area centred on Northwich in Cheshire. Caustic soda, however, can be produced by two methods; the soda ash produced by the Solvay process may be treated with lime, to yield caustic soda and calcium carbonate, and this is done on a large scale at Winnington; or an electric current may be passed through brine, yielding caustic soda, chlorine and hydrogen. I.C.I. are much the biggest operators of the electrolytic method, with their main works at Runcorn and Widnes; it is, however, used by some other firms, mainly for the sake of the chlorine.

This structure of production raises a number of interesting issues. First, why should production of such bulky products be so concentrated geographically, when sulphuric acid production is very dispersed? Secondly, why should it be so largely in the hands of one company— again in contrast to sulphuric acid—and what are the consequences? Thirdly, what determines the extent to which caustic soda is produced by the electrolytic method rather than the traditional one? Fourthly, what problems are there in ensuring an adequacy of supplies of the three products effectively involved—soda ash, caustic soda and chlorine?

(b) Geographical concentration

The short answer to the question of geographical concentration is that Cheshire is very well situated for bringing together the three materials primarily required—brine, limestone and coal—and is well provided with rail and water communications for distributing the product to home or export markets, and that the cost of assembling the raw materials near a big consuming centre (for example London) would usually far outweigh the saving in freight on the finished product.[1] To this must doubtless be added the usual forces favouring the location of additional plants at the traditional centre, but I.C.I. would have had little difficulty in siting them elsewhere if this had seemed advantageous.

It is interesting to note that the high cost of transporting soda ash and caustic soda, relative to their value, has had an influence on the location of some important *consumers*. One must not be dogmatic on such things, but it can hardly be a coincidence that such large amounts of soap and glass, for example, are produced in the north-western regions.

[1] The salt alone is heavier than the soda ash produced from it and the method of extracting it as brine virtually ties soda production to a salt-producing area. There is no *difficulty* over transporting soda ash, as there is with sulphuric acid.

Table 8. *Leading exporters of alkali* in 1955*

Exporting country	Value of exports (£ thousand)	Quantity (thousand tons)
United Kingdom	8,072	427
United States	7,039	368
France	4,768	276
Germany	940	38

* The definition varies slightly from country to country, but in each case covers soda ash and caustic soda.
Source: Trade Returns of each country.

(c) Predominance of I.C.I.

The concentration of production in the hands of I.C.I. requires more careful consideration. It is not a matter of patents, and the methods of production are well established and, in their main features, reasonably well known—though some details of their application are not common knowledge, and considerable research is continually being carried on to improve this eighty-year-old process. In the last resort, a would-be rival could obtain his 'know-how' through affiliation with an experienced foreign producer.

In effect, the simplest answer is probably the right one: although there is relatively little to *prevent* another firm—say a big consumer—from producing alkali, yet so long as I.C.I. is willing to supply the whole market and follow its present pricing policy there is no *incentive* to do so. In actual fact no other firm has tried to start an ammonia-soda works since the First World War, though some caustic soda has been produced as a by-product of chlorine, as noted above; this, together with the fact that the United Kingdom is the world's biggest exporter (see Table 8) supplies strong presumptive evidence that I.C.I. is an efficient producer with a moderate price policy.

There remains, however, the question of why I.C.I. has been willing to spend considerable capital sums on expanding its plant so as to continue to supply the whole market for this basic chemical, whilst stressing the need for big consumers of sulphuric acid to produce for themselves—and indeed adopting the same attitude in relation to chlorine, even though the consumers who were persuaded to produce their own chlorine inevitably sell caustic soda in competition with I.C.I. An outsider can only guess at the answer, which probably rests on a number of considerations. Thus the ammonia-soda process is very much an I.C.I. tradition, introduced to this country by Ludwig Mond; there are advantages in maintaining a 100 % share of the market which do not apply to one of 25 %; on transport grounds, expansion on existing sites is 'economically right', whereas acid for big consumers should be made on their site; the technical problems of introducing the ammonia-soda process are much greater than they are for sulphur-burning acid plants, and many of the big consumers of alkali are not even chemical firms, so that the 'social responsibility' argument that big consumers should look after themselves is further weakened; the expansion probably yields a reasonable profit, and a safe one, even if other ventures might yield a bigger one; and on the human side, the men in charge of the alkali division were 'entitled to' some share of the company's expansion, and had the personnel and organization to handle it.

From the national point of view, the consequences of this unified structure of production seem beneficial rather than the reverse—given that its persistence is not due to any artificial restrictions on entry of new producers, and the general reaction of I.C.I. to its responsibilities. It simplifies the problem of long-term planning, which is very necessary when expansion of capacity is a lengthy and expensive process; it places the responsibility for the supply of an essential basic material unequivocally on one body, and so *inter alia* facilitated the 'rationing' which was necessary after the war; research is in fact carried on with vigour, and neither its conduct nor its application suffers from any financial embarrassment of the producer; I.C.I.'s anxiety to avoid accusations of profiteering seems, at least in the prosperous times prevailing since the war, to increase with the degree to which it in fact controls the market for the product, so that its price policy for alkali is one of great moderation.

(d) Interlocking of production methods

In a static world it is clear that a proper balance between the two methods of producing alkali would be obtained by using the electrolytic process on a scale determined by the demand for chlorine; this would yield a certain amount of caustic soda, and the ammonia-soda process would produce enough carbonate for conversion into caustic to cover the remainder of the demand, as well as meeting the direct demand for soda ash and washing soda.[1]

This is in broad outline how the problem is tackled in the changing world in which the industry has to operate, but instead of a single equilibrium solution it has to be solved continuously. Moreover the production by one process or the other cannot be increased overnight to whatever level is indicated by the demand: plant extensions have to be planned years in advance on the basis of forward estimates. The

---

[1] Since the quantities demanded of all the products depend on their price, the above explanation is over-simplified, and of course the demand for chlorine might theoretically be so great that no caustic was needed from the ammonia-soda process. But given the demand curves for the products and the cost curves of the two processes, the theoretical problem of determining quantities and prices offers no difficulties.

inter-connexion between the processes means that the amount of plant laid down for the ammonia-soda process must depend on estimates of the future demand for chlorine as well as for soda ash and caustic soda.

Post-war developments have shown the difficulties in this field. Large-scale construction was clearly necessary after the war: the existing plant could not meet the existing demand for alkali; and a further rise in this was to be expected with the growth of the consuming industries. Expansion schemes were started for both processes, but before they were completed it became clear that new uses for chlorine were raising the demand so much that further electrolytic plant must be built. As a result the construction programme for ammonia-soda plant had to be reconsidered: some plans on which work had not started were put into cold storage, and some of the plant in course of erection was completed without the section for converting carbonate into caustic. Even so the completion of this plant created some excess capacity, and the fall in exports from the 1951 peak aggravated the position.

From the national point of view some reserve capacity for an essential material like alkali is a worth-while insurance policy against variations in demand: the previous limitation of exports and rationing of consumers had shown the danger of having too little (as a result of the impossibility of expansion during the war). Moreover we may reasonably expect that within a few years the growth of demand will provide a good use for any excessive reserve which now exists, and further extensions will have to be started in good time; but these may again have to be in electrolytic plant to supply more chlorine, and the ammonia-soda works may have to concentrate still more on soda ash. It will never be possible to dispose of the problem of estimating future demand for all the products and planning new plant accordingly: 'and so they lived happily ever after' are words which do not apply to the chemical industry.

7. DYES AND DYESTUFFS

The third case-study leaves the realms of single products altogether, and covers a group which numbers its products literally in thousands, without counting admixtures. The justification for treating all these together is partly the broad similarity of their use—to colour textiles, paper and other goods—and partly the links between them on the production side.

(a) The demand side

The basic reason for the enormous number of separate dyes is the enormous variety of colours and 'effects' which the users wish to impart to their wares. But the number of colours, etc., has to be multiplied by two further factors—one for the need to use different dyes for the various products, and a second to give the necessary price-and-quality range for each combination of colour and product.

The cost of the dye is a very small part of the user's selling price, whilst its quality can make a very great difference to the marketability of his product; consequently the user attaches great importance to the availability of a wide range of reliable dyestuffs, and also to the 'service' which the maker supplies—notably in finding and explaining the best technique for applying each dye. A dye may be priced 100 times as highly per ton as a basic chemical like sulphuric acid, but the user does not buy many tons and attaches more importance to quality in all its aspects than to price.

This does not mean, of course, that a wide difference in the prices quoted by reputable makers for products which yield similar results would have no effect—and this point is particularly important in the field of exports, which absorb a substantial part of the output. But moderate increases in one maker's price will not divert his customers *en bloc* to rival producers, whose dyes are unfamiliar, especially if the changed relationship is thought to be temporary.

So far as the home market is concerned, competition of foreign producers is strictly regulated under the Dyestuffs (Import Regulation) Acts, 1920–34. The First World War had shown the danger of being dependent on Germany for most of our dyes, and these Acts aimed at creating a British dyestuffs industry by prohibiting imports except under licence; such licences were (and still are) only given where the dye in question was either not produced at all in Britain or not produced in sufficient quantity or right quality. In considering the issue of a licence the question of relative prices charged by the British and foreign producer is in general disregarded, so that competition is only indirect —a foreign speciality dye against a slightly different British one.

(b) Production and international trade

The relationship between production, exports and imports in 1948 and 1951 (the years for which the Census of Production figures are available) is shown in Table 9. It will be seen that exports represented about 25 to 30 % of production by *weight*, but 40 % by the more important criterion of *value*—indicating (as might be expected) that a bigger proportion of the more highly priced types was exported than of the simpler bulk lines. Imports are even more concentrated on high-priced specialities, and since the war have mainly come from Switzerland.

Table 10 shows that both exports and imports rose to a peak in 1951, fell sharply with the textile recession of 1952, and rose again through 1953 and 1954. Production probably followed a similar course.

Table 10 also includes some pre-war figures for comparison, from which it will be seen that in 1937–8 the United Kingdom was a net *importer* of dyestuffs, reckoned by the more significant test of value; if allowance is made for price changes imports have never reached the pre-war level, whilst exports have more than doubled.

Table 9. *Production, exports and imports of dyestuffs**
in 1948 and 1951

	Quantity (Thousand cwt.)		Value (£ million)	
	1948	1951	1948	1951
Production	855	859	18·4	22·0
Exports	215	245	7·5	9·2
Imports	12	29	1·0	2·6
Approximate percentage of production exported	25	29	40	42
Approximate percentage of home market met by imports	2	5	8	17

* Defined in the census as 'finished dyestuffs obtained from coal-tar, other than pigment dyestuffs'. The trade figures may not be exactly comparable.
Sources: Census of Production Reports; Trade Returns.

Table 10. *United Kingdom exports and imports of*
dyestuffs, 1937–56

	Quantity (thousand cwt.)		Value (£ million)	
Year	Exports	Imports	Exports	Imports
1948	215	12	7·5	1·0
1949	219	9	8·7	0·8
1950	240	14	9·2	1·2
1951	244	29	9·2	2·6
1952	170	10	7·0	0·8
1953	207	18	8·3	1·7
1954	260	27	10·6	2·4
1955	211	26	9·7	2·3
1956	208	32	9·4	2·6
1937–8 average	97	45	1·3	1·4

Source: United Kingdom Trade Returns.
Note: Minor adjustments have been made to the figures for 1954 to 1956 so as to make them conform roughly to the definition for other years (and in Table 9).

This very important change-round reflects the fact that the British industry adopted a big programme of expansion at the end of the war with the main object of capturing some of the markets previously supplied by Germany—including the market in Britain. Estimates based on the Censuses of Production for 1935 and 1948 show the output of the dyemaking industry as having rather more than doubled in volume between those years.[1]

(c) Production methods

The overwhelming majority of dyes are very complex chemical products which are produced synthetically, the basic materials being mostly derived from coal-tar. Distillation of the tar itself is not regarded as part of the industry, but the subsequent chain of intermediate processes, which may be very long, is all included. Naturally these processes vary greatly from one dye to another, but the same intermediate products often serve as the basis for a considerable number of different dyes. Plant for producing these common intermediates may therefore sometimes be run continuously, even though the demand for individual dyes is often so limited that the later stages of their production have to be done on the 'intermittent' or 'batch' principle. Partly for this reason, smaller firms largely buy their intermediates ready-made, often at a stage in the chain where little further processing is needed.

Research is extremely important in this section of the chemical industry. Not only is there a continual struggle to find better methods of making existing dyes, but the search for new dyes is also unceasing.

(d) Structure of production

The making of dyes and dyestuffs is a sufficiently distinct branch of the chemical industry for it to be treated as a separate trade in the Census of Production—though the definition includes the production of tanning extracts.[2] However, the factories classified to the dyes and dyestuffs trade produce other chemicals, drugs, plastic goods, etc., on a scale which represents about one-quarter of their total sales; and in terms of *companies* the making of dyes could not possibly be treated as a separate industry since I.C.I. probably accounts for about two-thirds of the output.

In accordance with the general procedure of this chapter, the structure of production will be considered in relation to the *product* group—dyes and their 'intermediates'—rather than in relation to the whole output of the factories assigned to the dyemaking industry; and we shall consider companies, rather than factories.

---

[1] See article by B. C. Brown, 'Industrial Production in 1935 and 1948', in *London and Cambridge Economic Bulletin* for December, 1954 (p. v). The estimate is subject to a considerable margin of error because the average quality of dyes reported under the broad headings may have changed.

[2] The full particulars collected at a census may therefore be found in volume 2 of the Reports for 1948 and 1951.

The essential features of the picture are then simple. There are some sixteen companies making dyes, but I.C.I. produces about twice as much as the other fifteen put together—at any rate if one includes the intermediates which I.C.I. sells to the smaller companies. In a broad sense I.C.I. covers every section of the market, though naturally there are many individual dyestuffs which are specialities (often patented) of one of the other firms, and in general it performs all the intermediate stages for itself;[1] the other companies restrict their activities to a narrower range of dyes, and often buy a substantial proportion of their intermediates. The second largest producer is probably the Clayton Aniline Company, which has affiliations with a leading Swiss producer.

(e) *Nature of competition*

It is inevitable under such circumstances that I.C.I. should be mainly responsible for the general price level of dyestuffs, and that in the main the other producers will decide their policy in the light of the prices fixed by I.C.I. But with such a multitude of different products this generalization may on occasion be rather deceptive: in a particular subsection of the field, to which one of the other companies has devoted special attention, I.C.I. may in no sense be the 'price-leader'; and it is only in a limited way that one can apply a simple concept like a general price level or 'price structure' to a field where the firms' specialities clearly compete but are yet sufficiently different for their relative prices to change substantially without a very big switch of demand.

The small companies perform a variety of functions, but very broadly their ability to survive (and sometimes to flourish) seems to rest on one of two foundations: either they specialize in a particular field, often using well-established methods and 'not spending money on costly laboratories', so that by a close regard to details of the method's application they can quote very keen prices for some of the cheaper bulk products (so far as such a term can be applied to dyestuffs); or on the other hand they buy intermediates and produce admixtures in relatively small quantities for the speciality trade. In so complex a field as dyestuffs there is always likely to be room for such activities— in particular for the firm with low overheads which makes use of discoveries on which the patent has expired.

The dyestuffs market shows an interesting contrast in producers' attitudes to the results of their research. If these relate to the production of dyestuffs, they are patented as elaborately as possible; but the producers do a great deal of research into the problems of applying dyes, and

---

[1] It is interesting to note, however, that I.C.I. does no tar distillation at all; there is no rigid principle of self-sufficiency.

the results of these are made available to users free of charge as part of their 'service' to their customers.

Finally, competition must be considered in its international context. Table 11 compares the exports of the five leading countries, which probably account for over 80 % of the world total: it will be seen that the United Kingdom occupies third place, with about half the value recorded for Western Germany, and also of that estimated for Switzerland. The world's *imports* are naturally spread more evenly over a long list of countries, since the dye-using industries (notably textiles) are operated on a substantial scale even in relatively undeveloped countries, which may have little capacity for producing any but the simplest dyes. India is at the head of the list because of the vast size of its textile consumption, but in some ways it is more important to note that *every* country imports dyes, including the main exporters. In the case of the latter this is a reflexion of the importance attached by the using industries to a supply of foreign specialities, usually patented, to which reference has already been made; the governments of all the exporting countries give their home producers a very heavy degree of protection, whether by drastic quantitative restrictions or, as in the United States, by a tariff which may be over 100 %.

Table 11. *Leading exporters of dyestuffs in 1954 and 1955*

Exporting country	Value of exports ($£$ million)		Main markets
	1954	1955	
Switzerland	24	23	France, United States, Germany, India, Italy, United Kingdom
Western Germany	23	23	Hong Kong, India, Japan, Italy, France
United Kingdom	11	11	India, Hongkong, Australia, Netherlands
United States	8	8	Canada, Mexico, India, Japan
France	5	4	Brazil, India, Hong Kong

Source: United Nations *Commodity Trade Statistics*, Series D; Trade Returns for Switzerland.
Notes: (1) The definition of dyestuffs used in this table is rather wider than that in Tables 9 and 10, being no. 531 of the Standard International Trade Code; the Swiss statistics are not exactly comparable.
(2) No other country reported exports of much more than £1 million.

Competition in international markets is intensified by the great economy in production costs which can be obtained by having a longer run of production for any particular dye. The costs of changing over the plant from one dye to another—or of holding plant idle until sufficient orders for that dye have been accumulated to warrant making another batch—are a large part of the total cost of the batch; the incentive to secure further orders—whether by salesmanship, 'service', keen prices, or governmental intervention—is therefore extremely strong and the position is rendered more acute by the existence of substantial under-employed capacity, especially in Germany.

It is hard for an outsider to judge exactly what happens under such conditions. There is no international cartel for the sharing out of markets or price-fixing, so that one might expect to find an almost continuous tendency for prices to be cut down to levels which did little more than cover prime cost. But there are also forces tending to prevent this. Thus the number of important exporting firms in the world is relatively small, and each can well appreciate the consequences of an all-out price war when demand for dyes as a whole has a low elasticity and overhead costs absorb a large part of the price. Moreover the differentiation between the products sold by different makers under the same name is sufficient for consumers to prefer dealing continuously with the same producer, so that temporary price-cuts have to be very large to be effective—and even so run counter to the users' desire for stability in their costs.

In practice a firm's price-quotation and the intensity of its sales effort seem to vary somewhat from one country to another in accordance with the market situation there—which reflects largely the actions of the other exporters, though local producers may be important—and also in accordance with its long-run policy in that market. Sporadically a producer may virtually dump large amounts of certain dyes in particular markets, perhaps because he has taken the risk of producing a large batch in pursuit of economies of scale and found difficulty in selling it by ordinary methods. But in general export sales are expected to contribute a fair share of overheads, and no country can hope to remain a big exporter for very long unless its genuine competitive efficiency is high.

(f) Some general observations

The production of dyes in this country has advanced in forty years from the rudimentary state in which it stood at the beginning of the First World War to the position in which it not only supplies some 85 % of the home market but also occupies third place in the list of exporting countries. It has passed from the 'imitative' stage in which it merely adopted methods already used by the Germans or Swiss to increase (or start) the production of familiar dyes to one where it does a good share of the initiation of new products and new methods. The acid test of competition in international markets shows its progress as clearly substantial, although our continued inferiority to Switzerland also suggests that further progress should be possible.

It seems beyond doubt that this progress has been greatly facilitated by the existence of one large producer in the shape of I.C.I., especially as I.C.I.'s activities are not confined to dyestuffs. Research in the widest sense has been a key factor, and a big organization like I.C.I. has enormous advantages both for doing the research and for applying its results. It is not merely the size of I.C.I.'s dyestuffs production which is relevant here: the research done by the Dyestuffs Division might, and did, yield results which were of value in making other things than dyes; whether these were in fact produced by the Dyestuffs Division or another mattered little—their application was greatly facilitated by the spread of I.C.I.'s activities, and hence the incentive to do research was increased. Moreover on the financial side the greater ease of securing capital facilitated development and the existence of profits on other activities made it easier to maintain research expenditure in years like 1952 when dyestuffs were slumping.

As always, reliance on one organization for most of the development carries some risks with it, even if they have not proved serious up to now. The existence of more specialized firms is therefore welcome, if only as a spur to the big producer, and the liaison of Clayton Aniline with the leading Swiss producer is a special advantage.

The position might however be improved in its international aspects, though this is a matter which calls for action by the government rather than the producers. The dyestuffs industry is one in which there are great gains to be obtained from international trade, since the market for individual dyes is so limited that many should only be produced in one or two countries—perhaps even by one plant. All the major producing countries have, however, given drastic protection to their industry, and thereby limited the possibilities of specialization and exchange. A mutual agreement between the countries concerned to reduce progressively the scale of this protection (no matter what form it takes) should bring benefits to all of them, which would outweigh the transitional difficulties.

The scale of the protection is more important than its form, but the special system adopted under the Dyestuffs Acts might also be reviewed. It has the great advantage that where an import licence is granted the user obtains his supplies duty-free, and so is better able to face international competition in selling his product. But the system provides for no intermediate stage between 'duty-free' and 'prohibition', and so for virtually no price-competition between imports and home-produced goods. Prima facie it would seem better if a would-be importer who was unable to make out a case for a duty-free licence could still import the goods on payment of a prescribed tariff. Dyestuffs would, of course, come under the general provisions about anti-dumping duties like any other commodity.

8. PLASTICS MATERIALS

The final case-study relates to plastics materials, which are also a group containing a great number of separate products—though not as many as in the case of dyestuffs. The study is concerned with the production of plastics *materials* (for example moulding powders) not their fabrication into plastic *articles*.

The general characteristics of a plastics material are that it can be made to flow by the application of heat and/or pressure, and that it will retain the shape which it is thus made to assume. As a formal definition, however, this is not satisfactory: thus on the one hand it would cover metals, which can be melted by applying heat and then cast into all sorts of shapes, and also important 'natural plastics' like rubber and shellac; and on the other hand it does not indicate that we want to include under plastics 'materials' such things as rods, tubes and sheets, in which the flowing has already happened, and which will henceforward be treated by ordinary mechanical processes (sawing, drilling, etc.).

We can make the definition of the group more logical by specifying that the materials must be synthetic and by bringing in the chemical property which plastics have in common: they are all polymers, with molecules which contain many thousands of atoms. But the grouping is one based on convenience and historical usage, rather than chemical or economic logic: thus synthetic fibres used in textiles are omitted, though they conform to the general definition.

(a) The demand side

Plastics materials are defined in such general terms that it is not surprising to find that the group has an immense variety of uses.[1] A layman may perhaps find the following approach helpful in trying to understand the types of purpose for which they are used:

(i) Plastics are not in general *cheap* materials. The 1951 Census of Production showed that the average price of moulding powder was about £250 per ton which is a great deal higher than the price of an equal weight of steel, or timber, or earthenware. As an offset, the specific gravity of plastics is much lower than for metals, and the article can often be made much thinner than with wood or earthenware by the use of precision methods of moulding, so that on each count a smaller weight of material is needed. But even so the cost of the material will commonly be higher, and plastics will not be used in place of the 'traditional' materials unless there is some other advantage.

[1] An account of these is given in two Pelican books: *Plastics in the Service of Man* by E. G. Couzens and V. E. Yarsley, 1956; *The Chemical Industry* by T. I. Williams, 1953 (especially ch. 15).

(ii) This advantage frequently takes the form of economy in fabricating cost: because plastics can be made to flow, intricately shaped articles can be fabricated at much lower cost than would apply with (say) timber. But this economy is dependent on the demand being great enough to absorb a substantial output of the article.

(iii) In addition, plastics are frequently used for the sake of the special properties which they give to the finished article, rather than for the sake of cheapness. These properties range from attractive appearance to electrical insulation and resistance to damp.

Naturally this simple analysis does not tell the whole story, and in particular the two factors of *cost* and *special properties* have to be considered together in many cases. But it does point to some of the key factors, and it helps to explain why in 1955 all the innumerable uses of plastics put together still only absorbed about one-quarter of a million tons in the United Kingdom. Even with all due allowance for the lightness of plastics, the contrast between this figure and the millions of tons of cast iron, steel or timber shows how little is gained by vague general talk of plastics as a 'substitute' for such materials.

The analysis given above also helps to explain why plastics cannot simply be considered *en bloc* as a single material. The 'special properties' needed for different articles vary enormously, and call for materials which may be very different in appearance, cost, chemical composition and method of use. Thus the relative importance of cheapness and attractive appearance is quite different for an electric light switch (for which the dark hue of the cheap phenolic plastics matters very little) and for tableware, for which the greater colour range of amino plastics outweighs their higher price.

Nevertheless, the various types of plastics are far from being divisible into watertight compartments, with the materials included in each serving one set of purposes, and no competition between them. This is one of the numerous cases of overlapping spheres of application: each type of plastic competes with at least one other in at least a part of its uses, and in effect they are all linked together by this chain process.

Finally, one must emphasize that demand cannot simply be considered in terms of broad types of plastics—phenolic, aminoplastic, vinyl, etc. Within each of these types the user wants, and gets, a great number of different products or grades, varying in price and properties. Once again it is a matter of competition between materials which serve the same broad purpose, but which are sufficiently distinct in their characteristics (and often in their price) to be far from perfect substitutes in the economic sense.

(b) The structure of production

The structure of the plastics 'industry' has to be considered in the light of the fact that it has been developing very rapidly over the last thirty years or so: not only has the total output been multiplied more than ten-fold, but many new types have been evolved. This second point is indeed the more important of the two for understanding the structure of the industry. The various types of plastic have only a very broad connexion with each other so far as production problems are concerned: the fact that all are polymers is of some significance but not much; facilities for research and testing which a firm had installed for one type provide a reasonable starting-point for work on another, but do not give it any decisive advantage over a firm whose past experience related (say) to working with the raw materials in question.

In brief, the production of almost every type of plastic has natural links on the supply side with some other kind of chemical production, which may well be stronger than the links with other types of plastics. As a result no firm makes all types of plastics materials, even if we define 'types' fairly broadly, and many makers of plastics materials also produce other chemicals.

There are about forty firms who produce plastics materials. Their varying 'approach' to plastics production may be seen from the following illustrative list of firms of varying size:

The British Xylonite Company may claim to be the pioneers of plastics materials, having produced celluloid since 1877. They have developed from celluloid to produce various other plastics materials, and share with Distillers the ownership of B. X. Plastics which produces a further range. They have always been basically a plastics firm, with little or no outside activity, but unlike most manufacturers of plastics materials they also use them on a big scale to make plastic goods.

The Distillers Company on the other hand is a firm which embarked on the production of plastics materials as a logical extension of other activities—first plastics based on alcohol, which it has long produced by fermentation; then plastics based on acetylene, after it had erected a calcium carbide plant during the Second World War; and recently intermediates for newer plastics as a corollary to the synthetic production of alcohol which it does in partnership with The British Petroleum Company.

British Celanese and Courtaulds both concentrate on the cellulosic plastics in which they can make use of experience gained in their main activities as rayon-makers.

Cooper, McDougall and Robertson apply to the manufacture of phenolic plastics their experience in handling phenol which they gained in their original trade as sheep-dip makers.

British Industrial Plastics used to make cyanides for the gold-mining industry, which became depressed after the First World War. After some changes it developed the production of aminoplastics to provide an outlet for its sulphocyanides.

Birkbys started as moulders, and then developed the production of synthetic resins and later of moulding powder for their own consumption.

Bakelite is another basically 'plastics' firm, which manufactures many types besides those which are familiar in the household.

Finally, Imperial Chemical Industries is probably the biggest producer of plastics materials. Perhaps its greatest asset is its widespread experience in research and development; the discovery of polythene, for example, was made in the course of research into the influence of very high pressures on certain chemical reactions, done by the Alkali Division.

The great diversity of experience and interest of the firms concerned is one of the strengths of the plastics industry at a time when new developments are still so important; there is no danger of an over-stereotyped approach. It has also led to great variety in the combinations of plastics materials which firms include in their range; inspection of the *Buyers' Guide* published by the British Plastics Federation did not show any pair of firms which had developed the same combination of products even in terms of broad types.

In general the manufacture of plastics materials is in the hands of large or at least medium-sized firms. Some materials could be produced quite efficiently on a relatively small scale, but a small firm would lack the laboratory facilities needed for development, and would have no particular advantages.

(c) Competition and prices

It is not possible to give any useful answer to the question 'How far do particular firms have a monopoly of certain types of plastics materials?' Inspection of the *Buyers' Guide* reveals a fair number of categories with only one supplier—starting on p. 4 with alkyd resins in the form of moulding materials, which are supplied only by Bakelite. But such an approach gives a very exaggerated picture of the number of 'monopolies' in any significant sense. Quite apart from the ease with which potential competition could often be made actual (for example because firms are supplying the same type of plastics in another form), the type in question will normally be sold in close competition with other types. The answer to the question depends wholly on the degree of detail in the classification: further 'monopolies' could be added by subdividing the categories into various grades.

In effect, producers of plastics materials compete with one another more through the performance of their product than through price, especially in the newer types of plastics; even in the longer-established types there are differences of grade or performance which may make a consumer prefer one producer's wares to another's, despite the fact that the latter appear to be cheaper.

This does not of course mean that users are indifferent to prices, nor yet that progress in the industry consists wholly in new developments. Thus in the Board of Trade's wholesale price index the component for 'plastics materials and synthetic resins' is one of the relatively few which has shown a fairly marked drop in recent years: in September 1956 it was 124 (June 1949 = 100), against a peak of 134 at the beginning of 1952. Although a 'new' industry can be expected to show a downward trend in prices, relative to the general movement, this fall is in marked contrast to the continued rise from 135 to 158 shown over the same period by 'general chemicals', and that from 128 to 136 shown by the index for all manufactured products (excluding fuel, food and tobacco).

Comparatively few producers of plastics materials use them themselves to make plastic goods—and conversely few consumers have started up their own production of materials. The latter point suggests that the industry follows a price policy which may be considered moderate in view of the risks and research expenditures involved, but in itself it is not really strong evidence. The users are mostly not at all well placed to produce their own materials: they are both too small and unversed in the techniques involved, which are quite different from those of (say) a moulder.

Technically, it would be much easier for a material-producer to establish his own moulding department, but most of them 'stick to their last'. One reason for this is that the consuming department would not want to be confined to one source of supply, nor would it probably absorb the whole output of material; thus both sections would have to do 'outside' trade, and there is a tradition against the material-maker competing with his own customers. In effect, however, there is little more reason to expect the maker of plastics materials to enter the moulding trade than to expect a dyemaker to go into textile finishing.

(d) International trade

The international trade statistics show that in 1955 the United Kingdom was second only to the United States as an exporter of plastics materials (see Table 12), though Germany had been rapidly catching us up. The three exporters largely serve different markets, and for the United Kingdom to catch up the United States it would have to obtain a more significant share of the Canadian market, which is much the biggest and is dominated by the United States.

Exports have amounted to about one-quarter of total production in recent years so that they are an important element in the industry's economy. At the same time we import substantial amounts of plastics, mainly from the United States—indeed we are the biggest importers after Canada. These imports are essentially of kinds or grades which we do not (yet) make or do not make in sufficient quantity; it is most important that our users should have access to adequate supplies of the best materials, wherever produced.

Table 12. *Leading exporters of synthetic plastics in 1954 and 1955*

Exporting country	Value of exports ($£$ million)		Main markets (arranged in 1955 order)
	1954	1955	
United States	37	48	Canada, United Kingdom, Japan, Mexico, France, Colombia, Germany
United Kingdom	24	27	Australia, South Africa, New Zealand, India, Netherlands, Sweden, Denmark
Western Germany	18	25	United Kingdom, Netherlands, Sweden, Austria, Switzerland, Italy
Canada	7	10	Mexico, Colombia, United Kingdom
France	5	6	Switzerland, Argentina, Vietnam

Source: O.E.E.C. *Statistical Bulletins,* Foreign Trade Series IV.
Note: Synthetic plastics are taken as item 599.01 in the Standard International Trade Classification.

Table 13 gives the figures for our imports and exports in recent years. It shows that our exports have always substantially exceeded our imports, and also that they grew phenomenally between 1948 and 1951. The set-back in 1952 had been more than made good by 1954.

Table 13. *United Kingdom imports and exports of plastics materials*

Year	($£$ million) Imports	Exports
1948	3·7	4·7
1951	7·9	16·4
1952	6·1	13·6
1953	6·5	16·5
1954	9·3	20·5
1955	12·0	22·8
1956	10·7	26·1

Source: United Kingdom Trade Returns.
Note: Transparent cellulose wrappings are not included.

International trade statistics provide one of the acid tests by which we can judge an industry like plastics. On the whole they give re-assuring evidence of a progressive industry which has established a large export trade, though the way in which Germany has caught us up is rather disturbing—her *net* exports are bigger than ours. Complacency would be disastrous in an industry where progress is needed both in developing new products and in improving the ways of making existing ones.

The plastics industry has a number of characteristics in common with dyestuffs, such as the importance of research and development, but the structure which has evolved is different: I.C.I. is not, as in dyes, the dominating firm, producing almost every type, but simply one of the leaders, both in value of output and range of products. There are good reasons for the difference, such as the greater variety of products and of basic techniques, calling for variety of experience: the speed of advance has also been so rapid and along so many lines that a single organization would have found it hard to show the necessary versatility. As usual in the chemical industry, no single formula is applicable to all problems.

BIBLIOGRAPHY

Association of British Chemical Manufacturers, *Directory of British Chemicals and their Manufacturers*, London, A.B.C.M., biennial.
Report on the Chemical Industry, *1949* and *Report on the Chemical Industry, 1953: a Supplement to the 1949 Report*, London, A.B.C.M. 1950, 1954.
British Plastics Federation, *Buyers' Guide, 1955*.
Couzens, E. G. and Yarsley, V. E., *Plastics in the Service of Man*, Penguin Books, 1956 (Pelican Series).
Morell, A. J. H., Stevens, F. P. and Talbot, E. W., Chapter on 'The Chemical Industry' in Royal Statistical Society, *The Sources and Nature of the Statistics of the United Kingdom*, vol. I, ed. by Maurice G. Kendall, London, Edinburgh, Oliver and Boyd, 1952, p. 249.
Williams, T. I., *The Chemical Industry*, Penguin Books, 1953 (Pelican Series).

CHAPTER VII

STEEL

By Duncan Burn

1. INTRODUCTION

This chapter is concerned with the industry or industries which supply 'finished steel products', as they are somewhat ambiguously termed, as raw materials for other industries. It does not cover the making of iron castings, although these are within the province of the Iron and Steel Board which the government set up in 1953 to supervise the steel industry. The government's choice was determined by the fact that iron foundries and steelworks use broadly the same raw materials. Whether this was a compelling reason on administrative grounds was, as events proved, a matter for debate: it is not a compelling reason in economic classification (which can follow its own logic and convenience). The economic problems of iron founding are complex and of great interest, but in the main they are distinct from those of steelmaking.

For the economist the interest of the steel industry lies largely in the factors which have induced a widespread, almost universal, belief in Britain that the industry should be subject to some sort of public control or supervision (if not ownership), and in the forms of control which have been developed. The belief was generated in the inter-war years during which the industry suffered severely in international competition. How far this was owing to inherent weaknesses, how far to dumping by foreign firms, was in dispute. It was clear, however, that various factors—the severe impact of trade fluctuations (so that there was often heavy unemployment and apparently over-capacity), the high cost and the durability of plant, the growth of local monopolies of various kinds, the integration of makers and users—gave apparently high-cost plants great powers of survival, checked the advance of methods which (given a high level of utilization) reduced costs, and encouraged the formation of cartel-like organizations which often aimed at fixing prices profitable to the firms with higher costs. It was generally agreed by 1930 that drastic modernization was needed in the industry. Hence when the movement for renewed protection succeeded in the 1930's—everywhere a decade of rampant economic nationalism—the grant of protective duties was accompanied by the institution of public supervision intended to ensure that prices remained reasonable and the progress of re-equipment adequate.

Since the war different conditions have prevailed in many respects; there has consistently seemed to be too little steel, British prices instead of running above continental and parallel to American prices have been below both, exports have normally been restricted in the interests of home sales, imports have been sought to fill up the gaps in supply. In these different circumstances, the result largely of full employment policies everywhere, emphasis in arguments for public control or ownership has shifted. It has concentrated much more on securing an adequate rate of expansion and the organization of raw material supply —starting usually from the assumption that most of the steel used in Britain should be made there—and less on cost reduction.

These developments necessarily provide the focus for this chapter. At the outset the products and processes are described, and the limiting effect of variety of demand on scale of production is considered. The growth of demand in Britain, in particular the relation between actual and forecast demand since the war, is then traced. Section 4 discusses the dispersion of production, in regions, plants and firms, and explores the probability that this subdivision is inimical to efficiency by modern standards. Section 5 traces briefly the price and investment experience from 1945 to 1956: and provides a prelude to the survey of the central institutions, their genesis, their evolution since the war, and their apparent impact on efficiency. The last section concludes with a brief contrast of the situation in the United States, and also in 'Little Europe', where the European Coal and Steel Community has provided a different model of control, and opened the way to an extension of free competition which might have profound repercussions on the British industry.

2. PRODUCTS AND PROCESSES

'Finished steel products' vary greatly in shape and composition. Steel, it has been said, is not one but a family of metals, whose common character is that their main constituent is iron; but they include (apart from unwanted 'impurities') varying quantities of other elements. There is always some carbon (most steels are just carbon steels) and there may be manganese, silicon, nickel, molybdenum, chrome, boron, vanadium, titanium, tungsten, or other alloying metals. Phosphorus and sulphur are common unwanted inclusions (which must be reduced to negligible quantities) but occasionally both are deliberately used for the properties they give. These different steels are produced in various shapes—in flat plates or sheets or strips; in bars or rods of round, square, elliptical or hexagonal cross-section; in girder, beam or channel forms of varying weights, in tubes, in wire, and in miscellaneous complex and maybe unsymmetrical shapes (these being produced by casting or forging processes). Making these products thus involves both metallurgical processes for producing a material of the right chemical and physical composition (i.e. with the required proportions of different constituents and in a required crystal structure) and processes, more nearly mechanical, for giving the material the required shape.

Production involves a chain of processes. There are two main raw materials for steel: the primary one iron ore (in which iron is found as an oxide mixed with other materials such as alumina, silica, sulphur, phosphorus); the secondary one iron or steel 'scrap', that is iron or steel from discarded machinery or other discarded manufactures which include iron or steel (ships or bridges or tram lines for example) or the 'waste' from manufacturing processes—such as 'turnings'—and from steelmaking itself. Iron ore is mined or quarried. The iron in it is normally separated out in a blast furnace, a large tall furnace (the modern ones are 100 ft. high) into which ore and coke are charged at the top, a hot air blast is blown in near the base, and liquid pig-iron is drawn off at the base or hearth. The process is continuous, a blast furnace remaining active for several years before needing to be re-lined. It produces as by-products gas which is a source of power, and slag which represents unwanted materials in the ore, and may sometimes be used as road material, or for cement. This is a process where the product weighs much less than the raw materials: hence it is desirable as far as possible to keep down costs of assembling raw materials. The blast furnace metal is known usually, for historical reasons, as pig-iron: it has a high content of carbon and is not freed in the blast furnace from sulphur or phosphorus.

Pig-iron and scrap are made into steel by one of several steel melting processes, in which further removal of 'impurities' occurs and the constituents required apart from iron are added in the correct proportions. There are four major types of process. They may be thought of for convenience as being adapted to producing different quantities or qualities of steel and using different grades or mixtures of raw materials, but the position is not static. In the converter type, invented by Bessemer, air—supplemented or replaced in modern forms by oxygen —is blown through molten pig-iron; a vigorous combustion results from the reaction of the blast and the hot iron. Normally the converter uses little scrap. In the open hearth process (invented by Siemens) heat is provided by burning gas or oil; the flame, generated in the upper part of the furnace, is directed at an angle onto the iron and scrap in the lower part of the furnace—the hearth. The combustion temperature is raised by the use of preheated air, the preheating being accomplished in fire-brick regenerators heated by the gases escaping from the furnace. This process can use a lot of scrap. In the electric arc process heat is generated by an arc formed between electrodes and the metal in the 'charge' which is being refined. The charge is commonly all scrap. Finally steel may be melted (but only from exceptionally pure raw material and for very high-grade steel) in an 'induction' furnace where the heating of the raw material contained in a cylindrical refractory vessel is derived from an electric coil around the vessel. For very pure steel electric melting may be carried out in a vacuum.

These processes, particularly the first two, have variant forms. A fundamental advance was the introduction in 1878 of the 'basic' process (by Gilchrist Thomas) applicable in most types of furnace whereby, by the use of basic instead of silica refractories for the furnace, and by charging 'basic' reagents, phosphoric pig-iron could be refined. A high proportion of iron ores contain a lot of phosphorus. Most processes are in varying degrees still being developed to extend the range of steels they can make satisfactorily and the range of raw materials they can treat. The post-war years have seen particularly important advances in the status of the converter and arc processes.

Liquid steel from all types of furnace is normally poured into ladles and from these is poured ('teemed') into cast-iron moulds, where it solidifies into 'ingots', in various simple shapes, which when solid but hot enough to be plastic are either rolled between plain or grooved rollers or (much less usually) forged under a press. There are usually two or more stages of mechanical hot processing: and in these the molecular and grain structure of the metal is consolidated while the steel is also being given the required shape and size either as an intermediate or finished product. Ingots which are to be made into plates or sheets are first rolled into 'slabs' having an oblong cross-section: those destined for sections or bars are rolled first into 'blooms' having a square cross-section, and then into 'billets', also of square section— from 2 to 4 in. square.[1] For some products there are further processes —sheets and strip and special steel bars are often subjected to cold rolling or cold reduction (where the metal is rolled between plain or grooved rollers when cold); wire is made by 'drawing' rods through dies: some small bars and sectional shapes are 'extruded' through dies; tubes are made either by piercing solid rounds in special rolling mills, or by rolling up strip steel and welding it or by bending plates and welding them together. Some sheet is 'galvanized' (coated with zinc), some is coated with tin and made into tin-plate. The finishing thus becomes highly specialized.

Many ancillary processes form minor links in the chain of production. Iron ore, for example, is often pre-treated (especially 'sintered') before

[1] The primary rolling is normally in a 'cogging mill' or in a 'slabbing mill'.

smelting: by-products are recovered at several points. Between the hot-rolling or forging stages the metal must usually be reheated. Often intermediate products are subjected to cleaning operations; surface defects are chipped or ground out, oxide scale may be removed by 'pickling' in weak acid. Much steel is subjected to heat treatments (cycles of heating and cooling which vary greatly in length and type) which change its properties or restore properties which some of the processes impair.

The plant used in steelmaking at all stages is necessarily large and substantial because of the weights to be handled, the high temperatures encountered and (in rolling) the pressures that must be exerted. The plant is both costly and durable.

In general it is technically advantageous to integrate all the processes required to make a finished steel product from the blast furnace onwards in one works, and it is sometimes useful to include coke ovens and in some circumstances control and ownership of ore mines has technical advantages. The primary gains are the conserving of heat and avoidance of transport. Iron from the blast furnace can be taken molten to the steel furnaces, the ingots from the steel furnaces can be rolled as soon as they are solid but without becoming cold and requiring complete reheating: the blast furnace provides a surplus of gas to generate electrical power which it is economic to use on the spot in subsequent operations; and there is a considerable transport economy in an integrated works—if well planned—since most of the products at all stages are heavy in relation to their value, and they lose weight in processing: only 70 to 75 % of an ingot is made into a finished product—most of the rest is recovered as 'scrap' and provides part of the steel furnace charge. It circulates in the works. The avoidance of buying and selling intermediates no doubt also reduces administrative costs.

At all stages in steelmaking it is conspicuously cheaper to produce on a relatively large scale. Materials are now mainly handled mechanically. Hence, for example, the larger a furnace is the lower the labour cost—no more men are needed to look after it. There is usually also a saving of fuel partly because as the capacity of a furnace is enlarged its volume increases faster than its wall area, so that there is less radiation loss. For the same reason and because the material handling equipment can be used more intensively the capital cost of the structure is less in proportion to output. While technical considerations have progressively favoured larger furnaces it is also usually desirable to operate furnaces not in single units but in groups—partly because a furnace must be out of commission periodically for a month or so to be re-lined: and partly to supply 'batches' of metal at suitably frequent intervals through the day.

In rolling mills, too, provided that the manipulation of the metal being rolled is mechanized (which has been normal though not universal for many years), larger outputs involve, broadly speaking, no more workers. By rolling large ingots the machinery in all its stages can operate with less starting and stopping per ton of output, so that there is more working time: large pieces of steel retain their heat longer and can be subjected to more work in one heating, and faster working— greater speed in the mills, quicker reversing of rolls if they are reversed, quicker manipulation of the hot metal (all of which requires powerful motors and very substantial equipment)—makes it possible to do more work on the steel before it loses its heat. Steel is now often finished at a rate of 30 to 60 miles per hour. There are great advantages in working as continuously as possible not only to conserve heat and preserve furnace linings but to preserve uniformity in operation and in the product.

It is less uniformly advantageous to operate several rolling mills in parallel than to operate a group of melting or smelting furnaces. Cogging or slabbing mills, with a minimum capacity of upwards of 800,000 tons, can be quite effectively run as a single unit, and it is sometimes argued they are best so run, since a single unit provides the core of a sufficiently large integrated unit to extend the powers of a good manager. In subsequent rolling stages wide-strip mills which produce, for example, the sheets for motor-car bodies, or for tin containers, absorb the whole output of a slabbing mill—up to 2·5 million tons a year—but many finishing mills absorb far less than the full output of a primary mill and it is necessary therefore to run several in parallel if the whole output of primary or intermediate mills is to be absorbed. Their output is limited partly by technical reasons (for example, a narrow-strip mill rolling at the same speed as a wide-strip mill will roll a far smaller tonnage) and partly by market reasons. Provided the market is large enough it is of course advantageous to use a mill only for a narrow range of sizes, which are near its highest capacity:[1] where the range of a mill is thus limited it is necessary to have several mills if a wide range of even one type of finished product alone is to be made.

An integrated plant of modern design carrying out all the stages of production from coke manufacture to the production of finished steel products and making therefore at least 1 million tons of ingots a year will cost about £80 for each ingot ton to be made in a year (i.e. a total investment of £80 million) or nearly £110 a ton of finished steel. Capital cost will have to be reckoned at £12 to £15 a ton of finished product on a moderate estimate of interest and depreciation (the latter about 5 %), and after allowing for some of the capital cost to be carried

[1] I.e. which require most of its power.

by the by-products, and assuming fairly continuous operating and slow rate of obsolescence. The cost is much higher than it was twenty years ago, not only because of inflation but because the processes have been progressively made more elaborate and the plant (almost all entirely specialized for steelmaking only) therefore more costly in 'real' terms. Apart from extra cost involved in using the poorer raw materials which must often now be used, the compensating gains are partly better and different products, partly much lower fuel and labour costs.

A post-war development, 'continuous casting' may conceivably reverse the trend towards larger plants at least for some types of product. In this process liquid steel is poured into a tube which at the point where the liquid enters it is water cooled, so that the steel entering it quickly solidifies to form not an ingot but a sort of continuous billet, which moves down the tube and can be cut, as it descends, into lengths appropriate for use in a finishining mill. It is an attractive process, which would eliminate the heavy capital cost of making ingots and cogging and rolling them into billets: it would also eliminate the production of scrap which is unavoidable when ingots are cast, because in these a large area of unsound material is formed at the extremities, but mainly at the top, through the differential rate at which cooling takes place. Continuous casting would thus require a much smaller output of liquid steel for a ton of finished steel, and reduce both the capital cost of furnaces and processing costs. Continuous casting was developed first on the continent and then most intensively in America. It is only slowly coming into commercial use, and hardly at all in the United Kingdom. It is mainly used so far for high-grade steel in moderate quantities (up to 40 tons an hour, but usually less). It might prove economic to group many units together ultimately, but the economics of all this are obscure.

Steelmakers are faced with the problem of gaining as much of the advantages of large-scale operating as they can while providing the wide range of products which users of steel want to buy. This is not quite so terrifying as the list of products and sizes and qualities suggests —because a surprisingly large proportion of the steel that is used is wanted (or can reasonably be made to be wanted) in fairly uniform and simple specifications. Nevertheless a limit is set by markets to the scale of operations, so that it is by no means always, or even usually, possible —in any country—to operate on the scale which would give lowest costs if costs of distribution and sizes of orders were neglected. The restriction is almost invariably greater at the finishing end.

The scale of operations permitted by the market is smaller for high quality products which are to have special properties, exceptional toughness, hardness or elasticity for example, or resistance to high temperature or corrosion, than for more ordinary steels. But it is also often more difficult to make such special qualities, to control the composition or secure the required freedom from impurities, so that the technically advantageous scale of production is lower as well as the size of the market. The disparity between the scale of operations which gives relatively low costs and the size of market is not necessarily greater in degree with special steels than with more ordinary steels.

The scope given by markets for large-scale operations varies from country to country. In America the consumption in uniform sizes and shapes of some types of steel has been exceptionally large—owing (on the passive side of the account) to the confluence of a larger population, a disproportionately larger geographical area, and a distribution of raw material, power and food production which results in much long-distance transport on a large scale. Transport by rail, road and oil or gas pipeline creates immense markets for standard products. No doubt this market circumstance is one of the major reasons why, although modern steelmaking was born in Britain, Britain long ago lost her leadership in the industry, and the cumulative process of technical improvement has had more conspicuous successes elsewhere, above all in America where the most impressive advances in large-scale integrated operation to reduce costs and raise labour productivity have occurred. So much so that although the earnings of her workers were almost twice those of British steelworkers in 1939 the price of steel in the United States was by and large no higher: and though United States prices are now some 25 % higher, average earnings in the United States industry are nearly four times as high.

3. DEMAND FOR STEEL IN THE UNITED KINGDOM

The demand for steel is derived mainly from the activity of capital goods industries, which in turn depends on the volume of gross capital formation. The following table shows the main user industries in the United Kingdom in 1955. The pattern of distribution does not differ widely in other heavily industrialized countries. Transport, it will be seen, took 36 % of the steel whose final industrial use was specified. Motor vehicles took nearly 16 %, and if the use of drop forgings and springs for cars were separately available cars alone possibly took one-fifth of the steel supplied.

A large part of the demand for motor-cars is of course for consumers' capital goods: and some of the demand for electrical equipment likewise. The only large segment of the market for steel of which much is for direct consumption is the tin-plate trade, providing the material for containers—tin cans, for example, for food, tobacco, polishes, oil.

Table 1. *Domestic consumption of steel by industries, 1955**

	Thousand tons	%
Transport		
Motor vehicles, cycles, aircraft (including repairs and parts)	1,438	16
Shipbuilding and marine engineering	808	9
Locomotives and rolling stocks	731	8
Other railway uses	255	3
Constructional engineering, building and contracting	1,429	16
Mining	691	7
Iron and steel industry	465	5
Engineering		
(a) General	1,370	15
(b) Electrical	430	5
Gas, electricity, water (excluding plant)	92	1
Tools, instruments, implements, watches	82	1
Hollow-ware (excluding tin boxes, etc.), metal furniture, windows, springs, needles, pins, etc.	580	6
Tin-plate	656	7
Total	9,027	99

* Apart from this 4,538,000 tons of finished steel were used in making drop forgings and laminated springs (613,000 tons), bolts, nuts, screws, etc. (271,000 tons) wire and wire manufactures (924,000 tons), and in supplying stockholding merchants (1,668,000 tons) and small users and other unspecified consumers. Most of this steel was destined ultimately for the consuming industries in the table, but the distribution between them is unknown.

This dependence on the capital goods industries made the steel industry extremely susceptible to the ups and downs of the trade cycle. This was not an insular peculiarity. Attitudes and organizations in the industry were largely shaped by this risk. Since the Second World War cyclical fluctuations in demand have been modest in proportion, and only for short times and on a small scale has any capacity in Europe or America been idle for lack of orders. While such fluctuations have greatly lessened in amplitude the rate of increase in demand for steel has greatly increased. At the prices charged some demand—how much is uncertain—was often unsatisfied. An approximate measure of the

Table 2. *Steel consumption in the United Kingdom*
(from home sources and imports)

(Million ingot tons)

1911–15	5·56	1948	13·87
1916–20	7·32	1949	14·55
1921–5	5·05	1950	14·29
1926–30	7·41	1951	14·77
1931–5	6·81	1952	15·92
1936–40	11·67	1953	16·04
1941–5	14·53	1954	16·59
1946–50	13·43	1955	18·20
1951–5	16·30	1956	19·24

growth of consumption can be given, though the figures are only of steel supplied to consumers, not all necessarily used in the year of purchase.

The annual rate of increase of consumption was $2\frac{1}{2}$% from 1900 to 1938; from 1948 to 1952, 4%; in 1954 and 1955 it averaged 6 to 7%.[1]

As will be seen later the growth of demand outstripped the forecasts usually adopted in planning capital investment, though some forecasters always suspected these were too conservative. No accurate means of forecasting were evolved. Wartime forecasts of 'requirements' often proved very inflated. It was plausible to regard early post-war demands as being exceptionally high because of the transitory needs of reconstruction, and when demands continued exigent in the early 1950's this could be thought of as due to rearmament. It could also fairly be argued by the early 1950's that no further large increase in labour force was likely in the near future.

One crucial factor in forecasting, by the methods used, was to judge how far a given increase in the output of industries using steel as a raw material would increase the consumption of steel.[2] A persistent increase in the relative importance of steel-using industries could be foreseen. The first report of the Iron and Steel Board stated that 'a general tendency for engineering and similar products to become more complex' had meant that over a long period the output of these industries rose faster than their use of steel. A ratio of 10:8 in rates of increase had seemed a reasonable guide. But in some recent years it was nearer 10:10 than 10:8. This was almost certainly a reflex of certain features in recent technological development. Many of the newer industries which expand most—chemical and oil refining, and the nuclear industries, for example, which are only steel-using industries because they use steel in their plant, not as a processing material, nevertheless have a high consumption as plant consumers. The same would probably prove true (though the quantities would be smaller) of all industries where large advances in mechanical handling and automatic or remote controls, whether by way of transfer machinery or conveyors or by pressure or suction through pipes and conduits, have occurred. In the main these increased uses of steel for plant would be represented in the demands of the plant makers who used steel as a raw material. The adoption of mechanical handling and analogous procedures in some of the metal-using industries themselves—motor-car production is the outstanding instance—usually leads to a greatly increased use of steel in processing. The Iron and Steel Board decided in 1955 in forecasting

---

[1] Iron and Steel Board, *Annual Report for 1955*, (H.M.S.O. 1956), p. 3.

[2] The consumption of the steel-using industries would be largely to provide machinery and plant for investment—in all industries. Naturally the activities of the plant makers would be forecast in the light of probable rates of gross capital investment.

consumption in 1958 to use a ratio of 10:9; by the end of 1955 it was clear that in the short run this had already again proved insufficient. Similar forecasting errors were made on the continent and in the United States. The methods often had an air of refinement which belied the reality.

If industrial investment absorbed as much of the national income in Britain as in many competing industrial countries (which by the end of 1955 was widely deemed desirable) a still farther jump in demand for steel was seen in 1956 to be likely—a jump, rather than a further change of trend.

The seductive habit of discussing demand as 'requirements' often gives current estimates an air of fixity irrespective of cost. Some demands would be lessened if prices were higher. (Price policy will be discussed later.) For some purposes there are alternative materials—plastics, for example, aluminium and other light metals, timber and ferro-concrete can be used for some purposes in place of steel. There is also scope for saving steel by changes of design and the use, for example, of higher tensile steels. Higher prices would move the margin of substitution, and encourage the use of other materials and designs. Where there is no scope for substitution demand for steel is likely to be highly inelastic within the probable limits of price changes, and the degree of elasticity where there is scope is not high but is not to be disregarded. The cost of steel is usually a small part of the total cost of products in which it is used, so that movements in its price have only a negligible influence on the attractiveness of investment.

'Demand for steel' is an amalgam of demands for the different finished steel products. Some are joint demands: a ship's hull for example needs plates and sections, and welding rods, its engines need forgings, castings, and so on. Some products compete with each other for the same purposes. Demand for different products does not change at the same rate and some types of steel can be scarce when others are plentiful. Demand has expanded most in the last decade for flat products, sheets and plates, largely owing to the development of steel sheets which can be subjected to deep stamping, and to the spread of welding, whereby weldments of plates are used in place of heavy building sections and of large castings in industrial plant, for making tubes of large diameter, in high pressure vessels in place of forgings, and for other uses. Demand for plates has also grown with the persistent high activity of shipbuilding, and here the spread of welding has led to a demand not only for more plates but for wider plates, which the steel industry has not been well equipped to provide. Demand for heavy sections has also been reduced—less in Britain so far than elsewhere—by the use of ferro-concrete, which reduces the total weight of steel used in building but increases the demand for rods. The growth of the oil and chemical industries, and demand for high capacity boilers, heat exchangers and pressure vessels have greatly extended demand for tubes. Technological changes—in aircraft, for example, and nuclear energy—have required increasing quantities of steels with exceptional qualities.

Consumption of steel is dense in the principal engineering centres. A survey in 1950 gave the following regional distribution:

Table 3. *Steel consumption by region**
(percentage in last quarter of 1950)

Region	%	Region	%
Midland	19½	North Midland	6
London, etc.	17	Wales	4½
North-West	12	Southern ⎱	4
Scotland	11	South-West ⎰	
East and West Ridings	9	Eastern	3½
Northern	8	Northern Ireland	1½

* The regions are the Ministry of Labour's.

This has an important bearing naturally on problems of location, both because transport is a fairly heavy cost on bulk steel, and because steel using areas are scrap producing areas. A further analysis about the same time showed that 42 % of steel was sold to 186 buyers whose orders exceeded 2000 tons in a quarter, and a further 17 % to 1052 whose orders exceeded 500 tons. This does not of course indicate the size of orders for individual products. A considerable volume of the orders for steel are for small quantities. The difficulty arising from this is greater for sectional than for flat products. Often small orders are for relatively standard sections, and orders can be 'bulked'.[1] In most branches of the trade makers do not hold large stocks of finished products, but there is a large and growing trade in the hands of stock-holding merchants, who handled 11 % of the steel supplied in 1955. This is most important for tubes and sheets, where a large part of the output is made in a small range of standard sizes or gauges: the simplicity of the shapes eases this. Part of the output of all the more standard products is handled in this way. It facilitates the bulking of small orders for standard products and so enlarges the scope for large-scale production methods and it enables users to get the steel they want immediately, instead of waiting for it to be made to their order. Many orders are, of course, for non-standard products, and could not be supplied from stock, and large orders are almost invariably placed directly with makers.

[1] It is possible, for example, to tell regular customers when a particular section is going to be rolled.

Before the war the export trade was highly competitive, though it was coming increasingly under the influence of international cartels. Since the war, save for one or two brief interludes, export demands have been in excess of supply and several of the large exporters—the United Kingdom, United States and Germany—have on occasion been also large importers. This situation shows signs of persisting.

4. THE ORGANIZATION OF PRODUCTION

(a) Sources of the United Kingdom supply of steel and steelmaking raw materials

Most steel used in the United Kingdom is also made in the United Kingdom. Some is imported; but there has been a net export consistently since the war, higher than in the inter-war years.

Table 4. *Components of United Kingdom steel supplies*

(Annual averages or annual figures. Million ingot tons)

	Crude steel produced	Deliveries to or from stock	Re-usable material used	Imports	Total supply	Exports	Net import	Net export
1926–30	7·64	n.a.	n.a.	3·20	10·84	3·43	—	0·23
1931–5	7·24	n.a.	n.a.	1·55	8·79	1·98	—	0·43
1936–40	12·27	−0·27	n.a.	1·73	13·73	2·06	—	0·33
1941–5	12·45	+0·09	0·23	2·13	14·90	0·37	1·76	—
1946–50	14·43	+0·02	0·66	0·62	15·73	2·30	—	1·68
1951–5	17·60	n.a.	0·40	1·15	19·15	2·84	—	1·69
1956	20·66	−0·20	0·31	1·77	22·54	3·32	—	1·55

n.a. = not available.

Discussions of plans for the steel industry have usually implied that imports should be reduced, and that Britain should be almost self-sufficient in steel. This is plausible when steel is scarce, and British steel—in part for factitious reasons—is cheaper than imported, and imports are hard to obtain and cannot be bought at short notice in large quantities.

The economic justification of the assumption is not quite self-evident, since the natural advantage Britain has enjoyed for steelmaking has been declining. Originally Britain had cheap suitable coal and widely scattered deposits of iron ore. By their nature mineral deposits are wasting assets: the ore resources in the districts on which Britain's fame as a steelmaker was built have been almost all exhausted, and the most easily won coal in the older areas has been taken. An iron or steelmaking centre often gains new advantages as its raw material sources decline:

it may create a local market, which will also be a local source of scrap, it will have a trained labour supply, and possibly other 'external economies'. But because the industry is one where in the early processing there is a great loss of weight it is one for which location where raw materials can be cheaply assembled is an exceptional advantage.

More than half the metallic content of the iron ores used in iron and steelmaking comes from imported iron ore. The tonnage of home ore is still the higher, but its average iron content is approximately 27%, that of imported ore 57%.

Table 5. *Iron ore supplies*

	Iron ore produced in United Kingdom (million tons)	Imported iron ore	
		(million tons)	average value (shillings per ton)
1937	14·2	7·0	23
1946	12·2	6·5	56
1950	12·9	8·4	57
1951	14·8	8·8	85
1952	16·2	9·7	118
1953	15·8	11·0	114
1954	15·6	11·6	103
1955	16·2	12·9	107
1956	16·2	14·4	117

About 95% of the home ore comes from the East Midlands ore fields, the principal concentrations being in North and South Lincolnshire, Northamptonshire and Oxfordshire. Most of the ore is quarried, though an increasing proportion will in future be deep-mined. Mining is more costly: the cost, by French analogies, might be about 20s. a ton. Quarried ore costs much less. The average labour cost of home ore in 1955 was 2s. 9d. a ton.[1]

Imports of iron ore come from a wide range of countries, of which Sweden (29%) and French North Africa (25%) were the most important in 1955, followed by Newfoundland and France (7% each), Spain (6%), Sierra Leone, French West Africa, Labrador (5%), Brazil (3%), and a little from Spanish Morocco, Liberia, Venezuela, India, British West Africa, and South Africa. Some of the smaller sources are likely to grow in importance—for example, Venezuela and Labrador, where enormous deposits have been opened up primarily with United States capital for the United States industry. The British is thus not the only industry depending partly on imported ore: the West German is as dependent, the United States increasingly so.

---

[1] The output of 16·2 million tons was produced by an average of 4150 workers, whose average earnings were £11. 3s. a week.

Freights form an appreciable part of the cost of imported ore. To keep this cost down much larger ore carriers are being used or built (from 30,000 to 80,000 tons) where it is practicable; the Americans have pioneered in this, and the Swedes have followed.

Ore is imported into a great number of different ports in Britain, hence the average quantity at any one port tends to be small, and most of the ports are not suitable for big ships. For Germany the trade is more concentrated, a great proportion of ore entering by Rotterdam, which has facilitated the effective use of highly specialized plant.

The growing cost of coal production in the United Kingdom is dealt with in ch. IV. Coking coal is among the categories of coal whose production cost has risen most: Durham, South Wales, Lancashire and the relevant parts of Scotland are all in differing degrees (but especially Scotland) 'high cost' mining districts. Coking coal in Yorkshire, though poorer in quality, is much cheaper. Producer gas from coal for open hearth furnaces has been replaced since the war largely by oil.

Raw material assembly costs for pig-iron vary greatly in different regions of the United Kingdom, and the dispersion has become exceptionally wide with the sustained high price of imported ore. In 1950 when imported ore had fallen to its lowest post-war average price the British Iron and Steel Federation contrasted the assembly costs at well-placed sites respectively for using home ores, and imported ores. The results of the calculation were:

Table 6. *Raw material assembly costs (per ton of pig-iron)*

	Imported ore site (s.)	Home ore site (s.)
Ore	93	48
Coke	66*	94†

* 16 cwt. coke including low transport cost.
† 20 cwt. and including high transport cost.

Subsequent price changes require considerable modifications. The imported ore cost has been doubled: the home ore cost may have risen by one-third. Coking coal costs have risen more in the coastal districts than for home ore sites which can use a high proportion of cheaper coking coals. A revised comparision for 1955 would be approximately:

	Imported ore site (s.)	Home ore site (s.)
Ore	186	64
Coke	88	118
Total	274	182

The smelting of home ore required more blast furnace and sintering capacity per ton of iron: but though this excess may have amounted to from £5 to £7 for a capacity of 1 ton a year this represents at the most a capital charge of 15s. to 20s. a ton. The resulting pig-irons have slightly different properties: the home ore pig-iron may be slightly dearer to use in the open hearth, but it would be ideal for the basic Bessemer process whose value has been growing. Precise comparisons are difficult, but there is no doubt that a very substantial margin of advantage is now enjoyed by the user of home ore—provided he is allowed to retain it. The figures given here possibly minimize it:[1] an authoritative estimate within the industry in 1955 put the advantage at £5 a ton of steel.

Scrap, other than the circulating scrap arising within steelworks, is produced where steel is 'processed' by users or where machines or structures made (in part or whole) of steel wear out. The main centres of its production are thus the centres of the metal using industries. Scrap as produced commonly needs sorting, and cutting or baling. Most of the scrap is handled and prepared by large merchant firms.[2] The price of scrap, rigidly controlled, varies regionally, being lowest where much is produced, for example in the dense industrial Midlands, the Glasgow area and the North-East Coast, but highest in South Wales where demand greatly exceeds supply.

The major part of the scrap used by the United Kingdom industry is domestic scrap; but there have been substantial imports, which have been costly. In 1954, 760,000 tons were imported at a cost of £10·9 million (i.e. £14·4 a ton): in 1955, 1,277,000 tons at an average cost of £17 a ton. The sources of imports have varied greatly, and competition for this scrap from the continent grew acute.

The supply of process scrap is necessarily a function of steel consumption (thus, for example, the proportion of steel used for shipbuilding which becomes scrap is likely to be uniform from year to year). The supply of scrap arising from wearing out or obsolescence of old equipment or buildings is less predictable, but when steel consumption is rising fast this 'demolition' scrap is likely to be a falling proportion of consumption. In recent British experience fluctuations in availability of home-bought scrap seem to sustain this view: from 1949 to 1955 the home-bought scrap consumed in steel furnaces was on an average

---

[1] The full calculation is complex. For example, imported ores usually need flux, home ores are commonly used in 'self-fluxing' mixtures. The home ore cost in the table includes sintering, the imported ore cost does not. There is more by-product gas in using home ore.

[2] The larger of these, by logical evolution, now combine the scrap trade with many other activities—trade in non-ferrous scrap, second-hand steel and machinery, steel stockholding, contracting and constructional engineering, reconditioning of machinery, machine-tool making, crane making, steel casting manufacture, and so on.

26·7 % of home consumption (measured in ingot tons): but in 1952, when consumption jumped up sharply, it fell to 26 %, and again in 1955 when there was a sharp rise in consumption of ore the home-bought scrap consumed fell to 25·5 %. An expansion of steel output must (in the absence of temporary exceptional circumstances or import possibilities) depend on increased supplies of pig-iron or its equivalent.[1]

(b) Regional distribution of United Kingdom steelmaking

Steelmaking in Britain is remarkably dispersed, and this dispersion has in its broad features been sustained with remarkable constancy for a generation. The proportion of the total output of crude steel made in the different producing regions is shown in Table 7.

Table 7. *Regional outputs of crude steel as percentage of total, 1929–55**

District number	1929 (%)	1937 (%)	1955 (%)†	Increase in output 1937–55 (million tons)	Output in 1955 (million tons)
(1) South Wales and Monmouthshire	24	20	23 (*16*)	1·97	4·61
(2) North-East Coast	23	22	20 (*24*)	1·17	3·99
(3) Sheffield	13	14	13 (*1*)	0·90	2·64
(4) Scotland	16	15	12 (*8*)	0·45	2·34
(5) Lincolnshire	8	10	10 (*14*)	0·70	2·00
(6) South Lancashire, Cheshire, Flint, Yorkshire except Sheffield and North Riding	8	8	9 (*6*)	0·73	1·80
(7) Staffordshire, Shropshire, Worcestershire and Warwickshire	6	6	5 (*4*)	0·34	1·04
(8) Northamptonshire, Derbyshire, Leicestershire, Nottinghamshire and Essex	2	3	5 (*19*)	0·56	1·00
(9) North-West Coast	2	3	2 (*8*)	−0·02	0·36
Total (in million tons)	9·6	13·0	19·8	6·80	19·79

* The data all come from the statistics of the Iron and Steel Board and the British Iron and Steel Federation: but the districts are renumbered to put the most important areas first.

† Italic figures in brackets give percentage distribution of pig-iron output.

This almost static pattern is a structural feature of great interest because during this period the underlying cost factors have changed greatly, and the response to the change has been negligible. The greatest expansion of output has occurred in South Wales, one of the regions most distant from home ores, with dear (though good) coal,

---

[1] For example, sponge iron, or iron reduced from iron ore by a hydrogen reduction process.

where scrap is expensive because there is little local consumption of steel, and from which the main markets for steel are relatively distant. There are ports for export, though the shipping services are not as valuable an asset as, for example, those of Liverpool. Of the old major districts only Scotland has lost ground appreciably and this only in the last few years.[1] The home ore districts (5 and 8) have made proportionately little gain in relative importance after the small jump between 1929 and 1937 when steelmaking was started at Corby in Northamptonshire. Together these regions have provided one-fifth of the additional output from 1937 to 1955.[2]

The dispersion originally rested on the widely scattered distribution of iron ores as well as of coal. The districts which now have large ore deposits (possibly originally these were the largest deposits) were little developed in the early days of British iron or steelmaking: hence, among other things, they have no local market and no local scrap. Many of the older districts illustrate the process of adaptation described briefly earlier. Firms on or near the coast turned to imported ores—in South Wales, Scotland, the North-East and North-West Coasts, and in the Lancashire-Cheshire area. In South Wales most of the works at the heads of the valleys gave way to new works on the coast: in Scotland this did not happen. Here the steelworks depended more on scrap which was plentiful from the local market (which the Welsh lacked). The industry in the 'Black Country', though never one of the great steel areas, rested on the market (which had in turn rested on the wrought iron production which made the district famous) and on the cheap scrap which flowed therefrom. Sheffield was in part an anomaly: heavy steelmaking was in a sense built up on the back of high grade steelmaking, for which low raw material assembly costs are less important and in which Sheffield built a great reputation before modern methods of steelmaking were invented. (The tradition has been brilliantly maintained.) Sheffield made—and makes—no pig-iron, and the mass production side of its steelmaking relied largely on scrap as raw material, which was used in quantities far in excess of local supplies. As coal in the older coking coal areas became scarcer and dearer and imported ore prices rose steeply Sheffield became a better location for large-scale steelmaking, but the technical change to take advantage of this, the manufacture of pig-iron, has not yet been made.

The distribution of pig-iron output shows rather more response than that of steelmaking to changing raw material costs. The relative strength of the North-East Coast among coastal districts and the weakness of

[1] The North-West Coast, however, *was* a major district in a remoter past.

[2] Iron ore from Northamptonshire and Lincolnshire have been used for steelmaking in South Wales, Staffordshire and the North-East Coast.

the Scots position stand out: but with the completion of new large furnaces now being built in Scotland this weakness will be somewhat obscured.

The distribution of output of individual finished products differs widely from that of crude steel. There is for some products a large degree of regional specialization, as the following table for 1955 shows. It helps to explain some of the strength of areas where cost factors would seem otherwise unfavourable.

Table 8. *Regional distribution of production of principal types of finished steel (all qualities)*

District	Plates	Sheets	Heavy sections bars and rods	Light sections bars and rods (including wire rods)	Tubes	Tyres wheels axles	Other forgings	Cast-ings	Alloy steel ingots
(1) South Wales	16	62	4	15	8	n.a.	n.a.	7	4
(2) North-East Coast	35	3	40	13	5	2	8	19	1
(3) Sheffield and East and West Riding, Yorkshire	2	1	7	23	1	53	49	27	67
(4) Scotland	27	4	17	6	16	2	10	16	14
(5) Lincolnshire	16	n.a.	9	5	n.a.	n.a.	1	2	1
(6) Lancashire, etc., but excluding parts of Yorkshire (included in 3)	2	28*	1	12	n.a.	42	9	5	9
(7) Staffordshire, etc.	2	4	18	12	33	n.a.	14	16	1
(8) Northamptonshire, etc.	n.a.	—	n.a.	12	36	n.a.	7	9	2
(9) North-West Coast	n.a.	n.a.	5	1	n.a.	n.a.	n.a.	n.a.	n.a.
Million tons	2·5	2·2	3·1	2·2	1·3	0·3	0·2	0·3	1·2

n.a. = not available.
* Including District 8.

Thus the North-East Coast, Scotland and Lincolnshire are predominantly heavy steel producing areas and make 78 % of the plates and 68 % of the sectional products. Sheet production (with which tin-plate is linked, since the tin-plate is made from sheets) is almost wholly concentrated in South Wales and District 6. Tubes are made primarily in the East and West Midlands, with only Scotland otherwise much in the picture. Sheffield is responsible for half the forgings, over a quarter of the castings, and nearly a quarter of the light sectional products: it produces two-thirds of the alloy steel. The concentration of heavy plate production corresponds in part to the concentration of shipbuilding on the Clyde and the Tyne, Wear and Tees. There is much constructional engineering also on the North-East Coast. The concentration of sheet, tube and alloy steel production does not correspond with the location of markets. There is some concentration of wire rod production in Lancashire which reflects a large development of wire drawing near Warrington.

The concentration of production of light re-rolled sections and bars in the West Midlands is largely in the hands of re-rollers—about forty firms—who do not make their own steel but buy intermediate or semi-products (usually 'billets') some of which are imported; otherwise they are often made by steelmakers in other districts: a considerable tonnage for example comes from Sheffield. The re-rollers' consumption of 'semis' in excess of local production was about 550,000 tons in 1955. All this had to be transported from other districts or from abroad. In Sheffield too there are many 're-rollers', buying their semi-products from other steel firms; but they rely mainly on supplies from local steelmakers.

(c) The number and size of plants

Though the advantages of large-scale operations for a large proportion of the output of the steel industry are manifestly great, the number of 'establishments' coming within the industry—in the Census of Production sense—is surprisingly large. The core of the steel industry comes within the category Iron and Steel (Melting and Rolling), which includes integrated steelmakers and rollers, plus 're-rollers' and steel founders. The Census for 1951 records 398 establishments in this category. Outside this category there were fifty-one blast furnace establishments, 156 establishments making tubes, thirty-one making sheets, forty-four making tin-plates. These figures are liable to mislead. Where iron smelting, steelmaking and the making of sheets, tin-plates or tubes are carried on together in an integrated plant the main stages must appear as separate establishments.

The 398 'establishments' included ninety-nine which employed from ten to forty-nine workers, the average number employed in these being twenty-eight, whose net output was £2·8 million. A quarter of all the melting and rolling establishments contributed, that is, 1·8 % of the net output.[1] At the other end fifty-six establishments (about 14 % of the total number) employing upwards of 1000 work-people each produced nearly 70 % alike of the gross and net output, and employed

[1] They would include, for example, small toolmakers. During the war there were over forty firms (with only one or two exceptions Sheffield firms) who made high-speed steel, and of these just over thirty did not link it with any larger-scale steelmaking. Their weekly output averaged about 15 tons: ten larger makers averaged 50 tons a week, the rest about 3 tons a week. The Census Report, in an analysis according to specialization within the trade (Table 6), states there were 116 steel manufacturing plants (with melting) making non-alloy steel, and 70 making alloy steel. But foundries and ingot-making plants are not distinguished.

70 % of the persons employed (13,516 out of 204,897). Seven establishments with upwards of 4000 workers each and 19 % of all the workers in the industry produced 19 % of the net output.

It is likely that the fifty-six largest establishments were with one or two exceptions melting shops plus rolling mills. The intermediate group, 243 works with below 1000 workers but more than forty-nine, will have included most of the re-rolling works (which number in all about 120)[1] and the steel foundries which are not included in engineering works, etc. (some seventy), some forges,[2] plus some smallish steel melting and rolling plants which fell in between the 1000-workers-plus group and the forty-nine-workers-or-fewer group.

Thus while the greater part of the industry's output, even in unintegrated works, comes from the larger works there is a considerable range in size of establishment and no sign of a normal or representative size. Nor is there any orderly difference in the net output per person for works in different size groups, which might be expected if the establishments with larger outputs invariably employed more capital in relation to their output.[3] The largest average net outputs per person were in the smallest works of all—employing from eleven to twenty-four persons—where net output per head was £1264, and in the group employing 300 to 399 persons, where the average was £1008.[4]

For the production of steel of fairly standard qualities the scale of works is usefully compared in terms of tons of steel ingots made (and rolled) in a year. The wide range of sizes shown in the Census of Production figures is naturally reproduced if this criterion is adopted. In Table 9 is shown the distribution of ingot output between firms in different size groups in 1952,[5] with an estimate for 1955.

Two or more separate melting shops are operated in several of the plants counted as one in the table. In several instances the subdivision is a source of lower efficiency. In the nine largest steelworks listed above there were sixteen melting shops. It is normal and obviously often

---

[1] The Census (Table 6) identified 131 steel manufactures without melting. Perhaps they were all re-rollers: the author's lists do not show quite so many.

[2] The same source gives thirty-two forges.

[3] Nor is there an orderly difference in the percentage which net output forms of gross output. This would give an appearance of statistical support for the view that the larger establishments (according to number employed) carried out more processes, in which case the added value might be larger in proportion to material input. But though this difference exists between the four smallest sizes and the remainder it is not so otherwise. It is probably a fair generalization that in the larger-scale operations of integrated plants net output becomes a smaller part of gross value for each specific operation.

[4] The establishments with from 3000–3999 had the lowest average net output, £714. Although it is possible to guess at some plausible explanations—the products of the larger works were more subject to price controls, and in the smallest net output possibly in effect included remuneration for management more than for capital—the data do not provide any.

[5] The figures cover the outputs of all nationalized plants.

sensible to have an open hearth plant linked with basic Bessemer, which was done at both British Thomas steel plants. But the subdivision in other major works marked the retention of some old plant whose costs were relatively high. It usually limits the scope for economies of scale and complicates internal transport and heat economy.

Table 9. *Size of plants according to ingot outputs*

Output range (thousand tons)	Number of plants		
	1952		1955 (est.)
	Number	Percentage of ingot output	Number
50 but under 100*	8 (4)	*4*	7
100 but under 150	12 (3)	*9*	13
150 but under 250	12 (3)	*15*	10
250 but under 350	9	*17*	7
350 but under 500	5	*13*	7
500 but under 600	3	*10*	2
600 but under 750	2	*8*	3
750 but under 1,000	3	*16*	4
1,000 but under 1,500	1	*7*	1
Over 1,500	—	—	1

est. = estimate.

Note: Figures in brackets indicate the number of plants primarily making alloy and special steel.

* Apart from the very small tool steel producers referred to above (p. 279) there were several substantial plants making less than 50,000 tons a year—for example, J. Baker and Bessemer, Jessops, Darlington Forge, Clyde Alloy.

Between 1952 and 1955 there was an increase in the proportion of works of larger capacities but no reduction in the number of plants.[1] The average output rose from about 280,000 tons to 340,000 tons a year.

The greater proportion of the smaller melting plants, and a few of the larger, were not integrated with pig-iron production. Of the thirty-three works which made up to 250,000 tons a year in 1952 only six had blast furnaces attached. Nine of these unintegrated plants were primarily making alloy and special steels. Of the twenty-two larger plants five, making 2·6 million tons of steel, were unintegrated.[2] The proportion of steel in whose production cold pig-iron is used has been steadily declining though it still remains important. Of all pig-iron used 33·3 %

[1] One plant dropped out (Dorman Long's Britannia works) but the same firm built a new bigger and better plant (Lackenby).
[2] Steel Peech and Tozer's (United Steel Co.), Sheffield: Colvilles' Dalzell Glengarnock and Lanarkshire works: John Summers (Shotton). By 1955 one of these (Summers) had put up the first of two blast furnaces; Colvilles had some projects.

was used cold in 1946, 28·7 % in 1952, 25·5 % in 1955. The tonnage so used in 1955, 2·66 million tons, was substantially more than in 1946, and more even than in 1952: but the use of hot liquid iron was increasing faster.

The subdivision of steel melting and the extent to which steel ingots were made in plants not adjacent to pig-iron production and steel billets were re-rolled in small plants not making steel have been criticized as sources of avoidable high cost. The most notable recent comment was made by an Anglo-American Productivity Team in the report published in 1952, where they analysed carefully the size of plant which 'British works should attain in order to achieve a desirable level of efficiency'. They laid down an output of 500,000 to 600,000 tons of pig-iron from two blast furnaces, upwards of 800,000 tons of steel ingots, from 800,000 tons to 1·0 million tons a year for a primary mill rolling ingots to make 'blooms' and 1·2 million tons for a mill making slabs, as minima for an integrated plant. Up to these figures there were steady gains in cost reduction: beyond them there were further gains but small ones.

As to the cold metal plants, so common in the United Kingdom, the report argued that 'the loss in efficiency and productivity does not become serious' for making 'small tonnages of steels of odd compositions and sizes' until they get below 300,000 tons a year. Cold metal shops making heavy products should, however, make over 500,000 tons a year. The report did not explain how the under-employment of a modern primary mill could be avoided, even with an output of 500,000 tons, but presumably the 500,000 tons of heavy products would still be in 'odd compositions and sizes', and the plants not equipped with the high capacity mills.

In one respect these figures were indeed soon shown to be too low: it was generally accepted in a year or so that a continuous wide-strip mill's capacity should be 2·5 million tons a year[1]—otherwise extremely costly capital equipment was under-employed.

It would be wrong to regard these minima as even a guide for more than a few years: successive 'guides' over the last thirty years have continuously gone up. But they constituted a striking commentary on the distribution of production in the United Kingdom when the report was written, and (despite consequent changes) five years later.

The Productivity Report recognized that more standardization would be needed if British works were to work on the scale they laid down, but thought that much of the variety catered for was 'unnecessary on technical grounds'. It would mean also more specialization in works on a narrower range of products, hence more transport costs

---

[1] I.e. for a mill making the wider sizes, strip *c*. 7 ft. wide.

to markets: again this, they argued, would be more than offset by the reductions of cost.[1]

The team contrasted British production primarily with American— five years later it could have contrasted in some respects with that of Germany. In the United States in 1950 nearly 60 % of output came from seventeen plants with outputs of over 1·5 million tons a year, and an average of nearly 3 million tons. 75 % of ingots were made in plants with outputs of over 1 million tons each. The average output of all plants was three times the British figure: and alloy and special steel plants, as well as plants for the more standard qualities, were on a much larger scale. To this the report attributed the much higher productivity of plant and of labour found in the United States. It gave the ratios in the following—necessarily very approximate—figures.

Table 10. *Ratio of comparative productivities in United States and United Kingdom*

(U.K. = 1)

Process	Plant productivity	Labour productivity (per hour)
Blast furnace	2·8	3·5
Open hearth: Hot metal	1·8	2·6
Cold metal	1·4	2·2
Rolling	c. 1·5	1·5–2

Such data are always indications, not proof: and of these, those referring to productivity of plant are liable to mislead unless their content is carefully noted, for they merely show that larger capacity units are normally used. They do not mean that a given expenditure of capital per unit of capacity results in a larger output. For this, however, the report did also provide a guide: it pointed out that although earnings were on average three to four times as high in the United States, the cost of a wholly new plant, more or less identical in character, was not very different per ton of output per year in the two countries.

Their report was not the first to make this kind of criticism of British production: nor was this the only British industry subject to this sort of criticism, but it is the most recent one from within the industry. Since the strong central organization of the industry was set up (it will be examined later), criticism from inside has been less often published than in the days before the industry was supervised by a body acting in the public interest.

The report naturally raises the issue—how much is the saving which

[1] Anglo-American Council on Productivity (succeeded by British Productivity Council), *Iron and Steel*, Productivity Team Report, pp. 86–7.

changes of the kind suggested offer? Since it almost neglected the general issue of location, the possible reductions in labour cost are those most relevant. For 1955 the approximate average labour costs[1] in iron smelting, steel melting, and rolling mills (including re-rolling but excluding tin-plate or tube or wire making) were (respectively) 16s. 6d. a ton of pig-iron, 21s. a ton of liquid steel, £3. 15s. a ton of rolled product.[2] Thus if the increases of labour productivity which the Productivity Team spoke of (above, p. 283) were really achievable significant reductions of cost might be made if other cost factors were not seriously unfavourable (that is primarily if any additional capital cost involved did not exceed the reduction of labour cost).[3] In a period of expanding output the sum is a complex one; a comparison of different kinds of investment (not between one investment and no investment) and some of the investments can involve drastic reductions in raw material assembly costs,[4] reductions in fuel as well as in labour costs, and falls, as well as rises, in costs of delivery of finished products.[5] In an industry of giant plants, average costs have very limited significance. What is under consideration is always a small number of specific alternatives. It may reasonably be concluded that the rigidity of the production pattern, leading to excessive subdivision, and too little adaptation of location, has resulted in significantly higher costs: but it would be foolish to try and put this in precise figures.

(d) The size of firms

As the outcome mainly of a series of amalgamations during the last thirty years the production of steel though still divided between many often rather small plants is now concentrated largely in the hands of ten or a dozen large concerns. Thus in 1952 six firms, operating thirty-two works in which steel was made, had each an output of over 1 million tons (three made between 1·5 million and 1·7 million tons and one over 2·2 million tons) and in the aggregate an output of 9·5 million tons,

[1] Calculated from statistics of earnings published since the war by the British Iron and Steel Federation (now in conjunction with the Iron and Steel Board).

[2] The average 'net output' per ton of rolled and cast steel (including pig-iron production), sheet rolling and other re-rolling, but not tube, wire and tin-plate making, was c. £15 a ton in 1951: possibly it would be about £20 in 1955. But such averages are misleading.

[3] No doubt the reduction of labour would be followed by an increase of wages. But this should only affect the calculation slightly.

[4] See above, p. 274.

[5] For example, a sheet-works built nearer the home market would enjoy lower delivery cost than from Port Talbot. The Census of Production gave a rough indication of average transport costs in delivering finished products. In 1950 it was roughly £13 million for the delivery of 10·5 million tons of rolled steel excluding tin-plate, sheets and tubes, plus some transport of 'semis', plus deliveries of exports to ports. This implies an average of about 22s. a ton. For sheets and tubes the average was much higher—nearer 52s. a ton. The cost of transport has, of course, risen since then.

which was 58 % of total British output. A further five firms, operating twelve works, each firm having a yearly output of between 500,000 tons and 1 million tons of ingots, and the group having an aggregate of over 3 million tons, provided another 18 % of the total output. Thus eleven firms accounted for just over three-quarters of the ingot output. By 1955 their participation in this trade was probably higher.[1]

The first eleven fall into several contrasting types. There is first a group of predominantly heavy steelmakers, whose main products for sale are heavy plates, heavy sections, rails, together with some 'semi-products'—billets and bars for re-rolling, a proportion of which they may re-roll themselves. Colvilles and Dorman Long's are the largest firms of this type. The first is a regional consolidation of all Scots heavy steelmaking, with which it combines a moderate-scale production of alloy steel (much smaller than that of the major Sheffield works). Plates—for which there is a large local demand—probably comprise well over one-third of its rolled product (its production was c. 650,000 tons of plate in 1955), over one-quarter of the national output. Colville's heavy steel output is distributed among five melting plants, not one on deep water, and until 1957 only one supplied with hot metal. The supply of two others from a new blast furnace plant at an inland site, but using imported ore, started in 1957. Dorman Long's falls far short of a regional consolidation, but its five steelworks are more nearly contiguous than Colville's and are all on or near deep water, and have hot metal supplies. In each firm the individual works are in a greater or lesser degree specialized on different products in the companies' programmes. Both embrace constructional engineering, but this is of much greater importance for Dorman Long's who have derived a large part of their profit from it.[2] Consett and South Durham fall into the same category, on a much smaller scale. Consett is a one-plant company, on an inland hill site some miles south of Newcastle, where there was once ore and where there is still immediately adjacent some of the coking coal the company needs. Proposals to move to a deep water site on the Tyne were rejected. The South Durham company has two steelworks, one on the north bank of the Tees, and one on the south (at Cargo Fleet), specialized respectively on plates and sections. It makes part of its plate output into large welded tubes in a third plant.

Another group of firms are predominantly makers of one of the more advanced finished products—sheets, tin-plate, or tubes. One, the most recent, the Steel Company of Wales, is wholly in Wales, and is an outcome of the amalgamation during the war of Richard Thomas

---

[1] In 1929 the eleven largest firms had made 70 % of ingot output.

[2] The group includes both the Dorman Long constructional company and Redpath Brown.

(a leading tin-plate firm which was extending its sheet business) and Baldwins, who started as makers of sheets and had spread into heavy products and tin-plate. The amalgamation was formed to build the widest-strip mill in the United Kingdom, for which the site of Baldwins' obsolete plate mill was chosen (Port Talbot). It was a water-side site, but could only give access to ships of up to 8000 tons, though the greater economy of larger ships was already known. The Steel Company of Wales was divided from the parent company in 1955. There are three other major firms in this group. First, Richard Thomas and Baldwins; this comprises a fully integrated steelworks and continuous-strip mill and tin-plate works at Ebbw Vale (an inland site up a Welsh valley which has lost its former advantages) which was the first such mill to be built in this country, a large number of small old-style tin-plate plants, many with small unintegrated cold metal steel plants attached, in South Wales, and an integrated medium-sized steelworks in Scunthorpe (Lincolnshire). Its former Chairman, Sir William Firth, who introduced the continuous wide-strip mill into Britain, hoped to do so in the East Midlands whose low costs he knew from experience, but was prevented by political and industrial pressures. John Summers primarily makes sheets, though it has a small integrated plant at Stoke making heavy sections. Its main plant, at Shotton, near Chester, where the second British continuous wide-strip mill was installed in 1938–40, is located near neither coal nor ore, and it is not on deep water: nevertheless it has been deemed advisable to turn it from a cold to a hot metal shop by building blast furnaces to use ore imported via Birkenhead and its capacity has been rapidly increased. Stewarts and Lloyds make almost exclusively tubes; their largest plant is on the Northamptonshire ore fields, where they succeeded in starting in the early 1930's—a few years before Firth was prevented from carrying out a similar policy. Here the most modern integrated production of tubes made from welded steels was established. Corby also makes 'solid drawn tubes' by piercing and extruding billets. The firm has other much smaller and older plants at Bilston in the Black Country, Clydesdale and elsewhere in Scotland, and in South Wales. It also includes the Stanton Iron Works, one of the principal producers of cast-iron pipes, and it is one of the two firms with the largest home ore mining rights. With this group of firms it is convenient to class the Guest Keen Iron and Steel Company, which in its main Cardiff works makes mainly billets for the adjacent re-rolling plant of Guest Keen and Nettlefolds. It includes also the Brymbo Steelworks and John Lysaght's, Scunthorpe, which may be regarded as a product of the process whereby finished product makers in the past built up-to-date steelworks, though here the link has snapped. This happened as a result of the substitution of continuous strip for the sheet bars which Lysaght's made cheaply in Lincolnshire, and then carried to South Wales to use. Outside the 'first eleven' there is the Lancashire Steel Corporation which is partly analogous, making wire rods to supply affiliated wiremakers in Warrington, though also making some heavy steel—rails and sections. In all these instances of specialized finished product makers it may be said that in a large measure they have moved back from their finishing trade when this has expanded sufficiently to provide a market which would justify them in establishing for themselves a more efficient supply of steel than they could then get from other British sources.

The United Steel Company, the largest of all, by contrast with those so far described is a variegated company, with a foot in many trades and in three regions. Near Sheffield it has two plants (one itself a group of plants); one (S. Fox and Company) making high-grade alloy and special steels, the other making primarily mass produced billets of which it re-rolls a proportion, together with railway tyres and wheels. On the North-West coast it has an integrated acid Bessemer steel plant making mainly rails. In Lincolnshire it has a large steelworks (also with blast furnaces) in two sections (Appleby-Frodingham), one producing heavy plates, the other making rails and heavy sections. This uses the local Frodingham ores. In a sense this combine was the antithesis of both the popular principles of rationalization, regional and product specialization. In Lincolnshire it has the most extensive mining rights, and in this region it has expanded and modernized greatly since the war and enjoys very low costs in its steelmaking.

The first eleven includes one major alloy and special steel firm—the English Steel Corporation (E.S.C.), with a group of works (most of them adjacent) in Sheffield, and subsidiaries in Manchester and Darlington. It makes virtually the whole range of alloy and special products, including small tool steel products, large outputs of springs and of drop forgings, and the heaviest castings and forgings including pressure vessels and turbine rotors. E.S.C. is part of the Vickers concern. Though no other of the exclusively alloy and special steel firms come into the first eleven selected on a tonnage basis one other at least would presumably do so if turnover were the criterion, namely Thomas Firth and John Brown, whose range is almost as extensive. Before nationalization they were part of the John Brown group, but this link has not been reconstituted. They have, however, bought Beardmore's. They make, apart from steel products, small tools, large weldments, and steelworks plant—rolling mills, forging presses, etc., and rolls for rolling mills. There are several other alloy steel firms of considerable importance—all in Sheffield[1]— and a host of small ones whose specialization increases as their scale

[1] In particular Hadfield's, Brown Bayley's, Samuel Osborne's, and William Jessop's.

diminishes. Some of the medium-scale Sheffield firms have gone into the later stages of the titanium business.

Providing that part of the output not supplied by the eleven majors or the other firms so far mentioned are a considerable number of mainly small units (though by British standards three might count as medium-sized), including the many smaller alloy steel plants, a group of small unintegrated open hearth plants in South Wales founded to provide sheet and tin-plate bars on the old style but sometimes now providing billets, and four plants in other regions, two in the West Midlands, one in Scotland, one near Rotherham (Park Gate which is integrated), of which three make light bars and sections and one plate. Since de-nationalization two of these have been bought by Tube Investments, who are the other major tube makers apart from Stewarts and Lloyds. Here the steel user has not built an up-to-date works, but has bought existing units of a moderate size which have undergone considerable improvement since the war.[1] It is probably in part a means of ensuring regularity of supply and quality; the latter can in part be assured by using the firm's own scrap as far as possible.

The structure of most and especially of the larger companies is complicated by their participation in ancillary activities, providing some of their raw materials or supplies (such as refractory bricks) or disposing of by-products—blast furnace slag (for example in slag cement), steel-works slag (as fertilizer), coke oven by-products. A number of the larger companies have interests in oversea steelworks or construction companies, primarily within the Commonwealth.

It follows from this analysis of the size of firms that buyers are normally not in a position to buy steel of one particular kind from a large number of sellers, despite the surprisingly large number of plants. Often, because of the specialization within trades the number of potential suppliers is one or two only. Thus Stewarts and Lloyds are the sole important makers of butt welded tubes; they share with Tube Investments almost the whole production of solid drawn tubes, and Tube Investments are the sole important makers of precision tubes. There are only two producers of tin-plate by wholly modern processes, only three producers of wide-strip by modern methods (which alone give satisfactory deep 'drawing' properties) and only one making the widest widths of coil. In plates there are five suppliers of ship plates, but the production of boiler plate and of specially thick large plates is much more limited—largely to Colvilles and E.S.C. Only one firm so far, Cargo Fleet, makes 'universal' beams, though Dorman Long are

---

[1] The new owners soon announced that at Round Oak they would install large electric steel furnaces (arc furnaces) to make ordinary grade steel—following a practice started in the United States.

completing a mill to do so. There are only two or three firms who make the largest forgings or castings.

Where competition was limited to a very few firms attitudes towards getting or keeping business were noticeably different, though the post-war period has not in general put competitive methods to severe tests. Some big firms have, however, acquired a good reputation for making only such promises of delivery, either in the home market or for export, as they can keep, others have an unenviable record for break-ing promises; some have a reputation too for selling vigorously at a distance when trade is sagging but treating distant customers roughly when trade is good, whereas other firms nurse regular customers all the time. Unsatisfactory service, an unreadiness, for example, to supply small orders quickly, is a normal accompaniment of scarcity: in a fully competitive situation this would tend to be self-liquidating.

5. INVESTMENT PLANS AND PRICE TRENDS SINCE THE SECOND WORLD WAR

The increase of steel consumption depended, it has been seen, mainly on expansion of home production and hence on increase of capacity. With the prospect of full employment policies after the war, and the back log of requirements at home and abroad caused by the destruction and the deprivation of war, coupled with the expectation of sharper competition from America (which was misjudged), all the firms began to make plans for reconstruction and modernization in the last year or so of the war, and these, when collected together, formed the basis of a plan presented to the government late in 1945 and in due course accepted by the government as a basis for the industry's development. The plan incorporated a great part of the firms' proposals: but the comparisons of their plans led to a few significant alterations. There were some important additions (a large new home ore based plant, and a coastal plant in Scotland) and the plan established what was deemed a rational balance in the growth of pig-iron and steel capacity; and among other things made provision for the disappearance of some of the smaller plants after a transition period, the concentration of rail-making in four plants, and the dropping of plate-making by some ill-favoured producers. The largest single project was the wide-strip mill referred to above: there was also to be a new plant at Middlesbrough to make broad flange beams (a new product for Britain). The plan was partly to expand capacity, partly to introduce new products, partly to modernize and rationalize.

Investment over the next five years followed a strikingly different pattern from the one laid down in 1946. Thus, for example, the big projects injected in the plan, which did not originate in the firms' first thoughts, did not materialize: the plants that were to disappear were enlarged: the rail rationalization was apparently forgotten: the blast furnace programme went ahead rather slowly and development of home ore sites was especially slow. The volume of investment—in money terms, adjusted to changes in the value of money—did not differ greatly from that visualized in the plan. But in real terms what was done differed substantially. The period was one which naturally stimulated expansion—in retrospect less than was desirable—and the shadow of nationalization may have been an added irrational stimulus.

Though some of the changes from the first 'plan' were due to ungovernable circumstances and some were rational adaptations it was not reasonable to say that all were due to sound judgment, the flexible adaptation of plans to changing circumstances. Blast furnace developments went slowly[1] and some were deferred; the result was that in 1952 steel output fell because home pig-iron output had not grown fast enough to replace the scrap which was available from Germany before the German industry recovered and expanded. Later, the expansion of steel supply was again planned on what later was seen to be too small a scale: and the general pattern of expansion in the second five years of peace was declared to be the expansion of existing plants—all of them—which did not conduce to a rapid approach to the state of efficiency advocated in the Productivity Report. Nor did it lead to concentration in the best sites whether coastal or home ore based. Failure to develop home ore sites was often attributed to lack of houses or lack of fuel, but it was also vigorously defended on the ground that imported ore prices would provide steel from imported ore at least as cheaply—which was incorrect. This contention, though vigorously challenged in 1944–5, on what proved to be sound assessments, was not formally given up until 1956, when the Steel Board's Report pointed to the advantage of higher home ore consumption to save foreign exchange. Moreover there was conspicuous slowness in developing the supply of particular products: heavy plates were the outstanding example, and this scarcity was most acutely felt in shipbuilding although its effect was pervasive, and markets for heavy plates expanded in many industries. Shipbuilders wanted more plates and wider plates. The use of 'four high' mills for heavy plates (Germany had at least three in use in 1955, when the United Kingdom still had none) provided

---

[1] Some people attribute this exclusively to difficulty in getting turbo-blowers, through lack of capacity in face of the demands for large generators for the Electricity Authority and for export. This view seems to exaggerate.

plates better in some respects—more uniformly flat—and British makers were being asked for these qualities. The rate of expansion in the industry naturally allowed considerable improvements in average labour productivity without a reduction in number of works; there was, it has been seen, much room for improvement by simple changes. The index of output per man in 1937, 1950 and 1955 was 100:115:141. The investments also led to improved fuel economy. Within the pattern of what was done, much was impressive.

The cost of the annual investments in the industry are set out in Table 11, which gives both the actual expenditures and their approximate measure in 1955 prices.

Table 11. *Investments in iron and steel works, 1946–56*

(£ million)

	Actual prices	In 1955 prices		Actual prices	In 1955 prices
1946	—	—	1951	54	63
1947	—	—	1952	54	57
1948	32	43	1953	52	55
1949	42	56	1954	60	63
1950	49	64	1955	72	72
			1956	87	83

It was frequently claimed by those who advocated nationalization that without this step the industry would be unable to provide sufficient capital for modernization and expansion. The possibility of nationalization itself created difficulties throughout the post-war years, and still did so in 1957; the Labour Opposition tried to prevent denationalization, or so it seemed, by threatening to treat punitively those who bought steel company shares after the Steel Bill of 1953, and this necessarily made it more difficult and more expensive to raise money. The industry complained throughout the post-war years with some force that price control (and high taxation) limited the resources for self-finance, and that other industries were better placed. Nevertheless the bulk of the industry's investments have been self-financed: of the funds invested by firms representing three-quarters of the industry's capacity 81 % came from internal resources, only 19 % from external borrowing. Practically nothing came from ordinary share issues. The internal resources were, however, especially helped by two sources, one of which cannot be recurrent while the other is unlikely to be so. Many firms lost coal mines on nationalization—and therefore had compensation to invest. And for much of the time export prices carried a good premium, providing income above that from the fixed home prices. The largest single external source before nationalization was the Finance Corporation for Industry (F.C.I.) created in 1945, which had provided £40 million by 1951. Short-term advances from joint-stock banks have been considerable. Under nationalization from 1951 to 1953 advances of £30 million were secured from these banks, and where firms had surpluses these were 'pooled' for the use of firms needing capital. The agency set up on denationalization to re-sell the nationalized assets has continued to advance substantial sums for capital development.[1]

The major new plant which had to be financed, the Port Talbot strip mill, was financed largely by the F.C.I. and by a large (£15 million) debenture issue in 1947. Smaller-scale piecemeal expansion is possibly attractive partly because a larger part of it can be financed out of profits, especially the profits of a single concern. This not only avoids any immediate call for interest payments; it may be a means of avoiding lessening the control of existing interests. In early 1957 the prospects for loans and debentures were assessed as fairly good: the prospects for ordinary share issues negligible for expansion: the prospects for self-finance far below what was needed, unless price rises allowed wider margins. Price increases agreed in 1957 were partly to allow these.

The advance in 'labour productivity' was reflected in the comparatively favourable price record of the steel industry since the war, which contrasted sharply with pre-war trends. Fairly continuously since the war British home prices for most kinds of steel have been lower than home prices on the continent and in America. Table 12 gives international comparisons of prices for angles, plates and for sheets just before devaluation in 1949, and in 1956. These are only indications. The immense range of sizes and qualities of steel and in the sizes of orders rules out a comprehensive comparison.

Table 12. *British and foreign home trade prices for steel, 1949 and 1956*

	Angles		Plates		Sheets	
	March 1949	December 1956	March 1949	December 1956	March 1949	December 1956
	£ s. d.	£ s. d.	£ s. d.	£ s. d.	£ s. d.	£ s. d.
United Kingdom	19 1 6	37 14 0	21 14 6	41 9 6	28 6 0	49 6 0
United States	22 15 1	45 4 0	23 0 8	49 12 0	26 18 5	55 4 0
Germany	*	41 17 0	*	48 10 0	*	57 19 0
France	23 4 4	36 6 6	27 0 6	43 16 0	32 8 8	54 0 0
Belgium	19 3 2	39 3 0	20 11 4	47 2 6	27 18 0	52 13 0

Note: The prices include delivery to users' works, which is much more onerous, in distance, in the United States. The sizes taken are: *Angles*, 5 in. × 5 in. × ½ in., 5 tons of a size, 20-ton lots; *Plates*, 20 ft. × 5 ft. × ¼ in., 5 tons of a size, 20-ton lots; *Sheets*, 6 ft. × 3 ft. × 20 gauge, 25 tons of a size. French and Belgian prices are for Bessemer steel.

* The German figures are early 1950: they are exceptionally low owing to the relics of the influence of allied price control policies.

Sources: British Iron and Steel Federation (B.I.S.F.) *Monthly Statistical Bulletin*, May 1949, and B.I.S.F. *Annual Report* for 1956.

[1] Below, p. 298.

In 1949 American prices for heavy steel products were only a little above British; for sheets they were lower. The larger gap later (which extended to sheets) reflects the effect of devaluation. Wage levels were from three to four times as high, hence the relatively narrow price difference still implied in 1956 (as the Productivity Report stated in 1952) a strikingly greater combined efficiency in the use of the resources committed. *Vis-à-vis* the continent of Europe it is likely that the British investment did result in British costs moving favourably as against continental, largely because the German plant had run down badly since the rationalization of the 1920's and took time to catch up. There were other factors: coal prices and scrap prices were kept artificially low in Britain—more so than elsewhere; and for long periods the burden of high imported ore prices was lightened for British users at the expense of home ore users. Possibly, too, profit margins were lower. But these matters can better be considered after the development of the central institutions of the industry has been briefly traced.

6. THE CENTRAL ORGANIZATIONS

(a) Evolution

The most individual developments in the steel industry during the last twenty-five years, the elaboration of its central organs and the evolution of a system of public supervision, had their origin, it has been seen, in the difficulties encountered in the first thirty years of this century. By 1900 the British steel industry was already under severe criticism for inefficiency and was being outdistanced not only in output but in the development of new equipment both by the United States and Germany. For its part the industry was already complaining vigorously of dumping. The industry traced the inefficiency to the dumping, but that was certainly not the whole story.

The relative decline of the British industry in efficiency of production —as reflected in comparative costs—was due to a combination of internal weaknesses and inhibiting external conditions. As an industry supplying mainly capital goods steelmaking suffered acutely—everywhere—from the growing severity of the recurrent slumps. As an industry where the plant was costly but durable and prime costs thus much below total costs, when demand fell it suffered—again everywhere—from violent price-cutting. But the British industry was more vulnerable. Depending much more on exports, it suffered more acutely from slumps when the younger foreign industries were growing and progressively occupying protected home markets hitherto partly supplied by Britain. These industries moreover could often, particularly on the continent, keep up their home prices by cartel arrangements behind their tariffs and cut prices vigorously to get exports, not only in third countries but to a growing extent in free trade Britain whose markets were unprotected. The home markets in the United States and to a less extent in Germany grew faster than in the United Kingdom, and in the United States at any rate this was partly an inevitable outcome of geographical circumstances and the growth of population.

These things certainly slowed down the expansion of the British industry, which made adopting or developing new methods more difficult. As the older industry the British was also faced with the bigger problem of modernization, in possibly the least favourable circumstances. The British steel industry had grown on top of the iron industry, and this had started it off with a scattered, much subdivided structure. As seen above this was partly a reflexion of the original scattered distribution of iron ore as well as coal, but it also reflected the relative smallness of the units and the lack of vertical integration, which were both technically appropriate in the wrought iron age. At the time modern steel processes came in, the largest British ore deposits (in the East Midlands) were still hardly used, partly no doubt because they were not close to coal; but several of the ore deposits which had been worked were already becoming exhausted. Most were also unsuited to steel in the years from 1856 to 1878 when only ores low in phosphorus could be used. In the United Kingdom only the West Coast Hematite of Cumberland, Westmorland and North Lancashire were in this category, so that the early steel age saw the rapid growth of this virtually new centre. Other, older, iron centres began to look elsewhere for their ores. Thus the import of iron ores, at first from North Spain, started for the steel industry at an early date. They were cheap, they came in general as return cargoes in coal ships, and they came to a multitude of ports or sub-ports and continued the life of a great many widely dispersed works. The ports were large enough for the ships of the day. In some regions—South Wales for example—some of the firms were attracted from inland sites onto the coast: in other areas, Scotland for example, this did not happen.

In the early days of the open hearth process when furnaces were small and hot metal was not used, many malleable ironworks turned to steel melting and rolling and many small iron-rolling mills bought steel 'semi-products' and re-rolled them into finished products. It was enterprise, of a kind for which there was most scope in the United Kingdom where the open hearth process thrived more against Bessemer than on the continent. The small open-hearth shops thrived to some extent on using a high proportion of scrap. Since ironworks had often attracted iron-using industries around them, the steelworks which succeeded them were often in areas where scrap from consuming industries was fairly abundant. Some ironworks which became re-rolling plants were able to thrive for some time on cheap imported billets.

The younger foreign steel industries were less hampered by 'historical' forces. The malleable-iron industries in their background were smaller, and there were powerful centripetal forces. German coal, for example, was not widely scattered as the British, and the Ruhr field dominated: and though the steelmakers of the Ruhr had to use mainly imported ore it inevitably came through one or two ports only: there was an immense concentration of import at Rotterdam, followed by large-scale barge transport up the Rhine. In France expansion naturally concentrated on the vast Lorraine iron ore fields.

A dispersed, rather disintegrated structure once established in the steel industry was likely to prove rather rigid if demand grew relatively slowly, and was subject to acute fluctuations. The plant is very durable: for long periods it could therefore be used without need of money to replace it. Periods of boom, which make high-cost plant remunerative, recurred. Many plants made some specialities, special sections or a special quality (like boiler plate), sometimes for a local market and often involving some 'know-how', which earned profitable prices, and firms could use this as a basis for selling products more open to competition for small margins—or no margin if need be. The costs of transport gave most works some 'local monopoly', which groups of firms in a locality made use of by collective price agreements. Many firms had close links with some consumers, through common ownership or interlocking directorships and the like. Many also had good financial reserves to meet bad times; some proved strong almost for the reverse reason, that banks who had helped them by advances justified on past reputation and success seemed anxious to preserve them when they ran into difficulties. In these conditions competition seemed to result in stalemate: and this fostered price-fixing agreements, first local, then national, then international, sometimes with quota agreements added.

It was perhaps the reverse of the same medal that resulted in several large users of steel coming into the industry, particularly in the years before the First World War, though also in some notable instances between the wars. For while high-cost plants were kept alive the large consumer had an especial gain in putting up his own plant.

The 1920's brought new difficulties. War-time and early post-war reconstruction expansions, not all well conceived, imposed financial burdens which were desperately onerous when demand proved disappointing, and when deflation as well as foreign competition brought prices down. Continental rivals got their new plant rather later—as part of their reconstruction—and for them the financial burden was lightened by inflation, which was also a provocation to invest.

A Departmental Committee from the steel industry appointed in 1916 (and representing 'both sides') to consider the industry's position after the First World War declared in its report (which was the first overt acknowledgment from a group in the industry that there was leeway to make up, and the first plan for 'rationalization') that production should be mainly concentrated in plants making at least 300,000 tons of ingots a year. Unless there were, as they visualized there would be, a rapid growth of output, large modern style plants could only replace the existing ones if many existing firms lost their identity, whether by bankruptcy or amalgamation. In the ten years before the First World War the few horizontal amalgamations had been outnumbered by the inflow of new firms. Moreover some amalgamations, far from leading to concentration of production, strengthened the hold on life of weak plants.

After the First World War, under varying impulses, but primarily as an outcome of financial stringency and competitive difficulties, the pace of amalgamation increased; and by the end of the inter-war years the consolidation of firms which has just been surveyed had largely occurred, by several routes: some, as has been seen, regional consolidations to permit rationalizing of steelmaking, some inter-regional consolidations whose object was less simple, some consolidations of finishing which became the basis of new steelmaking.

Concentration in big firms was a necessary prelude to modernization, but did not ensure it. Most of the firms said that a tariff was also a necessary prelude, though this was widely contested, because it was familiar that in its heyday the industry had been backward (for example) in introducing fuel economies, had in other ways seemed unprogressive and had lacked scientifically trained staff and management. A further (unpublished) government report on the industry in 1930 by a committee under Lord Sankey took the view that rationalization must precede a tariff, otherwise rationalization would not be on an adequate scale.

The slump settled the issue—the tariff came first, but with safeguards. The Import Duties Advisory Committee (I.D.A.C.) appointed in 1932 was to ensure that when a tariff was imposed the public interest was served. Out of the negotiations between I.D.A.C., which exerted pressure on the industry to reorganize itself, and the steelmakers' central organization, which was reconstituted with greater powers in 1935 as the British Iron and Steel Federation (B.I.S.F.), a system was evolved which was to 'secure the systematic planning of the industry as a whole', eliminate 'unrestricted' competition at home or from abroad, develop internal co-ordination and co-operation with the aid of a tariff as far as was necessary and of international agreements—all of this while 'avoiding the evils of monopoly, safeguarding the public interest, and fostering efficiency'.

One feature of the constitution of the new B.I.S.F. of 1935 was the appointment of an Independent Chairman, whose function, not very clearly defined, was partly to act as an arbiter between firms in the industry but also in a wider sense to help the steelmakers to sublimate their desires, and to present to the public a symbol of the steelmakers' determination that this should be accomplished. Sir Andrew Duncan was cast for this role. He had already had experience in infusing his particular sense of public responsibility into industrial development in coal, electricity and shipbuilding. The system evolved also provided for supervision by a body of 'independent persons', a role which was given before the war to I.D.A.C. itself.

The positive impact of supervision before the war was limited, being most pronounced in respect of prices. The mere fact of protection (and the use of a so-called 'flexible tariff', which was put at a very high level, but reduced by agreement for imports from countries whose steelmakers were prepared to abide by a low import quota) naturally led to more investment and some modernization resulted. But much of what was done appeared to buttress high-cost location and stand in the way of radical change. Discussion of investment plans showed an immense preoccupation with avoiding for several reasons any disturbance of established sites: political forces weighed heavily in favour of this—to help depressed areas. The evolution of price control reached the point at which a central fund based on levies proportionate to the ingot output of firms was instituted to promote price stability. Arrangements were made for example to stop the export of scrap, which made it possible to keep the home price low and stable, and the excess costs of imported scrap and pig-iron above home prices were carried by the central fund —that is, the whole industry carried the marginal high costs of firms like Colville's who relied greatly on imported scrap and pig-iron. These were straws in the wind.

(b) Since the Second World War

The war strengthened the central organization. Devices for establishing stable prices, in greatly elaborated forms, were made a pillar of war-time price policy. Planning to modernize was necessarily abandoned during the war: but there was central planning for capital investments needed for war supplies. At the close of the war, partly because modernization had been stopped by it, partly because American technical advances were more fully appreciated and had gained impetus from the war, radical re-equipment was more generally regarded as necessary, and since resources were scarce the need to plan such changes centrally was almost universally taken for granted. So too it was assumed that the system of prices stabilized by a central fund, and fixed now by the government, must continue at least for a time if only to avoid violent but economically misleading price changes in the transition from war to peace and to avoid inflation. The application of the principles of the middle 1930's thus received new impetus.

Before post-war developments in planning and price-fixing are sketched in, the other thread of post-war policy can usefully be followed because it provided what for the moment must be regarded as an interlude which modified without reversing the general line of development. The programme of the Labour Government of 1945 promised to nationalize the steel industry. The government first appointed a supervisory board: but in 1950, after prolonged uncertainty, prolonged debates, and a second election, the major part of the industry was nationalized. In order to avoid great dislocation of managements, such as occurred in coal, the firms were left intact and a holding company, the Iron and Steel Corporation of Great Britain, was formed to take them over. The Corporation's powers were naturally greater than those of the Iron and Steel Board—indeed in a different category—but nevertheless it had to do initially in price-fixing and investment planning the sort of things the Board had done. The boards of the companies were able for various reasons quite legally to maintain in large measure their autonomy for the period in which the Corporation might have been influential—the period before the Conservatives were returned pledged to denationalize the industry—which they did, as far as it could be done in a bill, in 1953. They set up again a supervisory Iron and Steel Board, and an Iron and Steel Holding and Realization Agency, whose function it was to sell firms back to private ownership when it became practicable, and meantime to hold the assets of the nationalized industries and act as owners.

Because the steel firms were able to keep the Corporation in important respects at arm's length for sufficiently long, and because the whole episode was so short, it would be wrong to pass judgment on nationalization as from experience. The form in which nationalization was cast was intended, by preserving the existing firms initially, to avoid the disaster whereby in coal mining all the best managerial units (in which the proposals of the Reid Committee were evolved) were broken up. But this involved an immediate threat (which of course had no time to get worked out) that the manufacturing end of firms like Dorman Long's, with its large constructional engineering interests, would compete from an immensely privileged position against private firms in the same trades. Moreover Mr Hardie, the Chairman of the Corporation, planned to make drastic changes, in the shape of the firms and constitution of boards. He seemed likely to consolidate regionally, in Lincolnshire certainly, on the North-East Coast perhaps. He had plans to put all the home iron ore into the hands of a separate company (an interesting proposal). He had the idea (which he had toyed with for many years when he was in the scrap business) of putting down a new giant works at Rosyth—a site where Swedish ore could be brought in cheaply but whose only nearby coking coal was dear, and whose access to markets was not good. The Corporation based depreciation on replacement values and took good profits; but Mr Hardie in his final fling on retirement denounced this and said that steel prices were too high. The claim is sometimes made that the Corporation under his guidance saw for the first time the need to secure more foreign ore and to hurry the building of new blast furnaces. Possibly it pushed one or two projects, but by and large it was moving with the tide. It did not need proving that new personalities in control of an industry could make changes: but whether in this case the changes would be mainly for good or bad, what criteria of national interest would be followed, remained unknown or uncertain.

Despite political insecurity and threats the market proved relatively favourable for selling shares of many of the former companies, some publicly some privately, from mid-1953 until early 1955 when conditions grew less easy. The assets for re-sale were naturally greater (in real terms) than those originally bought, because there had been new net investment. New capital had been provided by the Corporation, and for firms still in public ownership by the Agency. Significantly the two major companies which had large works on home iron ore were sold early and successfully: their shares soon went to a considerable premium. It was necessary to sell on terms which promised a return above that normal because of the renationalization risks: on the other hand expanding trade plus inflation made it possible to sell on terms which at times represented more than the book values of the assets. A large proportion of sales have been preceded by a reorganization of the capital structure of the firms, and the agency retained large sums in preference shares and unsecured loan stocks in many companies. Control was returned to the companies by the sale of ordinary shares, but the capacity of the market to absorb the industry's capital would presumably have too greatly restricted the number of companies sold had the whole of their capital been offered. The financial return on the re-sale is primarily of political significance: but the extent of re-sale, until it is complete (or until the whole situation is, as it might be, again reversed), is a fact, in the structure of the industry, of significance, but now greatly diminished. It could influence the policy adopted by or for the industry, since this may be influenced by a desire to create conditions which will favour re-sale. It must influence the policies of the firms which remain unsold, because the Agency carries out 'holding company functions'. They operate through the appointment of directors, supervision of financial affairs, the machinery of company meetings, and they 'have arranged to be consulted on matters which by their magnitude or importance are outside the scope of normal management'. The only major unsold firm by the autumn of 1957 was Richard Thomas and Baldwins. The company is concerned in major investment decisions involving a touch of controversy. Its Lincolnshire site is too small for a modern-scale unit. It plans sensibly to diversify its output in a new works at Newport. The Steel Board and the government would have liked the company to start building a new strip mill sooner than it is prepared to do so. No firm not already making strip, it is said, is prepared to embark on such a mill.

The present Iron and Steel Board was set up in 1953 to 'provide public supervision' of the steel industry 'with a view to promoting the efficient, economic and adequate supply under competitive conditions of iron and steel products'. A number of subjects were to be kept under review—prices, raw material supplies and their distribution, capacity, research and training, safety, health and welfare, joint consultation except on the terms and conditions of employment. It was the second such Board: the first was the Labour Government's stop-gap arrangement of 1946. A Board of this kind had been recommended by the industry's trade union as far back as 1930; and there was already a fifteen-year experience of supervision by I.D.A.C., by the Ministry of Supply, by the first Board and by the Corporation, whose development cannot be examined in the space of this chapter.

The members of the Board (there are eleven, the first Chairman being Sir Archibald Forbes) were appointed at the outset by the Minister of Supply.[1] There are three full-time members, the rest are part-time members; and they are chosen partly from the steelmaking and steel-using industries, partly from persons in varying degree independent in the sense of having no direct interest.

The Board's chief functions concern planning and prices, but it has also a watching brief—or more—over most of the other central activities developed by the industry. It has to be satisfied, for example, that ore supplies will be expanded fast enough. One of its early decisions was to start a new survey of home ore resources. Imports of iron ore have been centrally purchased for the whole industry since the war by a subsidiary of the British Iron and Steel Corporation (B.I.S.C.(Ore)). Though not immune from criticism this has normally brought in all the ore which could be used, and such difficulties as have arisen have

[1] Later by the President of the Board of Trade and later again (1957) by the Minister of Power.

been from shipping rather than ore supplies. The nationalized Corporation believed too little was done to ensure supplies in the more distant future. The industry has a substantial research association which spends £500,000 a year: individual companies spend collectively £2 million in addition. Here, as in many matters, the Board merely observes, though if it thought it advisable it could intervene. The Steel Federation has since the war acted as a sort of clearing house through which orders for steel which are hard to place can be placed and where deliveries are urgently needed they can be expedited. Here again the Board observes.

For some products there appear to be informal arrangements—the steelmakers appear to supply the shipyards, for example, on a basis which preserves the relative importance of the yards: so that a reconstructed yard which can work faster cannot get enough steel to run at full capacity. This is not a good arrangement: the basic weakness is, however, lack of supply, and there is a price complication since imported plates are much dearer than home produced plates.

The Federation has built up the best regular series of statistics provided by any British industry (though of course they make the student ask for more). These are now the joint responsibility of the Board and Federation. The Federation maintains the relations of the industry with the public with exceptional skill. In the evolution of the economic devices of centralization, the Federation played a large part, under the guidance of Sir Andrew Duncan. His death greatly weakened it: and since Sir Robert Shone joined the new Board the power of the Federation has appeared to wane. In part this was possibly willed by the firms in the industry, who may prefer to avoid a two-tiered organization (or counting the government department even a three-tiered one) in which the firms' contacts with the supervising body are largely indirect.

In regard to planning the Board has to make regular reviews of capacity, and in consultation with firms and their trade associations to ensure the provision of such new plant and the organization of such new raw material resources as are needed for 'efficient economic and adequate supply'. If there are gaps in the firms' plans the Board may report to the appropriate Minister who may himself set out to fill the gaps. The Board has also to examine all the major plans of the firms and can veto those not conducive to the 'efficient, economic and adequate supply'. It has also to sanction any destruction of existing plant.

With regard to prices the Board has the power to fix maximum prices. This is permissive: the Board does not have to fix prices for any products, and needless to say prices do not need to be (and will not be) fixed for all products. The appropriate Minister can direct the Board to fix some prices, and can direct it to vary its decisions—if this is necessary 'in the public interest and for the efficient, economic and adequate supply of steel'. The Act goes no further in defining how the Board should fix prices than to say that the prices should not be inconsistent with promoting the said ideal state of supply. In the debates on the Bill it became clear that the Minister thought the price should be fixed in relation to the costs of efficient firms, so that inefficient firms would be forced out of business, but that Ministers supported the continuance of a central fund, which had now come to be known as the 'Industry Fund'. The Board 'considered various methods of price-fixing', and concluded that none was ideal or suited to all circumstances. In regard to 'the cost of production element—the overwhelming constituent' the Board 'adopted for the generality of products the average of the current cost of each product applicable to the bulk of production, but in doing so excluded those pertaining to a band of the highest-cost productions'. They decided in fact to do what their predecessors, who had also had Sir Robert Shone's guidance, had done.

The spread of the cost of different firms continued to be greatly narrowed by the processes of the Industry Fund. This, as described by the Board,

takes up the losses arising from the re-sale to producers of imported ore, scrap, pig-iron, and semi-finished steel at prices below the prices actually paid for these goods by the central buying organization....It also meets other outgoings such as losses on shipbreaking, assistance with high-cost transactions within the industry (mainly in respect of carriage charges on uneconomic hauls), central research and other central services. It is further used to correct the disparity in the cost of steelmaking which would otherwise occur from the control of the price of scrap at a level below its value in use. The Fund is fed by levies on producers at rates approved by the Board and which form part of the steelmaking costs on which the Board's maximum prices are based.[1]

There were two levies, organized and administered by the British Iron and Steel Federation—a levy on ingots covered all the operations except the correction of the disparity caused by the price control of scrap, which was covered by a levy on purchases of scrap (not on circulating scrap).

All firms paid equally in proportion to their ingot output (or scrap purchases) but they benefited differentially. For example a user of home ore paid as much per ton of ingots as users of imported ore, but the benefit in terms of lowered costs was limited to the latter. The fund was not used only to spread the incidence of high-cost raw materials at a given time—it was used to even out the incidence of periods of high and low import prices. This was done by keeping the ingot levy high enough in periods of relatively low import prices to provide a surplus in the fund which would be used to cushion the effect of relatively high prices later.

[1] *Annual Report* for 1955, p. 25.

In estimating capital cost for price-fixing the Board allows for the exhaustion of assets by normal wear and tear and by obsolescence before the end of their physical life, which is 'in many cases' probable. It is astonishing for how long steel plant goes on being remunerative, and it is a pity the Board gave no chapter or verse for the claim that loss through obsolescence is common.[1] The 'writing off' of assets is rightly based by the Board on replacement costs in assessing depreciation—but, oddly, when the right level of profits is being assessed the original cost of the assets written down at Inland Revenue rates is accepted.

The Board having arrived at what it deemed the allowance for depreciation and obsolescence 'necessary to preserve a healthy industry' stated that the industry should set aside at least these sums for replacements: a demand whose validity belongs to the realm of political rather than economic logic. 'The allowance for profit by each type of product,' the Board stated, 'was determined as a rate of return on the relevant capital which had regard *inter alia* to the nature of the industry, current interest rates and what might be expected to be a normal level of working in relation to capital over an extended period of time.'

The maximum prices are home prices only: in general, export prices have been higher than home prices since the war. But home prices are themselves designed to give adequate profit: and since (even if prices are kept stable) if demand falls the reduction of load will reduce the volume of profit, the prices give a margin at times of good trade which is high enough to offset this fall in volume.

Steel prices in the United Kingdom are by tradition delivered prices —the steelmaker pays the transport cost. Round each main steelmaking region there is a large zone in which delivered prices are uniform irrespective of the distance from any steelworks in or outside the zone, and they are the same in all these zones. In zones remote from a steelworks prices are higher. The uniformity of prices in the different producing regions is a legacy of the practice of inter-regional dumping based on local monopoly in the past. It greatly reduces the inducement to a steel user to take the cost of delivering steel into account in deciding where to locate his works. This differentiates the British system from that in most continental countries and in the United States.[2]

All steel prices because of the immense variety of sizes, qualities, and scale of orders, are made up of a base price (related to a particular size and quality and quantity) plus extras for departures from this.

---

[1] Of course some investments are bad but this is a different matter. A lot of rather ill-chosen new equipment was put in before the war; some has been since.

[2] The British system, however, has moved from a situation in which there was a uniform price almost through the whole country for some products.

The 'extras', like the base price, are agreed and fixed. The differences of cost in departing from standard sizes or qualities, however, vary from works to works according to their plant, raw materials, range of orders, managerial skill, and their manner of accounting. To fix standard extras therefore involves a compromise capable of having important effects. If the 'extras' are in general rather low, the price for the standard product, the basic price, will be higher, and vice versa. There is thus a difference in the financial incentives towards using standard sizes and large quantities. In the United States the 'extras' have commonly been a higher proportion of base prices than in the United Kingdom; so have the discounts for large quantities. In its review of prices in 1953–4 the Iron and Steel Board revised extras upwards, which was a wise step likely to encourage efficient production.

The Board has the duty of giving advice on the level of protection needed for the industry, and its Chairman is a member of the Council of Association between Britain and the European Coal and Steel Community. The Board did not appear to favour the elimination of tariff barriers in its early years, and was widely believed to favour a minimum protection of 15 % plus anti-dumping duties. The problem was generalized by the proposal that Britain should enter a free trade area, though how the Council of Association would then fit in had still to be worked out in 1957. Maximum duties of 10 % were agreed in 1957.

(c) Impact of supervision

It is sometimes suggested that these arrangements allow the steel industry to produce the results of competition while avoiding its dangers, by means of constructive co-ordination and public supervision, and that they constitute a particularly fruitful form of relation between the State and industry. There is, the argument runs, no lack of competition, although competition in its most familiar form is eliminated. Exporters have to compete with foreign steelmakers. At home steel competes with other materials, and though there is no price competition between steelmakers firms compete in cost reduction, expansion of capacity, and service to customers. Prices fixed by an outside authority rule out excessive profit and provide an inducement to efficiency (both by good management and good investment) since by reducing costs individual firms can increase their profits. The fixed price is itself therefore the source of a form of competition which can only be healthy. Price competition is necessarily liable to be destructive in an industry where capital costs are so high, and when investments in new capacity are so large and so durable that blind competitive investment involves the danger of great error. Moreover because the plants are often isolated decisions to close them may bring local distress. Discussions between steelmakers about their plans, and with a supervisory body, can avoid overlapping and duplicated investments, discourage investments which are not as good as they might be, and prevent changes which cause pockets of unemployment if the gains are incommensurate. If the gains *are* commensurate remedial action can at any rate be set in motion.

Where the risks appear great because past troubles have been so disturbing it is politically useful no doubt to have an institution which appears able to secure 'the public interest'. How much difference— apart from this—has the organization made? Have other countries lacking it done less well as a result?

To this pragmatic test there is no conclusive answer. The rising output and productivity are no proof that the central organization has had a significant effect, because in conditions of rising world demand, rising faster than before the war, with no prolonged interruptions and an almost continuous state of 'sellers' market' at home and abroad, the encouragement to expansion of capacity would always have been irresistible. All firms were stimulated. But were they stimulated enough or in the right ways? The estimates of demand published by the industry's planning bodies at various times proved too conservative. If the Board used Procrustean methods to limit expansion that would in retrospect be a mark against it: it is probable that it did not so act. In its last report (1957), the Board wants expansion to be slightly faster than the firms. The fact that the new schemes, including a new home ore based plant, injected into the Plan of 1946, the proposed rationalizations and the disappearance of some small plants were not realized suggests that the expansive force of individual firms in response to the market stimuli was not to a significant extent canalized by central plans. There are several possible interpretations: one that the plans not carried out were proved impracticable or wrong by events, or that those responsible for central decisions took this view of them; a second that initiative could not be injected from the centre; a third that it was politically unattractive—to all concerned—to press for radical change when plenty of change of some sort was taking place, and it was possible to argue that speed was everything.

During the war it was often accepted that efficiency would best be served by concentrating expansion and not proliferating it through all works. Though a common criticism of the form of planning body set up for steel is that it can stop things being done but cannot start them, the impression of the first ten years is that apart from some delays and minor adjustments it has neither stopped nor started things and has not brought about either a greater degree of concentration and specialization or more radical shifts to deep water sites or home ore sites. Discussions of plans in the Federation or Board provide a useful clearing house; firms know formally of each other's projects, and there is scope for sharing technical experience. But these things can and would be secured by less elaborate means if that is all that is wanted. It is of course possible that what is a legitimate deduction from the first plan period may not apply later—may not apply now: but one must wait for the evidence.

The cautious attitude on prospects of demand was probably shared by the leading firms and many of those responsible for central planning decisions (though a Treasury forecast in 1949 took a more expansive view). Early in 1955 the case against excessive expansion was set out elaborately, the main theme being that, since steel plant is costly, to expand too much is a serious waste of investment. The Board is now more expansive than the firms. Where expansion requires a new plant whose capacity is large in relation to total demand there is of course a real difficulty—one easier to face in a 'European' sized market.

The criticism is powerful, but the first ten years of planning were unusually unpredictable. Nationalization soon followed by denationalization, rearmament following the years of reconstruction, unchecked gradual inflation throughout have been obviously confusing and warping. It has not always seemed reasonable to base policies on economic criteria. But at the same time the economic prospects have been misjudged. It could be argued that the technique of planning and of getting plans carried out must be learned. Within the present frameworks of the system of supervision, planning and price-fixing can be based on a variety of principles and criteria (it may be thought that the government should have done more in legislation to define these), and the application of the principles already adopted can be applied with more skill.

Thus in fixing the scrap levy which is used to equate the cost of using pig-iron and scrap in open-hearth furnaces, the rise in the cost of making pig-iron appears frequently to have been underestimated, and the relative value of scrap compared with pig-iron has been in other respects set too low, so that steelmakers using a high proportion of scrap have been favoured when expansion of pig-iron manufacture was to be encouraged. Again in assessing the relative advantage of using home and imported ores the prospective cost of imported ore was for a long time put too low, and the users of imported ore have for long periods benefited from the Industry Fund to which the users of home ore were contributing. These can be regarded as avoidable administrative misjudgments, or as deliberate sacrifices of rational price incentives in order to preserve stable prices (in the belief that Britain was on the peak of a trade cycle) or to keep steel prices low. (This was advocated by socialists as a service to the rest of industry, and more generally as anti-inflationary, though its effect was more probably the reverse. Both 'sides' possibly strained after low prices for political reasons.) The second Board appeared quickly to react against the tactics which kept prices extremely low. The advantage of using scrap for example was lessened: and margins which covered depreciation and profit were widened.

This underlines the wide range of discretion which in this structure is given to those who are to supervise 'in the public interest'. To begin to assess the advantages gained it is desirable to observe what happens elsewhere. Neither on the continent nor in America is there the same system. In America there is no planning of investment or fixing of prices—and no supervision. At periods when more capacity has seemed necessary for defence the government has allowed quick 'write-offs' for expansions, which no doubt could lend itself to a spasmodic control of investment and its timing, and has exerted a stimulus. Prices are 'f.o.t.'—not 'uniform delivered' in the British sense. There is price leadership: at times of scarcity there are 'premiums', and if orders were scarce as they were in the 1930's no doubt there would be price concessions as there were then—on transport, extras, or on the base price. But this fell far short of the destructive competition the fear of which is put forward as making price-fixing essential in Britain. The stabilizing force is the usual recognition in conditions of oligopoly of the relative strength of the competitors. Price-cutting was used as a means of securing market gains, but was not continuous: it did, however, reflect —and reward—changes of comparative strength. But just as price-cutting was not in fact destructive so the general movement of prices in the period of high demand has not been marked by acute peaks (except for high-cost products of marginal firms): the policy of avoiding sharp changes has been normal with the big firms and price leaders. The margin of profit has been higher than in the United Kingdom: but that probably marks a sounder equilibrium. Expansion of capacity has occurred in spasms: but the rate of growth since 1939 has been impressive, and the speed with which new plants are erected is much faster than in the United Kingdom—there is, that is, more elasticity of supply in this sense. The way prices are formed is still subject to much criticism: but their main 'antitrust' interest seems to be to avoid a reduction in the number of competitors. On the continent the picture is different again: the European Coal and Steel Community sets out to establish rules for competition, which bear some resemblance to the rules implicit or explicit under the antitrust régime in the United States. There is some degree of collusion in fixing prices in most producing areas, but there is inter-regional competition. Profit margins again are probably higher than in the United Kingdom. The Community does not fix prices, though it can intervene: nor does it plan investment, though it examines projects, expresses judgments, and may advance capital on cheap terms. Its practice, however, is still developing, and there are conflicting influences, including a greater propensity to plan. What is clear is that the steel industry is healthy, thriving and expanding in the United States and in the Community under these other régimes.

BIBLIOGRAPHY

(a) Books, Periodicals and Year-books

Andrews, P. W. S. and Brunner, E., *Capital Development in Steel: a Study of the United Steel Companies Ltd.*, Oxford, Blackwell, 1951.

British Iron and Steel Federation, *Annual Reports*.
  Monthly Statistical Bulletin (which includes until the end of 1955 valuable if angled articles). Published jointly since 1956 by the B.I.S.F. and the Iron and Steel Board.
  The Statistical Handbook, annual (formerly *The Statistical Year-book*).
  Steel Review, quarterly (first published in January 1956).

Burn, D. L., *The Economic History of Steelmaking, 1867–1939*, Cambridge University Press, 1940. (A further volume covering the period 1940 to 1956 will be published shortly.)

Goldschmidt, Dietrich, *Stahl und Staat: das Britische Experiment*, Stuttgart und Düsseldorf, Ring Verlag, 1956.

Minchinton, W. E., *The British Tinplate Industry: a History*, Oxford University Press, 1957.

Pugh, Sir Arthur, *Men of Steel*, London, Iron and Steel Trades Confederation, 1951.

United States Steel Corporation, *Papers for the Temporary National Economic Committee*, New York, 1940.

(b) Official Publications
(All published by H.M.S.O. except where otherwise stated)

(i) United Kingdom

Iron and Steel Board, *Reports*.

Iron and Steel Corporation of Great Britain, *Report and Accounts for 1951–3*, annual.

Iron and Steel Holding and Realization Agency, *Reports*.

Ministry of Supply, *Iron and Steel Industry: Reports by the British Iron and Steel Federation and the Joint Iron Council*, Cmd. 6811, 1946.

Board of Trade, Import Duties Advisory Committee, *Report on the Present Position and Future Development of the Iron and Steel Industry*, Cmd. 5507, 1937.

(ii) International Organizations

European Coal and Steel Community, *Annual Reports*, Luxembourg, The Community.

CHAPTER VIII

THE BUILDING MATERIALS INDUSTRY

By B. R. WILLIAMS

I. GENERAL ACCOUNT OF THE INDUSTRY
AND COLLECTIVE AGREEMENTS

(a) The variety of materials

It is impossible to give either a tidy or adequate account of the building materials industry. There is a great variety of materials, which are produced in many different ways. The industry has an existence only in terms of the use, in some cases not an exclusive use, of this wide variety of materials and products. Census of Production material is distributed among several volumes of which the main ones are: *Building Materials* (Order III, 29, 2 and part of 29, 3 in the Standard Industrial Classification, i.e. covering the treatment of stone, the manufacture of slate goods, prefabricated concrete products, asbestos cement goods, lime, etc.), *Bricks and Fireclay* (Order III, 20 and part of 29, 3), *Cement* (Order III, 24), and *Timber* (Order XIV, 170 and 179). These materials account for roughly two-thirds of the cost of materials used in building a house. The remaining one-third are included or submerged in such volumes as *Non-Metalliferous Mines and Quarries, Glass, Roofing Felts, Paint and Varnish, Iron Foundries, Brass Manufactures,* and *Hardware, Hollow-ware, Metal Furniture and Sheet Metal.*

The Simon Committee Report[1] estimated that there were 150 different categories of building materials, and that the basic building materials were produced by at least 2500 firms. In the summary table on the production of building materials in the *Annual Abstract of Statistics* over thirty main categories are listed: namely, sand, gravel, lime, whiting, bricks, cement, clay and concrete roofing tiles, damp-course and roofing slates and felt, gypsum, gypseous plaster, plaster board, insulation board, laminated board, hard board, wall partition blocks, flooring and wall clay tiles, cast-iron soil pipes, manhole covers and frames, lead and copper sheet and pipe, and metal windows. There are in addition plain timber used in carcassing and floors, constructional steel, electricians' materials, and newer building materials such as plastics and aluminium.

The materials in this heterogeneous collection are produced in many

[1] Ministry of Works, *The Distribution of Building Materials and Components: Report of the Committee of Inquiry*, (H.M.S.O. 1948).

different ways ranging from open-cast mining in sand, through mining, crushing, and firing in bricks and cement, to modern methods of chemical processing in the case of plastics. The variety of processes used is reflected in wages, in hours of work, and in relative price movements. Average weekly earnings for men in April 1955[1] were 259s. 4d. for cement, 225s. 1d. for glass, 216s. 9d. for bricks and fireclay, 211s. 6d. for clay, sand, gravel and chalk pits, 191s. 4d. for miscellaneous wood and cork manufactures, 188s. 4d. for timber saw milling and 166s. 8d. for slate quarrying and mining. There were, however, significant differences in hours worked—57·6 in cement, 51·3 in clay, sand, gravel and chalk pits, 49·9 in bricks and fireclay, 48·4 in glass, 47·6 in saw milling, 47·2 in miscellaneous wood and cork manufactures, 42·9 in slate quarrying and mining. Average hourly earnings therefore show a smaller spread than weekly earnings.

(b) Competition between materials

Many of these building materials are competitive, and this competition has increased with the interrelated improvements in building techniques and materials. For external walls, other than for housing, bricks and concrete are competitive, and in addition a wide range of materials (such as plastics, glass, stove enamelled metal sheets, aluminium and timber) are used as claddings or infillings (for external walls) to framed buildings. This competition between wall materials is at the moment greatest in non-domestic building. For internal walls there is competition between clay bricks, bricks made from mixture of clay and pulverized fuel ash, breeze blocks, plaster board, wood, metal and plastic. In this field, as in external cladding, changing techniques of building whereby walls no longer need to support floors and roof have created new possibilities of using materials of lightweight construction. Development in building roof structures has had a similar effect. New methods of spanning large areas with light construction have created new use competition between steel, reinforced concrete, aluminium and timber.[2] For roofing there is competition between slates, clay tiles, concrete and aluminium. For windows and door-frames, there is competition between timber and metal. For flooring there is competition between materials such as timber, ceramic and plastic tiles, and cork.

Such competition between alternative materials can be as significant as competition between producers of the same material. Whether such competition between building materials is as significant as competition between producers of like materials is difficult to determine because of

[1] *Ministry of Labour Gazette*, vol. 63, no. 9, September 1955.
[2] See, for example, *The Financial Times Survey of the Building Industry 1955* (Supplement, 24 January 1955), pp. 18–19.

the peculiar relations between client, architect, and builder in the building industry. In the architects' building specifications particular materials are specified, in many cases particular subcontractors are nominated and, in addition, a particular maker of a building material 'or agreed equivalent design or quality' is often specified.[1] The architectural design of the building, the procedure of architects in choosing subcontractors and in nominating particular makers of building materials, are thus a crucial factor in determining the degree of competition throughout the building materials industry. The architect, except where he is a salaried member of a building firm, must by his professional code remain financially independent of the builder and the building materials producer, but whether this does lead him, in the interest of the client, to find the competitive price before nominating subcontractors or particular makers of materials is an open question, the answer to which could only be gained by a detailed study of procedure in architects' offices.

There have been significant changes in the constitution of production between 1938 and 1954. The production of bricks, clay roofing tiles and stoneware pipes and conduits has fallen by 8 %, 50 % and 20 % respectively. The production of the others has risen in varying degrees: sand and gravel by over 200 %, concrete roofing tiles by over 100 %, plaster board, cement, steel windows and doors by over 50 %. This change in the constitution of production is related to changes in relative prices as well as to change in building techniques and in the quality of newer materials. Thus, for example, the price of cement has risen 30 % since mid-1949 compared with 37 % for building bricks other than flettons, and 185 % since 1935 compared with 230 % for bricks.[2]

(c) Size of firms

There are great variations in capital and net output per worker in the different sections of the industry, as reflected in Table 1.

The size of establishment and degree of concentration also varies considerably from section to section of the industry. The largest company engaged predominantly in the manufacture of building materials, and the only one in the list[3] of the 100 largest public companies, is The Associated Portland Cement Manufacturers (A.P.C.M.), though the

[1] For estimates of the importance of subcontracts, see Monopolies Commission, *Report on the Supply of Buildings in the Greater London Area* (H.M.S.O. 1954), pp. 9, 10. Estimates range from 19 to 71 % of total cost on particular building projects.

[2] For the movement from 1935 to 1948 see B. C. Brown, 'Industrial Production in 1935 and 1948', *London and Cambridge Economic Bulletin*, December 1954, p. v.

[3] Included in *A Classified List of Large Companies Engaged in British Industry*, issued by the National Institute of Economic and Social Research (London, 1955). In 1954–5 the A.P.C.M. ranked 31 by asset size and 18 by income.

largest British public company, Imperial Chemical Industries, produces a large output and range of building materials.[1] Also British Plaster Board, the Tunnel Portland Cement Company, English China Clays, the London Brick Company, The Rugby Portland Cement Company, The Steetley Company, the Amalgamated Roadstone Corporation, Eastwoods, The Crittall Manufacturing Company and The Marley Tile (Holding) Company possess assets of over £4 million. Existing alongside these are many very small firms, particularly in bricks, non-metalliferous mines and quarries, timber and 'building materials', but also in sections which show a high degree of concentration—namely, cement, metal windows and plaster board.

Table 1. *Wages as percentage of net output and net output per worker*

Census trade	Net output per person employed (£) 1951	Wages and salaries as percentage of net output
Slate quarries and mines	430	75
Timber	572	61
Bricks and fireclay	601	66
Glass other than containers	647	59
Building materials	698	57
Non-metalliferous mines and quarries	795	50
Roofing felts	1,354	33
Cement	1,492	33

In cement, approximately two-thirds of total output is produced by the A.P.C.M., and nine-tenths by the A.P.C.M., the Tunnel Portland Cement Company and The Rugby Portland Cement Company. In metal windows, The Crittall Manufacturing Company produced 40% of output and together with Henry Hope and Sons, and Williams and Williams, rather more than two-thirds of the total. In bricks just over one-quarter of the output is produced by the London Brick Company, and the National Coal Board—the next largest maker—produces a further 10%. However, in contrast to the position in cement, metal windows, plaster board and aluminium, the remaining output is produced by a very large number of firms.

It is rare in building materials to find a high degree of concentration based on marked economies to scale of plant. The A.P.C.M. has grown very largely by the amalgamation or purchase of companies making cement.[2] The London Brick Company, the British Plaster Board

[1] See Imperial Chemical Industries, *Products for Building*, 1954.
[2] It has works at Hull, Ferriby, Kirkton Lindsey, Hope, Barnstone, Harbury, Cherry Hinton, Claydon, Sundon, Dunstable, Kidlington, Penarth, Rodmell, Upper Beeding, Grays, Stone, Greenhithe, Cliffe, Northfleet, Rochester, Wickham, Snodland and Sittingbourne.

(Holdings), the Tunnel Portland Cement Company, Amalgamated Roadstone Corporation, Eastwoods and Marley Tiles are likewise based on amalgamation and purchase. They are all multi-plant firms.

(d) Restrictive practices

Sir Herbert Manzoni has produced a list of building materials for which local authorities had received identical tenders.[1] This list includes cement and metal windows, and in addition bolts, nuts and washers, wire nails, sheet lead, pipes and traps, bitumen emulsion, road tar, pre-cast concrete goods, earthenware pipes, galvanized dustbins, spun-iron pipes and street lighting equipment. Cement prices are controlled by the Cement Federation; bolts, nuts and washers by the Black Bolt and Nut Association and the Bright Bolt and Nut Association who quote prices at a plusage on the standard list 'which at the moment appear to vary as between areas'; wire nails by the Nails Association which issues a standard price-list; sheet lead, pipes and traps by the Lead Sheet and Pipe Manufacturers' Association which issues standard price-lists; earthenware pipes by the National Pipe Federation which issues a standard price-list on which are based both manufacturers' and merchants' tenders, although there is sometimes a variation in the cash discount allowed. In some of the other cases there is evidence of local but not national price-fixing schemes. Thus in chain-link fencing the City of Birmingham received identical tenders from two manufacturers and three merchants, though the City of Liverpool received extremely unidentical tenders. There are also regional variations in the case of metal windows—and, for reasons given below, in some regions tenders are identical, in others not. In pre-cast concrete goods, and to a lesser extent in bitumen emulsion, there is evidence that prices of local tenderers are kept equal, with the prices of outside tenderers higher by the cost of freight involved.

None of the building materials in Sir Herbert's list, other than earthenware pipes, is in the Simon Committee List of Producer Associations that operate merchant agreements, and none is controlled by a producers' association whose members produce less than 85 % of United Kingdom output. In the Monopolies Commission report on *Collective Discrimination*,[2] exclusive dealing, collective boycotts, aggregated rebates and other discriminatory trade practices are said to exist in the production and distribution of the following building materials that have not already been mentioned—bricks, copper cylinders and boilers, damp courses, fibre board, flushing cisterns and copper balls, glazed and floor tiles, heating boilers and radiators (cast-iron), paint, plaster board,

---

[1] Reproduced in *The Builder*, 29 April 1955.
[2] Cmd. 9504 (H.M.S.O. 1955).

sanitary earthenware, sanitary fireclay and other clayware. As in the case of bricks, some of the arrangements affect only certain sections of the trade in these products, and are operated only in certain parts of the United Kingdom.

Price agreements and other 'restrictive practices' may be operated by producers, or they may be operated by either producer-merchant agreements or merchant-manufacturer agreements.

(e) Agreements between producers

The Cement Federation which controls prices of Portland cement is an association of all producers. Merchants' rebates and the conditions of rebate are fixed by the Federation. A description of the Cement Federation's price and distribution policy will be given in the next section.

The Glazed Wall and Floor Tile Manufacturers' Association, whose members produce over 90 % of home output, operates a common ex-factory price policy. Tiles are considered in the chapter on pottery.[1]

The Metal Window Association, whose members account for some 90 % of sales of standard metal windows in the home market, operates a common-price policy.[2] The (confidential) Standard Pricing Schedule consists of gross list prices with a rebate table known as the Price Adjustment Table. Gross list prices apply to sales up to £100 in gross value. Rebates on sales above this £100 rise to 25 % for orders of £600 and over. Prices are intended to apply to all orders placed in the United Kingdom, with no provision for a reduction if sold ex-works excepting an occasional allowance of 5 % on government orders.[3]

Members report inquiries over £616 in selling value. Where outside competition is not expected members quote equal prices in accordance with the Standard Pricing Schedule. Until July 1956, where outside competition was expected, the Secretariat of M.W.A. authorized one member to quote a price below the schedule price. This member decided on a price and the Secretariat instructed other members to quote a higher price. Since July 1956, members decide between them the extent of the cut to be made, subject to a maximum fixed each month.

Less than one-third of home sales are through merchants. The terms on which M.W.A. members are recommended to sell to merchants— 15 % off gross list prices for orders up to £100 rising to 25 % off on orders over £250, with the merchant allowing quantity rebates on resale in accordance with the Standard Pricing Schedule—are designed to encourage merchants to handle small orders, and in practice they rarely

[1] Ch. xvii.
[2] Monopolies Commission, *Report on the Supply of Standard Metal Windows and Doors* (H.M.S.O. 1956), ch. 3.   [3] *Ibid.*

compete for large orders. These terms are allowed only to 'signed up' merchants, that is those with whom they enter into an agreement concerning price maintenance. Normally metal windows are handled by merchants appointed as agents for a particular manufacturer. Because of this there is no Association enforcement of merchants' selling prices and no collective enforcement: a merchant employed by a member is considered by the M.W.A. to be that member's agent. In the conditions of 1937 a quota scheme was regarded by the M.W.A. as an essential part of its price policy. The quota scheme was abolished in 1947.

In these cases the proportion of output going to merchants' premises is very small, and the firms are grouped in very strong trade associations. Where this is not so, effective price control generally requires manufacturer-merchant agreements.

(f) Producer-merchant agreements

Builders' merchants have worked in close alliance with the manufacturers of building materials in resale price maintenance schemes, in several cases using association discounts and deferred rebates to maintain the strength of and loyalty to the agreement.

The bulk of building materials are distributed through builders' merchants; the rest are distributed through specialist merchants or go direct from manufacturer to builder.[1] Where distribution is through specialist merchants rather than through builders' merchants, the proportion of the material going direct to user tends to be high. Specialist merchants operate where, as in brass, copper or malleable tubes, paint, glass, timber, and boilers, there are important users other than builders, or where, as in glass, boilers, radiators, gas and electrical appliances, specialized services in shaping, assembling, fixing or servicing are required—services which large builders will often provide for themselves. Another case of specialist distribution is provided by sand and gravel merchants who act, in effect, as hauliers, often paying the full pit price. Direct-to-builder distribution is common in awkward materials such as sand and gravel and in bricks which can easily be stored on site. In bricks, however, although merchants do not store more than small lots, they often collect and place orders and deliver from railway sidings. The merchants take on a greater importance in the distribution of bricks at times of scarcity for by maintaining large orders with brick companies they are often able to 'quote' shorter deliveries than the brick companies themselves. Direct distribution results too from the preferences of large buyers and also from the preferences of strongly organized sellers, as is the case with metal windows, glass, Portland

[1] The proportion for various commodities is given in the Simon Committee Report, pp. 53–5.

and asbestos cement. In such cases, producers can develop their own selling organization or use direct distribution as a means of enforcing their own decisions concerning conditions of sale.

Builders' merchants perform several functions. They maintain stocks, which is convenient both to sellers and buyers—particularly to the smaller ones. It is convenient to sellers in that the merchant continues to buy during the winter and convenient to the buyer in that supplies from a wide variety of sources are gathered together for him. They act as a link between manufacturers and builders, develop a detailed knowledge of sources of supply, economize the use of transport and in some cases arrange for a phased delivery of various materials and components on site. Larger merchants are also able to provide technical advice and trade information to architects and builders, and provide credit to builders. The Simon Committee gives an estimate that before the war the average length of credit given by large merchants was sixteen weeks, and eleven and four weeks respectively in the case of medium and small merchants.

Table 2. *British Ironfounders Association rainwater goods rebates*

Discount, rebate or allowance	Large merchants (%)	Small merchants (%)	Large user consumers (%)	Small user consumers (%)	Government departments and structural engineers (%)	General public and unsigned consumers
Trade discount	20+4	20+2½	20	10	20	n.e.
Tonnage allowance	Nil−5	Nil−5	Nil−10	Nil−10	10	n.e.
Cash discount	5	5	2½	2½	2½	n.e.
Association rebate	5 if eligible	5 if eligible	n.e.	n.e.	n.e.	n.e.
Super rebate	Nil−7½	Unlikely to qualify	n.e.	n.e.	n.e.	n.e.

n.e. = not eligible.

The Monopolies Commission has described in some detail the operation of manufacturer-merchant agreements in cast-iron rainwater goods and imported timber. Members of the British Ironfounders Association (B.I.A.) produce about 90 % of the total output of cast-iron rainwater goods and distribute two-thirds through members of Distributors of Builders' Supplies Joint Council or Building Industry Distributors. When the Commission reported, there were agreements to provide for the maintenance by foundries and merchants of common minimum delivered selling-prices with discounts that vary according to the type of buyer, and for exclusive dealings between signatories. Table 2 gives the schedule of discounts, the discounts on the price to the public being deducted successively. The scale of discounts was such that no merchant could profitably trade in association goods unless he was a signatory to the 'rainwater agreements'.

Ten producers out of seventy-four produce one-third of the output of cast-iron rainwater goods. These ten are subsidiaries of Allied Iron-founders. The Allied group, the only user of fully mechanized methods before the war, has three of its ten foundries fully mechanized, and because of advantages gained from its combination of rationalized production and sales with mechanized production, it has lower costs than other producers.[1] The Monopolies Commission reported that the Allied group does not appear to have 'played any greater part in the creation or maintenance of restrictive practices in the trade than that which arises naturally from the participation in the Rainwater Agreements of a concern having so large a share of the trade'.[2] That this is so is due in some measure to competition from alternative materials.

During the years 1933–9, the British Ironfounders Association, to which was tied by exclusive dealing obligation the great majority of merchants, was yet not strong enough despite output quotas to avoid price competition. For competition came both from non-association foundries and from alternative materials such as asbestos cement. The Ironfounders Association sought an agreement with the asbestos cement manufacturers to fix prices and quotas for both types of material. Although in 1935 and 1936 the asbestos cement manufacturers showed some interest, later they displayed none.

Since the war the proportion of cast-iron rainwater goods produced by non-association firms has been very small. For though about 20 % of capacity of the light castings section of the foundry industry is non-association, rainwater goods form a smaller proportion of total production of these non-association members. Rainwater goods of alternative materials are now, however, a substantial part of production. The figures for 1949 are set out in Table 3.

Table 3. *Cast-iron pipes and substitutes*

Material	Rainwater		Soil		Smoke		Total output	
	Tons	%	Tons	%	Tons	%	Tons	%
Cast-iron	46,968	45	44,283	84	6,982	49	98,233	58
Aluminium*	12,589	12	–	–	–	–	12,589	7
Asbestos cement*	24,861	24	4,676	9	7,108	51	36,645	22
Pressed steel*	19,232	19	3,448	7	–	–	22,680	13

* Figures calculated in equivalent cast-iron tons.

[1] Monopolies Commission, *Report on the Supply of Cast Iron Rainwater Goods* (H.M.S.O. 1951), p. 62.
[2] *Ibid.* p. 62.

These alternative materials have substantially weakened the power of the association of makers of cast-iron rainwater pipes to control the market.

Following the Monopolies Commission Report, the Ministry of Works held discussions with producers and distributors and new trading arrangements were introduced by the industry from the beginning of 1952. These new arrangements reflect the Commission's recommendation that

> there should be no discrimination by foundries either as regards supplies or as regards trade terms on the ground that a merchant has or has not entered into an agreement with the foundries, or is or is not a member of a trade association; and that merchants who buy from non-members of the B.I.A. or who handle imported Rainwater Goods, should not as a result be deprived of supplies from members or obtain them only on less favourable terms.

The modifications have as yet made no significant difference.[1]

In the case of imported timber an Approved List System has been built up by an organization of agents and importers associated with the Timber Trade Federation. The admission of concerns to the approved lists is controlled by Joint Committees of agents and importers. The agents on each approved list agree to negotiate sales only to importers on the list and importers agree to buy only through agents on the list. By the operation of this system traders not admitted to the list are forced to operate as non-importing firms,[2] and all but a very small proportion of imported timber is forced to pass through at least one agent and one importer to the user.

This Approved List System was not built up by joint action of agents and importers on the one hand and merchants on the other. There was consultation with merchants but this affected only the detail and not the main principles of the system. The Monopolies Commission found that, in general, there is price competition among timber traders. 'There is competition among agents, among importers and non-importing firms. There is no form of price-ring on a national scale', although there are certain local price agreements between importers and merchants. Thus price-lists—'guides to the prices to be charged'—are issued in Scotland, Northern Ireland, Sussex, Devon and Cornwall. None of these local agreements is binding on members and there are no penalties for infringement, although local opinion in the trade exercises a pressure on members to observe the list prices. Over most of the country no such price-

---

[1] Monopolies Commission, *Collective Discrimination* (1955), p. 41.

[2] A brief outline of the system of admission to and exclusion from the list is given on pp. 26–8 of the Monopolies Commission *Report on the Supply of Imported Timber* (H.M.S.O. 1953). It is an essential feature of the scheme that timber users should be excluded from the importers' list.

lists exist. Following the Monopolies Commission Report criticizing the agreements of traders on the 'Approved Lists' to deal only with each other, the Timber Trade Federation abrogated these agreements.

(g) Merchant-manufacturer agreements

In the inter-war period a group of builders' merchants in London made agreements to observe common prices for goods sold over the counter, and price-lists were prepared and circulated among members. Soon after, merchant groups in other parts of London copied this practice and a common price-list for London was developed. Later the common monthly price-list became the responsibility of the Builders' and Plumbers' Merchants Association which had a membership extending beyond London into the South and Midlands. The Builders' Merchants Alliance, a London merchant organization, published a price-list for heavy materials. The preparation of these price-lists was taken over in 1943 by the Building Industry Distributors (B.I.D.), formed in 1942 to amalgamate the above-mentioned Association and Alliance and the National Federation of Builders' Merchants. The attempt to secure price maintenance for large-quantity sales, in contrast to over-the-counter sales, led to an attempt to involve manufacturers in the merchants' price-fixing arrangements. Agreements were made with manufacturers' associations whereby merchants agreed to observe resale prices fixed by (or agreed with) manufacturers and to handle only manufacturers' association products, and manufacturers agreed to adhere to these prices and to grant special terms to merchants who were party to the agreement. Thus, where these agreements were made between manufacturers' and merchants' associations a merchant received not only the usual merchant terms but an additional special rebate. Of course the strength of the merchants' associations depends in some measure on making their lists and the lists of the manufacturers identical, but the natural desire of the merchants' associations to administer such a 'closed shop' has not always been easy to satisfy. The position has been complicated by differing practices relating to distribution through merchants in the North and the South, and manufacturers wished to put on the merchant list those to whom for a variety of reasons special terms had been granted in the past, whether or not they conformed to the merchant association's definition of a genuine merchant—namely, a seller who has a showroom (or, for heavy building materials, a yard), carries stocks adequate to the needs of the district, and does not operate as a builder.

Although the merchants and manufacturers had certain disagreements about compiling a National List, there were serious discussions from 1936 to 1939 between the Distributors of Builders' Supplies Joint

Council and the Council of Building Materials Manufacturers, representing a wide range of building material manufacturers on the light side of the trade, concerning the creation of a price maintenance scheme covering a large group of building materials. The Council of Building Materials Manufacturers was prepared to accept a joint merchant-manufacturer scheme to regulate trade in the building industry, provided that each constituent manufacturers' association had a price maintenance scheme with merchant distributors and that the merchant organizations undertook that their members would sign the agreements for which they were eligible.[1] However, difficulties about drawing up an agreed list of merchants prevented any further progress before the war, since when negotiations have not been renewed.

The Distributors of Builders' Supplies Joint Council (D.B.S.J.C.) formed in 1936 is made up of the wholesale section of the National Federation of Ironmongers, the British Federation of Plumbers' Merchants Association whose 140 members are situated mainly in the north of England, the Scottish Metal and Plumbers' Merchants Federation and the Plumbers' Merchants Association of Northern Ireland. Ninety to ninety-five per cent of the distributors are members of one of these associations or of the Building Industry Distributors.[2] The constituent associations have continued to deal with the particular problems of their own section of the trade, to negotiate price-fixing arrangements with manufacturers' associations and to enforce these agreements. It has been the task of the Joint Council to represent the merchants in relations with the government and to prepare a national list of genuine merchants. The National List for the light side of the trade was published in 1939 and a list for the whole trade shortly after the war. For the reasons mentioned above, however, the particular manufacturers' associations have not been prepared to exclude from their list merchants not included in the Joint Council's original National List. In consequence, certain building firms which have for many years conducted a merchant trade and been given merchant terms by manufacturers are in practice included in the National List. Until 1950, the D.B.S.J.C. required a manufacturer to undertake to give wholesale merchant prices only to those (a) 'whose names are included in the National Wholesale Merchant list as qualified to deal and who are regularly dealing in our products', and (b) 'whose names appear upon an existing merchants' list agreed by a Joint Committee of Manufacturers and Merchants appointed to deal with the products of which we are manufacturers, and that no new names will be added to such lists unless they are included in the National Wholesale

---

[1] Monopolies Commission, *Report on the Supply of Cast Iron Rainwater Goods* (1951), p. 29.
[2] The Building Industry Distributors were members until 1949, but now co-operate on matters of common interest such as the National List.

Merchant List'. When this was withdrawn the D.B.S.J.C. explained that

a very large number of manufacturers were not taking copies of the National List because they were unable to sign the undertaking due to the fact that they manufactured products other than those handled by Builders' Merchants and obviously, by signing the undertaking they would be prevented from selling those products except through the Builders' Merchants channels, which would be an incorrect procedure.[1]

The effect of the National List has been mainly on newcomers who, lacking any established arrangement with particular manufacturers, must generally—generally, because manufacturers reserve the right to include merchants not on the list—conform to the Joint Council's definition of a bona fide merchant.[2] The Monopolies Commission reported that any concern that complies with the definition of a bona fide merchant is able to gain entry into the organized trade.

The effect of these various restrictive practices on the economic performance of the industry will be considered after a more detailed examination of the cement and brick sections of the industry.

2. CEMENT

(a) Processes of production

In 1824 Joseph Aspdin found that he could produce an hydraulic binding material by mixing finely pulverized chalk and clay, burning them at a high temperature and grinding the resulting clinker. This discovery took place at a time when intensive building activity was exhausting the only cementing material then known—a natural clayey chalk. About 1845 I.C. Johnson produced cement of the modern Portland type by fine-grinding the clinker produced by burning raw materials 'with unusually strong heat until the mass was nearly vitrified'. The foundation for the modern rotary kiln process, which has made possible an even burning of the clinker and great economies in fuel, was laid by the end of the century. This type of kiln was first built in the United States in 1886 and introduced into Europe about 1896. Among the first rotary kilns was one of 26 ft. in length and 5 ft. in diameter, which may be compared with modern kilns of 300 to 500 ft. in length and 9 to 14 ft. in diameter. These rotary kilns brought a transformation of the production process in the decade before the First World War, and led to changes in the structure of the industry. Rostas estimates that

---

[1] Monopolies Commission, *Report on the Supply of Cast Iron Rainwater Goods*, pp. 99–100.

[2] In the eighteen months from January 1949, twenty-eight out of seventy-four applications were accepted.

whereas in 1907 63·3 % of capacity was in the form of fixed kilns, by
1924 84·5% of that capacity and 90% of capacity in use were rotary kilns.[1]

In the 1930's the process of flotation, a method widely used in the
concentration of ore, was adapted to the concentration and beneficiation
of limestones. Previously the slurry mixtures were obtained by blending
natural raw materials, but the flotation process made it possible to use rock
deposits previously unusable and to produce cements for special purposes
such as low-heat-hydration cements and sulphate-resisting cements.

Instrumentation has also brought accurate control of kiln speed,
draft, and feed, with a consequent economy in kiln lining and fuel.
Developments such as these have made possible a vast increase in
output, quality, and output per man. Equally, they have turned cement
making into a highly capitalized industry.

In a modern cement undertaking,[2] chalk or limestone is mechanically
excavated or quarried and trucked to the crushing plant at the works.
Clay, the second raw material, is excavated and carried to the washmill
where any sand present settles to the bottom and is removed. This clay
is then pumped (or taken by tanker) to the cement works. At the works,
the clay and the chalk or crushed limestone are mixed with water to
form the cement slurry. The slurry, after screening to the correct degree

[1] L. Rostas, *Productivity, Prices and Distribution in Selected British Industries*, N.I.E.S.R.
Occasional Papers, 11 (Cambridge University Press, 1948), pp. 81–2. Sales of rotary kilns
from the four leading producers are given in Economic Commission for Europe, *Growth and
Stagnation in the European Economy*, by I. Svennilson (Geneva, 1954), p. 157.

*Rotary cement kilns delivered from four European manufacturers**

Period	Europe			Rest of world		
	Number of kilns	Total capacity†	Average capacity per kiln	Number of kilns	Total capacity†	Average capacity per kiln
		(Thousand tons)			(Thousand tons)	
Up to 1904	96	—	—	4	—	—
1905–14	292	—	(30)	49	—	(30)
1915–20	52	—	(60)	15	—	(60)
1921–9	216	16,570	77	99	7,560	76
1930–4	50	4,635	93	59	6,280	106
1935–8	53	5,155	97	54	5,290	98
1939–44	22	2,230	101	26	2,400	92
1945–50	51	6,080	119	102	12,415	122
1921–50	392	34,670	88	340	33,945	100

* Klöckner-Humboldt-Deutz, Germany; Polysius, Germany; F. L. Smidth and Com-
pany, Denmark (including American branch); Vickers-Armstrongs, United Kingdom.
† Annual capacity based upon 330 days/year.
Note: The figures in parentheses are tentative.

[2] For a graphic description of cement making, see *Cement in the Making*, London, Cement
and Concrete Association, 2nd ed., 1951.

of fineness, is pumped to large storage tanks where it is kept agitated by mechanical stirrers or compressed air. These slurry tanks perform a two-fold function. After analysis of the clay-to-chalk content, corrections may be made in the next clay-chalk mixture to ensure that when this is added to the slurry already in the storage tanks the mixture will be correct. Further, the slurry in store makes it possible to shut down grinding plant and washmills while allowing the kilns (into which the slurry is pumped) to continue in operation.

The rotary kiln is a revolving steel cylinder tilted down from the feeding (and drying end) to the firing zone to facilitate the through-put of the slurry. Pulverized coal is blown in at the firing end. As the slurry passes down the kiln the moisture is driven off, the clay is then dehydrated and the chalk or limestone is broken down into carbon dioxide (which is given off) and lime, and then the various chemicals combine at high temperature (approximately 2500° F.) to form clinker. This after partial cooling goes to the clinker store for final cooling and storage. The kiln works continuously and in Britain an average rotary kiln produces 500 tons of cement clinker every twenty-four hours.

The final stage of manufacture is grinding, and here the setting time of the cement is regulated by adding an appropriate quantity of gypsum to the clinker. The mixture is then fine-ground in very large and heavy grinding mills. Finally, the cement is forced by compressed air into storage silos which have capacities of up to 2500 tons. These silos are equipped for delivery direct to bulk cement lorries or by chain conveyors to the packing plant. Storage of one-quarter to one-half of the annual capacity of the plant is often thought desirable to provide for continuous and economical operation, and although it is no longer necessary to 'season' the cement, some large purchasers require a testing that lasts up to a month during which time the cement remains in store.

(b) Size of establishments

For cement, the census analysis by size is given in Table 4.

Table 4. Cement (Analysis by size, 1951. Larger establishments in the United Kingdom)

Average number employed	Establishments (number)	Gross output* (£ thousand)	Net output* (£ thousand)	Persons employed (number)	Net output per person employed* (£)
25–99	13	3,657	1,243	919	1,353
100–199	11	6,582	2,419	1,675	1,444
200–749	21	27,081	10,784	6,887	1,566
750 and over	3	8,968	3,933	2,837	1,386
Total	48	46,287	18,379	12,318	1,492

* The figures in this column (except the total) are mainly estimated.

As compared with 1948 this shows a relative rise in net output per person in the smallest establishments. The 1948 Census of Production, however, used an 11–99 category, thereby including alumina cement.

Table 5. *Percentage distribution of employment in cement*

	11–99	100–199	200–499	200 and over	500 and over
1935	15·2	28·2	24·7	—	32·0
1948	7·0	17·7	—	74·6	—
1951	7·4*	13·5	55·9†	—	23·0‡

    * 25–99.   † 200–749.   ‡ 750 and over.

The comparison of size distribution of employment in pre-war and post-war years is given in Table 5. As compared with 1935, the post-war figures show an increase in the 200-and-greater group, and there has been a further shift into that group between 1948 and 1951. This movement reflects the fuller use of capacity as well as the construction of new capacity. However, the cement industry is not a large employer of labour and the tendency to labour-saving equipment (in extraction, in materials handling, in size and in automatic control of kilns) is so distinct that movements of employment by size category are not very significant. For the same reason net output per person by size category is not a good indication of the relation between output per man and size of plant. In fact the installation of large-capacity equipment, employing much the same labour force as the smaller units, is the biggest single factor explaining the four-fold increase in output per man in the last fifty years.[1] However, the high cost of transporting the product forces a considerable dispersal of plant.

In the last fifty years cement production has grown rapidly. In round figures, production was 2,750,000 tons in 1907, 5,750,000 tons in 1935 and 12,500,000 tons in 1955. This expansion has involved both an increase in plant and a rise in labour productivity. For example, employment shown in the 1924 Census of Production was much the same as that in the 1951 Census but production in the latter year was more than three times greater. Between 1935 and 1951 the employees per ton of cement production fell from 1·6 to 1·15. Man-hours involved from winning raw materials to despatch from works were, per ton of cement, 2·75 in 1946 and 1·87 in 1954.

[1] Rostas, in *Comparative Productivity in British and American Industry*, N.I.E.S.R. Occasional Papers, 13 (Cambridge University Press, 1948), pp. 114, 115, gives figures for American industry that show a marked increase of output per man with size of plant.

(c) *Financial concentration*

More significant than movements in average employment per establishment is movement in control. Although employment per establishment is relatively small the degree of multi-establishment control is high. Thus the 'Blue Circle' group of companies produces just under two-thirds of the industry's home production and controls twenty-seven of the forty-nine cement works. There are now only ten independent financial interests in the industry and three of these are responsible for 90 % of the output.

Cement is a highly mechanized industry involving a large capital outlay. The existing degree of capitalization is difficult to assess, as cement-making plant does not deteriorate quickly and, apart from marked change in technique, it can be maintained on a repair and small-replacement basis. Dr T. Barna in a paper to the Royal Statistical Society[1] estimated that in 1955 the 'replacement cost new of fixed assets' was £3100 per person employed. In the light of the revaluation of assets by The Associated Portland Cement Manufacturers, Dr Barna has raised this figure to £5000. That this figure is too low for genuine replacement cost will be argued below.

During 1924 and 1934 The Associated Portland Cement Manufacturers re-invested £3·8 million and expanded capacity by nearly one million tons per annum. Allowing for investment in freehold and leasehold chalk and clay land, etc., the cost of installing new capacity was about £3 per ton.[2] In the five years before the war annual capacity of 125,000 tons was scrapped and modern plants with a capacity of 2,250,000 tons were built. The cost per ton of cement-making capacity was then about £5 per ton. In the post-war period the cost per ton has been much higher. The A.P.C.M. plant at Shoreham completed in 1950 with a capacity of 350,000 tons cost £2,500,000.[3] This is roughly £7 per ton of annual capacity and equivalent to £7000 per employee at 1947–9 prices, or £10,000 to £12,000 at 1956 prices. One can get comparable figures for the United States in 1950 from the plans submitted to the American government for additions to existing capacity or the building of new cement plants. The construction cost per ton of annual capacity varied from £3 to £13 with an average of £9·5 (or £12 to £13 at current prices).[4]

In 1955 the A.P.C.M. revalued its fixed assets so that the 'resultant valuation represents estimated present cost of replacement of fixed

---

[1] 'The Replacement Cost of Fixed Assets in British Manufacturing Industry in 1955', read 21 November 1956, and published in the Society's *Journal*, Series A (General), vol. 120, part 1, 1957, p. 1.

[2] Rostas, *Productivity, Prices and Distribution* (1948), pp. 85, 86.

[3] *The Economist*, 28 July 1951.   [4] The author owes this information to Dr T. Barna.

assets after taking into account their expired and estimated future lives'. Although the revaluation was conservative the value of 'land, buildings, plant less depreciation' was almost doubled. The implied figure of £5000 fixed assets per employee does not of course represent the cost of a new works. For on the one hand the figure is based on estimated net replacement cost and on the other hand the valuation of the easily exploited Thames and Medway lands is low.[1]

The Rugby Portland Cement Company probably has the highest proportion of post-war equipment—between 1938 and 1955 it increased deliveries by 275 % compared with 65 % for the industry. In 1955 the balance-sheet valuation of fixed assets was £6¼ million. This was estimated by Mr Halford Reddish to be £4 million less than value in 1956 prices.[2] Assuming that The Rugby Portland Cement Company produces 7 % of the output of the industry the revaluation of assets at current prices would imply a figure of £12 per ton capacity. Clearly, however, where old equipment forms the backbone of the industry any such estimate is largely arbitrary in times of inflation. The only reliable figures are those for recent extensions and new works.

The combined effects of the longevity of plant, the high capital outlay per unit of output, a rapidly increasing output per man with mechanization, improved fuel efficiency and greater size of kilns, a homogeneous product, and fluctuating markets, have produced a strong financial concentration in the industry.

The capital outlay per unit of output and the low proportion of wage costs to gross output—it has fallen almost continuously from 25 % in 1907 to 13 % in 1951—gives an incentive to work at full capacity. In the past when demand was not expanding with capacity this led to price-cutting. As this did not produce much increase in demand, there was a movement to amalgamation. On three occasions in Britain 'price war' has produced amalgamations which engineered higher prices. These higher prices, however, led to the growth of new firms and, before 1935, to the collapse of voluntary endeavours to enforce a common selling policy. The number of firms, however, fell from 109 in 1924 to forty-six in 1935, to ten in 1956.

The history of the A.P.C.M. gives some indication of the process of financial consolidation. It was founded in 1900 to amalgamate some thirty companies. In the next decade, associated with the expanding demand for cement and the introduction of the rotary kiln, new companies were started. In 1912 the A.P.C.M. bought up thirty-three of

---

[1] The new A.P.C.M. works at Cauldon in Staffordshire was in 1954 expected to cost £3,000,000 for an output of 175,000 tons. This cost of £17 per ton is misleading as the works is designed so that it can easily be trebled in size, with the cost of extension much less than the cost of the original works. Even so the relevant cost per ton capacity was certainly greater than £10.   [2] Chairman's speech, Annual General Meeting, 1956.

its competitors and merged them into a new company, the British Portland Cement Manufacturers, in which it has a controlling interest. In this way, A.P.C.M. came to control four-fifths of output at that time. After 1919 there were new competitors and renewed competition. In 1932, when production fell by about 15 % the 'Red Triangle' group got into financial difficulties and the A.P.C.M. acquired its assets. In 1938 there was an agreement and exchange of shares between the three leading companies—the A.P.C.M. group controlling 55 % of output, the Alpha Cement group controlling 15 %, and the Tunnel Cement group (originally financed by F. L. Smidth and Company and other Danish firms) controlling 12½ %. A.P.C.M. purchased all the Alpha Ordinary Shares in return for shares in A.P.C.M., and transferred 26 % of these Alpha shares to the Tunnel Portland Cement Company in exchange for (non-voting) shares of the Tunnel Company.[1]

The fforde Report (1947)[2] listed the member firms of the Cement Makers' Federation. These were classified into financially interlocking groups. The first, the A.P.C.M. group, consisted of the A.P.C.M. and its subsidiaries B.P.C.M., Alpha Cement (then owned in part by Tunnel Portland Cement), G. and T. Earle, South Wales Portland Cement and Barnstone Cement Company. This group now produces about two-thirds of the industry's output.[3] The Cement Marketing Company is a selling organization for the group. The second group consisted of the Tunnel Portland Cement Company, which had a part ownership of Alpha in exchange for its own shares with A.P.C.M., a direct controlling interest in the Clyde Portland Cement Company, and a 50 % interest in Ribblesdale Cement, which it founded jointly in 1935 with the Ketton Portland Cement Company. This group now produces about one-sixth of the industry's output. The third group comprised Eastwoods Cement, Eastwoods Lewes Cement, and Eastwoods Humber Cement. These are all subsidiaries of Eastwoods, makers of bricks and tiles, and in 1949 the parent company sold its assets concerned with the cement industry to its wholly-owned subsidiary Eastwoods Cement (controlling Eastwoods Lewes and Eastwoods Humber Cement). The fourth group was The Rugby Portland Cement Company, and its subsidiary, Charles Nelson and Company, which it acquired in 1945. It produces about 7 % of cement output. The fifth group consisted of three Scottish companies engaged in the manufacture of blast-furnace cement with sales made through the Caledonian Portland Cement Company. There was

[1] In 1949, A.P.C.M. disposed of the greater part of its holding in Tunnel Portland Cement Company and re-purchased the Alpha shares from them.
[2] Ministry of Works, *Cement Costs* (the report of the fforde Committee), H.M.S.O. 1947.
[3] In 1955 this 'Blue Circle' group delivered just over 8 million tons of cement from their twenty-seven home works and exported nearly 1¼ million tons, i.e. roughly two-thirds of both production and of exports.

in addition the Ketton Portland Cement Company (with a half interest in Ribblesdale Cement Company), the Aberthaw and Bristol Channel Portland Cement Company, the South Wales Portland Cement Company, I.C.I., Chinnor Cement and Lime Company, and Mason's Portland Cement Company.

Since 1947 there have been certain changes. The number of member firms in the Cement Makers' Federation has fallen from twenty-two to nineteen. The three Scottish companies are now represented by the Caledonian Portland Cement Company. The Barnstone Cement Company (a subsidiary of A.P.C.M.) is no longer represented and Mason's Portland Cement Company has been absorbed by A.P.C.M., while Amalgamated Limestone Corporation (which during 1953 constructed a small cement works near Plymouth with a capacity of approximately 40,000 tons per annum) is a new member. The Tunnel Portland Cement Company has sold its holding in Alpha Cement and in turn the A.P.C.M. has sold most of its holding in the Tunnel Portland Cement Company. There are thus now ten independent financial groups. In addition two companies (one, Marchon Products, now a subsidiary of Albright and Wilson, from outside the nine financial groups) are now selling to A.P.C.M. cement or cement clinker, derived from the extraction of sulphuric acid from anhydrites.

(d) The Cement Makers' Federation

All manufacturers of Portland cement are members of the Federation which controls price policy, and until recently quotas. The Federation was formed in 1918, but it was not until 1934, as a result of intense competition during depression, that complete federation was achieved. From 1935 manufacturers made an agreement to fix prices and sales quotas. It should be borne in mind that apart from the recent war years, the Cement Makers' Federation has operated only during years of expanding output. Total production was at its minimum in 1932 and thereafter rose, on average, 600,000 tons a year up to 1939. It was in this period that old plant was scrapped and modern plant with a capacity of $2\frac{1}{4}$ million tons built. In the post-war years output was expanded from pre-war works and in addition, after 1950, from increased capacity. Prices of building materials also rose throughout the period from 1935, excepting a very slight check in 1938.

The main function of the Federation is to fix prices for ordinary Portland cement. Prices are fixed by voting on the part of the members and, in practice, a decision needs the votes of at least four members or groups.[1] (Resolutions to amend quotas required unanimous approval.)

---

[1] For voting provision see fforde Committee Report, par. 15.

The delivered-to-site price in any locality is based on delivery from the nearest works or coastal 'importing centre' and applies whether or not the cement is delivered from such a point. The base price is the ex-works price and varies partly with the region and partly with the raw material used—price being higher where limestone rather than chalk is used.[1] To this base price, or imported price, is added a sum that varies with distance from the works. In England, Wales and Northern Ireland 2s. is added for deliveries 5 to 10 miles from base. Thereafter additional costs are 2s. for the 10 to 15 miles radius, 1s. 6d. for the 15 to 20, 1s. 6d. for the 20 to 25, and then 1s. for each succeeding radius of 5 miles, i.e. for each 5 miles beyond 25. Where circles meet the lower price is taken.[2] In Scotland prices are fixed at particular centres and haulage costs added.

These delivered prices are increased for loads of less than 6 tons. Prices are quoted as delivered packed cement, but if delivered in bulk[3] or if collected from works 8s. 6d. and 11s. 6d. per ton are allowed. There is also a cash discount. Additional rebates are allowed to certain departments of state and to merchants who do not use cement, own or occupy a wharf or depot, and handle at least 300 tons per annum.[4] This last provision may be waived where a merchant is sponsored by a manufacturer or can show that he is a genuine builder's merchant. A larger rebate is given where cement is taken into store than where (as with 40 to 50 % of cement manufacturers' sales) it is simply brass plated.[5] A general deferred rebate scheme applies to users of cement. For any purchases between 1000 tons and 10,000 tons per annum the deferred rebate is 1s. per ton, and on quantities in excess of that 2s. per ton, except in Northern Ireland where the rebate is 1s. per ton provided the aggregate purchased is in excess of 1000 tons. Where the cement is supplied by a merchant the rebate is paid out of his margin.

'The variation between one base price and another is very considerably narrower than the variation between the cost of production at one works and another. Not only is this the case, but the base price for a given works does not necessarily reflect the cost of production at that works.'[6] There is nothing surprising in this, since with few exceptions the base prices of 1934 have been adjusted to meet the average

---

[1] A list of base prices for 1934, 1938 and 1945 is given in Appendix VI of the fforde Report.

[2] Until recently an exception was made in the Greater London Area where the base price for the Thames and Medway works (the lowest base price) applied throughout.

[3] 20 % is now delivered in bulk.

[4] Certain rebates mentioned in the fforde Report have since been changed. The provisions relating to resale price maintenance and to exclusive dealings with members of the Cement Federation have been struck out and the special rebate schemes for London and approved concrete product manufactures have been abolished.

[5] The percentage rebate varies with base prices since the rebate is given 'per ton', but the full rebate averages about 6 %.   [6] fforde Report, p. 16.

increase in costs. In those few cases where the relation between base prices has been changed the reason, it would appear, is to be found mainly in the location of new works.

The location of works makes possible substantial variations in area prices.[1] The necessary raw materials are calcium carbonate, which occurs in the form of limestone or chalk, and alumina and silica, which are present in certain clays. Suitable clay is found in most parts of the country, and though the main and best deposits of chalk are in South-East England, there are limestone deposits in many parts of South-West, Midland and North England and in Wales. However, there is a strong concentration in South Essex and North Kent on the banks of the Thames and Medway, where there are thirteen works, out of the forty-eight making Portland cement, producing 40 % of output. This concentration of production in South Essex and North Kent is due not only to the proximity of the London market which absorbs 15 to 20 % of cement output, but also to an easy access to excellent chalk and clay deposits, and good transport facilities.

The delivered prices do not in general reflect the works price plus cost of haulage. There is a considerable element of subsidy to those points of delivery that are remote at the expense of points of delivery close to cement works. This policy, in itself, makes the incentive to establish works in high-price areas less than it would be if users distant from the works were not subsidized. But more important than this has been the general aspect of price policy, namely the association of base price itself with the 'price circles'. For when a new works is started in a formerly remote area, to fit in with the price structure the works price must be significantly below that previously charged there; and this base price applies for deliveries within 5 miles of the factory whether or not that factory can supply it. The fforde Report mentions a proposal to establish a new works that was abandoned when the Federation made it clear that the opening of the new works would entail a base price lower than the existing delivered price. This difficulty would not apply if a non-Federation firm were set up. There are now no exclusive dealing provisions but until these provisions were eliminated from the Federation arrangements after the war it was difficult to establish a non-Federation firm since any customer purchasing from such a firm lost the right to any rebates from Federation firms.

As there is no public information about costs in particular localities it is not possible to judge the precise impact of price structure on location. The fforde Committee examined cost figures but simply commented that it 'found in them no readily discernible pattern'. It is worth noting, however, that there has been a growth of works in

---

[1] fforde Report, p. 18.

new areas since the war—at Pomplett, Mold, Cauldon (Staffordshire) and Whitehaven—and this tendency may grow with the end of exclusive dealing provisions.

'Probably 25 % of the cost of cement at destination represents cost of transport'[1] and although the Federation tries to supply from the nearest works, the price structure itself may have maintained an unnecessarily high element of transport cost.

In commenting on the barrier of 'exclusive dealing' to the creation of a non-Federation firm, the fforde Committee reported that

competition from an outside interest which concentrated itself on supplying only in those localities which best suited it and took no share in the less profitable deliveries at greater distances from the convenient points might well be claimed to be unfair competition. We regard this as a reasonable and a logical answer to the criticism, provided always that the protection which the Federation thus affords to its members is not used so as to increase prices above what is reasonable or to allow the survival of inefficient works [p. 21].

This qualifying clause is an admirable statement of what is really the beginning of the problem.

In judging the impact of the Cement Makers' Federation, it would be foolish to rely on a doctrinaire assertion that, since the Federation Scheme has abolished price competition, it must be against the public interest. It is true that price competition has been non-existent except for special cements, but proof that this has been against the public interest depends on establishing a plausible deduction that efficiency would have been greater in the absence of the Federation Scheme.

The case for competition is quite simply stated—that it makes possible free entry and the expansion of the more efficient firms, or works, at the expense of the less efficient, and so acts as to raise the average level of efficiency and to lower prices. This competitive pressure works through the downward effect on the level of profits, which gives existing firms an incentive to make a more careful study of existing processes to eliminate waste and increase efficiency and gives existing and potential firms an incentive to find new processes that will create a gap between prices and costs. Once such an innovation is made by some firm or firms the others must follow or suffer losses.

It is difficult to apply this competitive model to the cement industry. Cement-making plant lasts a long time, and the proportion of overhead to direct cost is high. Once old plants have been amortized it may well pay to keep them in action even though much more efficient plant has been developed. Even stationary kilns are still in use in most European

[1] fforde Report, p. 18.

countries.[1] Apart from strong cyclical variations in the demand for cement, excess capacity was built up with the introduction of new kilns.[2] For Europe in 1927 capacity was 35 million tons and actual production 28·5 million tons; in 1938 capacity was 60 million and production 45 million tons. In these conditions falling prices give the financially stronger companies an incentive and an opportunity to buy up the weaker companies and to make price and quota agreements. Price and quota agreements and further amalgamations tended to become alternatives. Such agreements were also the basis of restrictions on international trade in cement. Excess capacity in one or several countries would have led to 'dumping'—a practice which producers eager to gain stability in their home market were keen to avoid. As early as 1904 Belgian and German producers agreed on the principle of exclusive national markets. With the excess capacity and falling prices that developed in the 1920's, agreements on the principle of exclusive national markets became general. Competition in third markets in Europe and overseas was also regulated by various agreements such as the German-Belgian-British-French agreements regulating competition in the Dutch market, in the Baltic countries and in the Argentine (in 1928), in the Irish market (1935) and in the United States (1938).[3] Intercement, an organization to cover all export trade, was formed in 1937. This was followed in 1946 by the present organization, Cembureau.

For the inter-war period the capacity of the European cement industry as a whole exceeded effective demand by one-third. By a variety of methods output came to be regulated but was not concentrated in the most efficient plants. In Britain, however, the housing boom produced a different situation. The war years apart, the British Cement Federation has operated within an expanding market. The quota scheme (which was abolished in 1951) was not operated to restrict

[1] Economic Commission for Europe, *Growth and Stagnation in the European Economy* (Geneva, 1954), p. 156 n. 3.

[2] Rostas, using census reports for 1907 and 1924, estimated in *Productivity, Prices and Distribution* that capacity in the British cement trade was 3,700,000 tons and 4,250,000 tons in those years compared with outputs of 2,886,000 and 3,240,000 respectively. For 1935 and 1939 he estimated (the latter estimate based on the *Report of the Committee on Cement Production*, Cmd. 6282, H.M.S.O. 1941) capacity at 7,000,000 and 8,750,000 tons with production at 5,949,000 and 7,715,000. As compared with France, Italy, Belgium and Poland, Britain showed little excess capacity during the 1930's. In Europe from 1928 to 1934 capacity continued to grow rapidly, despite a fall in output. 'The increase in capacity in the 1920's had been stimulated by a rapid technical progress and, before the end of the decade, the industry was planning for a continued expansion combined with modernization.... It was some time before the expansion plans of the late 'twenties matured in the shape of new plants, but meanwhile the depression had set in...' E.C.E., *Growth and Stagnation in the European Economy*, p. 60.

[3] Before the agreements the Netherlands and Ireland benefited from the dumping policies of exporting countries. After the agreements these countries established the production of cement.

production. Since the war at least, the biggest handicap to the entry of new producers has been the lowness of prices made possible by a mass of equipment bought at the much lower pre-war prices.

The fforde Committee estimated that profits on average capital employed was $10\frac{1}{2}\%$ in 1938, 12 % in 1943 and $6\frac{1}{2}\%$ in 1945. Since then profits have been higher. From 1952 to 1955 A.P.C.M. trading profits averaged 29 % of sales. In 1954 its profit (trading profit less depreciation) was £11 million which was equal to 35 % of its trading capital (stocks, land, buildings, plant and capital work in progress) and 38 % of its net tangible assets. In 1955 profit was 22 % of trading capital as re-valued at January 1955, and 24 % of net tangible assets. For the Tunnel Portland Cement Company profits were 22 % and 24 % of trading capital in 1955 and 1956, while for The Rugby Portland Cement Company profits were 15 % and 13 % of trading capital in 1954 and 1955, or 9 % and $8\frac{1}{2}\%$ if assets were re-valued in 1956 prices.

In contrast to the position in the 10 years before the war, the cement industry has financed the major part of growth without raising new capital. Net tangible assets of the A.P.C.M. increased from £12 million in 1945 to £29 million in 1954, and (after revaluation) to £49 million in 1955. In that time no new capital has been raised and debentures have been reduced by almost £1 million. In the Tunnel Portland Cement Company net tangible assets have increased from £3½ million in 1945 to £5½ million in 1947 to £12 million in 1956. The only new capital raised was £1½ million in 1946. In The Rugby Portland Cement Company net tangible assets have increased from £1½ million in 1946 to £6½ million in 1955. In this case £2½ million has been raised— £1 million in 1947 and in 1954 and £½ million in 1953.

This power to finance expansion from profits is not a good guide to the profitability of entry to the industry. The trading capital of A.P.C.M. as re-valued in 1955 gives a lower capital cost per ton capacity than would a new works if only because much of the equipment has been written down over many years. Thus if profit is calculated on trading capital net of depreciation, the older the age of the equipment the greater the percentage profit on trading capital. The significance of this is shown by comparing the (partially re-valued) fixed-asset cost per ton capacity of £5 for the A.P.C.M. and £12 for The Rugby Portland Cement Company with its younger equipment. Furthermore, accounting profits in cement include a substantial return from ownership of land and natural resources. As the most productive known chalk and limestone deposits are owned by existing companies, new entrants would not have such a profitable 'rent' income.

We have then a situation where due to inflation and rents, established companies can make large profits at existing prices, though these prices are not high enough to encourage the growth of new firms. It is significant that the post-war outside entry to the industry has consisted of cement production as a by-product to sulphuric acid extraction from anhydrites or, as in one case, of a small-scale plant associated with extensive limestone quarrying.

In the absence of the Federation price control scheme the price of cement, in the post-war period, would probably have been higher, and the proportion of exports greater. Exports during the five years 1950–4 have varied between 15 and 20 % of production and have been valued at £85,000,000. The price in export markets (with which the Federation is not concerned) has been significantly higher than the price in the home market, and although export margins have been falling there is little doubt that more could have been exported. In this case the home price would have been higher, and the conditions more favourable to new entrants. But whether this would have been in the public interest is doubtful.

(e) Incentive to efficiency

Perhaps the best way to get at the probable effect on the public interest of Federation arrangements is to examine the incentives to efficiency that may exist within it. There appear to be four factors making for efficiency—expansion, research, competition from other industries, and political sensitiveness.

There has been a tendency for output per man to increase with size of plant. This economy of size of plant depends on full running and therefore on a large market. Technical developments have made possible larger and more efficient rotary kilns but, given the longevity of the equipment and the low labour cost per unit of output, the introduction of these depends not simply on a large market but also an expanding market. Such a market has existed—the production of cement has increased from 5·81 million tons in 1935 (when there was excess capacity) to 8·2 million tons in 1939 (when there was not excess capacity) to 12·5 million tons in 1955—and made it possible to install larger kilns alongside the pre-war kilns.[1] The fact that investment in recent works does not show a rate of profit as high as that for profits on trading capital as a whole is not a sign that they are being built too big. The explanation is simply that construction costs have risen because of inflation and that prices are based on cost averaged over pre-war and post-war equipment. War-time apart, the Cement Federation has operated within a period of building boom. This the Federation has

[1] The capacity of rotary kilns at the beginning of the century was 10,000 to 20,000 tons; of recent years it has averaged 130,000 (E.C.E., *Growth and Stagnation in the European Economy*, 1954, p. 156). The post-war A.P.C.M. plant at Shoreham has a capacity of 350,000 tons.

not been able to influence. Its arrangements may, however, have helped to increase the average size of plant. First, its price structure has given existing firms an incentive to expand scale of operation at particular works. Second, through the Cement and Concrete Association which is financed by members of the Federation and conducts research into and acts as consultants on the uses of concrete (as, for example, in pre-cast reinforced concrete, concrete shell and barrel roofs, pre-stressed concrete, construction of concrete or soil-concrete roads), the demand for concrete has been extended.[1]

Research and development work in processes of manufacture and quality of product is a condition of continuing efficiency. The fforde Committee mentioned criticism from witnesses of the industry's provision for research, although this was directed rather to its failure to develop alternative uses. Research into the use of cement is conducted by the Building Research Station and the Road Research Laboratory of the D.S.I.R., and by the Cement and Concrete Association. The Cement and Concrete Association was formed in 1935 but it was not until after the war that it conducted research. It is now a well-established and valuable research and development organization which not only publishes its results in forms suitable to different types of readers, but arranges conferences of scientists, and of specialist groups such as the Pre-stressed Concrete Development Group which brings together engineers, architects, contractors and plant manufacturers interested in pre-stressing. The work of the Cement and Concrete Association, however, is concerned almost entirely with the use of cement. For the cement itself research is left to the individual manufacturers—there is no central research establishment. At the works research is an extension of technical testing and control. Thus it is necessary to analyse the clay-to-chalk content of the slurry, to add the appropriate quantity of gypsum to the clinker to determine the setting time of the cement, and to test the properties of cement after 'seasoning'. Out of this testing and control has come research into the properties of the raw materials used in cement manufacture, the constitution of cement clinker, the ash content of the coal and chemical composition of the ash which mixes with the raw material in the kilns and affects the quality of the cement. In 1955 the A.P.C.M. spent £300,000 on research and development which was between $\frac{1}{2}$ and 1 % of turnover. The research centre of this Group now includes provision for training men in cement technology to ensure a supply of men capable of putting the results of research into practice. This is a recent and promising development.

Developments in such things as rotary kilns and quarrying do not depend on the direct efforts of the cement producers. In kilns the

---

[1] The Federation has also endowed a Chair in concrete technology at the Imperial Institute.

development is made by engineering firms. The engineering talent of the firms that produce kilns (in Britain, Vickers-Armstrongs and Edgar-Allen and Company) is, in this sense, placed at the disposal of the cement industry.[1] The same applies to firms that produce excavators and handling equipment for quarrying.

Competition from other industries is also important. There have been technical developments in substitute materials—for example, bricks, timber, aluminium—and in methods of building, that exert a pressure to efficiency on the cement industry.

These incentives to efficiency are not created by the Federation, in the sense that they could all exist without it, but the Federation has worked within them—it has not reduced them. The Federation has, however, made possible a fairly free exchange between cement firms on technical matters, though not of detailed costings.[2] The Federation has also, in some measure, created political sensitiveness. This induces heightened consciousness of and attention to that important (though vague and variously interpreted) concept, the 'public interest'. Through attention to the public interest we may expect a downward pressure on prices through an exclusion of the least efficient works, when reckoning the average costs on which prices are to be based or when estimating what increased costs can be absorbed, as well as a greater allocation to process research and development than would otherwise take place. The efficacy of political sensitiveness, however, depends on an optimum excitation of it—a matter about which we know little.

Because it has created a national organization, the cement industry is involved in problems of national importance and must look beyond the problems of a particular maker. Whether the industry has, in accordance with Keynes's dictum,[3] socialized itself and thereby achieved the right (or expected) blend of virtue and vice is a matter on which there are wide differences of view. It is clear, however, that in some ways the cement industry does act like a national undertaking. This is clear from its view that it provides supplies at all places at prices which are calculated to absorb the cost of affording that service to the public at all places. In the post-war years when, at Federation prices, cement was in short supply, more expensive imported cement was sold at Federation prices and the difference financed by a levy on home producers. This procedure was maintained after the end of government price control in 1951. Likewise, the basis of the delivered price system

---

[1] The leading kiln producers have provided designs for new factories and the technical knowledge for production. Such firms produce not only the kilns but in general 'equipment for cement production'. 'As a consequence, new plant efficiency has been very similar in different countries.' E.C.E., *Growth and Stagnation in the European Economy*, p. 157.

[2] This, however, has doubtless taken place within the groups.

[3] *Essays in Persuasion* (London, Macmillan, 1931), p. 314.

involves a considerable element of subsidy to those points of delivery that are remote at the expense of points of delivery close to cement works. This position grew up somewhat by accident, but the Federation now thinks of its subsidy to distant users as a part of its duty to meet in full from the nearest source of supply the demand at all points of the country.

Although a quota scheme was part of the original Federation agreement (the object of which was to ensure the maintenance of the agreed prices) it has not concerned itself with the efficiency of particular firms and has not therefore been concerned with shutting down inefficient works or with seeing that the most efficient methods are used. The quota scheme did not stop some firms expanding relative to others. As the quota scheme operated during periods of rising demand it was not difficult for energetic firms to increase their quotas. The fforde Committee found that 'the effect of the quota scheme coupled with the establishment of the Cement Makers' Federation has been that competition on price has been eliminated since 1934 except on special cements'. The quota scheme has since been abolished, without any effect on the degree of price competition, for the abolition of quotas will not tend to create price competition unless there is excess capacity.

The fact that the Federation has not concerned itself with the efficiency of particular firms does not mean that prices were agreed at levels sufficient to cover any inefficiency. They were not. Prices fixed have been adjustments to the 1934 levels in accordance with increases in costs. An increase in coal prices and wages rates has a different impact on the efficient and inefficient, but there is some evidence that the relevant 'increase in cost' was that for the average concern.

On the fixing of prices the fforde Committee recommended that the Federation should be prepared (a) to review production costs of particular works to ensure that the retention of high-cost works is essential, (b) to disseminate cost information so that each firm will have a yardstick by which to judge its own, and (c) to submit its price schedules to an independent body.

The Federation acted on these recommendations and appointed a chairman, at present Sir Malcom Trustram Eve, and an independent firm of chartered accountants which examines the costs of individual firms. The average costs of production derived from the costs of the individual firms are supplied to the Federation members, though it is for the chairman in association with the accountants to decide the 'average cost' figure to be used for the price review. Thus they may judge that there are too many works with unnecessarily high costs and exclude them, or some of them, from the average. A review of prices is made periodically, but a rise in prices is only likely to be recommended when there is a marked increase in some cost element such as coal, electricity or transport, which together constitute almost one-half the cost of producing cement.

Some informal price control schemes may be used to ensure that the least efficient get a living. Such an object is, however, inconsistent with another possible object which is here operative, namely, to prevent a rise in the profits of the industry above a level deemed reasonable, whenever there is a wide gap between the efficient and the inefficient. There is another possible object, which is to use the price control as a means of exerting pressure towards efficiency. The Cement Federation pricing scheme appears to have an element of this 'pressure towards efficiency' in it, but it would seem that this element will remain relatively small until there is a wider use of efficiency audits and less secrecy about comparative cost data.

3. BRICKS

(a) Trends in output

There are certain obvious differences, which in some measure reflect differences in the nature of production, between the production of cement and the production of bricks. In 1951 output per worker was £1492 in cement and £601 in brick and fireclay, and the ratio of 'administrative, technical and clerical employees' to operatives was one in five in cement, and one in nine in bricks and fireclay. In cement a net output of £18,379,000 was produced from forty-eight establishments whereas in brick and fireclay a net output of £46,578,000 was produced from 1050 establishments. The production of bricks is also much more dispersed,[1] which reflects the higher transport cost of the products and the more generous natural distribution of brick-making materials.

There are several classes of building brick—common, facing and engineering, and within the first class in particular there is a clear distinction to be made between fletton (made from 'Oxford' clays which facilitate a high degree of mechanization and give, because of the high carbonaceous matter, substantial fuel economy in firing)[2] and the non-fletton.

[1] See National Brick Advisory Council Paper No. 6 (H.M.S.O. 1950) for a map of brick-works throughout England.

[2] 'These are a series of blue or greyish marine clays with subordinate beds of clayey limestone and bituminous shales stretching from Lincolnshire through Northamptonshire to Huntingdonshire, Bedfordshire and Buckinghamshire. The great depth and extent of the deposits have led to their exploitation for brickmaking on a considerable scale. The shaley nature of the clay and its behaviour on grinding make it excellently suited to the semi-dry-pressed process of manufacture. It is an example of a deposit in which variations in properties and composition of individual seams are of minor importance provided thorough mixing of

Common bricks are those suitable for use, externally or internally, in general construction, usually above damp-course level. In 1938 commons were 85 % of total output and in 1951 70 %. By 1951 the output of fletton and non-fletton commons was almost equal. Facing bricks are those which meet the minimum requirements of commons but are manufactured or selected specially to provide an architectural feature. They were 12 % of output in 1938 and about twice that in 1951. Engineering bricks have a minimum compressive strength and a low water absorption. They constituted $2\frac{1}{2}$ % of production in 1938, and $3\frac{1}{2}$ % in 1951. Thus as compared with 1938, there was a substantial increase in the production of facing bricks relative to commons. This change in proportion was, however, mainly due to a lower output of commons. Whereas in 1938 the production of bricks (excluding refractory and glazed) reached 7500 million, in 1951 it was 6080 million. By 1954 output had almost reached the 1938 level.

That production is not above pre-war levels is due to two main things —a growth of substitute materials for walling and the closure of a large number of small brickworks quite unsuited to the post-war condition of labour and fuel shortage. For the whole of brick and fireclay in 1947 there were, including firms employing less than ten, 1250 establishments of which not more than 950 were brickworks, whereas there were twelve to thirteen hundred brickworks before the war.[1] Whereas in 1937 the employment was almost 96,000, in 1951 it was 77,500. This is a marked change from the 1930–8 period when the output of bricks was doubled and the labour force increased by 50 %.

Even after making allowance for war-time disruption in the brick industry, this change in the output trend in bricks is significant and particularly so in relation to the output trend in alternative walling materials. The fact that brick production has not expanded at the same rate as building activity is related both to the method of using bricks on site (which in turn is related to the size of the traditional 'hand brick') and to the method of making bricks—a method on which the very long established craft of brick-making still exerts a strong influence in many works.

the whole depth of face is carried out and limestone fragments are sufficiently reduced in size on grinding. In this respect it may be contrasted with the Lias clays lower in the system, in which careful selection of the seams is necessary and contamination with pyrites fragments must be prevented. The relatively high carbon content of the Oxford Clay is particularly noteworthy, since this reduces the fuel required for burning.' *Third Report of the Committee on the Brick Industry* (1943), p. 22.

[1] *Report of the Committee on Amenities in the Brick Industry* (H.M.S.O. 1947). Here an estimate is given of 1358 pre-war brickworks. This, as compared with the estimate of 1147 brickworks in the First Report of the Committee on the Brick Industry, includes very small works.

(b) Methods of production

Clays suitable for bricks are widely distributed throughout Britain.[1] In the manufacture of heavy clay products the works are almost always sited as near as possible to the clay quarry, and the manufacture has generally been carried on as close as possible to the chief centres of population. Brick earth, clay and shale, used in the manufacture of building bricks, are obtained from open clay holes, though clay or shale obtained incidentally during coal mining is used to a certain extent. With refractories the position is different, as most of the refractory fire-clays of the country are associated with and in general immediately underlie particular seams of coal. In several districts, this association of clay suitable for brick-making with productive coal seams has made available clay that would otherwise have been uneconomic because of depth, and has led to the development of brick-making as an important auxiliary to coal or iron-ore mining.[2]

In the ancient craft of brick-making a considerable fund of knowledge about the behaviour of different types of raw material was slowly accumulated, but it was not until hand-making methods and firing in intermittent kilns began to be replaced that there was a significant attempt to make a technical study of clay properties, reactions of clays to firing, and control of firing temperatures in kilns. The introduction of more efficient continuous kilns made a big change, but this was not a sufficient condition for a transformation of the technical outlook of the industry and the introduction of the most efficient methods of production.

There is a great disparity between methods and costs at different works. This disparity is due to a variety of factors such as size and age of the plant, degree of mechanization in handling, extent of technical knowledge and efficiency of management. But costs vary also with the nature of the raw material used. In the winning of the clay or shale many methods are used varying from hand to mechanical excavators. The movement of the clay to the preparation plant is equally varied. In both winning and moving clay, however, there was a great increase in mechanization during the period of 1920–38, when the output of bricks was doubled, while since the war both shortage of labour and improvements in excavating and handling equipment have encouraged mechanization. In many works, however, complex strata provide problems not yet solved by the mechanical systems available.

[1] See National Brick Advisory Council Paper No. 6 (H.M.S.O. 1950) for a map of brick-works throughout England.

[2] See F. H. Clews, *Heavy Clay Technology* (Stoke-on-Trent, British Ceramic Research Association, 1955), chs. I and II. See also for the properties of the clays used, Paper 5 of the National Brick Advisory Council (H.M.S.O. 1950).

Both the preparation of the clay or shale for shaping and the shaping itself vary with the nature of the raw material. There have, however, been considerable improvements in crushing and grinding in new or modernized works and in the movement of material from process to process. Not all the processes of shaping are equally adapted to mechanization. In the processes of clay preparation and shaping the consistency of the mixture at which moulding takes place is the determining factor and this has largely depended on the nature of the clays used.

In hand-making the clay must be soft and easy to work. Some bricks are still made by hand as there is some demand for the rough and slightly uneven surface texture produced by the act of throwing the clay into the mould. The process is known as the 'soft-mud process'.[1] This process is also used for the production of 'stock' (or London) bricks which are made, though not by hand, from the clay-chalk deposits near the Thames in Kent and Essex. The clay is mechanically pressed into shape and then dried either in the open air or in tunnel driers.

Machinery has made it possible to use harder clay or shale and provided new ways of forming the bricks. The oldest machine process is the 'wire-cut process'. Here the clay is usually fairly soft and of a fine texture but a stiffer mixture than that of the wet-mud process is needed as the clay is consolidated and extruded from the pug in a rectangular column and cut into the proper shapes by a wire-cutting mechanism. The design of the pug has changed little since it was first invented. Numerous adjustments have been introduced on a trial and error basis as the laws governing extrusion are incompletely known.[2] De-airing extrusion machines, an important innovation with poorly plastic clays, were developed in the United States about 1930 and have been copied in Britain, mainly for salt-glazed pipes. As in the wet-mud process the bricks are too soft to be set directly into the kiln from the machine.

In the 'stiff plastic process', used mainly for colliery shales and certain other clays and shales which do not easily develop a high degree of plasticity, the clay is used in a stiffer condition than in the wire-cut process and is forced into moulds forming brick-shaped clots. These clots are then automatically brought under a press which gives them the exact shape and size required. The bricks are removed directly to kilns to be dried and fired.

In the semi-dry process, used for making 'fletton' from the Oxford clays and for a number of other shales and clays with a low natural plasticity, there is a break with tradition in that the clay is used in the form not of plastic paste but of moist grains which are pressed directly

---

[1] The aesthetic properties of the hand-made brick are not its only advantage. It is superior to some machine-made bricks and of course can be made for special purposes.
[2] See F. H. Clews, *Heavy Clay Technology*, ch. v.

into moulds in the making machine and then, after the escape of air from among the grains of clay, repressed.

There are considerable differences in practice in drying (in the case of the first two processes) and in firing. Hot floor drying is used considerably for wire-cut bricks and although as an intermittent drying method it is thermally inefficient, it is convenient when output is varied. Tunnel driers are thermally more efficient and adapted to labour-saving devices but their advantages depend to a certain extent on the ability to arrange an appropriate layout of the works.

About 90 % of common bricks are fired in continuous kilns mainly on the Hoffman principle. These kilns are of varying age, design and efficiency and the majority were designed before 1900.[1] Many improvements have been made in the firing efficiency of these kilns but the greatest advance in firing has come from the car tunnel kilns following Dressler's muffle kiln (1910) and Faugeron's direct fired kiln (1913). Unlike the United States, however, this country uses few car tunnel kilns for building bricks. These car tunnel kilns although they are not always as economical in fuel as the Hoffman continuous kilns do give greatly improved setting and drawing conditions. They are better adapted to the continuous method of production, but because of the high capital cost they are not adopted except where the more costly products such as refractories are being fired, or where, as most obviously in new works, layout can be arranged to facilitate that smooth flow from making to despatch which is essential for working plant efficiently with a minimum of labour. It appears that the car tunnel kiln does show substantial advantages if an efficient drier and works are designed in relation to it.

In the Third Report of the Committee on the Brick Industry, it was estimated that one-half of the labour used in brick production is concerned with handling, and the major portion of this in handling the green and fired bricks. The great waste of labour in handling bricks is due to the old non-continuous conception of production or to the difficulties of arranging, in the very durable old works, a layout suited to mechanized handling. Even with an old layout, however, much can be done to improve handling as, for example, by paving the approach to and adjusting the openings of kilns to enable the use of fork-lift trucks for placing and drawing. The shortage of labour since the war has started such a development in a number of works.[2]

---

[1] See E. Rowden, 'Firing in the Heavy Clay and Refractories Industries, 1900–1950', in *Ceramics: a Symposium*, ed. by A. T. Green and G. H. Stewart (Stoke-on-Trent, British Ceramic Society, 1953), pp. 771–823.

[2] There is a valuable table showing trends of developments in Appendix I of the Third Report of the Committee on the Brick Industry. An extract from the Chairman's speech at the 1955 Annual General Meeting of Eastwoods—manufacturers of flettons, stock bricks,

(c) Size of establishments

The Census analysis by size and distribution of employment for bricks and fireclay is given in Tables 6 and 7.

Table 6. *Bricks and fireclay (Analysis by size 1951. Larger establishments in the United Kingdom)*

Average number employed	Estab-lishments (number)	Gross output (£ thousand)	Net output (£ thousand)	Persons employed (number)	Net output per person employed (£)	Net output per person employed 1948 (£)
11–24	212	3,532	2,049	3,967	516	489
25–49	374	13,091	7,582	13,371	567	462
50–99	279	20,451	11,730	19,215	610	494
100–199	123	18,481	10,005	16,680	600	530
200–299	31	8,391	4,959	7,487	662	548
300–399	14	5,304	2,521	4,815	523	472
400–499	7	3,365	1,886	3,241	582	503
500–749	5	3,729	1,839	2,950	623	534
750 and over	5	7,376	4,007	5,760	696	576
Total	1,050	83,720	46,578	77,486	601	504

The establishments covered in Table 6 are not a homogeneous group. Of the 1050 establishments 644 were specialist producers of building bricks, and in these establishments net output per person was £598, which differs little from net output per person for the whole trade. However, even within building bricks there are significant differences in manufacturing techniques between the fletton and non-fletton bricks. The production of fletton bricks is the more highly mechanized, the firing is easier and the net output per person employed is correspondingly higher.

Table 7. *Percentage distribution of employment in bricks and fireclay*

	11–24	25–49	50–99	100–199	200–299	300–499	500–749	750 and over
1935	6·5	20·8	24·2	24·8	18·6		5·5	
1948	6·1	17·8	22·2	24·1	9·4	9·7	3·4	7·3
1951	5·1	17·3	24·8	21·5	9·7	10·4	3·8	7·4

cement, roofing tiles and concrete products—enables us to appreciate the significance of this change. 'Brick outputs at Fletton works were further expanded during the past financial year. Also at various stock brickworks another £200,000 was spent during the twelve months on new plants. Additional kilns and drying chambers and these extensions at a cost of about £1 million have not only provided outputs of higher quality but have at the same time converted seasonal yards into factory units giving continuous productions and all year round employment.'

Table 7 shows the distribution of employment by size. There is no marked tendency for the distribution of employment by size to change. Such a table, however, obscures a definite tendency (related to labour-saving innovations) to an increase in size as judged by output. Mechanization can lead to great increases in output without an increase in persons employed, and the degree of mechanization throughout the industry is so uneven that the summarized Census of Production figures often conceal more than they reveal.

In the fletton section of the industry, the size of the average works is larger,[1] though because of the degree of mechanization net output per person does not show an increase with the size as measured by numbers employed. There are five firms, of which one—the London Brick Company (L.B.C.)—produces approximately two-thirds of the output. Although the fletton section of the industry has achieved economies of scale, each of the larger companies has a number of works. Economy of working does not increase indefinitely with size. The output of the L.B.C. for example, has grown both from a better flow of production and from an extension of the number of works, largely through acquisition between 1924 and 1950.[2]

The contrast between the fletton and non-fletton sections of the industry is shown by the 1948 Census analysis according to specialization within the trade. There were seventy-two specialist establishments producing fletton-type bricks employing 9427 persons. There were 524 other specialist producers of building bricks employing 23,403. Thus roughly one-third of the output of specialist producers come from seventy-two 'fletton' establishments, and the other two-thirds from 524 non-fletton establishments. A comparison of the L.B.C. and the National Coal Board, which is the second largest firm producing bricks,

---

[1] In 1938 when fletton production was one-third of the whole there were ninety-six plants using the semi-dry process out of 1472 brick-making plants. The number of works was 1316 (National Brick Advisory Council, Paper 6, Table 2). The London Brick Company produced one-quarter of the national output from its twenty-seven works.

[2] The London Brick Company was registered in 1900 as B. J. Forder and Son. Its name was changed in 1923 to London Brick Company and Forders on amalgamation with The London Brick Company, Dogsthorpe Star Brick Company, Northam Brick Company, Star Pressed Brick Company (Whittlesea), United Brick Company, and the Warboys Brick Company, and changed to above April 1936. The assets of New Peterborough Brick Company and Saxon Brick Company were acquired in December 1923, the works of Millbrook Brick and Tile Company and Somersham Brickworks in 1927, the businesses of Plowman's Brick-fields, Arlesay Brick Company (Bearts), Hicks and Company and Fletton in 1928. Share capital in Itter's Brick Company and a controlling interest in Beeby's Brick Company were also acquired in 1928, but during 1936 these companies were wound up and their assets transferred to the L.B.C. Business of the Bletchley Brick Company was acquired in 1929 and that of the Bedford Brick Company in December 1936. During 1941, the company acquired the share capital of Clock House Brick Company (in liquidation) and assets of Aylesford Pottery Company and in 1942 Grovebury Brick Works Company. During 1950, the company acquired brickworks at Skew Bridge, Bletchley, from Bletchley Flettons.

helps to point the contrast. The Board took over eighty-three brickworks and two pipe works employing 2943 people and producing about 10 % of the total output of bricks. The brickworks vary widely in age, type and size. The largest, Niddrie brickworks in the Scottish division, produced over 25 million bricks in 1952, while twenty-nine works had outputs of less than 5 million bricks.[1] The Coal Board produced an average of just under 7 million bricks per works in 1952, which is less than the national average but more than for the non-fletton section. Approximating from 1948 Census figures, it would appear that non-fletton works produced an average of 5 million bricks per annum, and the average fletton works produced over 20 million.

(d) Pricing policy

When in 1935 the turnover of the industry was £16 million the capital invested was 'variously estimated at sums upwards of £15 million'.[2] Turnover has increased in relation to capital investment since 1935, and now the industry as a whole probably 'turns over its capital' a little more than once a year. In the fletton section the turnover is nearer twice a year. This higher rate of turnover reflects changes in methods of production and the higher rate of investment in labour-saving devices. This reduces ease of entry,[3] which together with the growth of non-local distribution will intensify the trend towards large scale of operation and a reduction in the number of producers.

The price arrangements of the industry are not easy to describe, as the breakdown of the local markets is creating new price arrangements. While the industry was local there could be no national policy of co-ordination among producers, and machinery for relating production to demand or for the fixing of minimum selling prices did not exist. There were a number of local brick associations but the amount of price-fixing was small. The National Federation of Clay Industries was formed in 1928 to promote the welfare and protect the interest of all trades in or connected with the clay industries, but not to deal with prices or wages. The Federation has 859 members, not all of whom produce building bricks. Practically all producers of non-fletton building bricks are members of the Federation. (The fletton producers are members of the Pressed Brick Makers' Association which is not a member of the National Federation. Some companies produce both fletton and non-fletton bricks and are members of the Federation.)[4]

---

[1] National Coal Board, *Report and Accounts for 1952* (H.M.S.O. 1953), p. 45.

[2] *First Report of the Committee on the Brick Industry* (1942), p. 7.

[3] The capital cost of a new brickworks is now about £20,000 per million bricks output.

[4] There was before the war some disagreement between fletton and non-fletton producers on price and distribution policy.

The Federation has not since its creation acquired powers to fix wages and prices, though it does provide export services to the clay industry on five out of nine industrial councils, and in the review of price policies except in the cases of bricks, roofing tiles and clay pipes.

The National Federation of Clay Industries, like the British Pottery Manufacturers Federation, has as members individual firms as well as trade associations. The main trade associations, some of which are themselves federations of trade associations, are the Northern Brick Federation with 325 members covering 26 % of brick output, the Midland Federation of Brick and Tile Manufacturers (seventy-eight members and 7 % of the output), the East Midlands Brick Association (thirty-six members and $4\frac{1}{2}$ % of the output), the South-Western Brick and Tile Federation (ninety-six members and 4 % of the output), the South-Eastern Brick and Tile Federation (134 members and $9\frac{1}{2}$ % of the output), and the Scottish Employers' Council for the Clay Industries (forty-nine members and 9 % of the output).

Several of the member associations are empowered to deal with prices, but price-fixing occurs only in a few areas. The Stock Brick Manufacturers Association with fourteen member firms producing all the 'London' stock bricks[1] does fix prices, as was shown by the announcement at the end of 1955 that stock brick prices would not be raised for six months. The Manchester Brick Association and the West Riding Brick Association operate a common delivered price policy within specified areas. This, however, is not the typical procedure in the brick associations. Bricks tend to be sold ex-works, plus delivery charges.

According to the Simon Committee Report, 50 % of bricks go direct to the user, 49 % are ordered but not stored by merchants and 1 % go to merchants' premises. Ordering through a merchant is a custom of the South rather than of the North, though Ministry of Works contracts in the North often entail ordering through specified merchants.

In many districts, there are considerable variations in quoted delivered prices, due to differences in either works prices or distance from site. At times when a sudden increase in building activities produces scarcity, the number of weeks' delivery is often more important than these price differences. (During one such period of scarcity, similar National Coal Board bricks were being quoted 10 % cheaper by the Board than by a merchant, but the merchant was offering very much shorter delivery.) However, apart from these periods of acute scarcity, due in the immediate post-war years to price control and short capacity and more recently to fluctuations in the building programme, there is a growing number of districts where non-local bricks are cheaper than

[1] Simon Committee Report on *The Distribution of Building Materials and Components* (1948), p. 56.

local. In this, larger wire-cut brick makers such as the National Coal Board are now having an effect similar to that of fletton producers. Where previously the main effect of competition was price-cutting in time of building recession, now, owing to improved training facilities and more adequate research, competition will exert a significant pressure towards mechanization and raw material control.

(e) Incentives to efficiency

The rate at which modern techniques are introduced has been greatly affected by the size and longevity of brickworks and the local nature of the market. In the older works, the layout and cost of replacing durable kilns and equipment impose limitations on economic modification. Modernization has come dominantly from an increase in capacity —from the construction of new works and the extension of old ones.[1] The great expansion in output between 1920 and 1938 was thus a major factor in modernization. In general 'advance has gone hand in hand with a tendency towards large works laid down on raw material of easy working and large extent'.[2] With the apparent end of the period of expansion the mechanism of expansion will depend increasingly on the break-up of the local market which has provided shelter for a large number of small producers who have not been greatly affected by the trend towards mechanization.

While methods of production are dominantly traditional the differences in efficiency between different works are not likely to be sufficient to overcome the high cost of moving bricks between regions: the market is inevitably local or regional. The introduction of mechanization and scientific control in an old industry is, however, almost certain to increase the effective size of the market by creating a wide gap between the more and the less efficient. In building bricks this gap has been created particularly by fletton producers.

The fletton brick is made from Oxford clay which, with its high carbonaceous content, gives economy in burning. This prime economic asset gave the fletton producers a unique opportunity to transform the brick industry. At a time of rising brick output adequate financial resources were available and a high degree of mechanization to which the raw material also lends itself was achieved. Rostas in *Comparative Productivity in British and American Industry* gives an estimate, derived from 1935 Census information, of output per man in fletton and non-fletton bricks. For the industry as a whole in 1935 man-hours per 1000 bricks were 15·4, for producers other than fletton and sand-lime producers

---

[1] Before the war non-single-unit brickworks produced 70 % of output and this proportion has since increased.
[2] *Third Report of the Committee on the Brick Industry* (1943), p. 7.

20·8, for fletton producers 9·6. Comparable figures for 1955 are 7 for fletton (with some works as low as 5·8), 11 for stiff plastic and 12 for wire-cut.

The fletton brick weighs less than the non-fletton and this fact together with the quantities involved enabled the L.B.C. to get advantageous transport terms and develop before the war a wide-spread direct distribution of bricks. This, together with attention to scientific analysis of materials at the works, enabled full advantage to be taken of large-scale continuous production methods. The old attitude that brick production is a local affair was discarded,[1] and the L.B.C., in creating a nation-wide system of distribution by rail and by its own fleet of lorries, has had an important effect in making many small local works uneconomic and in facing other producers with a hitherto unknown competitive pressure. The L.B.C. is not now the only firm with a wide-spread system of distribution. Eastwoods, who are in both the fletton and non-fletton section, and also produce cement and tiles, have already been quoted. The Western Counties Brick Company, which was formed in 1928 to amalgamate a number of brick manfacturers and building merchants in Exeter, Ottery St Mary, Torquay, Paignton, Plymouth and East Cornwall and which is known for its high strength bricks made from Devonian clays, distributes over a wide area. Blockleys, making wire-cut, engineering and chimney bricks with works near Wellington, Bloxwich and Bedworth, 'is sending bricks to all parts of the country from Scotland to the South Coast, where good class buildings are being erected'.[2] The Sussex Brick Company[3] and the Yorkshire Brick Company[4] are other examples of firms that have developed large output and distribution methods.

[1] See *Second Report of the Committee on the Brick Industry.*
[2] Chairman's Review issued with 1954–5 accounts.
[3] Registered 1927 as Sussex Brick Company (1927) to acquire business of Sussex Brick and Estates Company (registered 1930). In 1929, acquired assets and undertaking of Thomas Mitchell and Sons (Guildford). In August 1935, acquired entire Share Capital of Dorking Brick Company for £257,500 cash. In March 1940 formed Sussex and Dorking United Brick Company, a wholly-owned subsidiary which took over all manufacturing operations of Sussex Brick Company and Dorking Brick Company. The group now comprises: *Subsidiary Companies*, The Sussex and Dorking United Brick Companies, Lunsford Company, Nutbourne Brickworks, Dorking Brick Company, Sussex Waggon Company, Southwater Brick, Tile, Terracotta, Pipe and Clay Company, Ightham Tile (Holdings) (acquired 1953), The Ightham Brick and Tile Company, Alfred Hardy and Company. *Principal Products*, Engineering, facing and other high-grade building bricks, roofing tiles and fireplace briquettes. *Brick and Tile Works*, Warnham, Southwater, Bexhill and Horsham in Sussex, Lingfield, Guildford, Farnham, North Holmwood, Beare Green and Hambledon in Surrey, Tonbridge and Ightham in Kent, Crondall in Hampshire and Rugby in Warwickshire.
[4] Registered 1920 as private, made public June, 1933. The Company and its subsidiaries own and operate sixteen brick and tile works in Yorkshire, Staffordshire, Wiltshire and Lincolnshire. The Company owns all shares of Askern Brick and Tile Company, Castleford Brick Company, Cocking and Sons; David Sharratt and Sons, Glossop Brickworks;

Both the craft tradition and the local tradition in the brick industry have entailed an inadequate development of research, education and training facilities. In this situation, we cannot expect to find a widespread use of modern management techniques. Except in the few larger firms that have developed technical control facilities and flow principles of production the methods of management are very similar to those of the pottery industry.[1] The small family business is the typical form of organization. The impact of death duties has brought a tendency to create public companies while maintaining as far as possible family control, with a consequent tendency to be shy of outside capital. In the fletton section, where the typical size of the five firms is larger, public companies are usual. The rise of the fletton section has in fact been a very potent factor in breaking up the old forms of production and organization.

While markets were local the community of interest in developing technical training and research into both the basic properties of the raw material and more efficient methods of production was not obvious. 'The heavy clay industry labours under a distinct handicap in the lack of adequate training of its future technical personnel and in this regard may be compared unfavourably with other industries.'[2] Although there has been an improvement in educational and training facilities since this was written in 1943, it would not be true to say that the position has been transformed. Little by way of research into clay properties and into more efficient methods of production was achieved by the small firms that dominated the industry until recently. One would not expect them to conduct research, unless they developed a co-operative research association. This, for reasons mentioned, they did not do. Innovations such as the Hoffman kiln, the car tunnel kiln and de-airing have come from outside the country; while in cutting off and handling appliances British brick manufacturers have utilized continental and American plant to a considerable extent.

The growth of interest in scientific and technical matters affecting the clay industries led to the formation of ceramic societies in the United States (1899) and England (1900). Till quite recently however,

Holbeck Brick and Fireclay Works, Northampton Brick Company, South Emsall Brick Company, Staffordshire Brick Company (owning all shares of Cheshire Brick Company), Selby Brick and Tile Company and Stairfoot Brickworks. Also controls J. R. Mitchell and Company and (jointly with Yorkshire Amalgamated Products) Brick Marketing Company. Also has substantial interest in Metropolitan Brick Company and Wiltshire Brick and Tile Company. Brick Marketing Company, in which the Company is jointly interested with Yorkshire Amalgamated Products, now distributes the whole of the company's goods. *Products* include varieties of facing, building and engineering bricks, tiles, firebricks, etc.

[1] See ch. XVII.

[2] *Third Report of the Committee on the Brick Industry* (1943), p. 7.

the predominating interest was in pottery and refractories. Butterworth[1] has pointed out that of the 170 papers in the *Transactions of the British Ceramic Society* for the years 1935–9, twenty-four only dealt wholly or mainly with products, materials or processes of the heavy clay industry; of these twenty-four, nine described machinery, works equipment or processes, nine were summaries of existing knowledge or recommended practice, leaving only six with any claim, however humble, to be regarded as original contributions to scientific knowledge.

There has been since the 1930's a considerable improvement in the technical outlook in the industry and more adequate research, education and training facilities are being developed. A research association for refractories was formed in 1921: there is a distinction between users of refractory and building bricks. The users of refractories in the iron and steel and carbonizing industries in seeking greater heat inputs and operating temperatures must take a great interest in the properties of the bricks and demand from the suppliers bricks of specific technical qualities. Further, refractory bricks must be fired to a much higher temperature and this causes a steep rise in fuel cost and gives an added incentive to research into firing and control. The pressure to research in building bricks is less in both counts. In 1947 the British Ceramic Research Association was formed by combining the Refractories Research Association and the Pottery Research Association. A heavy clay section was added in 1948 when makers of building bricks and roof tiles agreed to pay a fixed levy. The British Ceramic Research Association and the Building Research Station are adding to the scientific knowledge of clays, and some of the larger brickworks have developed works laboratories to enable a continuous analysis of the clay samples. The need for such works laboratories has increased with mechanization. As modern manufacturing became more removed from the old handicraft methods, the need for close control over materials increases, for the machine is unable to cope so readily as the hand with variations in the material fed to it from hour to hour or day to day. Further, the need to control quality of product has been increased by the tendency to a more detailed specification of purchasers' requirements. There has been a growth of closer specification in building and a consequent tendency for higher selection of building bricks on the basis of strength. This creates an obvious need for control over raw materials and manufacturing process. This control requires analysis of the materials and the finished product and a search for the causes of any substantial variations that may arise in manufacture. Such a search creates the opportunity to bring improvements in the process of production—an opportunity which the

[1] B. Butterworth, *Bricks and Modern Research* (London, Crosby Lockwood, 1948), pp. 16–17.

few companies with works laboratories for testing and research have used.[1]

The influence of customer specification is, as we have already mentioned, most obvious not in building bricks but in refractory bricks. The demand from the metallurgical industries and more recently from atomic energy establishments for refractory bricks that would stand up to higher furnace temperatures had led in the past thirty years to a substantial change in the technical outlook and performance in the production of refractory bricks. There are still firms producing low quality refractories by craft methods but the general transformation of the industry has been rapid.[2] In this it was helped by the existence of firms which combined the production of refractories not with common bricks and pipes but with furnaces or steel or foundry or electrical requisites.

A change in the technical outlook of the industry is also required for the development of new clay building units. The traditional brick has already met competition from alternative materials and forms of construction. Traditional building bricks have many advantages in price and appearance, but they also have certain disadvantages: their thermal insulation is poor, and their use involves the hand craft of bricklaying. Yet it is possible to produce a clay brick with improved thermal insulation which has the advantage of a smaller moisture movement than cement products. Such bricks have been produced on an experimental scale, but so far the brick industry does not seem to have been as conscious as the cement industry of the need for such developments. Yet new products must come if burnt clay is to maintain its position. 'The building industry is being rapidly educated to demand materials that will meet scientifically defined standards and will not indefinitely

[1] For one example see *The Economist*, 21 July 1951. There is there a short comment of the impact of works laboratories on the process of production at the L.B.C. Cf. the following extract from the Chairman's speech at the Annual General Meeting of the London Brick Company in 1956: 'A matter of pronounced importance is that the background of knowledge of the properties of our materials and of our processes, which is being steadily built up by our Technical and Research Department, becomes more important as the range of our products grows. Let me illustrate what this means. In 1950 we built a kiln to produce 57 million bricks per annum. This, of course, is a good-size kiln. As a result of research and scientific control, this kiln is now yielding bricks at the rate of 78 millions per annum so that we have gained an increase in production from this unit of 21 million bricks per year without any considerable extra capital cost. To erect a kiln to produce 21 million bricks per year the capital cost would be in the region of £60,000. As our knowledge grows so will the expansion of kiln firing instrumentation widen and, under scientific control, lead to still greater efficiency. As a result of the research and regular testing, reliable data is constantly becoming available for the use of our customers who, in their effort to achieve economy in the use of building materials, must of necessity have detailed knowledge of the properties of the goods they specify and use.'

[2] Cf. the comments on electrical porcelain in the chapter on the pottery industry (ch. XVII). See also 'Refractories in Great Britain: a survey of Recent Progress' in *The Times Review of Industry*, March 1954, p. 10.

remain blind to the fact that bricks have faults as well as solid virtues'.[1]
The mechanization of building will doubtless increase. With increased
mechanization will come a demand for building materials suited to
mechanical methods. The hand brick is not: hollow blocks much larger
than hand bricks have been developed, though their use in Britain has
not proceeded as far as in Europe and America owing to the restrictive
effect of building by-laws and to conservative views on the part of
users. But even these blocks are far from being *the* material for mechanized assembly. For that a much larger unit would seem to be required.[2]

Such developments have been made more feasible by the recent
expansion of research into the properties of clay and processes of
production, and by the break-up of the local market.

4. CONCLUSION

(a) Opportunities to progress

Opportunities to increase output per man are provided by the invention
or adoption of new techniques of production and new methods of
management. The invention of new techniques of production has become increasingly dependent on industrial research and development.
Apart from plastics, however, building materials are not laboratory crea-
tions. The process of applying science to this industry is more difficult
than in science-based industries where there is a vast amount of relevant
scientific data in existence as well as, from the normal processes of
higher education, a supply of scientists trained in the relevant field.[3] The
attempt to overcome this difficulty has been slight. In 1955 only 0·28 %
of workers in the treatment of non-metalliferous mining products other
than coal, bricks, china, glass, cement, etc., were employed on research
and development. The British Ceramic Research Association, the
Forest Products Research Laboratory of D.S.I.R., the Timber Development Association, the Cement and Concrete Association, the Building
Research Station, and the Chalk Lime and Allied Industry Research
Association provide very important additions to research and development. Though research and development in building materials is low,

---

[1] Butterworth, *Bricks and Modern Research* (1948), p. 150.

[2] Cf. *ibid.* p. 153: 'If a really light-weight clay product is developed in really large units
it will be practicable to trim the units to standard sizes with a carborundum or diamond
saw, so overcoming the main obstacles to standardization of sizes of clay products—namely,
variations due to uneven shrinkage in drying and firing.' He suggests that the improved
methods of making stable foams in recent years for fire fighting could be adapted to the manufacture of light-weight clay products.

[3] See B. R. Williams, 'Science and Industrial Innovation' in *The Advancement of Science*,
vol. 13, no. 51, December 1956, pp. 156–62.

it has grown considerably in the last ten years, and this growth has created new opportunities for technical change.

Opportunities are also created by invention in other industries. Thus engineering and metallurgical research in other industries has made possible great improvements in cement kilns, while the need for closer control over the properties of refractory bricks has led to the creation of new techniques which have been applied to non-refractory bricks. In the same way new methods of management developed in other industries can be utilized by the building materials industry.

How far available new techniques of production and management are used depends in considerable measure on two inter-connected things—knowledge of them and capacity to use them.[1] In bricks the break-up of the local market and the development of co-operative research and technical education have created an opportunity to make use of the practices of other industries, and provided men with the technical skills capable of using them.

In a different sense the opportunity to progress is provided by an expanding market. For then output can be expanded by using the techniques in new plants. Equally, the expanding market generally provides profits adequate to finance, or to attract the finance for, such expansion. We have noted the importance of this in both bricks and cement.

(b) Pressures to progress

The most common pressure to progress is provided by competition. This competition may be direct or indirect: it may come from the producers of the same commodity or from the producers of a substitute. In the brick industry there is in most regions direct competition between producers. In Portland cement there is no price competition between producers though there is competition in special cements and competition for market shares. The same is true of tiles. In metal windows and in cast-iron rainwater goods there is no price competition between members of the Association but there is competition between non-members (who supply 10% of output) and members.

Indirect competition exists in varying degrees between bricks, cement, aluminium, glass and timber for walling; between clay tiles and asbestos tiles for roofing; between metal and wood windows and doors; between cast iron, aluminium, asbestos cement and pressed steel for rainwater goods. The strength of this indirect competition does largely depend on the extent to which indirect competitors are cutting costs and prices and this depends on the extent of change in technique. This in turn depends on the extent of invention in that industry (or in its supplying

[1] See C. F. Carter and B. R. Williams, *Industry and Technical Progress* (Oxford University Press, 1957), ch. 10.

industries) which in turn depends on the extent of research and development in, and the educational level of, the industry. Such things provide the conditions of creative competition.[1] The relative weakness of these conditions in the building materials industry has meant that the extent of indirect competition was weak except in so far as other industries have provided new knowledge. This indirect provision for indirect competition did exist, and it is becoming stronger with the growth of provision for education, research and development within industry. For this makes the industry as a whole less parochial and better able to draw on developments elsewhere.

The creation of research or development departments within firms also creates a pressure to progress. For then the employed scientists and technologists have an interest in justifying their employment or in increasing their power and influence. This helps to create a new climate of opinion in which an improvement in methods of production becomes a matter of pride. This can be particularly important in a regulated industry such as cement.

Industries which either supply machines or materials or purchase the product may exert pressures to progress. If a supplying industry develops better machines or materials it will press these on the buying industry, and perhaps provide technical knowledge and service to encourage use. A purchasing industry (as, for example, the steel industry in the case of refractories) may on the other hand press the supplying industry to improve methods of production and quality of product.

(c) Restrictive practices

The preceding treatment of the opportunities and pressures to progress provides the context for the analysis of the effect of restrictive practices. Restrictive practices will be judged to be bad if, on balance, they restrict opportunities or pressures to progress.

The Metal Windows Association operates a common price policy. Before the war the M.W.A. regarded a quota system as an essential part of its price policy, but quotas were abolished during the boom conditions after the war. As a result of pressure from Crittalls to keep prices down, prices are based on a formula which disregards the high-cost producers.[2]

The M.W.A. rests its main case for the common price system on the two interdependent measures of co-operation thereby made possible—namely the exchange of information on costs and on production methods. Since members know, it is argued, that selling prices are in fact properly

---

[1] Carter and Williams, *op. cit.* ch. 15.
[2] See Monopolies Commission *Report on the Supply of Standard Metal Windows and Doors*, ch. 7 and app. 8.

related to the cost of efficient manufacture, they can with confidence co-operate to increase efficiency and improve quality. Such co-operation has led to complete rationalization of sections used in the window trade, to a detailed exchange of information about production techniques and cost which has greatly reduced the spread between the highest- and lowest-cost plants, to a development of exports, and to competition in the fields of service, quality and design.

The practice of cutting prices when faced with competition from outsiders, the Association describes as a defensive operation which it does not like but was led to adopt when non-members obtained copies of the Association price list and made a practice of quoting just below Association prices. The Association regards its 'defensive operation' in this situation, not as a restriction on competition, but as 'simply a limitation of the Association price agreement'.

The Monopolies Commission argued (p. 81) that such a 'defensive operation', using the collective resources of the majority to defeat the competition of the minority, involves an anti-social use of monopoly power. In evaluating the Association's claims for its common-price system, it points out that although the system has been in operation for over twenty years, it was only in 1949 that members began to exchange costs, and only since 1953 that they have done this systematically for price-fixing; and that it is only since this information has been exchanged that its members have felt sufficient confidence in one another to share technical knowledge freely. Thus the Association's claims to have achieved remarkable savings in its members' costs in recent years reflect adversely on its operation on the common-price system up to 1949. Until recently the common-price system protected some manufacturers from the consequences of their own inefficiency (p. 80). As it now operates, following efforts to establish a uniform system of costing, the exchange of costing information, and the fixation of prices on the basis of an average cost heavily weighted by the lowest costs, the Commission does not think that common pricing operates against the public interest.

The reasons for the improvement in the Metal Window Association's procedure seem to have been three—a new (post-war) attitude to the exchange of technical information, the desire of the largest producer to expand its sales, and government investigations into monopoly. Thus the publication of the fforde Report on cement costs influenced the M.W.A. attitude on the operation of its quota and price policy (p. 17), and the impending legislation on monopolies and restrictive practices so influenced both the Association and the largest producer that quotas and allocations were abandoned, and new procedures were introduced on costing and pricing (pp. 17, 38).

Merchants 'signed up' to distribute metal windows make an agree-

ment with the manufacturer concerned. As there is no Association
enforcement of merchants' selling prices and no collective enforcement,
the Metal Windows Association has not restricted competition with
wooden windows, nor set up a barrier to the entry of new producers.
Indeed one company which started in 1945 and is not a member of the
M.W.A. is now among the five largest producers.

The Monopolies Commission deduces from the extent of improvements in efficiency in recent years that previously inefficient producers
were protected by the way in which the common-price policy was
administered. The change of procedure was connected with the (short-
lived) resignation of Crittalls from the Association at the end of 1948
and its decision in 1952 to reduce prices contrary to Association decisions.
The successful pressure from Crittalls to base prices on costs in efficient
plants shows that in the absence of quotas and collective discrimination
common pricing does not hinder the expansion of the efficient so long
as efficient producers have an incentive to expand. Then, where output
is expanding, common pricing is quite consistent with competition and
the freedom to introduce new techniques.

Where there is excess capacity, as in depression, the maintenance of
common pricing is likely to involve quotas, which quotas seldom lead
to a concentration of production in the most efficient plants. This leads
to waste. However, the absence of quotas in industries with a high
proportion of overhead to direct costs does not ensure such a concentration (except as a result of amalgamation), while in the absence of
collective discrimination, quotas set no barrier to the introduction of
more efficient methods of production or lower prices by non-association
firms. Furthermore, if a community of interest in new techniques is
generated or fostered by association policy, common pricing may be
associated with the creation of new opportunities to progress. This
appears to have happened in the tile industry and to a lesser extent in
metal windows. Once, however, provision is made for industrial
research and development and for the training and recruitment of
technologists and technicians, such a link between common pricing
and technical progress is likely to weaken.

In the case of cast-iron rainwater goods common minimum prices
were reinforced by exclusive-dealing provisions. Such a policy makes
it difficult for enterprising firms to ensure that a common pricing policy
does not protect inefficiency. The Monopolies Commission found that
the exclusive-dealing provisions were contrary to the public interest in
that merchants and manufacturers who did not subscribe to the rainwater agreements were excluded from the bulk of the trade, in that
owing to the operation of the minimum price agreement the introduction
of low-cost methods of production was retarded, and in that no adequate

incentive was given to buyers so to bulk and standardize their demands as to encourage foundries to specialize their production, nor any means provided to pass on consequential savings to consumers. The exclusive-dealing provisions have now been abolished. However, even when they operated, average profits of signatories to the agreement were not high: the extent of competition from goods of alternative materials such as asbestos cement, aluminium and pressed steel ensured that. Indirect competition thus severely limited the power of the B.I.A. to act restrictively. Pre-war negotiations between manufacturers (including the B.I.A.) and merchants (through the D.B.S.J.C.) to make a comprehensive price maintenance scheme covering a large group of building materials were of course intended to reduce indirect competition. Such agreements could have operated only on the basis of far-reaching collective discrimination and would certainly have been contrary to the public interest.

The cement industry raises other issues. The provision for quotas and exclusive dealings were abolished after the fforde Committee inquiry in 1947, and an independent chairman and firm of chartered accountants were appointed to decide the appropriate 'average cost' figure to be used for price reviews. The most important remaining issue is the basis of the price scheme. However, in the absence of provision for exclusive dealing, that price scheme does not discourage entry except regionally, and in the sense that under the Federation Scheme the desire to avoid 'excessive-profit' pricing leads in time of inflation to a strong emphasis on historical cost rather than on replacement cost.

The Cement Federation has not reduced indirect competition, but rather, through encouragement of research into the uses of cement, increased it. In this it has a better record than the more directly competitive brick industry which has not yet, for reasons given above, developed such a sense of community interest in technical progress. Of course, the effect of public inquiry or the anticipation of public inquiry on the policy of the Cement Federation, should not be forgotten. The abolition of quotas and discriminatory dealings, and the institution of a new system of price-fixing in the cement industry, and in the metal windows industry too, followed the fforde Committee Report.

It is clear from the Monopolies Commission reports that many of the restrictive practices in distribution were engendered by depression. Several of these have not been operated in the boom conditions since the war, though the machinery of restriction has been kept in being for fear of depression. The avoidance of depression is thus likely, of itself, to diminish the importance of restrictive practices. An effective full employment policy is not however simply a matter of government *will*: the conditions of full employment must be created. Among these are the expansion of industrial research and development and of technological education, which expansion should increase both the opportunities and the pressures to technical progress in old established as well as in new industries.

BIBLIOGRAPHY

(a) Books

Butterworth, B., *Bricks and Modern Research*, London, Crosby Lockwood, 1948.
Clews, F. H., *Heavy Clay Technology*, Stoke-on-Trent, British Ceramic Research Association, 1955.
Green, A. T. and Stewart, G. H. (eds.), *Ceramics: a Symposium*, Stoke-on-Trent, British Ceramic Society, 1953 (section on Heavy Clay Wares, pp. 738–871).
Rostas, L., *Productivity, Prices and Distribution in Selected British Industries*, National Institute of Economic and Social Research, Occasional Papers, 11, Cambridge University Press, 1948, chs. 3 and 4.
Comparative Productivity in British and American Industry, N.I.E.S.R. Occasional Papers, 13, Cambridge University Press, 1948, apps. 5 and 6.

(b) Official Publications
(All published by H.M.S.O.)

Monopolies and Restrictive Practices Commission, *Collective Discrimination*, Cmd. 9504, 1955.
Report on the Supply of Buildings in the Greater London Area, 1954.
Report on the Supply of Cast Iron Rainwater Goods, 1951.
Report on the Supply of Imported Timber, 1953.
Report on the Supply of Standard Metal Windows and Doors, 1956.
Ministry of Works, *Cement Costs* (the fforde Committee Report), 1947, reprinted 1950.
Clay Building Bricks of the United Kingdom, National Brick Advisory Council, paper no. 5, 1950.
Clay Brickmaking in Great Britain, National Brick Advisory Council, paper no. 6, 1950.
The Distribution of Building Materials and Components: Report of the Committee of Inquiry (the Simon Committee Report), 1948.
First, Second, Third Reports of the Committee on the Brick Industry, 1942, 1942, 1943.

CHAPTER IX

THE MACHINE TOOL INDUSTRY

By M. E. Beesley and G. W. Troup

I. INTRODUCTION

In this chapter, the relations between elements in the structure of the present day machine tool industry and some aspects of its performance are explored. While demonstrating relations of this kind is a legitimate aim in studies of individual industries, to pronounce final judgments upon what is disclosed often cannot be achieved without bringing in criteria implying judgments of economic issues wider than those dealt with by a single industry study. This study centres upon aspects of competition and monopoly in the machine tool industry, and its findings may play a part, with those of other studies, in helping to form opinions on, say, government action in the monopoly field. But any attempt to evaluate other aspects of the industry's performance must be forgone.

More than any other industry perhaps, the machine tool industry carries the hope of raising productivity in manufacturing generally. It is thus not surprising that the industry has been the target of criticisms for many years on the score of its supposed lagging in technical advance —and that this criticism has had the support, at different times, of such diverse interests as motor-car manufacturers and trade unions. To pronounce on this, however, would be to raise the very difficult historical issue, which cannot be settled here, of what precisely were the relative roles of the machine tool-makers and their customers in a closely inter-dependent process.[1] Again, the British machine tool industry has sometimes been accused by user industries of a failure to expand as fast as it might have done; in the last few years frequent publication of news of a large back-log of orders has been interpreted on occasion as unwillingness to expand.[2]

Connected with this criticism are two more judgments—that the

---

[1] It is extremely difficult to pin down the way in which any given advance was made. Centreless grinding, according to one of our informants, was introduced into Great Britain, only after lag, from America in the 1920's. According to B. H. Tripp, however, Hans Renold in Great Britain developed a machine for this purpose long before it came into general use. Compare *Renold Chains: a History* (London, Allen and Unwin, 1956), p. 86.

[2] A recent example of this is to be found in the *Manchester Guardian*, 2 June 1956: 'To judge from appearances output has been remarkably slow to respond to the stimulus of very heavy demand.'

industry should be 'flexible' enough to expand to meet rearmament demands, as in 1951, without recourse to extra imports and that the industry should have done more than it has to replace imports at more normal times—by 'closing the gap' in the types of tools produced in Britain. Neither has the machine tool industry escaped the widespread criticism that exports and productivity in manufacturing should rise faster. More concretely it has frequently been said by critics inside and outside the industry that the industry should standardize its products and their components and reap the benefits of larger-scale production of parts; it should thus decrease costs and, by implication, aid the expansion of machine tool using industries and improve upon the present level of exports. These latter judgments are all the more weighty for having the support of the Anglo-American Productivity Team in Machine Tools.[1]

Institutions of the industry, attitudes to risk and the size distribution of firms in the industry are among the factors which underlie the competitive processes. They affect innovation and the prospects for an expansion of investment in the industry, and its possible consequences in terms of lower prices and exports. For example, the machine tool industry has a selling structure largely built up in response to inter-war conditions. The question of how adequate this is to deal with possible changes in the demand for machine tools may legitimately be explored. It is shown later that the expansion of the industry to meet short-run increases in orders depends on the expansion of subcontracting, another outstanding feature of the machine tool structure. And in the course of the discussion some of the criticisms made about the industry are shown to be, in part at least, inconsistent. Thus it is argued here, in effect, that the desire for a substantial increase in the economies of scale within the industry may conflict with a desire that the industry should contribute more to the extension of economies of scale in the plants of its major customers, since the types of machines made for the latter purpose tend increasingly to be of individual and specific design, which limits the scope for large-scale production in machine tool establishments.

But in all of these individual criticisms there are implied views extraneous to the present interest. Thus a judgment on exports involves a view about what constitutes health in the British balance of payments and on the broad question of the merits of international specialization as against the advantages on strategic grounds of self-sufficiency. The judgment about rearmament involves answering the question of whether the carrying of periodic excess capacity in subcontracting is justifiable, because suppliers of the machine tool industry, which typically also

---

[1] Cf. Anglo-American Council on Productivity, *Metalworking Machine Tools*, Productivity Team Report (London, 1953), p. 53.

supply many other industries, have been at least since the war generally fully occupied.[1] The case for increased investment cannot be settled by reference to the machine tool industry alone; it brings up the whole question of the returns on alternative industrial uses. The conclusions here are therefore confined to matters of wider policy on which the argument can throw light—in particular the usefulness of certain kinds of anti-monopoly policy in promoting competitive behaviour.

Competition in the machine tool industry, as in others, depends principally upon the way in which the demand for its products affects the expectations of the firms in the industry; the conditions of entry into the industry; and the degree of concentration within it. These aspects of the industry are each discussed in separate sections. The sections deal with: the characteristics of demand, to show the main factors influencing change; the effect which economies of scale have upon entry; the extent to which entry may be affected by the actual or potential control by existing machine tool manufacturers of supplies of the factors of production; the effect on entry of institutional arrangements such as patents and tariffs, and of access by newcomers to the markets already served by machine tool builders. This discussion is followed by an examination of the degree of concentration within the industry in terms of the production, financial control and marketing arrangements.

2. DEMAND, EXPECTATIONS AND THE SCALE OF PRODUCTION

The term 'machine tool' covers a wide field: there is no universally accepted definition, though broadly it covers all power-driven machinery used for cutting and forming metal.[2] In its widest sense, it conventionally embraces both wood- and metal-working machines, but generally, machines which work in wood are referred to as 'wood-working machinery' and not as 'machine tools' and the production of the two types of machines is largely by separate processes. Machine tools, then, perform six basic arts: drilling and boring; milling; turning; planing and shaping; grinding; and shearing and pressing.[3] They transform manual skills in metal-working into mechanical skills, with the attendant advantage of accuracy and interchangeability of articles made. Demand for machine tools is thus primarily a demand for aid to, or replacement of, human skills.

[1] Especially the Midlands subcontractors. Cf. E. C. Parsons and M. Beesley, 'Report on the Midlands', *Manchester Guardian Survey of Industry, Trade and Finance 1955*, p. 34.
[2] The writers wil be concerned principally in this study with new machine tools. Except where otherwise specified, the term 'machine tool' means a new machine.
[3] R. J. Kraut, *Mechanical Engineering*, vol. 74, March 1952, p. 212.

The steady technical evolution of the machine tool over the past century, resulting from demands for increased accuracy, speed, safety and ease of operation, has meant also that machinery required to perform given jobs has become cheaper in real terms. Much has been gained in accuracy by improvements in the construction of the machines. The incorporation of auxiliary devices in connexion with moving the component that is being machined—the tendency towards making the machine automatic—has made possible an increase in the speed of tool operation. The speed of cutting tools has also been increased by the use of new metals; for example tungsten carbide has increased the speed and life of milling cutters and reamers. Improvements have occurred in the electrical equipment of machine tools, and particularly in electric motors; these have widened the range of operating speeds to take advantage of the higher possible cutting speeds.

Since the technical development of machine tools thus makes possible a great range of substitution both of machines for labour and of more productive for less productive machines, demand for machine tools is intrinsically heterogeneous; a hererogeneity which, in setting limits to the objective possibilities of technical economies within the machine tool industry, provides the basis for a proliferation of small firms and makes a specialization by most firms in certain classes of machine tools a marked feature of the industry. This diversity of demand, and its concomitant diversity of supply, was such, for example, as to defeat all attempts in the 1930's to prepare schedules of classes of machinery to be automatically subject to or exempt from exceptional import duties. In spite of the prolonged attentions of the Import Duties Advisory Committee and much work by the Machine Tool Trades Association —and, one may add, the strong interest which the manufacturers had in seeing precise schedules established—the Committee, in 1937, 'stated that they had found that the technical difficulties of defining the machinery which should be included in such schedules were insuperable'.[1] (Individual applications had therefore to be dealt with, for particular machines or consignments.)

To describe more fully the character of the demand facing the industry and, more important, to consider its effect on entrepreneurial[2] expectations in the industry, its history must briefly be summarized.

First the growth of total demand may be considered; second, those changes in government taxation policy which have often been assumed to be important in the demand for machine tools; and third the changing

---

[1] Quoted in *The Duty-Free Entry of Machinery into the United Kingdom: Report of a Committee appointed by the President of the Board of Trade* (H.M.S.O. 1954), p. 5. This was a committee to review the system of duty-free admission of machinery into the United Kingdom.

[2] The term 'entrepreneurial' is used advisedly. As seen later control in general goes with risk taking in this industry.

character of demand over time. In the latter is found the most significant factor affecting the structure of the industry.

The first most immediately obvious fact about demand for machine tools is, to judge from production figures, its great increase since the 1930's. United Kingdom production of machine tools rose from £6½ million in 1935 to about £47 million in 1951—an extremely sharp rise even allowing for price changes.[1] Second, there has been a much slower rate of growth since the war, and third, to judge from production and the state of order-books, there has been a great fluctuation in that demand due, in the pre-war years, to the slump and in later years to war-time and rearmament production.

These last characteristics would lead one to expect cautious expectations on the part of firms. The slump experiences, particularly, look at first sight to be a plausible explanation of the facts that, in spite of the long-run growth in demand, since the war firms in the industry have, as a whole, aimed at a slowly increasing capacity and have reacted to fluctuating demands both by subcontracting the manufacture of machines[2] and by allowing delivery dates to lengthen.[3] Nevertheless, in view of the lapse of time since the slump, and the known changed attitudes of governments it is difficult to believe that cyclical fluctuations in demand are a very active element in present-day attitudes.

[1] Production figures for machine tools are unusually difficult to compare over time. The following are the values for United Kingdom production in various years: 1935, £6,531,000; 1937, £10,800,000; 1942 (height of war boom), £33,540,000; 1946, £20,024,000; 1951, £46,993,000 (Central Statistical Office, *Annual Abstract of Statistics*). The changing composition prohibits any attempt at price deflation. From 1941 we have, from the same source, numbers of tools produced. Thus 1942: 95,780; 1946: 44,845; 1951: 53,213. From 1951 onwards, figures are available on a different base. Before 1951 'low cost' tools are omitted (under £50 up to 1935, under £75 afterwards). After 1951 'low cost' tools are included. Production figures, including these, are: 1951: £48,590,000 and 133,019 tons; 1953: £66,180,000 and 151,608 tons; 1955: £75,384,000 and 150,240 tons; and 1956: £85,476,000 and 154,812 tons.

[2] For example, to the textile and printing machinery makers. Only about three-quarters of the peak war-time production was made by the established industry.

[3] Outstanding machine tool orders in the United Kingdom at the end of 1949 were £48·0 million (home £26·0 million, export £21·0 million). Since 1953, the figures have fluctuated between £88·7 million and £70·4 million (early 1954). (*Source*: Machine Tool Trades Association.) The outstanding orders for export contain a large element of guess-work and are particularly liable to inflation through duplicate orders when world capacity is strained, as in the Korean boom. Orders fell in 1954, for example, when much American capacity became available.

During the rearmament programme following the Korean crisis some 35,000 additional tools were required for use in Great Britain. Since the British industry was already fully extended and exporting about a third of the 55,000 tools produced each year at that time, the government placed orders abroad for about half of the tools needed. Armament industries could thus tool up more speedily and reduce the extra load on the British machine tool manufacturers in order to preserve that export position. Some diversion from home civilian industries was still necessary, but was minimized by a substantial increase in domestic machine tool output from £40 million in 1950 to £66 million in 1953. This increase in output was achieved largely by subcontracting.

This is certainly borne out by interviews with members of the industry: indeed one manufacturer of power presses went so far as to say, when asked about the effects of the 1931 slump, that the industry had hardly been affected. He remembered that in spite of the admittedly bad general state of trade, Russian orders for machine tools had saved the industry from serious contraction. It is true, indeed, that Russian orders arrived opportunely: but hardly in such quantity as to support the assertion.[1] The explanation may be that slumps of the size of that in the 1930's are fast receding from business calculations in this as in other industries.

It has often been argued that a very important factor causing changes in the demand for machine tools in recent years has been the adoption by British governments of a more lenient taxation policy (in the shape of initial and investment allowances) towards industrial investment in plant or machinery. It is argued here, however, that these allowances, though they may have had certain effects on that demand for a very short time, have tended to be ignored, by and large, in machine tool users' investment plans. The reasons are these.

Initial allowances, it will be recalled, were introduced in 1946, and granted tax relief of 20 % on the cost of plant and machinery instead of the lower conventional annual allowances. The effect of such allowances on demand for machine tools would have worked, it appears, through the prospective availability of funds to firms at the time of buying machinery. A firm receiving news of the allowances in a given year could, on their account, expect to have more cash available to buy machine tools in about eighteen months' time—during the period when tax on the year's earnings would be payable. Its forward plans, therefore, might be affected; an increase of the prospective liquidity would be foreseen, to enable it to extend investment. But a forecast of liquidity in general can at best be very uncertain, involving as it does predictions of such things as realized profits. Initial allowances did not reduce this uncertainty. They were in any case normally small in relation to funds required for investment, and they had the condition attached to them that they were loans from the government (though admittedly interest-free ones) which had to be repaid. (In effect they speeded up de-

---

[1] Employment in 'general engineering' (including machine tools) declined by 27 % between 1929 and 1932 and did not reach the 1929 level again until 1937. No separate employment figures are available for the machine tool industry but an index of the volume of output in the 1935 Census of Production gives the following series (1935: 100): 1924: 69; 1930: 72; 1933: 47; 1934: 74. Thus, although the machine tool industry probably recovered from the depression more speedily than any other section of general engineering the decline in production between 1930 and 1933 was of the order of 35 %. Statistics for the United States machine tool industry show by comparison a phenomenal decline in machine tool employment at about the same period. In 1929 the American industry employed 47,000; in 1931, 21,300 and in 1933, 12,700 (Biennial Census of Manufacturers).

preciation allowances.)[1] Most important, however, has been the fact that the allowances have been subject to rather unpredictable changes. The allowances were increased to 40 % in 1949; but were suspended in 1952, and then re-established at 20 % in 1953. These factors would dispose firms to regard the allowances as unhelpful to investment plans.

The investment allowances, it is true, were in a different category. They were fixed at 20 % in April 1954 and could perhaps be regarded at first as a permanent government subsidy to business which involved no ultimate repayment. (They were, in effect, additional to depreciation allowances.) But they were to prove as uncertain a boon as initial allowances had been—they were withdrawn in February 1956 and initial allowances were reinstated at 10 %. It is likely that firms would feel it prudent to ignore such doubtful 'assistance'[2] in their long-term investment planning.[3]

The changing character of demand for machine tools over the years is undoubtedly much more important in shaping expectations than past slumps and fiscal policy. In it are found objective conditions of demand which have limited, and will continue to limit, the realizing of internal economies of scale in the industry.

The machine tool industry began to assume its present characteristics at the beginning of this century, with the widespread growth of the use of certain general purpose machines to aid skilled men for a variety of operations. Examples of this type of machine are centre lathes and planers, which were the chief tools of the engineering workshop, though other tools, including shapers, slotters, and drillers had by that time been replaced by stronger and more accurate models.[4] Methods of accurate measurement had spread through engineering and this, together with improvements in the quality of castings and forgings,

[1] A provision was written into the United States tax laws in 1954 allowing machine tool buyers to recover two-thirds of the cost of a new tool within the first half of the depreciation period.

[2] The authors are indebted to Mr A. Mackintosh here for giving them the benefit of his experience in investigating investment policies in manufacturing industry.

[3] This is not to deny that, in the future, the government could seek to stabilize demand for machine tools through fiscal policy of this type. Initial allowances, small in relation to normal requirements for investment funds, would merely have the effect of a slight reinforcement or check to 'business sentiment' about investment; investment allowances, on the other hand, could well influence the timing of investment markedly and thus be a useful support in attempts to smooth out fluctuations in machine tool demand.

[4] Ever since the development of the steam engine in the second half of the eighteenth century—which called for parallel developments in the accurate working of components—the gradual movement towards modern machine shop methods has been due to a constant interaction of progress in engineering based at first on steam and then on electrical power and improvements in the performance of machine tools. By the middle of the nineteenth century machine tool making was an established industry, but most of the leading firms of today, including Alfred Herbert and Charles Churchill and Company, had their origin at the end of the nineteenth century or beginning of the twentieth.

permitted a wide range of work to be produced. There was thus a growing complexity of machine tool design, though the great majority of tools were still made for general purposes.

Since that time, the machine tool industry has been continually assisting in a process of reducing labour costs per unit of output. In Britain between the wars the demand for general purpose machines was overlain by a new demand for more highly productive machines which could be used by the semi-skilled operator. Increasingly women, for example, were being drawn into the labour force to work in new industries such as the making of motor-car parts, and electrical engineering. The lathe, to take one example, became the 'capstan' lathe. These machines allowed pre-setting, and the use of different tools on a given piece of work; each machine was operated by a single semi-skilled worker. Both of these early types could be used for many different kinds of work and so still justified the name 'general purpose' machines. The late 1920's and 1930's, however, saw the emergence of 'special purpose' machines used, for example, in the production of radio parts. These machines had a rather more limited field of work than had the previous ones and this limited range was made possible by the growth of simplification, standardization and large-scale production of components in the major tool using industries. Special purpose machines reduced the need for semi-skilled workers. In such cases the capstan lathe was replaced by the automatic lathe, a battery of which might be in the charge of one machine minder.

At the same time, in specially favourable circumstances and notably in the motor-car industry, special purpose machines began to be used for performing linked processes in a sequence. Here the machines became *specific* to the particular production conditions in which they were used. Design to individual specification became necessary, as distinct from the production of tools (general or special purpose) to be employed by a variety of firms where shorter runs required flexible multi-purpose machines, or where the production conditions of long runs were similar for a number of users. When machine tools are employed in mass production of, for example, motor-cars, radios or meters and in their accessory industries, the problem of the production line is largely one of accuracy in the component and of a continuous flow of output. The development of mechanization in mass production factories has not, so far, changed the fundamental principle of division of labour and specialization of skills, since machines have been introduced into production processes already designed round human skills. The use of special purpose machinery has led to further division of processes and further specialization at each stage. But as a result of intensive subdivision of operations in engineering workshops, the problems and costs involved in loading, unloading and transferring the work-piece have assumed a greater relative importance and have increased the need for co-ordination between the various stages of production lines. These factors have encouraged a trend towards transfer machines: and, more important, have accelerated the trend towards juxtaposing special purpose machinery and thus raised the demand for 'specific' machine tools.[1]

The tendency for demand for machine tools to change in the way just described is partly reflected in the figures given in the following table.

Table 1. *Distribution of British machine tool production for the home market by major types*

	Number of machine tools*	
	1947	1955
All machines	28,749	41,171
Lathes		
Automatic	552	1,569
Capstan and turret	1,464	2,905
Other	4,689	6,905
Drilling machines	4,012	5,193
Presses	4,063	4,190
Grinding machines	2,792	5,016
Milling machines	1,483	4,159
Shearing machines	1,742	1,405
Boring and broaching machines	1,589	873

* 'Major cost' tools. In 1947, those over £50; in 1955, over £75.
Source: Ministry of Supply; Board of Trade.

Though the relevant figures are available only for 1947 and 1955, this is a long enough period to show the trend. The data of the table can give only a rough indication of the qualitative changes in demand, for only broad categories and quantities of machine tools are represented.

In the home market, the delivery by the domestic industry of presses, which represent an old metal-working technique, where in general each machine has one semi-skilled operator, has hardly increased at all since 1947, in spite of the 43 % increase in the whole of home deliveries by the domestic industry. The milling machine and grinding categories on the other hand, more closely identified with highly productive investment, have increased in numbers markedly. Within the 'lathes' category, the shift to the use of less labour and towards

[1] The only information of the relative size of the machine tool industry's domestic customers is to be inferred from Census of Production data on 'investment in new plant and machinery'. The 1948 Census gives motor vehicles as the largest of such investments with £12·4 million and the mechanical engineering industry next with £11·3 million and the various branches of the electrical industry with £9·6 million. These are of course only the most indirect indications.

more intensive production techniques is clear from a comparison of the different rates of growth of autos, capstan and 'other' lathes.[1]

A substantial proportion of the demand for machine tools will continue to be for multi-purpose tools, but if, as seems justifiable, we may look in the future for increasing demands from domestic industries moving in the same line of historical development—towards automatic production—the field for special purpose and, particularly, 'specific' machine tools, will become relatively more important. These kinds of development undoubtedly provide the chief underlying reason why the American machine tool industry has gone very little farther than the British industry in adopting large-scale production techniques: the Productivity Team reported that 'batch' production of machine tools was the limit of American technical achievement and that 'there are no outstanding differences in the American machine tool industry as we saw it and the British machine tool industry as we know it'.[2] (This impression of relatively small American advantage in manufacturing techniques is indeed a rare occurence in Productivity Team reports!) America, of course, has had very much the same type of development in the structure of demand during the present century as Great Britain has had, though at an earlier stage and on a much larger scale.Thus although the American industry enjoys a larger internal market than does its British counterpart and although in the United States industry there is proportionately a rather larger number of big establishments[3], the size of plants in general is not dissimilar.

[1] During recent years a number of British machine tool firms have begun to produce American-designed machines under licence and some American machine tool firms (the most important example of which is Cincinnati Milling Machines) have established branch units in Britain. This movement has 'narrowed the gap' in the machine tools produced in Britain, particularly in special purpose machines. Before the war the bulk of the motor industry's special purpose machinery was obtained from the United States where automatic gear cutters, multiple cylinder borers and special purpose milling machines were made in fairly large quantities. The 'gap' in British production is not very wide in terms of the number of types, but it is significant that the 'gap' machines are frequently of the type which reflect leadership in the design of tools required for advanced production techniques.

[2] Anglo-American Council on Productivity, *Metalworking Machine Tools* (1953), p. 1.

[3] Comparisons between the establishment size distributions of the British and American industries are beset by difficulties of the field covered, the size of establishment recorded, and the size categories selected in official statistics. In the British data, which are presented in Table 2 (p. 374), the 1947 figures have also a particular but not fatal difficulty in defining the unit recorded. However, the following comparisons, which will indicate rough orders of magnitude, may be made: the American Census of Manufactures for 1947 recorded that sixteen establishments employed more than 1000 workers out of a total of 258 employing ten or more. Table 2 below records eleven 'firms' employing more than 750 workers out of 224 employing eleven or more for the British industry in that year. But the British industry, as defined, covers a larger field than does the American. Most other establishments in America which would come into the British definition are to be found in 'Other metal-working machinery' in the United States Census. In this category nine out of 290 establishments employed more than 1000 workers in 1947. Including 'Other metal-working machinery' the American industry employed some 126,000 workers.

The British industry, however, has since the war exported between one-fifth and one-half of its production; before the war it also relied heavily upon export markets as a means of achieving a larger scale of output than could be supported by the domestic trade alone. (In 1935 one-third of the industry's production was exported.) In so far as these exports go to countries at an earlier stage of industrial development than this country, the scope for 'non-specific' machines—and especially general purpose—increases. Since 1946, in fact, the chief destinations of British machine tools have been India and Pakistan, Australia, Canada, the Union of South Africa and France.[1] Deliveries of lathes for export, for example, when compared with deliveries to the home market, usually show a lower proportion of automatics than of other kinds such as capstans and turrets, though the export of automatics is tending to increase absolutely. The exports of capstan and other lathes are both much larger than the exports of automatics and more stable over time.[2]

It is likely, then, that the total future domestic demand will be increasingly 'specific' whereas growing opportunities for selling non-specific machines, if they occur at all, will probably occur largely in oversea markets, where of course they are likely to meet the full blast of international competition.[3]

In spite of the British industry's dependence on exports, it has never been the leader in international trade in machine tools. During the inter-war years the world export market was dominated first by Germany and then by the United States. Between 1924 and 1933, German exports, principally of general purpose tools, rose from 37 % to 70 % of the world total, though as a result of rearmament Germany's share of world exports declined after 1933. In the field of general purpose tools Germany is once again increasing its share of the world export markets.[4]

[1] From 1946–54 inclusive, total exports were £158 million. India and Pakistan took £20·9 million; Australia £20·7 million; Canada £11·2 million; South Africa £12·5 million; France £10·2 million. In 1938, on the other hand, of a total of £4·5 million the U.S.S.R. took £1·7 million machine tools. (Trade and Navigation Accounts.)

[2] Numbers of lathes exported

	1947	1955
Automatics	212	490
Capstan and turret	1,316	1,068
Other	2,783	2,541

In 1955 lathes represented 32 % of the total exports of machine tools by value. *Source:* Ministry of Supply.

[3] The growth of domestic machine tool industries in British export markets may, however, reduce the scope for exports of standard types and increase the need to export more specialized machinery.

[4] The German industry in the late 1930's and in the war underwent a forcible rationalization of output. The number of types of automatic lathes made was reduced from thirty-seven to eleven, for example; the number of large lathes from 216 to 115. This experience has probably helped the industry's more recent successes in the export markets.

The American industry, on the other hand, has traditionally led in international trade in special purpose (but 'non-specific') machine tools, and there is no reason to suppose that its position, built as it is on an early start in the field and accumulated 'know-how', will be seriously undermined.

For all these reasons, then, the diversity and trend of demand are not, it seems, favourable to a marked increase in internal economies of scale in the British industry and indeed may be expected increasingly to reward more costly improvements of individual products rather than lead to a large growth in the numbers of machines produced. Whether the industry can take advantage of this situation depends on the resources devoted to technical development, and on factors in the marketing structure, which are taken up later. It is true that a growing concentration upon 'specific' machinery does not necessarily conflict in all cases with an aim to increase the volume and reduce the costs of 'non-specific' tools. 'Specific' machinery may include standard machines specially modified for the purpose (but not tools producing individual components at high speed such as automatic lathes). It is known, for example, that the Austin Motor Company, in setting up production sequences involving transfer machinery, has used standard tools and has managed to introduce a unit construction principle in the design of certain elements of transfer machines. Nevertheless, on the one hand, the direct cost incentive to the machine tool producers to incorporate standard tools must remain weak in a field where, essentially, technical knowledge is to be sold, and on the other, it seems equally unlikely that 'specific' tools alone would provide the necessary additional volume to get unit cost of tools down markedly. Other difficulties of securing that volume are also discussed later.

Two further factors reinforce this view of the shape of expectations in the industry—the relatively long life of most machine tools and the question of the rate of obsolescence. Many machine tools not only have a long life but may after use in industries demanding very exacting limits of accuracy be sold to other users with less exacting needs.[1] Second-hand machines may be renovated and though not embodying the latest technical advance may still be able to compete with new machine tools. (Many small firms have entered the machine tool industry by this avenue.)[2] Moreover, machine tool makers have the

---

[1] Replacement demand may, however, at times be very high, as, for example, after the recent war when the machine tools of civilian industries in Great Britain and overseas had reached abnormally high average age. This of course is another source of instability in demand.

[2] L. A. Ferney in *The Engineer*, vol. 186, 1948, p. 640, makes the interesting suggestion that machine tool users may be divided into four 'use sectors': (1) 'high production'; including motor-cars, refrigerators, wireless: this sector requires modern high production machinery

opportunity, which is perhaps not so strong in any other industry, of influencing the rate of obsolescence in their customers' plants. They can to a great degree influence demand in their own favour by introducing technically better types of machines. In this they are helped by the fact that the largest tool users are among the most competitive industries and are continually seeking reductions in their unit costs. Hence the interests of the machine tool manufacturers also lie against that stability of design in the machine which is essential to a great increase in the scale of operations in individual establishments.

3. THE CONDITIONS OF ENTRY

From the point of view of demand, therefore, opportunities for large-scale economies are limited. Nevertheless, entry is, at the time of writing this chapter, difficult. The reasons for this do not lie in the nature of the productive processes or in the scale of capital needed for effective production in competition with existing machine tool manufacturers, but partly in factors affecting the general supply of materials and labour to the industry, partly in institutional arrangements such as patents and tariffs, and partly in the effect of certain selling arrangements. The last are more conveniently dealt with when the marketing structure of the industry falls to be considered; the first may be dealt with here.

The capital investment used for machine tool production is adaptable and so is no great hindrance to entry. Thus machine tools can be, and are, produced outside the specialist industry (i.e. those manufacturers who think of themselves as primarily machine tool manufacturers) by other firms in engineering. 'Outside firms' make in normal times about 15 % of the tools which are sold on the 'open market' (i.e. not made and transferred within integrated concerns.) Again, some of the machine tool industry's most important customers are themselves producers or potential producers of machine tools. Outside firms proposing to enter the field would not necessarily be handicapped by difficulties of access to suppliers of raw materials for machine tool products other than those affecting the whole of the industry. In its supplies of machined components, and complete tools by subcontract, the specialist industry

of not more than eight years old. (2) 'Intensive production'; including manufacture of prime movers, heavy lorries and chemical plant: the machines here require to be not more than twenty-four years old. (3) 'Intermittent production'; the jobbing engineers and railway repair shops: this sector requires machinery between twenty-four and forty-eight years old. (4) 'Occasional' sector, with machines forty to sixty years old. New machine tools are chiefly sold in the first and second sectors—mainly the first; and this pattern fits well with the description above of the structure of demand and its trend. It also underlines the size of the market for second-hand tools and their competition with new tools in large parts of engineering.

itself is often in a competitive position *vis-à-vis* other industries demanding engineering capacity. In times of full boom there is coincidence of demands on this capacity from several other industries besides machine tool makers; the latter—as well as would-be entrants—find themselves up against a reluctance on the part of suppliers to accept work on contract basis. Moreover, much of the work done for machine tool builders requires standards of precision that are too high for many engineering firms. This is a case, therefore, where competition for productive factors, and not a possible monopolistic control, may tend to discourage new entrants. On the other hand, the machine tool industry's output (and its 45,000 employees) are a very small section of engineering; it is difficult to conceive of any strict control on entry being exercised by this bottle-neck in supply. In so far as access to materials does influence entry, it influences it in favour of the integrated concern, and some entries since the war have been of this character.

The same kind of difficulties, but more serious ones, apply in the case of the supply of skilled labour. Owing to the high degree of precision work and complexity in many of its products, the machine tool industry employs an exceptionally large proportion of skilled men. Fitters and machine men take several years to train. Though there has been a steady recruitment of apprentices many skilled men have left the industry in recent years for employment in semi-skilled work at other engineering and vehicle machine shops. There has also been an acute shortage of skilled designer draughtsmen, many of whom have been drawn away to the aircraft industry. These difficulties have been aggravated by the location of the machine tool industry, and especially by its connexion in the Midlands and London with their intense shortage of labour since the war. Consequently there has been a persistent dearth of skilled labour which has not only acted as a deterrent to entry from outside the industry, but has also made it difficult at times for the industry to expand its own production and to utilize fully its existing capacity. Thus most newcomers to the industry during the post-war period have been either small firms already established in other branches of engineering or new 'one-man' enterprises, set up by skilled craftsmen previously trained in the large units. Here again, therefore, it is possible to argue that competition for supply of a scarce factor during a prolonged boom period has been of more significance in its effect on entry than any monopolistic controls are likely to have been. Were this scarcity eased but slightly, however, supply of factors would present few problems to the would-be entrant.

Since tariff protection was introduced in 1932 the British machine tool industry has enjoyed a moderate scale of duties on imported tools. Provision has been made from time to time for exemption from import duty of foreign machines that are officially accepted as being necessary and not immediately procurable in Britain, and a large volume of machinery has thus been brought into this country duty-free.[1] On the other hand, import licences for machines not basically different from types of machines made in this country have often been difficult to obtain; and conversely many of the British industry's oversea markets have from time to time been restricted or closed by quotas and licensing procedure. The difficulties of operating tariff policy have already been referred to, however, and these institutional arrangements do not appear to have any great significance in restricting competitive developments in internal, or indeed in international, trade.

Heterogeneity also undermines the effectiveness of patent rights. In a few cases, where an entirely new principle of performing a given machine tool skill has been found, patent protection has been made the chief basis of market superiority. The outstanding example of this in the last twenty years is probably gear-shaving. Generally, however, patent protection has been much less important than skill in design and ingenuity in applying available principles in machine tools. Patents are less important than the organization and performance of development work: they are to some extent an innovatory incentive, but a rather weak one, for diligent development work in a firm usually finds an alternative to another firm's patents. Development of new designs reduces a firm's dependence on, and therefore the effect of, patent rights.

In support of this general view an article may be quoted which discussed the characteristics of the products a United States machine tool manufacturer would find most attractive to adopt in attempting to diversify his production. After pointing to the need for products which would engage highly skilled labour and heavy machinery and equipment, the author put first on his list the need for a 'separate division under top management for developing new fields of industrial enterprise'—with the ultimate aim of setting up a division separate from the original manufacturing group. The list then added 'industrial innovations sufficient to provide a foundation for new business'; only last came 'patentability' or patent protection which will give five years 'before competition may be expected to enter'. (The legal life of a patent is seventeen years.)[2]

---

[1] In the financial year 1937–8, of total imports of machinery of £21·8 million, 30 % was exempt from duty. In 1946–7 the respective figures were £15·0 million and 36 % and in 1950–1 £42·8 million and 38 %. In these last two periods 'machine tools, metal-working and wood-working' accounted for just under one-half of the value of Treasury licences remitting duty on imported machinery. Board of Trade, *The Duty-Free Entry of Machinery into the United Kingdom* (H.M.S.O. 1954), Appendix D, Tables I and III.

[2] Review of paper by H. H. Langdon, 'Machine Designs and Problems, Before and After' *Mechanical Engineering*, vol. 75, 1953, p. 1012.

4. THE STRUCTURE OF MANUFACTURING

A most useful way to approach a description of the competitive relationships between firms in the industry would be to proceed by way of a series of 'concentration ratios' which are now a familiar shorthand for recording the size distribution of units. Thus, one would describe how far the industry is concentrated in the largest establishments (the technical units), then describe concentration in the largest firms (the units of financial control), and third, since this is an industry with substantial imports,[1] consider the concentration of control in the supply to the domestic market as a whole (a 'concentration ratio' for the control of distribution). Unfortunately, the available statistics do not permit exact calculations of this kind, principally because in most official statistics, machine tools are included with engineers' small tools which are used with machine tools.[2] However, certain indirect indications enable one to build up a fairly complete picture.

Table 2. *Size of establishments and 'firms', 1935, 1947, 1955*

Average number employed	Number of establishments 1935	Number of 'firms' 1947	Number of 'firms' 1955	Number of persons employed 1935 Number	%	1947* Number	%	1955 Number	%
11–24	17	49	55	304	1·4	1,050	2·3	986	2·2
25–49	31	55	70	1,118	5·3	2,570	5·6	2,520	5·6
50–99	28	38	56	2,124	10·0	3,610	7·9	3,852	8·7
100–199	23	42	38	3,065	14·6	7,380	16·3	5,092	11·4
200–299	11	13	20	2,713	12·9	4,100	9·1	4,838	10·8
300–499	3	13	20	1,221	5·8	6,430	14·2	7,472	16·7
500–749	3	3	4	1,846	8·7	2,240	4·9	2,347	5·2
750 and over	7	11	12	8,691	41·3	18,050	39·7	17,645	39·4
Total	123	224	275	21,082	100·0	45,430	100·0	44,752	100·0

* Estimate to nearest ten.

Source: 1935, Census of Production; 1947, Ministry of Supply; 1955, Board of Trade.

The 1935 Census of Production gives a size distribution of establishments. To this can be added an estimate of the size distribution of 'firms' for 1947 by the Ministry of Supply and for 1955 by the Board of Trade (Table 2).[3] These three estimates, though they cover the

[1] Imports in the years 1948; 1951; 1952, 1953 (the peak 'rearmament' years) and 1955 were as follows (c.i.f.): £4·8 million; £15·3 million; £60·0 million; £47·0 million and £17·0 million: and exports in the same years (f.o.b.) were £15·7 million; £18·0 million; £22·9 million; £23·2 million and £20·8 million. Domestic production in 1955 was about £74·0 million.

[2] This is the category represented by 'CDM' in the Standard Industrial Classification.

[3] The authors are grateful for the help given by members of the Board of Trade, Ministry of Supply, and PEP (Political and Economic Planning) in procuring statistics for this and other analyses.

same product field, use differing criteria of the unit recorded. The 'establishment' (1935 data) is the technical unit in the normal sense of the term; the 'firm' (1947 data) aggregates establishments owned by a firm under the same trading name; and the 'firm' (1955 data) aggregates establishments known to be owned by the same firm, disregarding trading name. It will be seen that these differences do not invalidate general comparisons because of the rareness with which these aggregates occur, and the character of the few that do.

To deal first with the changes between 1935 and 1947: the totals for the two years are not strictly comparable because of the difference in definition of unit, but inspection of the lists of 'larger' establishments (those employing over 100 workers) in the various regions of Great Britain (collected by the Ministry of Labour) is stated to have shown that in 1954 there were only four cases of firms having more than one such establishment under the same trading name. It may be assumed from this that the phenomenon is rare in the distribution of 1947; for it is unlikely that there were more cases of aggregates then, and any such aggregates are much more likely to occur among larger 'establishments' than among smaller. (In no case in 1954 did a firm have, under the same name, more than two establishments in total; and in no case did *both* establishments employ more than 500 workers.) For comparing the change in the size distribution between the years, then, one is on safe ground in treating the data, broadly, as if it covered the same unit for the two years. In so far as inaccuracy does occur, it tends to exaggerate the size of the larger units in 1947.

Between 1935 and 1947, therefore, the size of the industry was doubled in terms of employment, and in both years the labour force was approximately equally divided between a small number of establishments with more than 300 employees, and a large number with less than 300. Growth in the industry has been spread fairly evenly over the different size classes. (The average size of the largest establishments increased from about 1200 to 1600 employees, but the latter average includes three of the aggregate cases.) The most striking feature of the size distribution is that there was no great tendency, in this period of fast growth, for any particular size class to become more dominant; and the largest size class, if anything, tended to lose ground relatively to the others. Had there been a tendency, over this period, for technical economies of scale to be asserting themselves more strongly, we would have expected to observe a shift in the proportions towards the larger size categories.[1] This has not been the case.

The data for 1955 confirm these conclusions, though again the com-

---

[1] The measurement of size by number of workers is not good for this purpose, of course. But it is the only one possible and not too misleading taken in broad terms.

parisons are between different units. Here too, however, such in-accuracies as are imported into a comparison of size classes between 1947 and 1955 are in the direction of lessening the decrease shown in the share of the total number of workers employed in the largest size class. Besides including the four 'same trading names' cases of 1954, the 1955 data include another four cases (but only four) where large firms are recorded as each having one establishment or establishments, smaller than their main works, under a different trading name.[1]

All this is, of course, consistent with what was said earlier about the effects of changing demand on internal economies of scale. There are indeed large plants in the industry—one employs over 3000—but these plants, though they produce some types of machine tools in batches, are agglomerations of different engineering processes and make many different specifications of machine tools.[2]

Such is the diversity of product and the tendency of firms in the industry to specialize, however, that concentration in the manufacture of individual types of machines is much higher. This is the kind of picture partially disclosed in the Leak and Maizels study of concentration in British industry for 1935.[3]

Measuring concentration in terms of 'units of control', defined upon the criterion of legal control through a majority shareholding, they found examples of fairly high concentration in the production of 'lathes, automatic and semi-automatic, complete', and, to a lesser extent, in 'vertical drilling machines, complete'. The three largest 'units' in the industry controlled 80 % and 53 % of the total output of these products respectively.[4] On the other hand, no machine tool product features in their list of commodities, 'the output of which was concentrated in one or two firms'.[5] Neither were machine tools one of the trades or subdivisions in which the three largest units accounted for 70 % or more of the employment.[6] All these figures neglect the presence on the market of imports, and also the fact that part of the British production was exported: the effect of these omissions in total is that concentration is somewhat understated as a whole.

---

[1] One firm had five establishments in total, one four, one three and one two.

[2] As noticed earlier (p. 368 n. 3) there is evidence to show that the American industry, though about three times as large as the British in terms of total employment, has a rather similar size distribution of establishments. The four largest units there in 1947 had, however, an employment of more than 4000 workers, which is larger than any British units with the exception of Alfred Herbert. This incidence of a few very large units in the United States may well confer, and help to perpetuate, advantages in leadership in research.

[3] H. Leak and A. Maizels, 'The Structure of British Industry', *Journal of the Royal Statistical Society*, vol. 108, parts 1–2, 1945, p. 142.

[4] *Ibid*. Table XIV. Their industry covered engineers' small tools; but one may be sure that the largest units were not small tool-makers.

[5] *Ibid*. Table XV.   [6] *Ibid*. Table XIII.

Even so, it is clear that while there is a fairly low degree of concentration in terms of control over physical plant, there is a much higher 'product' concentration. Since the plant and machinery in the industry are readily adaptable to different products, this represents a type of situation which throws most of the burden of market control first on the ability to differentiate the firm's product, and second on control of the marketing arrangements. Competition through price-cutting has apparently rarely, if ever, troubled the industry: there has never been any suggestion, so far as the authors are aware, that the leading formal association in the industry—the Machine Tool Trades Association[1]— has attempted to control pricing arrangements, or has ever, as in the case of trade associations in other durable goods industries, attempted systematically to control the terms on which second-hand tools may be exchanged.[2] (This would in any case probably be a prohibitively complex undertaking.) Such close associations in the industry as there are—the Associated British Machine Tool Makers (A.B.M.T.M.) is the leading example—are organized on a principle of membership by product specialization, where each member produces a different class of product. It is significant that a search through textbooks on American monopoly history and policy has failed to disclose a single case where government action was taken against a machine tool maker. This inaction may conceivably have been due to the equivocal attitude of the antitrust laws to the use of patent rights, but it was more likely to have been due to the fact that price is not a competitive weapon which could be used by itself with much success in the machine tool industry.

This limitation on the use of price as a competitive weapon does not mean that competitive forces emerge in the guise of 'useless' variation of product or 'superfluous' service. Machine tool firms sell to know-

---

[1] The M.T.T.A., whose members include producers of both metal-working and wood-working machine tools, importers of foreign machine tools and some firms in related industries (e.g. cutting tools), is an advisory and consultative body. It represents the industry on the Machine Tool Advisory Council established after the Second World War to maintain contact between the industry and government departments. In 1946, in conjunction with the Institute of Production Engineers, the National Federation of Engineers' Tool Manufacturers, and the Gauge and Tool Makers Association, M.T.T.A. set up a new research body, known as the Production Engineering Research Association of Great Britain. P.E.R.A., partly supported by public funds, has as its main object the discovery of improvement in production methods and equipment by means of practical research for the machine tool and other engineering activities. M.T.T.A. has also recently formed a number of Production Efficiency Panels for the interchange of ideas, information and general aid, with the object of increasing the productive efficiency of members of the industry.

[2] The important exception to this was the Government Disposals scheme, supported by M.T.T.A., for a programme of gradual releases of war-time surplus tools after the Second World War. This, together with a high level of demand for machine tools at home and overseas, prevented a repetition of the dislocation of the market for new machine tools which occurred after the First World War. Cf. PEP (Political and Economic Planning) Broadsheet, 'The Machine Tool Industry', *Planning*, vol. 15, no. 292, 1948.

ledgeable customers. These often have their own means of servicing their purchases; where this is not the case, expert servicing by machine tool makers or their agents is necessary. But it does imply that market positions, once built up, are made the more difficult to assault because one possible strategy—price-cutting—is relatively ineffective. (Control of the market based ultimately upon differentiation of, and specialization in, products also reduces the prospect of a wider adoption of a principle of unit construction and standardization—and lowering cost.) The more standardized the products, the more useful—and dangerous—is price as a competitive weapon. Only a prospectively very large increase in output of standard tools would induce firms to alter fundamentally present market positions. The system of marketing, which is an outstanding characteristic of the industry's structure, is examined more closely later. Certain changes in that system, it is suggested, may well lead to a greater competitive effort. The chief benefits of this competition would probably be felt, however, not in the form of lower prices—at least so far as the home market is concerned—but in a quickening tempo of technical application to customers' requirements.

A study of the financial control of firms and the progress of amalgamations since the war does not fundamentally alter the description of the industry built up on establishment data. Most of the (approximately) 250 firms in the industry are private limited companies or partnerships and thus are closely held by individuals. There are some twenty or so public companies each with issued share capital of up to about £800,000 in which family holdings are also predominant. (These are not always majority holdings, but are large enough to form a basis of control.) Shareholding in the largest company which has grown up in, and is specialized to, machine tools—Alfred Herbert—is rather more widespread; but in 1955 25% of the issued share capital of £6,000,000 still belonged to the founder—and active head—of the company. Some of the other leading firms owe their origin to men who, early in this century, broke away from the established firms and who are still active; there have also been established notable American-led enterprises. Independence in manufacturing is a strong tradition in the industry. And control, in general, still goes with risk-taking: the 'golden rule' has not yet been broken (though through the growing weight of taxation it may not remain unmodified for long). More important, the firms are still small enough in terms of employment to have a simple internal organizational structure; the lines of communication within the manufacturing units in the industry are short.

Since the war, however, there has been a movement towards amalgamation which, while it has left the main structure of the industry unchanged, has changed the relationship of some of the larger firms to other industries. Partly this has been in the direction of backward integration outside the industry; this is most probably simply a reflexion of that competition for supplies noted earlier.[1] But backward integration of supplies is not a remarkable feature of the firms in the industry.[2] Some of the biggest firms, it is true, own iron foundries, but most firms are not large enough individually to establish foundries on a scale which would yield lower costs than the price charged by independent foundries, and jobbing foundries supply the greater part of the industry with castings. Since part of the production of machine tool castings is highly skilled work, however, there is room for the emergence of the specialist founder. Modern Foundries, for example, a subsidiary of the machine tool firm William Asquith, supplies a number of other machine tool firms with castings. In general, however, the very diversity of components and parts has tended to restrict the degree of backward integration.[3]

[1] Arnott and Harrison, for example, have acquired Omes, electro-forgings manufacturers, and Faulkners, specialist drop forgers.

[2] The Census of Production gives an analysis of purchased materials showing that during 1948, 'larger' machine tools establishments purchased 69,800 tons of iron castings, 15,100 tons of pig-iron, 25,000 tons of ferrous rods, 20,200 tons of ferrous wire, and 44,200 tons of other ferrous materials; and 6600 tons of non-ferrous materials. Other important items were ball- and roller-bearings, nuts, bolts, and electric motors. The 'conversion factor', or the ratio of raw material input to value of output, is very high in machine tools; hence the incentive to backward integration is limited by this as well as other factors mentioned elsewhere.

A few machine tool firms make their own forgings but only the more specialized and complex types. Standard types are bought out. There is some subcontracting of shaping work—rough shaping for later precision finishing in the machine tool works. Precision work is itself more difficult to subcontract.

[3] It is most unfortunate that there are no data for the industry in the country with which to illustrate the degree of backward integration. In the United States, however, the industry, as has been argued above, has a similar productive pattern to the British industry. The 1947 Census of Manufactures yields the following comparison between the machine tool industry and the motor-car and heating and cooking apparatus industries—two of the major 'assembly' type industries:

Number of establishments performing selected metal-working operations

Operation	Machine tools	Motor vehicles and parts	Heating and cooking apparatus
Founding	19	24	9
Die casting	3	25	1
Forging and presswork	10	74	8
Electroplating	12	88	24
Galvanizing	1	55	6
Heat treatment of metals	85	190	31
Automatic saw machine department	55	145	18
Machine shop	256	412	86
Tool-die room	75	258	43
Pattern shop	69	42	83
Plate or structural fabrication	24	51	22
Stamping, blanking, forming and drawing	23	305	59

Establishments in the motor and heating industries are clearly more integrated technically.

Partly also, the movement towards amalgamation has been in the direction of increasing the stake in the industry of firms whose main interests lie outside it. This has affected a few of the leading firms within the industry; for example John Brown and Company, shipbuilders, acquired a controlling interest in Wickman in 1947; other post-war acquisitions are those of The Staveley Coal and Iron Company, in James Archdale and Company and George Richards and Company.[1] These acquisitions have left the pattern of manufacturing concentration within the industry much as it was; their significance is that there has been a considerable increase in the capital resources available to the industry, and, perhaps more important, an increased possibility of access to capital.[2] This outside 'backing' was not entirely unknown in the industry before the war—the Birmingham Small Arms Company (B.S.A.) was the chief case—but the new developments mean that there are more independent points in the industry at which large capital resources could be deployed.[3]

Less strong links between certain companies do occur; the members of the A.B.M.T.M. are connected indirectly by their interest in that organization, through interlocking directorships; this form of link is also found between one or two other companies. Their function appears to be to back up certain divisions of the market: interlocking directorships within the industry are however not at all widespread.[4]

5. THE MARKETING STRUCTURE

The marketing structure of the industry is extremely complex and its roots go far back into the origins of the specialist manufacturing industry. Its chief features are that it is rather more concentrated than the production side of the industry, and that it is built up largely on a system of sole agencies, which give the marketing organization exclusive rights to sell and service a manufacturer's products, or rarely, individual items in his range.

---

[1] Cf. *A Survey of the United Kingdom Machine Tool Industry*, Noble Lowndes Finance Company, October 1955. Staveley have also acquired two Canadian firms: Standard Machine and Tool Company, and Modern Tool Works Toronto. Cf. *Engineering*, vol. 129, 1955, pp. 141–2.

[2] The Staveley Coal and Iron Company has interests in many fields from fruit juices to oil. Its chief function must be that of investor. This was one of the companies most affected by post-war nationalization measures.

[3] Metal Industries, J. Brockhouse and Company, and The David Brown Corporation are other examples of engineering combines with machine tool interests.

[4] There has also been a certain consolidation of product specialization through amalgamation. In 1954 two examples occurred. Thos. W. Ward and Company acquired Fredk. Town and Sons, manufacturers of radial drillers, and Coventry Gauge and Tool Company took over Pitter Gauge and Precision Tool Company. Cf. *Engineering*, 1955, p. 141.

Building up agencies for the home market and export was one of the earliest innovatory activities of the large manufacturing firms, and was one of the chief reasons for their expansion. The largest selling organization, as one might expect, is that of Alfred Herbert; other organizations were built around such firms as Asquith, B.S.A., Wickman, and Charles Churchill. (In the last two cases, large importing agencies from German and American manufacturers respectively were obtained in the 1920's.) These organizations act as agents for other smaller machine tool specialist manufacturers and for some of the major engineering firms who make machine tools as a 'sideline'. The ambit of manufacturing control of the market is thus widened. There are other centres of agency control; the major ones are those represented by A.B.M.T.M., and a large firm of specialist importers which is not directly concerned with manufacturing.[1]

The A.B.M.T.M. is perhaps the most well-known of the agencies, it has a form unique in the industry.[2] Formed in 1917, it then consisted of eleven manufacturers, including several of those now among the leading manufacturers. It was originally formed as an export agency but it turned its attention to the home market soon after its formation: each of the eleven had an equal number of shares in the company and a director on its board. There have been certain variations in membership since, and the members in 1955 numbered six, with a total issued share capital of over £1,400,000 between them. The A.B.M.T.M. deals with practically the whole of the products of its constituent members; it does not accept other agencies, although one of its members has an associated company in another agency group.

In sum, then, there exists for the home manufacturers a small number of what may be called 'leading agents'. There are many independent agencies, of course, but this does not alter the picture of domination by a few. The latter have the weight of manufacturing behind them and their position is further strengthened by a tendency for the functions of exporting and importing to be divided between them, as well as for them to have the agencies of leading manufacturers outside the machine tool industry (these manufacturers are among those firms which, as noted earlier, make some 15 % of total machine tool output).

An agency, once granted, apparently changes hands infrequently, though there were some notable changes at the times when large outside firms began to invest in the industry. After the Staveley Coal and Iron

---

[1] The 'specialist importer' has built up agencies with a number of domestic manufacturers of small, but not negligible, size. Nine of these manufacturers, in 1954, had establishments employing between 100 and 500 workers.

[2] The Scottish Machine Tool Corporation—an amalgamation of small firms formed in 1937—was somewhat analogous, but is now a single manufacturing firm; its issued capital is £400,000.

Company had made its investments in the industry, James Archdale and Company and George Richards seceded from the A.B.M.T.M. (in 1948 and 1954 respectively) and joined the Herbert group of agencies. Similar kinds of change attended the other investments by outside firms in the industry, but the net effect of these was to increase concentration in the leading agents' hands, for the agents which were already the largest increased further in size.

The principle of membership of the A.B.M.T.M.—that of specialization to product—is, in essentials, followed by each of the leading agents. Each, indeed, attempts to represent a whole range of specialist manufacturers: to a considerable extent they duplicate one another's range. The bigger leading agents carry on a far-reaching agency system throughout the world and were pioneers in the provision of spares and sales service. They were built up at a time when the leading manufacturing firms were concentrating on the production of general purpose machines and, later, the relatively non-specific but special purpose machinery.[1]

The organizations are thus geared principally to sell machines made on batch production principles and not the highly specific machinery referred to earlier. They gain economies of selling on a large scale— with important pooling of risks—in export markets; but the members of their selling forces, though nowadays often trained engineers, cannot, of course, be experts in the solving of the individual problems of every potential customer, especially where specific machinery may be required. Service is available to customers but the initiative to make use of it lies with the would-be customer.

Import agents, on the other hand, are extremely numerous, as is to be expected in view of the fact that imports tend to lie in the fields not covered by domestic batch production. Here, too, the sole agency system is dominant, though agencies for individual products of foreign manufacturers are rather more frequently granted than they are among home agencies. There do occur a few cases of manufacturers granting selling agencies which are not exclusively held by one firm; these are mainly given by American manufacturers.

The Machine Tool Trades Association issues a *Guide to Members' Activities* which amongst other things records the agents in the domestic market of some 800 foreign firms. In 1954, these were held by about fifty members. In less than ten cases were foreign manufacturers listed as having more than one British agent; about fifteen are recorded as granting agencies to different firms for different types of tool.[2] In

---

[1] Capstan and automatic lathes respectively were given earlier as examples of these.

[2] These figures, and those that follow, are only approximate. An unknown number of small tool agencies are included, though these will not invalidate the generalization.

general, import agents specialize in importing tools from certain countries. The three chief agents for American firms (to judge from the number of agencies held) covered 40 % of all the American agencies recorded in the *Guide*, and these represented about 90 % of the agencies held by these companies. Importers of German tools were rather less specialized; the three chief German importers (again judging solely on number of agencies held) covered 32 % of all recorded German agencies; these represented 68 % of their agencies.[1] The specialization to country may be put in the following way: the top twelve 'United States' agents, who held 86 % of all United States agencies, held only 17 % of the German ones; conversely the top twelve 'German' agents, who held 78 % of all German agencies, held only 11 % of American agencies. Agents who do *not* specialize to countries (they are not among the largest few importers in terms of numbers of agencies), are on the whole those firms which have very strong domestic manufacturing interests. Thus four of the leading domestic manufacturing groups had between them about fifty American agencies, sixty-five German and twenty-six from the rest of the world.

Specialization to country implies also a specialization in the type of machine tool imported: for example, agents for American tools specialize in certain types of milling machines, gear cutting machines and automatics, and Swiss agents in such tools as sliding head automatic lathes, used for work demanding very fine tolerances.

As with domestic marketing agencies, import agencies seem to change hands rather seldom. By comparing the *Guide* for 1954 with a somewhat similar publication for 1956,[2] it is possible to trace the firms holding some 230 agencies. Only some ten of these agencies appear to have changed hands entirely in the two years, although a somewhat larger number have been split between different agents to provide sole agencies in different classes of machines.

Import agencies then, are less highly concentrated than the domestic ones; the pattern does however serve to reinforce, rather than compete with, the domestic agency structure. The sole agency system applies in the import field too; it seems to be stable over time. The leading agents have agencies which extend their range of specialized products, and the other major importers tend to be concerned with importing those types of machines which are not manufactured at home.

---

[1] The United States and Germany are the main sources of machine tool imports. In 1954, imports were £5·2 million from the United States and £5·1 million from Germany. The total imports in that year were £16·1 million. This year was selected for analysis because it avoids the abnormally high import years of 1952 and 1953, when total imports were £60 million and £47 million respectively.

[2] *Guide to the International Tool Exhibition London, 1956* (Machine Tool Trades Association).

6. CONCLUSIONS

Since the war, the British machine tool industry has been operating in conditions of chronic shortage of factors of production and over-full order books. Over neither of these conditions has it had a significant degree of control. Comparisons of the general 'performance' of the industry with machine tool industries of other countries—which have often been to the detriment of the British industry—are unrewarding. For example, the recent and spectacular German performances in volume of production exports and developments of new designs has taken place in a context of rebuilding an industry virtually from scratch—with adequate labour supplies, almost complete re-equipment and time in which to think about and research into design of new and improved machines. Constant pressure on resources in the British industry has undoubtedly limited research efforts and development of the 'specific' type of machine tools. Nevertheless the conditions of competition in the industry have relevance to the problem of meeting the changing character of demands, for the present structure and practices have evolved largely as a consequence of pre-war development, and can be expected to persist even in a situation where the pressures on the supply of factors may be relaxed. The question of what the development of the British industry would have been in the absence of those pressures is a sterile one; whilst recognizing the difficulties under which the industry has laboured, the possibilities inherent in the industry's present structure may be brought out.

A number of arguments and conclusions may be drawn from the description of marketing arrangements and the structure of domestic manufacturing. The effect of the system of leading agents on the rivalry between *established* domestic manufacturers seems to be rather small. It has already been argued that this rivalry must inevitably take the form of product rather than price competition. Each leading agent represents non-competing specialist 'clients', and there tends to be a matching of ranges between the leaders. Consumers' choice between existing manufacturers in a given product field is not materially lessened by the existence of the leaders. Product competition between members of different leading agents remains. On the other hand, the structure does tend to discourage a specialist manufacturer from extending consumers' choice by making products outside his conventional range. If a manufacturer wishes to market a new product competitive with another client of his agent, he may be faced with the necessity of withdrawing from the agency entirely in order to do so. Such cases have indeed occurred. Between the wars, for example, there were certain resignations from membership of the A.B.M.T.M. because of disagreements about the legitimate confines of product specialization.

It might be argued that the case is nowadays more serious for a new firm wishing to enter the market for the first time with an innovation, or wishing to expand the sales of its product through innovation. An agency with one of the leaders is, of course, a most valuable asset and one which, if it can be secured, has very favourable effects upon a firm's prospects of growth. There are relatively few leading agents to choose from, however, and it is quite likely that developments going on within a given leading agent's sphere would, or would appear to be, similar to the new firm's product, from which, under the principles of non-competing membership, the new firm would be excluded. (Some agents are very anxious, of course, to secure the representation of firms who develop a type of product which does compete with existing agencies and there are examples where this has occurred since the war.)

With any new untried product, however, it is essential that as many favourable prospects of outlets as possible should be available. The chances of acceptance of new producers would, perhaps, be higher were there less concentration in the control of agencies. Moreover, it could be argued that the sole agency system oppressively limits the speed of development of sales for the new firm. A new machine tool, once it is ranked in the selling organization alongside many other products, may not perhaps be pushed as vigorously as it would be if more agents were appointed.

This is a point at which the American and British machine tool selling structures differ widely. The exclusive agency is, at best, of doubtful legality in America; it is certainly difficult to uphold in a court. The American industry lacks that concentration of selling agencies which is typical of the British industry; there the jobber of machine tools—a firm which may specialize on the marketing of certain classes of machines—is much in evidence. (Older established machine tool firms in America find that they have to by-pass the jobber and sell direct to customers. This may be a wasteful procedure in terms of sales forces and time compared with the British structure, but it has advantages which are taken up later.) A newcomer in America, dissatisfied with his first agent, can appoint others without difficulty. The jobbers, in their turn, have to face intense competition among themselves. This must, on the whole, give the new firm a rather higher chance of establishing itself and growing than its counterpart in Great Britain.[1]

This defect of the present structure does not seem to the authors to be so serious, however, as the problem of the development and sale of the 'specific' type of machine tool. This type of tool, as industrialization

---

[1] Curiously enough, the Productivity Team on Machine Tools failed to mention this striking difference between the two industries, though strictly it was outside its terms of reference.

proceeds, is likely to become of ever-growing importance in the highly productive sector of engineering. The ultimate limit in the development of 'specific' machinery is the fully automated process where the machines themselves are controlled and directed by other machines, thus governing the movement of the workpiece and virtually eliminating labour. This process has gone most far in motor-car production, and its implications for machinery design and manufacture have been well summarized by M. Pierre Bézier.[1] He wrote that the purchase of this type of machine

requires, first of all, a very close liaison between the customer and his [machine tool] suppliers, because their design has to take account of the buildings in which they will be installed, means of materials handling, either automatic, semi-automatic or manual, which are to be utilized for the transport of work, the processing of chips, scrap disposal, the arrangement of the distribution of services such as compressed air, setting liquids and electrical current....It can happen that the design of the [motor-car] product may be modified during the designing or manufacture of machines, because the drawing office has decided on some last minute improvement. The machine tools in the course of manufacture, will also have to be modified.

The present 'leading agent' structure of marketing in the British industry is, it seems, ill-adapted to foster this kind of extremely close liaison, even though it does leave open to individual members the option of direct contact with customers. Though, as we have argued, the organizational structure of the individual manufacturing firms is simple, lines of communication between the customer and the manufacturing plant are lengthened by the selling structures; and in the selling organizations themselves representing many different classes of tools, the very economy in centralized representation is at odds with the pressure towards elaborate and continued consultation and willingness to modify existing products which the development of 'specific' machinery creates. It is significant that machine tool manufacturers sometimes consider themselves 'handicapped' by delay in the final design of the end product and its components by user industries. Late modifications in design are frequently at least a potential source of conflict between machine tool manufacturers and users, especially in the motor and aircraft industries, where owing to the speed of progress in technical knowledge, new designs may be delayed on the drawing board in the interests of perfection. Users also often appear to the machine tool manufacturers to be unduly reluctant to adapt machines, suitably modified, from the existing ranges of production. All this seems to point to a need not simply for different attitudes on the part of user industries, but for much earlier and continuing consultation so that

---

[1] Of the Renault motor firm, at the British Institute of Management Conference on Automation in October 1954.

considerations of appropriateness and economy in machine tool requirements enter design planning from the start. Moreover, experimental
and developmental work in machine tools, which is concentrated in the
manufacturing firms, tends to be directed towards the existing range of
tools rather than to be utilized to deal with the problems arising from
the users' needs and plans, or to the accumulation of knowledge of
'specific' tools. (The fact that many of the leading British firms import
foreign machines reduces the incentive to produce these machines ni
this country.) This is not universal: some companies are in fact extremely alive to the need to shorten the lines of communication and to
simplify them. But the general position may be summed up by para-
phrasing the view of a manufacturer of long American experience.[1]
Comparing the British and American selling systems, he remarked that,
in contrast to most British firms, the American machine tool manufacturers believe in direct selling; that they not only make it their business
to keep themselves informed of potential customers' investment plans,
but would, if possible, be 'in there making the plans with them'; and
that they will not only have their representatives at the customers'
works, but will also make sure that their own subcontractors would be
there to assist deliberations, to make modifications and to give suggestions.
American business methods and businessmen are, of course, oriented in
general differently from British, but in this contrast the force of institutions must be recognized.

One result of this is that there has been an increasing tendency for
machine tool users such as motor-car and aircraft industries to integrate
backwards to machine tools. As M. Bézier (whose company took up
this policy, in the first instance, because of lack of suitable French-made
machinery) said, an 'advantage derived from making our own machines
is that liaison between the drawing office and the machine maker is
simplified because both belong to the same firm'. But users do this
reluctantly: many other claims exist for their capital resources;
especially as they are, in the main, assembly industries they have many
other possibilities of integration, and such a policy of integration
would be labour-intensive. They may also fail, by having to act on their
own initiative, to realize the potential benefit of that concentrated
research into machine tool problems—albeit mainly on lines much
influenced by existing products—which is being performed by the
leading machine tool manufacturers.[2]

---

[1] Given in an interview.

[2] In addition to some of the individual large machine tool firms, the Production Engineering
Research Association of Great Britain carries on research into new and improved designs and
methods. The facilities of P.E.R.A. are available to the smaller machine tool manufacturers at
a low cost.

Again, as opportunities for automatic plant arise, the need grows for the union of knowledge of machine tool designs and expertise in electronic control devices. At its most effective, this will be applied through individual machine tool manufacturers closely connected with developments in prospective customers' works. And, particularly as this is a youthful development, there is in general a need for the most flexible means by which knowledge in electronics can be applied.

This is illustrated by the developments in electronic machine tool control in America. There, knowledge has been applied not only by machine tool manufacturers through their own electronic departments, but also by machine tool manufacturers subcontracting the design of electronic equipment. Some users such as the aircraft industry have developed their own equipment. However, the machine tool industry itself has had to provide the main initiative, and is increasing rapidly its electronic resources.[1] This is most important in Britain because it is unlikely that electronics firms here will attempt to enter the machine tool industry in strength, for it contains very different processes, techniques and expertise. In this country, electronic specialists have originated in electrical engineering,[2] office equipment,[3] or as users of office equipment.[4] Some of these and other companies have shown much interest and initiative in extending the application of electronics to machine tools; but the use of such techniques often involves a fundamental change of machine design and the new ideas have been spreading only slowly.

This analysis appears to pose something of a dilemma. For having argued the shortcomings of the existing selling structure, its great advantage—in particular in export markets—must also be recognized. At home, in the sales of non-specific tools the system has the merit of economies of man-power in marketing and supports a high standard of after-sales service. It does indeed perpetuate and support specialization by manufacturers in individual types of tools, but it may be urged that this is in any case inevitable, since these incorporate different principles of operation, for example boring and turning. Difficulties appear where problems arise—as they do frequently in the field of 'specific' machinery —demanding a willingness to experiment with new principles, or to

[1] Cf. an article by B. K. Ledgerwood in *Control Engineering*, June 1956, p. 65. 'The machine tool field [in New England] is really changing. All the firms I visited had at least one qualified control engineer doing design work.'

[2] For example, Ferranti, Elliott Brothers (London), Electric and Musical Industries, and English Electric Company. The Ferranti development of a computer to control milling machines is particularly interesting in that it promises much cheaper production of very small quantities.

[3] For example, British Tabulating Machine Company, and Powers-Samas Accounting Machines.

[4] For example, Leo Computers, a subsidiary set up by J. Lyons and Company.

produce more complicated machinery or to incorporate different principles in the same machine.

In export markets, where, as has been seen, the dominant need is to sell general purpose machinery, the structure enables manufacturers to realize important selling economies in addition to those secured at home—the most significant being a lessening of risks, through their pooling, to individual manufacturers. However, the Productivity Team stressed, as have many others, the possibilities for reducing production costs and selling prices in the industry.[1] What is the significance of the selling structure in this problem?

The defenders of the present system see in it the germ, at least, of a method of reducing the prices of general purpose tools markedly. A fall in prices in the export markets might well give some competitive advantage to British manufacturers in international trade. (Such a fall would mainly be effective against German competition—American labour costs are too high for that country to match European prices. Customers for batch-produced, non-specific and fairly simple tools, once they had decided to invest, might well be attracted by differences in relative prices.) The Productivity Team argued, for example, that to make lower prices possible there was a great need for standardization of parts and components.[2] The leading agent structure, as has been seen, encourages specialization upon different classes of tools by the 'client' manufacturers; here, it could be argued, is satisfied one precondition for standardization.

The main difficulty, on the other hand, is to extend the sphere of standardized components further than the plants of individual clients of marketing organizations: standardization of components within the existing product ranges in the individual firms is already quite common in this country, as it is in America. But the prospects for setting up permanently expanded markets on the basis of low prices are, it has been argued here, weak and the trends of development in demand in general against the likelihood of large sales of batch-produced tools. Moreover, even if this estimate of the prospects for demand for non-specific tools is wrong, and it is true that there is in fact an objective possibility of much larger markets, then the conclusion must still be that the existing leading agent structure would be likely to act against such expansion through retarding a fall in costs. This would not necessarily be owing to lack of capital; the tendency of the capital available to the large firms to increase was noted earlier. It would be owing to the following factors.

[1] The Productivity Team apparently deemed the selling structure outside its terms of reference.
[2] The Productivity Team's arguments met with little favour in the trade in general, mainly on the score of their 'lack of realism'.

A widening of the movement towards standardization could be achieved either by further backward integration of part-making by machine tool manufacturers, or by the emergence of specialist suppliers serving a number of the existing large manufacturers. (Standardization would have to spread to many of the multifarious components of the machine tools to exercise a marked effect on costs.) But neither of these seems likely to take place. It is most unlikely that specialist firms would emerge spontaneously because of the large commercial risks involved in tying capacity to machine tool production. Thus, the burden would be thrown on to backward integration by individual manufacturers. But for large-scale capital to be drawn into individual firms for this purpose, there would have to be assurance of expanded home markets for those firms; expansion based on an anticipated increase of foreign trade alone would, it seems, appear to be prohibitively risky. Moreover, machine tool manufacturers would be unwilling to be dependent upon one another for large-scale supplies of components; hence there would be extra pressure for a larger and assured domestic market in order to justify backward integration by individual producers. To reach a new situation of greatly enlarged volume and lower costs, then, there would have to be a radical redistribution of existing domestic markets. Firms which would lose markets in this redistribution would be forced to take on other products to survive; thus the leading agent structure would be undermined from within, and the structure as a whole could certainly not absorb such market changes in its present form. Manufacturers, at present, would be unwilling, it may be argued, to face such an upheaval of marketing arrangements; the existing structure represents some assurance of security in markets.

The main trend of the arguments in this chapter, however, points towards three principal needs—an easing of access to distribution outlets in the home market, a closer link between manufacturing and user development, and the maintenance, on the other hand, of a large-scale selling structure for the export markets.[1] This points to a divorce of the home from the foreign agency systems of selling, and, closely tied to manufacturing as they are, this is doubtless far too radical a departure from the traditional institutions to emerge—at any rate with any speed—from the industry itself without some form of outside intervention. What form should that intervention take to serve the needs demonstrated here? The choice here is restricted to those forms of intervention comprehended under the term 'anti-monopoly legislation', though it is possible that changes in the general conditions under which

---

[1] Quite apart from the question of technical developments, it will be noticed that a closer link between manufacturing and user development would go some way towards reducing the uncertainty in forecasting total demands which the manufacturers now face.

machine tool manufacturers now work—such as a disappearance of excess demands, or a growing threat of backward integration by consumers—might, in time, serve those needs.

One must admit straight away to pessimism about the outcome of any such intervention. Experience in American anti-trust legislation has shown that the most consistent and effective action can be taken where collective action is essential to a monopolistic control. The strength of the present arrangements of the machine tool industry lies not in overt conspiracy in restraint of trade but in custom, the concentration of technical knowledge and the fact that the various aspects of the structure discussed are, as they act at present, self-reinforcing—among them the agency system, the representation by different classes of machine tool, and the close links between domestic manufacture and the leading agents. There are indeed few formidable obstacles to entry, as has been seen, along many of the conventional lines which industries adopt to protect members. Competitive pressures can only make themselves felt effectively at home through product competition: new entrants are channelled into a distribution system already set up to serve the aims of the existing manufacturing and selling firms. One possible measure, a reform of the patent law along American lines—to prevent the attaching of onerous conditions of marketing to shared licences—would have effect only in a limited part of the field.

The only practicable and effective step seems to be action to make the exclusive agency legally unenforceable in the home market. This would make it easier for a manufacturer to use competitive agents: its principal benefit might well be felt in the case of new entrants and innovatory activity, as it would encourage the growth of alternative selling outlets. But to alter English law in this direction clearly would not prevent manufacturers from appointing only one agent; while the distribution system is structured as it is at present, few established manufacturers would wish or have an incentive to change their methods of selling. If the reform were made, the exclusive agency would decline only slowly—as new firms, by their growth, proved the worthwhileness of the change. Meanwhile, the exporting agency system would remain, unattacked at least directly. Eventually domestic competition might threaten some of the existing export institutions too: if so this would be the price paid for an increased innovation. If the earlier arguments about their essential economy are correct, however, some substitute organizations, limited to the exporting functions, should find it possible to enter, and be profitable enough to survive.

BIBLIOGRAPHY

(a) *Books, Pamphlets and Articles*

Anglo-American Council on Productivity (succeeded by British Productivity Council), *Metalworking Machine Tools*, Productivity Team Report, London, 1953.

Ferney, L. A., 'The British Machine Tool Industry', *Engineer*, vol. 186, 1948, pp. 629 ff., 640 ff.

Jefferys, J. B., *The Story of the Engineers, 1800–1945*, London, Lawrence and Wishart, 1946.

Noble Lowndes Finance Company, *A Survey of the United Kingdom Machine Tool Industry*, October 1955.

PEP (Political and Economic Planning), 'The Machine Tool Industry', *Planning*, vol. 15, no. 292, 1948.

(b) *Official Publications*

Board of Trade, Report on *The Duty-Free Entry of Machinery into the United Kingdom*, H.M.S.O. 1954.

INDEX

Names of persons in capitals.
Titles of articles, Acts of Parliament and works in italics.
Abbreviations: footnote, n.; tabular statement, t.

PUBLICATIONS OF THE
NATIONAL INSTITUTE OF ECONOMIC
AND SOCIAL RESEARCH

published by

THE CAMBRIDGE UNIVERSITY PRESS

None of the Institute's books is sold direct by the Institute. They are available through the ordinary booksellers, and inquiry can be made of the Cambridge University Press, Bentley House, 200 Euston Road, London, N.W. 1.

ECONOMIC & SOCIAL STUDIES

*I   *Studies in the National Income, 1924–1938*
Edited by A. L. BOWLEY. Reprinted with corrections, 1944. pp. 256. 15s. net.

*II   *The Burden of British Taxation*
By G. FINDLAY SHIRRAS and L. ROSTAS. 1942. pp. 140. 15s. net.

*III   *Trade Regulations and Commercial Policy of the United Kingdom*
By the RESEARCH STAFF OF THE NATIONAL INSTITUTE OF ECONOMIC AND SOCIAL RESEARCH. 1943. pp. 275. 15s. net.

*IV   *National Health Insurance: A Critical Study*
By HERMANN LEVY. 1944. pp. 356. 18s. net.

V   *The Development of the Soviet Economic System: An Essay on the Experience of Planning in the U.S.S.R.*
By ALEXANDER BAYKOV. 1946. pp. 530. 37s. 6d. net.

VI   *Studies in Financial Organization*
By T. A. BALOGH. 1948. pp. 328. 30s. net.

*VII   *Investment, Location, and Size of Plant: A Realistic Inquiry into the Structure of British and American Industries*
By P. SARGANT FLORENCE, assisted by W. BALDAMUS. 1948. pp. 230. 18s. net.

VIII   *A Statistical Analysis of Advertising Expenditure and of the Revenue of the Press.*
By NICHOLAS KALDOR and RODNEY SILVERMAN. 1948. pp. 200. 18s. net.

IX   *The Distribution of Consumer Goods*
By JAMES B. JEFFERYS, assisted by MARGARET MACCOLL and G. L. LEVETT. 1950. pp. 430. 40s. net.

X   *Lessons of the British War Economy*
Edited by D. N. CHESTER. 1951. pp. 260. 25s. net.

XI   *Colonial Social Accounting*
By PHYLLIS DEANE. 1953. pp. 360. 50s. net.

* At present out of print.

* At present out of print.

STUDIES IN THE NATIONAL INCOME AND EXPENDITURE OF THE UNITED KINGDOM

Published under the joint auspices of the National Institute and the Department of Applied Economics, Cambridge.

Information about the *Register of Research in the Social Sciences* and the Institute's Reprint Series and other pamphlets can be obtained direct from the Institute.